D0564513

The **Rough Guide** to the World's Best Festivals

World Party

ROUGH GUIDES

worldparty.roughguides.com

Publishing Information

World Party
The Rough Guide to the World's Best Festivals

Published January 2007 by **Rough Guides Ltd**,
80 Strand, London WC2R 0RL

345 Hudson St, 4th Floor,
New York, NY 10014, USA

14 Local Shopping Centre, Panchsheel Park, New Delhi 110017, India

Distributed by the Penguin Group

Penguin Books Ltd,
80 Strand, London WC2R 0RL

Penguin Putnam, Inc.
375 Hudson Street, NY 10014, USA

Penguin Group (Australia)
250 Camberwell Road, Camberwell,
Victoria 3124, Australia

Penguin Books Canada Ltd,
10 Alcorn Avenue, Toronto, Ontario,
Canada M4V 1E4

Penguin Group (NZ)
67 Apollo Drive, Mairangi Bay, Auckland 1310, New Zealand

Typeset in Egyptian, Rockwell and Helvetica to an
original design by Diana Jarvis.

Printed in Slovakia

© Big Cat Press 2007

400pp includes index

A catalogue record for this book is available from the British Library

ISBN 1-84353-528-9

ISBN 13: 9781843535287

The publishers and authors have done their best to ensure the accuracy and currency of all the
information in **World Party: The Rough Guide to the World's Best Festivals**, however, they can
accept no responsibility for any loss, injury, or inconvenience sustained by any traveller as a result
of information or advice contained in the guide.

1   3   5   7   9   8   6   4   2

Acknowledgements

Thanks are due to Diana Jarvis for her great design and layout, Mark Thomas for sourcing
such fantastic photos, Katie Lloyd-Jones for the beautiful maps, and Keith Drew
for skilfully keeping the book on its editorial track; and, of course, to the
legendary Dave Dakota, whose idea it was in the first place.

This book is dedicated to Daisy, who will enjoy many parties.

worldparty.roughguides.com

The **Rough Guide** to the World's Best Festivals

World Party

Contents

INTRODUCTION 6

EUROPE
Common Ridings 19
Festa do São João...........................25
Fiesta de San Fermin 31
Galway International Oyster Festival....41
Glastonbury Festival 47
Hogmanay....................................53
Ibiza Closing Parties 59
Il Palio 65
La Tomatina 75
Las Fallas 81
Lewes Bonfire Night 87
Love Parade 93
Monaco Grand Prix.........................99
Notting Hill Carnival 105
Oktoberfest.................................113
Queen's Day................................121
St Patrick's Day............................127
Tenerife Carnival 133
Venice Carnival 139
Best of the rest **145**

THE AMERICAS AND THE CARIBBEAN
Burning Man 181
Crop Over...................................189
Day of the Dead 195
Fantasy Fest.................................201
Fiesta de Merengue 207
Halloween Parade 213

Junkanoo 219
Mardi Gras 225
Reggae Sumfest 233
Rio Carnival 239
Trinidad Carnival..........................249
Best of the rest **259**

AFRICA AND THE MIDDLE EAST
Festival in the Desert......................275
Rustler's Valley Festivals 281
Best of the rest **285**

ASIA
Ati-Atihan...................................299
Esala Perahera 305
Full Moon Party 311
Gion Matsuri 317
Holi 323
Kumbh Mela 329
Naadam......................................335
Phalgun Festivals..........................343
Pushkar Camel Fair 349
Best of the rest **355**

AUSTRALIA AND NEW ZEALAND
Birdsville Races............................367
Sydney Gay and Lesbian Mardi Gras 373
Best of the rest **381**

END MATTER **387**

Introduction

There's nothing like the life-affirming buzz of a major festival, whether it's toasting the arrival of summer in Iceland, chugging beers at Munich's Oktoberfest, or joining in the orgy of beats at Ibiza's closing parties. This book is a guide to over two hundred of the greatest events on earth, and represents the culmination of years of research, travelling and party-hopping by Rough Guide authors and contributors. Armed with this book, you'll find out all you need to know before you go, and what to do while you're there, as well as the practical details that can make or break your trip.

Every country in the world has its own festivals and celebrations. They're a colourful key to unlocking local cultures and can make for a fantastic travel experience. Many travellers have their own special memories of spectacular events they have attended, whether it's a long-planned visit to the Fiesta de San Fermín, or a stumbled-upon saint's-day procession in a dusty southern Italian town. The festivals in this book come in all shapes and sizes. Many have been around, in one form or another, for decades – some, such as Kumbh Mela and Naadam, for centuries – and have deep roots in the culture of the country they take place in. Others, such as Burning Man, will be following, perhaps even initiating, newer traditions. Some, like Sri Lanka's Esala Perahera, will have deep religious significance; others will be secular occasions based on a key, history-changing event – Lewes Bonfire Night, for example. Some, like Pushkar Camel Fair, will be a mixture of all of these things. And some, like Spain's La Tomatina, will be no more than a massive food-fight. However, nearly all the festivals in this book draw people from local communities together and demonstrate tangibly the

Fiesta de San Fermin

Top 20 festivals

These are the top 20 festivals around the world, as voted for by readers of the Rough Guides website ⓦworldparty.roughguides.com.

1. Rio Carnival
2. Fantasy Fest
3. Fiesta de San Fermin
4. Glastonbury Festival
5. Oktoberfest
6. Love Parade
7. Mardi Gras
8. Trinidad Carnival
9. Queen's Day
10. Burning Man
11. Notting Hill Carnival
12. Crop Over
13. Ati-Atihan
14. Westmann Islands Festival
15. Reggae Sumfest
16. Sydney Gay and Lesbian Mardi Gras
17. Las Fallas
18. St Patrick's Day
19. Rustler's Valley Festivals
20. Il Palio

values and priorities of local cultures – and, as such, they almost all involve some sort of cultural exchange; attending and getting involved in a sensitive and non-voyeuristic way offers a travel experience like no other.

The **philosophy** of this book, indeed of Rough Guides in general, is a relatively simple one: to get out there and see the world – responsibly – and to enjoy yourself while you're doing it. Which is definitely something you can do at all the festivals featured in this book. The list of events we've included is fairly subjective and inevitably highly selective. So how did we choose? Well, the list in part reflects the interests and preferences of our writers, and of visitors to our website. Also, we have tried to make sure that cultures and traditions from most, if not all, parts of the world are represented. We've also only included festivals that are annual and well established – attended by thousands rather than hundreds of people, and that have a big focus on participation. So, although you won't find all of the big music festivals, sports events and one-off parties here, you will find the classics – Rio Carnival, Glastonbury and Mardi Gras – as well as smaller events such as Scotland's Common Ridings and Australia's Birdsville Races. Arguably, these are the real gold dust in this book – all big enough to produce a great vibe in their own individual way, but small enough to retain a sense of community, authenticity and accessibility that many of the mega-events have lost.

How to find the perfect party

Before you pick that perfect festival to begin your conquest of the World Party circuit, it's worth remembering that there are some significant **barriers** in the way. All too often, festivals can be the worst time for travelling to – and staying in – the place in which the event is held. Accommodation prices rocket and the huge crowds can leave you feeling alienated while the festival bangs away somewhere in the distance. The golden rule, therefore, is to make your plans and book your accommodation at least six months in advance. This may not sit with

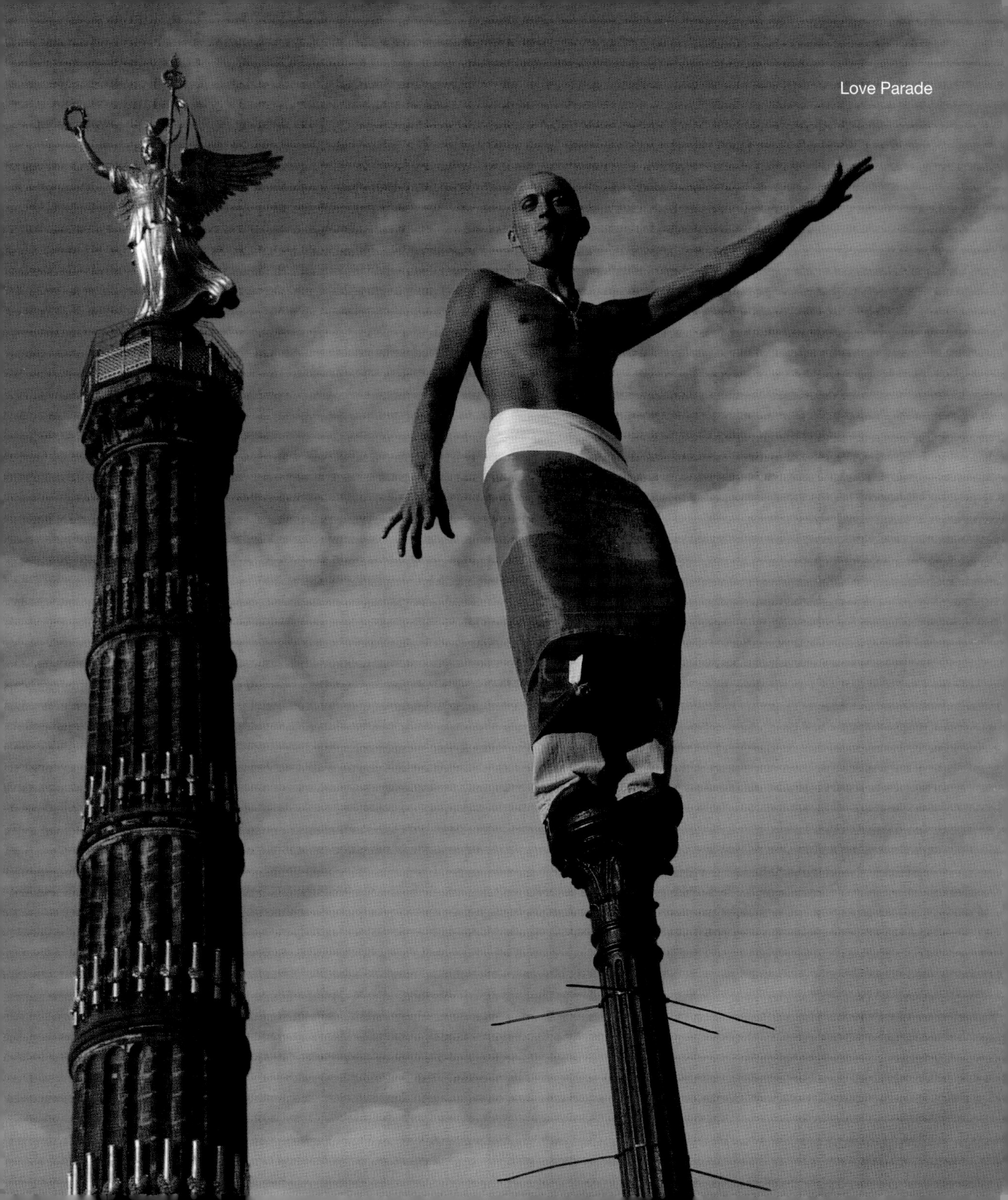

Love Parade

La Tomati

the "life's too short, live for the moment" feeling that sees you packing your party costume in the first place, but it will prevent you having to fork out a fortune for the only vacant hotel room in town. The "Doing..." section of each event provides advice and suggestions on overnight options (including good park benches, where appropriate) for all budgets.

Halloween Parade

   The other main concern is **safety**. Some events, such as the running of the bulls at Pamplona's Fiesta de San Fermin, are inherently dangerous. Don't feel pressured into thinking you've got to take part in the *encierro*: it's a great thrill if you get away with it, but, every year, dozens of runners – mainly drunk tourists – are injured (and occasionally killed). Another risk lies with being in a place where thousands of partygoers are losing their inhibitions at the same time. People occasionally freak out, pickpockets can relieve you of your cash and passport before you've cracked open your first beer, and, most importantly, crowds can stampede. Finally, trying a cocktail of drink and drugs for the first time is almost certainly best not done in the middle of a crowd of half a million people. Nothing in life is risk-free, and, ultimately, it's up to you.

   Our **aim** is that you'll be inspired to experience at least one of the events in this book. Maybe you'll get carried away and make it your life's mission to go to them all. If you do, the experiences can be memorable: swigging vodka on the banks of an extinct volcano before skinny-dipping at 3am during the Westmann Islands Festival; staggering down New Orleans' Bourbon Street during Mardi Gras with a bucket-sized iced Sazerac cocktail and a pocket-full of throws; waking up to the scent of a thousand camels in Pushkar; and wild, celebratory beers at 9am following the survival of another bum-clinchingly terrifying Pamplona bull run. We hope that this book will be your well-thumbed companion to many festivals and parties around the world. Happy travels!

Help us update

On any given day of the year there will be tens, perhaps hundreds of festivals happening somewhere in the world, and you will no doubt have come across some on your travels that we have missed. If you feel there's a festival or event that should be included in the book, or at least mentioned on the website, contact us at ⓦworldparty.roughguides.com and tell us about it. Enclose some photos if you have them. World Party is an interactive project and depends on the feedback of its readers. If your contribution makes it into the next edition, you will receive a free Rough Guide of your choice – and, of course, a copy of the new *World Party*.

Carnival

Carnival, carnaval, carnevale. Call it what you like, but the first huge global parties of the year are the celebrations that lead up to **Mardi Gras**, or Fat Tuesday, which marks the beginning of Lent. Traditionally, this pre-Lenten build-up is a full-on session of drinking, parades, partying and all-round riotous revellery. Carnival celebrations evolved through a combination of influences; pagan rituals, the Latin feast of Bacchus, the Roman Saturnalia, and variously celebrations of food, wine, virility, fertility and springtime renewal. Most events usually get going seriously four or five days before Mardi Gras itself, although, with the larger carnivals, preparations and some initial low-key events may have been taking place for months.

The term "carnival" derives from the Latin "*carne vale*", or "farewell to the flesh", a final celebration before Ash Wednesday and the temperance that follows. Mardi Gras is also known in some countries as "Shrove Tuesday" – an altogether more acceptable appellation to the Church, which has never been comfortable with carnival. So successful were the pre-Lenten celebrations that over the centuries the term "carnival" has become used to describe any kind of celebration, usually completely unrelated and taking place throughout the year – Notting Hill Carnival, for example. But it's the original, genuine events that shine the brightest.

The **dates of carnival** vary each year and are excruciatingly complicated to work out. Mardi Gras occurs 47 days before Easter Sunday, which allows for the forty days of fasting for Lent (excluding Sundays). Easter Sunday takes place on the first Sunday after the official full moon that occurs after the vernal equinox (March 21). The "official" bit of the full moon refers to some erudite fiddling around needed to reconcile the lunar and Gregorian calendars. The upshot, anyhow, and the important bit as far as this book is concerned, is that from year to year Mardi Gras can fall anywhere between February 3 and March 9. There are moves afoot to fix Easter as the second Sunday in April, which would make Mardi Gras the third Tuesday in February each year, but don't hold your breath…

So where should you be living it up before Lent? Well, there's the "Big Three" – **Rio** (right), **New Orleans** and **Trinidad** – or you could opt for one of the more traditional, quirky European events. **Spain** tends to do carnival best, with the raunchy affairs in Tenerife and Cadiz spilling over well beyond Shrove Tuesday, although **Belgium** and **Germany** also like to party come carnival time, laying on some of the most extraordinary events of all. For a double carnival whammy, note that the Orthodox Church calculates Easter differently, resulting in carnival celebrations in **Greece** and **Cyprus** that are generally at least a week out of synch with the others.

The festival year

The year kicks off, as you might expect, with **New Year** celebrations – most famously in Scotland, but everywhere in the world greets its arrival in some way or another. The volume is cranked up a notch further come **carnival** season, usually a month later. **Spring** and then **summer** see major sporting events, including the Monaco Grand Prix, as well as big music festivals such as Glastonbury, and the Love Parade in Berlin. There are, of course, also May–Day celebrations, midsummer festivals – enjoyed with particular gusto in Scandinavia and the Baltics – and assorted events that squeeze the most out of those last few summer months: Notting Hill Carnival, Spain's La Tomatina, and Italy's Il Palio. For some reason, **September** is the preserve of full-on, relatively recent entrants in the festival calendar such as Burning Man, Florida's Fantasy Fest and Ibiza's Closing Parties, while **October** and **November** are more rooted in tradition, with All Souls' Day being celebrated in wildly differing ways as Halloween in New York (and elsewhere) and as the Day of the Dead in Mexico, followed closely by the bizarre celebrations of Britain's Bonfire Night.

The Christian year

Carnival is the biggest "Christian" celebration worldwide, and although **Easter** is also celebrated with as much vigour around the world, it's a dour event on the whole, enjoyable as a spectacle – for example, in Seville – but not something in which you'd participate unless you're a believer. Instead, **saints' days**, particularly in Catholic countries, provide an excuse for a celebration on both a lavish and a local scale. This book only captures the very best and most spectacular of the world's saints' day festivals; wherever you travel, there is sure to be something interesting happening locally.

The Hindu year

Like Catholicism, Hinduism and its legends are the basis of thousands of festivals every year, of which the largest are the **Kumbh Mela**, a huge pilgrimage – it's the biggest gathering of humanity on earth – that descends on four holy sites in central India, and **Diwali**, the Festival

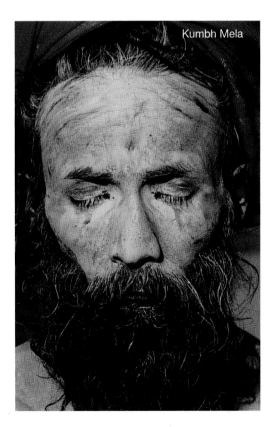
Kumbh Mela

of Lights, a smaller, more home-based affair that takes place in October or November and celebrates the return from exile of Lord Rama. Three weeks before Diwali, there's the more vigorous celebration of **Dussehra**, to honour Rama's victory over the demon Ravana, while earlier in the year, **Holi**, a commemoration of yet another Hindu legend, is celebrated on the first day after the new moon in March by the riotous splashing of colour over everyone and everything. There's also the camel fair in Pushkar, held in November at one of Hinduism's most sacred sites. In between all of these there's a festival for virtually every day of the week in India: we've listed some of the best known in the book, but there's nothing stopping you from discovering your own few days of religious revelry.

The Buddhist year

The Buddhist year is littered with festivals marking a significant event in the life of Buddha, but celebrations can vary wildly from country to country. Buddhist New Year is no exception, which is celebrated – as **Losar** – in February in Tibet and Nepal, but in April in Southeast Asia and Sri Lanka, and in January in India. Others, such as Thailand's **Loi Krathong**, are magical local events, although Sri Lanka's festival celebrating the Buddha's sacred tooth, Kandy's **Esala Perahera**, is perhaps the most spectacular Buddhist event you could attend.

The Muslim year

Islam doesn't have the same packed festival calendar as other religions. Indeed, its main annual religious observance, **Ramadan**, held during the ninth month of the Islamic lunar calendar, is when all devout Muslims are supposed to refrain from eating, drinking, smoking and any kind of sexual contact during daylight hours. This makes Ramadan a peculiarly downbeat time to travel through the Islamic world, although the feast of **Eid al-Fitr**, the three-day festival that celebrates the end of Ramadan, can be fittingly raucous.

Europe

Europe

Common Ridings
Festa do São João
Fiesta de San Fermin
Galway International Oyster Festival
Glastonbury Festival
Hogmanay
Ibiza Closing Parties
Il Palio
La Tomatina
Las Fallas
Lewes Bonfire Night
Love Parade
Monaco Grand Prix
Oktoberfest
Queen's Day
St Patrick's Day
Tenerife Carnival
Venice Carnival
BEST OF THE REST

Common Ridings

One of Britain's best-kept secrets

Common Ridings

Where?
Hawick, Scotland

When?
First weekend in June

How long?
3 days

Hawick

UK

The Common Ridings of the Scottish Border towns of Hawick, Selkirk, Jedburgh and Lauder are one of Britain's best-kept secrets. The focus of each event is a dawn horseback patrol of the fields that mark each town's boundaries – an equestrian extravaganza that combines the thrills of Pamplona's Fiesta de San Fermin with the concentrated drinking of Munich's Oktoberfest. Selkirk may boast the largest number of riders and Lauder might be the oldest event, but Hawick is always the first – and best attended – of the Common Ridings. The rides themselves and what they stand for are absolutely central to life in the Borders: as well as evoking the fierce independence of the region, they display the great sense of camaraderie amongst Border towns, each of which sends a number of representative riders and a small army of thirsty "Foot Soldiers" to their neighbours' events.

History

The Common Ridings are centuries-old costumed re-enactments of the horseback patrol of town boundaries that were undertaken more than four hundred years ago by towns on the Scottish–English border to give the Scots early warning of attacks from their expansionist neighbours; indeed, the large statue of a young man on horseback (known simply as "The Horse") that stands in the centre of Hawick High Street was built to commemorate one such skirmish. In his hand the young man brandishes the captured **flag** of a band of vanquished English soldiers, who had been beaten back at nearby Hornshole in 1514 by a brave group of local lads, known as "Callants". It's this flag – or at least a replica of it – that is solemnly handed over to the Cornet at the start of the Common Ridings on the Thursday evening, and returned on Saturday afternoon to mark the closure of the festival.

The **origins** of Common Ridings can be traced back to the thirteenth century, when they were a simple life-or-death necessity to retain claims on pastureland. By 1537, when Hawick received its town charter granting ownership of the surrounding commons, the Ridings were more of a large-scale civic chore, for which non-participants could be fined. The patriotic and more debauched aspects of the event began a lot later.

Thereafter, the event became less about your right to do what you like to your land and more about your right to do what you like to your liver – to the extent that in 1856 the council voted to **ban the event** "because of bad behaviour and drunkenness". Needless to say, the townsfolk simply ignored this edict and carried on regardless. The event was soon officially recognized again, and 150 years or so later has morphed into a spectacular amalgamation of horse-riding, boozing and civic ceremonies, of which every *Teri*, as the inhabitants of Hawick are known, is rightly proud. The Ridings have traditionally been a male-only preserve, but following a successful High Court appeal in 1997 that split town opinion, **women** are now welcome to participate in the morning rides.

Each of the Border towns has developed its own distinct Common Ridings traditions, but every event follows roughly the same formula as the one in Hawick (pronounced Hoik). The first evening, Thursday, witnesses the ceremony of **"colour-bussing"**, a huge reception at the town hall during which the town provost hands over the flag to the chief rider, or Cornet, with the words "safe oot, safe in" and the best lady, a representative from the town's young, female population, ties a ribbon in the town's colours to the flag. Entrance is by ticket only, so if you can't get in, join the huge crowd that assembles around The Horse statue on the High Street to watch the Cornet climb up to "buss", or decorate, the statue.

The morning rides

After the colour-bussing, attention then turns to the pubs. The standard closing time during the Common Ridings is 3am, and no sooner have most people stumbled out onto Hawick High Street than they're back again – the pubs open at 6am to allow plenty of time for the riders, plus virtually the entire town population, to get themselves suitably fortified

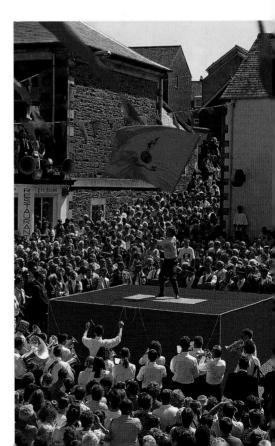

Insider info Most people come to Common Ridings to watch, but if you're confident you can ride a beast at full gallop cross-country and through Hawick's winding streets, the local tourist office (see p.24) may be able to arrange for you to join the ride.

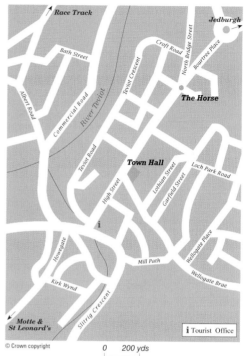

for Friday's **morning ride** around town, which involves a group of local young men plus anyone who is mad enough to join them. Don't worry about not waking up in time for the early start – the rides get going at around 7.30am – as a colourful and incredibly noisy drum and fife band marches around the streets at dawn to shake people from their sleep. You might feel a little underdressed as most of the riders are exquisitely attired in a formal costume of cream jodhpurs, black riding boots, tweed jackets and white silk neckerchiefs, but you don't have to be wearing traditional Common Ridings garb to try the traditional Common Ridings morning drink of "Curds and Cream" (rum and milk). It doesn't taste half as bad as it sounds – more like a kind of alcoholic milkshake – and slips down remarkably well with breakfast. Each rider will knock back between four and ten rum and milks before mounting their horses and galloping

mounting their horses, the riders gallop at breakneck speed around the ancient lanes and narrow streets of the town

at breakneck speed around the ancient lanes and narrow streets of the town. You have to be able to ride quite well to take part in this, as the pace can be thunderous, so most people just go along to spectate; the sight of nearly two hundred horses galloping at full pelt is amazing, and, as the horses race off, the crowds follow on behind, more to see who'll be the first rider to fall off than out of any particular sense of duty. Accidents can, and very often do, happen – not surprising given the amount of rum that has been consumed

The Cornet

The central character in the Hawick Common Ridings is the **Cornet**, a local male aged 19–24, who is chosen from the town's population of young horsemen, and who leads the rides, flanked by his Right- and Left-Hand Men. These guys are the cream of Hawick's young population and all three must be unmarried – indeed, you're not allowed to marry for three years if you're chosen. Last year's Cornet becomes this year's Right-Hand Man and then next year's Left-Hand Man. The first recorded Cornet was in 1703, and other than during the World Wars there has been an unbroken line to the present day. The female interest is represented by the two-dozen "Hawick Ladies", chosen from the same age range as the men.

– but the only recorded fatality occurred back in 1876. The morning riders are mainly Hawick locals, but representatives from other national, and occasionally international, riding clubs often attend, too.

The final destination of the riders is the local racetrack, a two-mile, half-hour walk north of town, where a series of **horse races** are held throughout day. The jockeys here are all professionals who forgo the temptations of alcohol – at least, until the races are over – unlike their amateur counterparts and the Foot Soldiers (the name given to anyone who walks up from the town) who throng the colossal beer tents that are erected alongside the course; indeed, the focus is just as much on the action in the beer tents as on the track.

Evening entertainment

The races finish around 5pm, after which the Foot Soldiers stagger back into town to reacquaint themselves with Hawick's pubs or – for those lucky enough to get tickets – don their finery for the highlight of the festival, the **Common Ridings Ball**, a black-tie affair held in the town hall, and an event so debauched that the antics of some years have reached mythical status (tickets cost £20, and are best bought from the tourist office in advance; see p.24). Outside, towards dawn, you can experience the bizarre sight of torch-lit Scottish **reel dancing** performed on top of the twelfth-century fortified "motte" by people who haven't stopped drinking for 24 hours and may not have slept in 48. If a testament were ever needed to the guts, glory and unbridled *joie de vivre* of the Scots, then this, surely, is it. You should have just enough time for an hour or two of shut-eye before the fife band strikes up once more and it's time to do it all again on the Saturday, at least until the Hornshole flag is returned to the provost and the riders can pack away their jodhpurs for another year.

Hitting the Hut

One unique feature of the Hawick event is the experience of the "**Hut**", a large cricket pavilion in St Leonards, on the outskirts of town, that houses some of the rowdiest early-morning piss-ups you may ever experience. After patrolling the town's boundaries on the Thursday and Friday mornings, the Cornet and riders arrive at the Hut at around 8.30am to a rapturous reception. They then settle down for the traditional breakfast snack of rum and milk, accompanied by rowdy songs and alcohol-soaked male bonding, before attempting to head off to the racecourse a couple of hours later. Inside, the Hut is filled with long trestle tables, and only one type of order is taken at the bar – a "crate", which contains a case of McEwans lager, a large bottle of rum and two pints of milk. Groups of five or six usually split the cost, although some bravehearts order a crate for themselves.

The Hut is a fairly male environment, as you might expect: the only way of getting around inside is by walking on the tables and grabbing hold of the overhead beams, while the urinals largely consist of a solitary open window. There's space for 700 or so revellers inside the Hut, but you'll need a **ticket** to get in; tickets go on sale at the pavilion the week before the event on a first-come, first-served basis and are invariably snapped up within hours. Good luck with getting one – it's worth it.

Other Common Ridings

Common Ridings events are held at each border town throughout the summer, starting with Hawick in early June. The principal men are elected annually and honoured with such titles as Standard Bearer (Selkirk), Cornet (Hawick), Callant (Jedburgh), Braw Lad (Galashiels), Reiver (Duns), Whipman (West Linton) and Melrosian (Melrose).

Selkirk Common Riding, generally held a few weeks after the Hawick event, is recognized as one of the oldest of the Borders festivals, with formalities dating from the Battle of Flodden in 1513 (commemorating, in this case, a miserable pasting received by the locals from English marauders). The Selkirk event also attracts the most horse riders – up to five hundred have been known to follow the Standard Bearer "safe oot and safe in" on the ride around town boundaries, making it one of the largest equestrian gatherings in Europe. For more information, see ⓦwww.selkirk.bordernet.co.uk.

Basics

Hawick is around fifty miles southeast of Edinburgh – the nearest **airport** – and forty miles north of Carlisle on the A7. There are no train services but **buses** run regularly from Edinburgh and Carlisle, and there is also a good bus service between the border towns should you want to check out other sights and Common Ridings events while you're in the area. Hawick's **tourist office** is at Drumlanrig's Tower Knowe (Mon–Sat 10am–5pm, Sun noon–3pm; ☎0870 6080404, ✉bordersinfo@visitscotland.com).

Accommodation

There's an abundance of B&B, hotel and guesthouse **accommodation** in and around Hawick; great close-to-town B&Bs include *Ellistrin*, 6 Fenwick Park (☎01450 374216); *Hopehill*, on Wilton Crescent (☎01450 375042); and *Oakwood*, on Buccleuch Road (☎01450 372814). All charge around £40 per night for a double room. For slightly more upmarket, you could try the comfortable *Mansfield House Hotel* (☎01450 373988 or 360400, ⌨www.mansfield-house.com), a mile outside Hawick on the A698 to Jedburgh, whose double rooms start at £60 per night.

Eating and drinking

Scotland is not renowned for its fine **food** at the best of times and Common Ridings does little to dispel this image. Let's face it, if you start drinking at 6am, you're unlikely to appreciate a gourmet lunch. You'll want hot, fried food, and a number of cafés, pubs and takeaway joints around Hawick's High Street do just that. For a curious Scottish treat, you can try the deep-fried pizza served at *Di Nallo's*, at the west end of the High Street. It looks as disgusting as it sounds, but is curiously satisfying after a skinful. For higher-quality cuisine, try one of the pubs in town for reasonable pub grub, or those just outside town, such as *Auld Cross Keys Inn* (☎01450 870305) in Denholm village on the A6 towards Jedburgh, whose specialities include chicken stuffed with haggis in a whisky cream sauce.

You're spoilt for choice for **drinking**, with more than twenty pubs crowding the High Street alone. *Robbie's*, on the High Street, and *Stampers*, on North Bridge Street, are sweaty, heaving places full of young bucks on the razzle, (the latter has occasional live music); the *Imperial Bar*, Croft Road, the *Exchange Bar*, 1 Silver St, and the *Queens Head*, 4 Cross Wynd, are more sedate, traditional establishments.

Useful websites

Hawick Callants Club (⌨www.hawickcallantsclub.co.uk) A must-read for anyone thinking of attending, this encyclopedic website gives more detail, history and reference information on the event than any one person could possibly need to know.

Hawick (⌨www.teribus.com/common.htm) Hawick's official website, with information on and photos of the Common Ridings.

Time zone GMT   **Country code** +44   **Currency** Pound sterling (£)

Festa do São João

The smell of grilling peppers and sardines wafts through the warm June air

Festa do São João

Where?
Porto, Portugal
When?
June 23 and 24
How long?
2 days

• Porto

• Lisbon

PORTUGAL

The old cliché that Porto works while Lisbon plays is redundant on June 24, when Portugal's second city teaches the capital a thing or two about having fun. The Festa do São João is a magnificent display of midsummer madness – one giant street party, with every available outdoor space in Porto given over to a full night of eating, drinking and dancing to welcome in the city's saint's day. Fireworks, bonfires and roaming bands of hammer- and leek-wielding lunatics keep the crowds entertained all night – traditionally, you're meant to witness the first majestic rays of dawn down on the beaches of Foz do Douro, with the day of São João itself spent recovering, a regatta of traditional boats down the Rio Douro providing a gentle antidote to the night before.

The celebrations

Preparations for the party begin several days before June 23, with virtually every *bairro* (district) of Porto decorating its streets with coloured ribbons. You'll also see *cascatas* – models representing everything from religious figures to workers to whole townscapes – which are constructed by various *bairros*, schools and businesses, with a prize given for the best one. The **morning of June 23** sees a series of frantic preparations, involving not only the council setting up stages and illuminations, but all the *tripeiros*, or tripe-eaters, as the residents of Porto are known. This really is a citywide party, as virtually every household plays its part with its own decorations or improvised stalls on the street outside their homes.

Festivities are already under way by the **late afternoon** of June 23, with people of all ages promenading round town. Outdoor braziers are lit on virtually every residential street, and the smell of grilling peppers and sardines wafts through the warm June air. Everything is flung open – windows and doors of cafés, bars, houses and restaurants; tables, chairs and benches line every available space, as squares, cobbled alleys and the riverfront become one giant open-air café. The early part of the evening sees old grannies tottering around with sticks, families pushing babies in prams, and small children asking passers-by for coins for São João, before the chanting male youths in replica Porto football shirts begin to get the upper hand. All night long, though, there's a mixture of people and ages out on the streets – this is the one party that no one in Porto wants to miss.

By **8pm** or so, the *tripeiros* are already in the party mood. A tide of whistle-blowing, hammer-wielding people begins to seep down the steep streets towards the river. No one seems to know the origin of the tradition of hitting people over the head on this day, but what was traditionally a rather harmless pat with a leek has evolved into a somewhat firmer clout with a plastic hammer that squeaks if hit with the correct force. You should know that everyone has a plastic hammer, and everyone wants to hit someone else with it – something that is done with remarkable restraint by even the most macho locals. (As a rule, if you are extremely attractive, expect to be the target for extra hits.)

People begin dancing to the live music by the Rio Douro while it's still light, banging their hammers on metal café tables to the rhythm of the Latin and African sounds. Elsewhere, live music performances vary from pop and rock to traditional folk music and choral singing – basically, there's something for everyone. As darkness falls, exploding

History

Every village in Portugal has an adopted saint – usually one of the **santos populares**, the popular saints of António (Anthony), João (John) or Pedro (Peter) – who is fervently celebrated on their annual saint's day; Lisbon's main saint is António, while Porto and many other towns in northern Portugal celebrate João. All these saints' days are in June, probably a Christian adaptation of pagan Summer Solstice celebrations, and there remains a strong religious element to the festivals, with decorations set up in churches and offerings made to the saints in the form of lighted candles and plastic body parts, donated as thanks or to ask the saints for cures. Special church services are given on the saints' days, often followed by a procession carrying an effigy of the saint, but in an increasingly secular country, the religious side is often forgotten in favour of the party element.

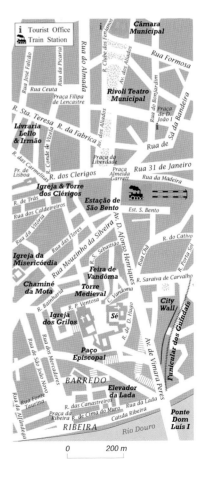

fireworks begin to rumble through the night sky above the glowing neon of the port-wine lodges over the Douro. The makeshift riverfront stalls do a roaring trade, and the whole city becomes a frenzy of dancing, whistling, and singing people of all ages. By now, you may be in the mood to participate more fully by getting hold of your own plastic hammer from one of the many stalls selling them. Indeed, the periphery of Avenida dos Aliados becomes a night-time market, with stall after stall selling everything from fresh bread to flowers to illuminated balloons, which periodically drift eerily into the night sky.

Midnight sees the inevitable climax of fireworks and illuminations, but the night is far from over. As dawn approaches, the emphasis shifts west to the beach of Praia dos Ingleses in the suburb of Foz do Douro, at the end of the Douro estuary. Here there's space to participate in the tradition of lighting bonfires for São João, with youths challenging each other to jump over the largest flames (casualties are surprisingly rare). The whole area then becomes one big beach party, with revellers dancing to ghetto blasters round the roaring fires. Pace yourself and before you know it the crowds will start to thin slightly and the first signs of daylight will appear on the horizon. It is now St John's Day.

Insider info If you're staying the night outside Porto's central grid, familiarize yourself with the route back to your hotel on foot – taxis on the night of June 23 are virtually non-existent.

Though most areas of Porto have some sort of celebration, there are three main places to head for: the central square made up of **Avenida dos Aliados**, the administrative heart of Porto, which during the festival becomes a traffic-free area of stalls and live-music stages; the precipitous warren of atmospheric, narrow alleys tumbling downhill from **São Bento station to the riverfront**, the earthiest and most historic part of town and, beyond here, the **Douro riverfront**, which is Porto's liveliest area all year and is a further heaving focal point for the festivities, with another stage set up on Praça da Ribeira for live music. The riverfront is home to many of the city's best bars and restaurants, which complement the array of hastily erected barbecues and stalls selling beer, and the river also forms the backdrop for fireworks that light up the sky after dark. A fourth area to head for – if you have the stamina – is **Foz do Douro**, out by the sea 5km to the west of the centre. This becomes the focus for a giant beach party, which kicks off at around 3 or 4am.

fireworks, bonfires and roaming bands of hammer- and leek-wielding lunatics

The boat regatta

Luckily for everyone involved, June 24 (St John's Day) is a public holiday. A few people attend morning church services, but the streets generally remain deserted as revellers recover from the night before. The afternoon, however, sees somewhat more gentle action by the riverfront with a **boat regatta**, usually starting at around 3pm. This is a race for the *barcos rabelos*, the low, wooden boats traditionally used to transport port wine from the mountainous Douro valley to the port lodges in Vila Nova de Gaia, opposite Porto. The best place to see the regatta is from Porto's riverfront, Cais da Ribeira, an atmospheric strip where kids cool off by plunging into the filthy waters from the double-decker Ponte Luis I bridge. Alternatively, walk over the bridge (or take bus #32 from Avenida dos Aliados) to the riverfront at Vila Nova de Gaia, from where the dense Porto cityscape makes a dramatic backdrop to the boat race.

Basics

Porto's **airport** is 13km north of the city in Maia and is linked by frequent trains and buses. Most long-distance **trains** stop at Campanha station; others use the more central São Bento station, while international **buses** pull up at Campo 24 Agosto, just east of the city centre. The top end of the Avenida dos Aliados houses the central **tourist office** (see below), where you can get free maps of the city.

Accommodation

Finding **accommodation** is not usually a problem in Porto, but you should consider whether a hotel bed is actually a worthwhile investment for the night of June 23 – most locals stay up at least until it gets light, and even if you do want a night's sleep, the central area is so noisy that an undisturbed kip is highly unlikely. For those deciding against a night in a hotel, the most central place for **left luggage** is São Bento station.

Relative peace and quiet can be had at the *Pousada da Juventude*, Rua Paulo da Gama, 551 (☎ 226/177257, ✆ www.pousadasjuventude. pt), the youth hostel 4km west of the city. This low-rise, modern building overlooks the Douro and has doubles from €42 and four-bed dorms from €15 per person. *Hotel América*, Rua de Santa Catarina 1018 (☎ 223/392 930, ✆ www.hotel-america.net), just clear of the night's noisiest activity and with its own bar, restaurant and parking, has spacious doubles for €55, while *Residencial Portofoz*, Rua do Farol 155 (☎ 226/172 357, ✆ www.portofoz.com), is a simple guesthouse out near the beach festivities, with its own bar – €52 for a double room, and €72 for one with glimpses of the Atlantic.

Eating and drinking

Forget **eating** at a restaurant on the evening of June 23 – just tuck into the grilled fish, meat, peppers and bread that are sold on every street corner. Sardines are the most common dish and some locals may even hand them out for free and show you how to eat them like a corn on the cob, nibbling the flesh off the rib cage with your teeth – a feat that becomes harder as the night gets darker and you get drunker. There are usually plenty of alcoholic **drinks** to be had. Cafés and bars sell good local *vinho tinto* (red wine), and entrepreneurial locals make a euro or two on the side by selling bottles of *Superbock* beer from washing-up bowls packed with ice. Don't worry about closing time – most places stay open until at least 4 or 5am.

Event info

Porto Tourist Office (✆ www.portoturismo.pt). Rua Clube dos Fenianos 25 (☎ 223/393472); Rua Infante Dom Henrique 63 (☎ 222 009 770).

Time zone GMT+1   **Country code** +351   **Currency** euro (€)

Fiesta de San Fermin

The scariest, loudest and most raucous party you'll ever come across

Fiesta de San Fermin

Where?
Pamplona, Spain

When?
July 6–14

How long?
9 days

For one week every year, the Spanish town of Pamplona parties so hard that the foothills of the nearby Pyrenees start to shake. Nothing can prepare you for your first Pamplona experience: the constant flow of beer and sangria, the outrageous drunken partying, the hordes of excited people in the streets, and, most of all, the early morning terror of the *encierro*, the daily bull run. You've got to hand it to the Spanish; they certainly know how to host a phenomenal party, and the Fiesta de San Fermin is simply the scariest, loudest and most raucous one you'll ever come across. It's the Bruce Lee of world festivals: it hits you hard and fast and leaves you feeling like you've been run over by a bus – or, more accurately in the case of the slower runners, a bull.

The San Fermin antics could only take place in Spain. No other country would tolerate an entire town being taken over for more than a week of non-stop drunken partying. And that's before you consider the reckless irresponsibility of letting people take part in the bull run. The Spanish, however, just take it all in their stride.

The **timetable** runs as follows. The fiesta is officially declared open at noon on July 6, but, like kids at Christmas, the locals can't wait for the start of the biggest bash of the year so the partying is already going strong by nightfall on the 5th. The first bull run is held on the morning of July 7. Then the ritual of all-night partying followed by a morning bull run followed by a few hours of sleep is repeated until July 14, when, after the last *encierro* has been run, adrenalin and alcohol levels recede to normal and the town gets on with the business of clearing up.

So intense is the partying at Pamplona that you are wildly optimistic if you think you can make it from start to finish. The best schedule would be to take in four days including the off-the-Richter-scale partying of the weekend. Things calm down a little after this, but whenever you come, the action is guaranteed to be going strong.

History

The festival is a celebration of Pamplona's **patron saint**, San Fermin, who was excruciatingly beheaded – the bright red neckerchief worn at festival time serves as a reminder of this. His official day, July 7, has been celebrated with a religious ceremony, fiesta and bullfights since the early sixteenth century. No one is sure when the daily ritual of the *encierro* began, but it has been the most prominent feature of the event for at least two hundred years. However it came about, the bull run was soon adopted as something of a rite of passage for young men of the region who still see it as an important step in adulthood.

Orientation

There are really only three areas you will need to know to make the most of the fiesta. The first is the main town square, **Plaza del Castillo**, which is surrounded by packed bars and is the focal point of the partying for the locals. The bandstand in the middle of the square is a great place to take your afternoon siesta in the sun and a good rendezvous spot when you inevitably get split up. It's also only a few hundred metres away from the start of the bull run.

Party kit

The first thing you'll notice when you arrive in Pamplona is the **uniform** that just about everyone is wearing: white trousers and T-shirt with a red neckerchief, red sash for your waist, and an optional comedy red beret. White is a strange choice of colour considering this can be one of the messiest events you'll ever go to, but it's traditional Basque attire. There are loads of stalls selling these outfits, and for less than €25 you're guaranteed a much warmer reception by the locals wherever you go. Another great accessory is a **wine skin**. These cost about €12 and save the hassle of carrying around glass bottles of sangria. It's also a highly effective method of soaking someone during the flour and sangria fights after the opening ceremony.

The dos and don'ts of Running with the Bulls

Do:

- Choose your day carefully – at the weekend *encierros*, there are twice as many runners, and twice as many casualties.
- Take time picking your starting spot – accident black spots are the corner after the Ayuntamiento, the death-trap alley of La Estafeta, and the Callejon bottleneck at the entrance to the bull ring.
- Give the bulls space – the bulls quite often turn around and run backwards, which is pretty terrifying for the people running closely behind them.
- Prepare to take evasive action – bulls can move incredibly fast. If one is right behind you, don't even spend an extra second climbing over the wooden barrier. Hit the floor and roll underneath. You'll be covered in grime, but your backside should be intact.
- Plan for the worst – if you fall over, don't get up: cover your head and don't move until someone gives you the all clear.

Don't:

- Be so drunk that you either think you're invincible or don't care.
- Don't call your mates on your mobile.
- Try to frame a good picture for the folks at home.
- Pretend to be a *matador*.
- Carry anything at all, apart from the optional rolled-up newspaper.
- Hide in a doorway and hope you won't be noticed.
- Try to run into the bullring just in front of the bulls.

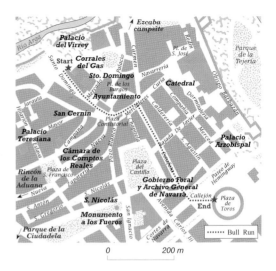

Up the road from the square lies the Casco Viejo, the old part of town, which houses another slew of bars including the famous *Mussel Bar* at the top end. The bar itself is nothing special – in fact, it's usually shut and just serves beer and sangria through a window. The attraction lies in its location on a small square, the **Plaza de San José**, and the suicidal sport of leaping from the top of the five-metre-tall St Cecilia statue, often wearing only a thin veil of bravado, into the arms (or not) of the crowd below – a favourite pastime of Aussies, South Africans and Kiwis (see box opposite). Even if you're not into diving yourself, the courtyard is a great place to hang out any time of day, as you will always find a big group of people drinking, singing and egging each other on to climb the statue. The atmosphere is very much of the party-till-you-puke-or-pass-out variety – a tiny part of Australia in Spain.

Finally, you'll spend some time around the **Plaza del Toros** bullring, either by charging triumphantly through the narrow entrance with a snorting bull hot on your tail (unlikely) or by watching other fools attempt the same thing from the safety of a ringside seat (more fun). Bullfights are held every evening (see box on p.39), involving the six bulls that ran earlier in the day – worth watching if you've had the shit scared out of you by them during the morning's *encierro*.

The build-up

The town's mayor makes a speech at noon on July 6 from the balcony of the *ayuntamiento* (town hall) in Plaza Consistorial, for which the crowds gather from 10am. After the speech, the mayor lets off a rocket to announce the **start of the Fiesta**, and the assembled mob erupts in a shower of champagne, beer, sangria, eggs and flour bombs. Running wine-battles carry on for a good couple of hours, and conga lines dance through the narrow side-streets shouting "*agua, agua, agua*" as they pass under a balcony, the occupants of which come out and oblige by emptying buckets of cold water over the mob. The hardcore revellers carry on for a few hours after this, but before long most start to drift away to eat and get a siesta before the first real night of partying begins – and, of course, the next day's bull run.

it's sheer terror sprinting through the blind alley of Estafeta with half a ton of rampaging beef hot on your heels

As the day wears on, more people empty on to the streets and rejoin the party that has been building since midday. Most arrive fresh faced with reasonably clean clothes, but the few who have kept on partying since the lunchtime food-fight now look like the living dead and stagger around the plaza in disoriented packs. Don't look down on this dilapidated street trash – it's only a matter of time before you join them. Like all endurance sports, the key to survival in Pamplona is to pace yourself. The locals have the art perfected and it pays to follow their lead. Around 10pm, crowds drift away from the town square and head up to the Parque de la Ciudadela, where an enormous fireworks display is held every night. If you're still going strong, head back to the Casco Viejo and the raging partying, which will by now be gathering pace. As dawn approaches, the atmosphere gets even more feverish. Groups of people have teamed up to run the *encierro* together and are knocking back the brandy to harden their resolve; others are nervously knocking back a few more drinks to help them decide. Of course, the really serious runners went to bed hours ago and are now dreaming of lightning dashes and *matador* heroics.

Statue diving

If the ambulance team engraved the name on the St Cecilia statue of every injury that had occurred as a result of the **statue diving** that takes place there, they would have run out of space years ago. Every afternoon during the festival, once the sangria and beer has really soaked in, people, almost exclusively foreign tourists, start scaling the fountain ready to entrust their spread-eagled flying bodies to the mob of drunken catchers below. The two most popular ways of getting carted off on a stretcher are either to get so drunk that you fall off backwards whilst scaling the statue, or to launch yourself into the crowd and land flat on your face in a pile of broken bottles because the catchers are too drunk or too busy drinking to pay any attention to you. To spice up the antics, girls usually do the jump topless – in fact, the crowd often refuses to catch female jumpers until at least the T-shirts come off – and there are always a few naked leaps before nightfall.

The Running of the Bulls: Spectating

Every day from July 6 onwards – from 5am – spectators are already in their places, watching the careful erection of the sturdy wooden gates that define the eight-hundred-metre bull run. The atmosphere is still a carnival one, but tense, with runners already strolling anxiously up and down the course, inspecting the ground and checking for danger spots. Loud brass bands get the crowds going from 7am onwards as they march around town to wake everyone up. The most popular drink for spectators and runners alike is a *carajillo* – a hot, strong coffee injected with a huge measure of brandy. Excellent for raising your spirits after a taxing night.

For a guaranteed **view of the bulls**, get a ticket for the bullring early in the morning. This is the end destination of the *encierro* and the scene of utter mayhem when the bulls and runners arrive, both competing to squeeze through the narrow opening. It costs about €3 for the best seats in the house and saves hanging around on the streets where you risk seeing nothing at all. For those who would rather take their chances outside, arguably the **best place to stand** is in front of the *Zaldiko* bar, just up the road from the Coralles del Gas where the bulls are kept, on Santo Domingo, but you need to get there early to bag your spot. The road slopes up towards the bullring in front of the bar, and you get an excellent view of the start and the first 300m of the course.

Minutes before the run the atmosphere is electric. Runners either limber up or totter around nervously, depending on the state they're in. Some look confident and determined, most are pretty twitchy, but the majority are completely petrified. Nearly all clutch the only **weapon of self-defence** permitted: a tightly rolled-up copy of the morning's newspaper – totally useless against half a ton of rampaging beef, but a good way to let out tension if squeezed tightly enough. Once the rocket signalling the start of the run is fired, the bulls shoot out of the corrals in seconds, and every runner's fate is truly in the lap of the gods.

> **Insider info** If you decide to run, the golden rule to surviving the *encierro* is to have a look at the course beforehand and decide which barrier you are going to duck under in an emergency.

The Running of the Bulls: Participating

It's up to you whether or not you want to **run with the bulls**. But if you do, take it seriously. The people who get injured or killed each year are almost always tourists. There have been 14 deaths and 205 serious "horn injuries" between 1924 and 2006. You really don't want to be added to that list. The six leading bulls (followed by a herd of tame bulls to keep them moving) run the 825m from the Coralles del Gas to the bullring in an average of 3 minutes 55 seconds. In this short period

A survivor's tale

Thousands run with the bulls, and every year many are injured. One of them was Scott Kelley. Here's his story.

The morning of July 9 dawned wet and chilly as we struggled out of our bed – basically a sheet we had spread on the ground underneath a building overhang – to prepare for the morning's *encierro*. We were hungover from large amounts of sangria, tired from dancing until four in the morning, and cold after getting soaked from the night's rainstorm, but who cares about such minor discomforts when you might get gored or trampled? Such is the fun and prestige of San Fermin. Fun because it's a week of non-stop drinking, dancing, parades, fireworks and bullfights. Prestigious because once you've taken part in the scary yet thrilling *encierro*, you've got yourself a tale that will trump the "Guess what we did this summer?" stories of all your friends combined.

July 9 was going to be my fifth *encierro* and as I hadn't gotten a scratch my previous times, I was brimming with excitement and confidence. I spent all morning giving tips to my friends – all Americans I had met a few days earlier in Barcelona – and allaying their fears. My advice seemed simple enough: run fast, watch for other runners and keep tabs on the bulls at all times. At 8am, we heard the explosion of a rocket, signalling that the pack of six bulls (and six female heifers) were out of their pens and heading our way. The tension in the air was electric. People gave each other quick, nervous glances. Some people immediately began running; others jumped up and down, trying to keep their muscles loose or trying to keep their adrenaline rush under some sort of control.

My starting point for this day was Estafeta, just past the Mercaderes corner. This is a good place to start – the street is long and straight, and you can spot the bulls coming from some distance away. As the seconds ticked by, the flow of men moving past went from a jog to a run to a full-out sprint. The crowd in the balconies overhead began cheering louder, and soon I could feel and hear the thunder of approaching hooves merged in with the other runners. Before I knew it, I was at a full-out sprint.

My travel companions were lost in the ensuing chaos. I'm a fast runner, but the bulls are much faster (they've been clocked at 35mph), and soon the main pack passed to my left. I could smell their musky odour and feel the rumbling as they charged past. This feeling, combined with the roar of the crowd and the beating of my own heart, made for an exhilarating moment, and I found myself shouting and cheering as I ran onward. As I headed into the bullring at the end of Estafeta I spotted a pile-up of ten runners ahead. Pile-ups are dangerous because they block the way and prevent runners from avoiding the bulls and other oncoming runners. Leaping over two or three fallen runners is easy, but a pile-up is different, and I had no choice but to dodge to the left. Just as I cleared the fallen bodies I glanced behind me and was shocked at the sight: an enormous black bull was bearing down on me. There was no time to jump out of the way and the bull ploughed into my left side.

It felt like someone hit me with a baseball bat. The thud of the impact took my breath away and I lost consciousness for a few seconds. When I came to I was lying against the tunnel just inside the bullring. I was disoriented but knew enough to stay flat on the ground and let other runners and bulls stream past. After waiting a few seconds I felt a pair of hands lift me to my feet. The final bull had just run past and people were already starting to slow down. I was lucky because the bull's horns hadn't connected – only its massive head. I had a bloody nose, my shirt was smeared with blood and mud, and the left side of my body ached horribly. I could stand, but my legs were too wobbly to walk so I was carried over to several Spanish medics, who cleaned me up and checked my eyes for responsiveness. I hurt, but it wasn't anything life-threatening, so I was led over to a bench where I sat down and took a moment to rest my aching body.

Thousands of runners had made it inside the bullring and it was impossible to spot my friends, so I made my way outside and picked a grassy knoll to lie down on. We met up later on to exchange our "war stories" (a favourite San Fermin pastime) – my bloody shirt and terrifying experience made for a good tale.

Looking back, I realized how lucky I was not to have been gored. Others weren't so fortunate: three people were gored that same day, and a dozen more during the entire festival. Coming face-to-face with a bull only deepened my respect and affection for the *encierro*. I used to view the morning's run as an adventurous game. Not any more. Take the running seriously, regardless of whether it's your first, fifth or fiftieth time. And, once that final bull has passed and the all clear is given, prepare yourself for what many consider an even greater challenge – keeping up with the city's outrageous partying.

The Running of the Nudes

In 2002, animal rights campaigners People for the Ethical Treatment of Animals (PETA) got a couple of dozen volunteers to streak through the streets of Pamplona in protest at the cruelty of the *encierro*, and indeed of bullfighting in general – their aim to change the Fiesta de San Fermin forever. PETA's so-called **Running of the Nudes** has since become an annual event, and nowadays around a thousand people join in the demonstration a few days before the bull runs. Despite the serious message, it's a fun occasion, and although the participants aren't always totally naked – in 2006, they had to don a pair of pants to be allowed to run – the sight of a thousand people running through the streets in little more than some fake horns and a red neckerchief is enough to get them noticed – and the issues raised. If you agree with them, you might want to join in. Even if you don't, the run is accompanied by lots of music, dancing – and a great party afterwards. For more **information**, see ⓦwww.runningofthenudes.com.

they have time to gore a few people, turn around and scare the shit out of some of the runners who think the danger has passed, and generally wreak havoc.

About ten minutes before the start of the run, stewards patrol the route and remove anyone in an unfit state. As they pass, this is pretty much your last chance to opt out as the spectators press so hard against the barriers you'll effectively be hemmed in until the start of the run. Traditionally, women don't run the *encierro*, but these days plenty take part. Stewards often ask **women** to leave, but if you want to run, just say you're OK, stand your ground, and hope for the best like everyone else.

Nobody can outrun the bulls for more than fifty metres. The **deadliest area** is about halfway along Estafeta, where the route is defined for twenty metres or so by a stone alleyway. If you get caught in the doorways that line this, and a bull takes a fancy to you, there's no escape. Your best bet is to either position yourself quite close to the start and jump aside as soon as the bulls pass, or start off a good couple of hundred metres up the road so you'll make it past Estafeta – and quite possibly into the actual bullring – before the beasts catch up with you. You may get booed by the crowd for starting so far up, but the sheer terror you feel as you sprint through the blind alley of Estafeta after the rocket has gone off is one hundred percent real. Finally, be really careful about trying to make it through the final tunnel into the bullring. It's an amazing experience storming into the ring to the roars of the crowd, but there's always a huge pile-up in the tunnel as people who have made it through slowdown. The bulls manage to catch up with this flailing scrummage and hit someone just about every day.

Once all the bulls have made it into the ring, another rocket is fired to give the all clear to those still on the course. If you're still cowering in the gutter with your hands clamped over your head, now is the time to get up and pretend you just tripped over. Back inside the ring, the bulls are quickly ushered into pens, where they will wait until the evening's bullfight. To please the crowds, the *novillas* – baby bulls with padded horns – are released and the mob of runners play **matador games** for half an hour or so. Every now and then, a big roar

goes up in the crowd as one of the young but immensely strong bulls manages to catch a tourist by surprise and toss them clean over its back. After about an hour, the arena gradually empties as people head off to clean up, get something to eat or just go back to bed. The first bull run is over – last night's carnage can now be cleaned up, the wooden barriers along the route taken down and the town can relax for a few hours before the evening's events – and before everyone has to go through it all again in tomorrow's *encierro*.

The closing ceremony

The Fiesta de San Fermin officially ends at midnight on July 14, with the red-and-white-clad revellers, each carrying a single burning candle, bidding farewell to the fiesta in the Plaza del Ayuntamiento, whilst chanting "*pobre de mí*" (literally, "poor me"). The party continues until the early hours of the morning, when the countdown commences for the next year's celebration.

Bullfights

Some people see a **bullfight** as a heroic ballet of man versus beast; others think it's a barbaric and undignified form of torturing innocent animals. Whatever you think, bullfighting is the raison d'être of the festival and the choice to see it is yours alone. A bullfight takes place around 6pm each day of the festival – lasting about three hours – and the locals head towards the **Plaza de Toros** (the bullring) from mid-afternoon with crates of chilled beer and armfuls of sandwiches. Brass, drums and other instruments make up the bands, which burst into song from different parts of the crowd to liven up the fight. **Tickets** are sold from the box office at the Plaza de Toros the day before each fight, although queues are very long – expect to wait at least an hour. If you don't fancy queuing, there are plenty of touts who will sell you tickets at slightly inflated prices. Once the fight has started, the prices fall pretty fast, and as there are six bulls, with each *matador* getting two each, you'll still see plenty of action.

Doing Fiesta de San Fermin

Basics

There are flights from Madrid and Barcelona to the local **airport** at Noáin, 6km from Pamplona, and there are regular **bus** and **train** services from major destinations around the country. The first three things to do when you get in to town are: get rid of your bags at your hotel or the central left-luggage locker facility on Plaza de San Francisco; sort your party kit out; and head for the town square, Plaza del Castillo, to get your free map – which shows where showers and other crucial facilities are located – and list of activities from the mobile tourist office. Then you're ready to let rip.

Accommodation

Due to the relatively small size of the town, finding accommodation during the festival on spec is a hopeless task and you'll pay three times the normal rate; even the **campsite**, *Ezcaba*, about five miles north of town, gets booked up months in advance, although a patch of land next to it allows camper vans to park up. Many of the town's inhabitants turn their houses and apartments into impromptu hostels during the fiesta, charging around €24 per night, but it's more likely that you'll end up joining the thousands of others who sleep in the many parks, plazas, and shopping arcades in the town. Showers and left-luggage facilities are available, so as long as you bring a sleeping bag, stamina and a sense of humour it's really no big deal. It also means you can stay right in the thick of things throughout your stay, but be careful with your stuff and try to sleep in groups – theft during the fiesta is rife.

Central, reasonably-priced **hostels** can be found around Calle San Nicolás: the *Hostal Otano* (☏ 948/225095), and *Hostal Beaván* (☏ 948/223428) are two good options, with double rooms for around €100. If you have more money to spend, you could stay in one of the **hotels** close to the action – the *Eslava*, in the Plaza Virgen de la O, west along the Rio Arga (☏ 948/222270), has a magnificent view over the city walls and charges around €130. The *Europa*, on c/Espoz y Mina 11 (☏ 948/221800), is very close to the Plaza del Castillo and the bullring and has a wide range of rooms, some of which overlook Estafeta, for around €270. Outside Pamplona, the *Parador de Olite* is half an hour away by car, and charges around €400 (obligatory during San Fermin), but is an amazing place to escape the mayhem if you want a bit of luxury.

Eating and drinking

Eating in **restaurants** is difficult unless you look reasonably respectable, and in any case most of the cheap restaurants simply turn into sandwich factories for seven days; apart from the *tapas* served in **bars**, you'll be lucky to find much else in the centre of town. Bars are open virtually all hours in Pamplona. However, buying sangria or beer from the various shops in the Casco Viejo is a lot cheaper. Of the bars on Plaza del Castillo, *Bar Iruña* is probably the best, with a sweaty dance floor that is heaving from around 8pm to 7am. One of the best post-run places is *Bodegón Sarria* bar on Estafeta.

Event info

San Fermin (ⓦ www.sanfermin.com). Excellent festival site with some great photos of fiestas past.

Useful websites

Pamplona Tourist Office (ⓦ www.pamplona.net). The official site of the tourist office. Packed with useful information on transport, accommodation and eating, as well as a programme of fiesta events.
Navarra Tourist Office (ⓦ www.cfnavarra.es). The regional tourist office website, offering information on the area as a whole.

Time zone GMT+1   **Country code** +34   **Currency** euro (€)

Galway International Oyster Festival

One of the greatest Irish pub-crawls ever devised

Galway International Oyster Festival

Where?
Galway, Ireland

When?
Last full weekend in September

How long?
3 days

Ireland's longest-running and best gourmet extravaganza, the Galway Interntaional Oyster Festival celebrates the arrival of the new oyster season with a three-day furore of drinking, dancing and crustacean guzzling. Most of the official events are based in the enormous red-and-white striped festival marquee, specially erected by the picturesque mouth of the River Corrib, next to small Claddagh harbour, but it's just as much fun to join the informal carousing and guzzling that takes place across the city centre, as visitors and residents alike attempt to tackle the Guinness Oyster Trail. If you've ever wondered what the Irish *craic* was all about, you'll find it here, in glorious technicolour, as you're whirled away into the fun, madness and mayhem of one of the greatest Irish pub-crawls ever devised.

The opening parade

The **opening parade** at noon on Saturday is a must-see and, unlike many of the other organized events, it doesn't cost a dime. Just after midday in Eyre Square, Galway's mayor cracks open the first oyster of the season, knocks it back in one gulp, and declares the festival officially open. A parade of marching bands, vintage cars, oyster openers, dignitaries and oyster "Pearls" – a dozen of the town's beauties, young and old – then make their way down the main street, past the thousands of locals and visitors lining the street corners, pub doorways, and the banks of the River Corrib.

The World Oyster Opening Championship

The parade's destination is the festival marquee, and more specifically the **World Oyster Opening Championship**, which, for the oyster aficionados who come from far and wide, is the highlight of the festival. Tickets cost €100 – you need to buy them in advance from the festival website (see p.46) – but this includes oyster tasting, a sumptuous seafood lunch and a ringside seat for the Championships at 2pm.

History

The **first Galway International Oyster Festival** was held in 1954, the brainchild of Brian Collins, the manager of Galway's *Great Southern Hotel* – then the largest hotel in the west of Ireland – who saw it as a way to extend the tourist season into September. Collins also spotted an opportunity to promote Galway's native oysters to a wider market and to capitalize on the city's reputation as the centre of the arts in Ireland. Convincing an Irish brewer, one Arthur Guinness, to sponsor the event, also helped.

If Collins was the brains behind the festival, Paddy Burke was its heart. He organized the opening and presentation of the 3500 oysters that were consumed during the first festival, and his eponymous pub, in the middle of Clarenbridge village, nine miles outside Galway, entertained the hundred or so visitors all afternoon. Come evening, the dignitaries returned to the *Great Southern* for dinner while the rest of the rabble raised hell in *Paddy's* bar until the early hours. There have been some refinements since – a striped marquee has housed other special events, including the World Oyster Opening Championships, since 1968 – but the spirit of Burke's original Guinness- and oyster-fuelled bash remains.

In recent years, the event has attracted an increasingly international audience, and in 1984 the marquee and ceremonies were transferred to their present location on the outskirts of **Galway City** and the rest of the carousing to Galway's numerous pubs.

The "Mardi Gras" Party and the Oyster Festival Gala Ball

Those with deep pockets who hanker after something more refined than Guinness-guzzling can attend the gala nights on Friday and Saturday. The **"Mardi Gras" Party**, held at the festival marquee on Friday from 7.30pm, is a gourmet dinner-dance, preceded by a champagne and oyster reception and hosted by the town mayor. Tickets cost €120, and the dress code is smart casual. Saturday night sees the **Oyster Festival Gala Ball** at the *Radisson SAS Hotel*, just east of Eyre Square on Lough Atalia Road, at 8pm. Tickets for this cost a hefty €150 each, but you get the chance to mingle with Galway's great and good over a champagne reception, dinner and cabaret. Dress is strictly black tie, but colour is provided by the spectacle of the oyster-opening competitors parading the flags of their countries – the cue for dancing till dawn. Tickets for both events are available from the festival website (see p.46).

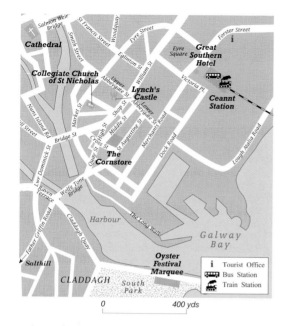

As soon as the parade has disappeared inside, usually by around 1pm, the barrels of Guinness are tapped, the champagne corks fly, and the oysters are shucked from their shells. Up to fifteen countries compete in the Championship, with teams from the USA, Canada, Scandinavia, France, Belgium, Germany, Italy, the UK and, of course, Ireland – the local representative is chosen at the Irish Oyster Opening Championship, held on the previous Thursday evening at *Quays Bar* on Quay Street (8pm; free). The objective is to open thirty native oysters as quickly as possible, but time is not the only criterion – points are also awarded (or deducted) for the final presentation of the tray of oysters. In case you were wondering just how long it takes a pro to do this, the 2005 World Oyster Opening Champion, the aptly named Oystein Reinsborg from Norway, needed only 2min 43sec to complete the task – though this is still some way off former world champion Willie Morans' amazing time of 1min 31sec, set in 1977.

The Guinness Oyster Trail

Even if you can't get into the festival marquee, you're still likely to have a ball. Entertainment for the masses comes in the form of the **Guinness Oyster Trail** – the real backbone of the party and a permanent feature for the past forty years. The Trail consists of some thirty pubs dotted around the town, each offering free oysters with a

pint of Guinness, not to mention a host of live music, comedy and dance acts over the entire three-day period. Almost the entire population of Galway, along with visitors from all over the world, cram into the pubs along the Trail to drink the dark stuff and knock back the slippery bivalves – every pub on the Oyster Trail employs a full-time oyster-opener throughout the weekend, who frantically and ceaselessly liberates the delicious creatures from their shells.

if you can down thirty pints and up to one hundred oysters and still attend the Farewell Party, you need never prove yourself again

The traditional objective is to down a pint and a couple of oysters in every pub along the Trail over the three days – that's around thirty pints and up to one hundred oysters. If you can do this and still attend the Sunday Farewell Party, you need never prove yourself again. If it sounds like your kind of challenge, just get hold of a **Trail Map**, available from any featured pub, and start drinking. Bear in mind that one of the main obstacles to completing the trail is the weather; perched on the west coast of Ireland, Galway is exposed to the unrelenting gales of the North Atlantic, and the weather at the end of September is usually wet and bitterly cold. It's all too easy to get stuck in one pub – everyone is usually very friendly and there's often a roaring log fire. The Trail isn't especially long – many of the pubs on its route are clustered around High and Quay streets and Eyre Square – but its pubs vary enormously in quality, size and the effort they make to get in to the festive spirit.

(see p.46).

Farewell Party

Final confirmation, if it was needed, that the organizers are on your wavelength comes on Sunday morning with the **Farewell Party**, held in the festival marquee from 1pm; tickets cost €20 – you need to buy them in advance from the festival website (see p.46). It goes without saying that oysters are on the menu – either fried, served with scrambled eggs, or raw – but it takes a cast-iron constitution to face the slippery shellfish after Saturday's excesses, so most people plump for the full Irish breakfast – the mammoth helpings of sausage, bacon, eggs, et al are just the job after the night before, especially when washed down with a few pints of the dark stuff.

Top Trail pubs

For atmosphere
Busker Browne's Cross Street. Multistorey pub in a former Dominican convent, with original fireplaces and plenty of comfy alcoves.
Neachtain's Cnr of Quay and Cross streets. Galway's finest traditional pub, a homely warren of small bars and snugs.

For live music
The King's Head High Street. Busy pub in an impressive medieval building, featuring anything from rock to big bands.
Tigh Choili Mainguard Street. Sociable traditional pub with twice-daily sessions.

Clarenbridge: the "original" oyster festival

Clarenbridge, the village where it all began, a few miles outside Galway, hosts its own oyster festival two weeks before the Galway event, which to some extent retains the intimate charm of the early days. Sadly, the man himself is no longer with us, but you can raise a glass to his memory in *Paddy Burke's*, the pub where it all started.

Held over ten days, the **Clarenbridge Oyster Festival** is basically a mini Galway, with plenty of traditional music and other special oyster-related events, not least the Oyster Gala Celebration on the second Saturday lunchtime, for which tickets cost €100. Later on, there's a festival barbecue to round the day off, and the next day yet another lunchtime celebration, at which more oysters are knocked back. For more **information**, see ⓦ www.clarenbridge.com.

Basics

Galway's **airport**, Carnmore, is just five miles outside of the city – taxis into the centre cost around €15 – while Shannon Airport is fifty miles to the south. From Dublin, **trains** (3hr) and **buses** (3hr 40min) run to Galway. The town's tourist office is on Forster street, near Eyre Square (℡091/563 081, Ⓦwww.irelandwest.ie)

Accommodation

Galway has a variety of **accommodation**, for all budgets. You could damn the expense and stay in the heart of the action at the *Great Southern Hotel* on Eyre Square, an opulent railway hotel that's recently been renovated in a crisp, modern style (℡091/564 041, Ⓦwww.greatsouthernhotelgalway.com; doubles from €200), or go really mad and stay at Philip Treacy's sumptuous *g hotel*, on the outskirts of town at Wellpark (℡091/865 200, Ⓦwww.theghotel.ie), though doubles here are stratospherically expensive at €400 or so. *Jurys Inn* is also perfectly positioned, at the bottom of Quay Street on the banks of the River Corrib (℡091/566 444, Ⓦwww.jurysinns.com), and is much cheaper at €130 for a double. Or there's the *Kinlay House Hostel* just off Eyre Square on Merchants Rd (℡091/565 244, Ⓦwww.kinlaygalway.ie), where you can get a dorm bed for €15. You can

also find cheaper accommodation in the city's many B&Bs, which are nearly all on the outskirts, including large concentrations on College and Dublin roads to the east of the centre, and in the coastal resort of Salthill to the southwest (accessible on city buses #1 and #8 from Eyre Square).

Eating and drinking

If, like most of the population of Galway, you're following the Oyster Trail for the weekend or attending the gala dinners, then finding places to **eat** and drink isn't an issue. Most of the pubs mentioned previously serve up hearty fare – notably *Busker Browne's* and *The King's Head* – as well as dishing out the oysters; and, come last orders, there's always *McDonagh's* fish and chip shop on Quay Street to fall back on – often literally.

Event info

Galway International Oyster Festival (℡091/527 282, Ⓦwww.galwayoysterfest.com). The official festival site, with event information and booking forms.

Time zone GMT   **Country code** +353   **Currency** euro (€)

Glastonbury Festival

It's time to rediscover your free-spirited, tree-hugging side

Glastonbury Festival

Where?
Glastonbury, England

When?
End of June

How long?
3 days

Glastonbury is quite simply the finest music festival in the world. It may not always attract the biggest-name bands, but there's something special about the vibe in the surrounding countryside of southwest England – Druid burial mounds, crop circles, converging ley lines and the like – and the festival digs right into that groove. As well as taking in some great sounds, it's a time to rediscover your free-spirited, tree-hugging side, sleeping under canvas, losing your shoes in the mud and sharing toilet facilities with a hundred thousand other people. There's a lot of drugs, a lot of young people and a great buzz, but Ibiza it ain't – you can still smile at people and hug strangers, but the person you're doing it to may be dressed as a Womble or the Earth Mother Goddess.

Glastonbury officially runs from Friday morning to Sunday night, with the majority of punters arriving on Thursday and struggling home Monday afternoon. It's a real camping experience, so you need to organize a tent, sleeping bag and ideally a ground mat if you want to avoid waking up freezing at 4.30am. These days, everything you might possibly need – spare tent pegs, blankets, toilet roll, gas cylinders, even a new tent – is available from the expanse of market stalls inside the festival grounds.

Pitching your tent

Your first big decision will be where to stick your tent. Arriving late Friday or on Saturday means your choice will be extremely limited, and you may find yourself walking around for hours looking for a spare patch of land. The area northeast of the **Pyramid Stage** (Row Mead, Big Ground and Kidney Mead) is hugely popular and very noisy, but gives you the buzz of being smack bang in the middle of things. The further south you go the more peaceful the fields are, with the areas surrounding the **Green Field** (Pennard Hill Ground, Dragon Field and William's Greenfield) particularly mellow. Romantics should pitch their tent in the west fields facing east, to receive the first golden rays of dawn. Once you've settled on somewhere, it's a good idea to rig up some kind of flagpole or marker to make your tent stand out from the fifteen thousand other identical ones in your field.

History

The **first Glastonbury festival** was held in 1970, when dairy farmer Michael Eavis persuaded T-Rex to play a gig in his fields on Worthy Farm, paying the £500 fee in monthly installments from his sales of milk. Intermittent versions of the festival were held in the same place throughout the 1970s, but numbers didn't really take off until 1981 when eighteen thousand people witnessed its relaunch as the Glastonbury CND Festival, with its distinctive new pyramid stage that conveniently doubled as a cowshed in winter. The event has been **cancelled** several times – first in 1988 following outbreaks of violence between New Age travellers and festival security, once in 1991 after the event was swamped by Acid House ravers, and again in 2001 and 2006, due to ongoing concerns about safety after numbers had rocketed to as many as one hundred and fifty thousand.

Other **key dates** are the launch of the festival's own station – Radio Avalon – in 1983, the introduction of the Green Field as a showcase for environmentally friendly technology in 1984, and the name change to "Glastonbury Festival for Contemporary Performing Arts" in 1990 to reflect the huge array of entertainment on offer. Music-wise, headline highlights have included Oasis in 1994, Massive Attack playing the first dance tent in 1995 and the Chemical Brothers' pyrotechnics of 2000 – though, as any old timer will tell you, the buzz caused by David Bowie's first appearance in 1971 is nearly impossible to outdo. The fields have been turned to mud several times, most recently in 2005 when two months' worth of rain fell in two hours, resulting in the bizarre sight of rubber dinghies ferrying stranded revellers across the fields.

In recent times, Glastonbury has become more and more commercialized. In 2002, **Mean Fiddler**, one of the UK's biggest live music promoters – which also runs other major British festivals such as Reading and Leeds (see p.150) – took a twenty percent stake in the Glastonbury Festival, and assumed full operational control of the event. Some people claim the subsequent festivals have been the best ever – and they've certainly prevented the unsavoury elements that have blighted Glastonbury in previous years. Others, though, feel that the big steel fences, sponsored tents, and sprawling market stalls now selling anything from bongs and bongos to iPods and mini DVD players anaesthetizes the festival. Not to mention the fact that you can see much of it on Channel Four these days.

However, the original feel-good vibe of the event still flows through the festival – over £1m is donated each year to **charity** at the insistence of Michael Eavis, to the likes of Greenpeace, Water Aid, Oxfam and local good causes.

If it's going to rain – and this being Britain in summer, there's every chance it will – don't pitch your tent at the bottom of a hill or you'll get soaked. And if it's going to be hot, don't set up too close to **toilet blocks**. The toilets at Glastonbury are almost as legendary as some of the bands that have played there. Combine the digestive systems of one hundred thousand people who have lived on a diet of junk food, veggie burgers and strong cider for three days, with sanitary arrangements that wouldn't pass muster at a refugee camp and you get an idea of what's in store. In recent years, however, there have been huge improvements, with the introduction of blocks of airplane-style flush toilets. Plenty of the old-style toilets are still around, though, to give you a true "flavour" of yesteryear.

Insider info Leave your mobile phone at home. One of the quintessential Glastonbury experiences is getting separated from your friends and wandering around hopelessly on your own, meeting all sorts of interesting characters in the process.

What's going on?

One of the greatest aspects of Glastonbury is the huge array of **entertainment** available to suit all tastes and all states of mind. In fact, it's entirely possible to go the whole festival without taking in a single big-name band. Instead, you can watch bizarre theatre performances, holler at the outdoor comedy acts, try out your skills on the trapeze, play the bongos in a tepee, check out a solar-powered shower, take in a low-key set at the acoustic stage, get your freak-on to some big beats in the dance tents, catch an open-air movie in the cinema field or just sit in the stone circle at the top of the Green Field and meditate on the whole sprawling spectacle below. And then get to see David Bowie headlining the Pyramid Stage. Priceless.

sit in the stone circle at the top of the Green Field and take in the whole sprawling spectacle below

As there's so much on offer, it's really worth keeping hold of a copy of the **festival guide** that comes with your ticket – it has great maps and a huge timetable. Read up beforehand, but stay calm – you can't possibly see and hear everything going on around Glastonbury so don't even bother trying. Alternatively, take a **radio** and tune into the official channel, Radio Avalon (87.7FM), which has regular news, music and timetable updates. The festival website (see p.52) posts a line-up of acts as and when they sign up, so check it regularly in the run-up.

What's in a name?

What is the Glastonbury Festival actually called? Some call it **"Glasto"**, which indicates that you're a city type just down for the weekend, having borrowed your parents' car to get there. West Country locals refer to it as **"Glasters"**, so perhaps everyone else should. The **"Pilton Festival"** would be the most accurate name, since Worthy Farm is actually located in the village of Pilton, six miles east of Glastonbury. Anyone caught talking about their imminent trip to the **"Glastonbury Festival for Contemporary Performing Arts"** should do the decent thing and give up their ticket to someone much more deserving.

Glastonbury: The movie

Julien Temple's film *Glastonbury* is the most complete collection of festival footage ever put together. The director, whose past achievements include the rockumentary classics *The Great Rock 'n' Roll Swindle* and *The Filth and the Fury*, had complete access to all aspects of the festival from 2002 to 2005, plus thousands of hours of personal footage dug out from under beds, from the cellars and the corners of mouldy wigwams festering in the attic. The result, released at the start of 2006, is claimed by many to be as good as attending the mud-and-love fest for yourself. It'll certainly bring back some great memories for regular festivalgoers, and whet the appetite of the uninitiated. As good as the real thing? You'll just have to go and decide for yourself.

Basics

The festival site is located six miles outside Glastonbury, on the A361, in the village of Pilton. Its bus station – beside Gate 1, in the northwest corner of the site – is served by National Express **buses**, which connect with major UK cities, including London, Manchester, Birmingham and Bristol, and First Badgerline buses, which connect with Bristol, Bath, Wells, Glastonbury and Castle Cary. The nearest **train** station is Castle Cary, five miles to the south. If you're coming by **car**, you'll need to buy a ticket to park in the secure car parks located in fields to the east and west of the festival site, or use one of the expensive unofficial parking fields nearby.

If you want to do it all in style, you could arrive by **helicopter** and stay in nearby caravan, log cabin or medieval tent accommodation. It's not really rock 'n' roll, but it will set you back around £1500 per person. See ⊛ www.flyglastonbury.com for details.

Accommodation

The best thing to do is bring a **tent**, although caravans, campervans and mobile homes are accommodated in designated fields to the east of the festival site. **Campervan** passes cost an additional £25 per person, and the demand for them is usually high, so you should get yours when you get your tickets.

If you can't stand the idea of camping, you may well be able to book a reasonably priced local **guesthouse** in Shepton Mallet or Glastonbury; regular buses connect both towns to the festival site. Alternatively, there are lots of comfortable **B&Bs** in the villages around, among them the fairly traditional *Tynings House*, Pillmoor Lane, Coxley (☎01749 675368, ⊛www.tynings.co.uk), with doubles from £56 a night, and *Clanville Manor*, Castle Cary (☎01963 350124, ⊛www.clanvillemanor. co.uk), for around the same price; or the very cool and slightly more expensive *Wookey Hole Inn*, in Wookey Hole (☎01749 676677, ⊛www. wookeyholeinn.com), which has stylish double rooms for around £80.

Eating and drinking

Food standards have improved enormously on site – where you used to be charged £5 for a cremated veggie burger, you now have the choice of Japanese noodles, curried goat, fish and chips, Thai fried rice, bacon baguettes, and much, much more from the stalls of the huge central market. This may be blatant commercialism to the festival purists, but it means you don't need to lug any heating and cooking equipment around with you and can get on with the business of enjoying yourself. **Beer** is widely available from the large centralized beer tents run by the Workers Beer Company, which also serve wine, Coke, orange juice and the infamous Burrow Hill Cider – enjoyed on its own or mixed with half a pint of lager as a "snakebite", a name you'll understand after drinking three of them.

Safety

Take it easy. Over the years, dozens of people have needed emergency treatment at Glastonbury from **drug overdoses** or from taking contaminated drugs, and there have been several fatalities. The festival is also occasionally plagued by petty **theft**, with entire tents and all their contents disappearing. Property lock-ups are available at each entrance, with others dotted around the site.

Event info

Glastonbury Festival (☎01458 834596, ⊛www.glastonburyfestivals. co.uk). Official festival website with ticket info, photos and the line-up.
Glastonbury Tourist Information Centre The Tribunal, 9 High St, Glastonbury BA6 9DP (☎01458 832954 or 949, ⊛www.glastonbury. co.uk).

Time zone GMT   **Country code** +44   **Currency** Pound sterling (£)

Hogmanay

The rain may have turned to sleet, but there's no better setting for a New Year's knees-up

Hogmanay

Where?
Edinburgh, Scotland

When?
Hogmanay is the name Scots give to New Year's Eve, although events are organized between December 29 and January 1

How long?
4 days

For a wild mix of fireworks, whisky, music and mass dancing, there's nothing like the street party in Edinburgh to celebrate New Year's Eve. They greet the arrival of New Year elsewhere around the world of course, but nowhere quite manages the blend of tradition, hedonism, sentimentality and enthusiasm achieved by the Scots; indeed, Edinburgh's Hogmanay – as well as similar events in Glasgow, Aberdeen and all across Scotland – has become a major world event, with a mass of processions, concerts and parties taking place in the days leading up to and immediately after the night itself. It may have been dark since 3.30pm in the afternoon, and the rain may have turned to sleet, but there's no better setting for a New Year's knees-up, which sees over one-hundred-thousand people crammed into the Scottish capital with one thing on their mind: midnight.

The build-up

It's a good idea to arrive in Edinburgh a few days before Hogmanay, to catch the various events taking place, and it's worth giving yourself the chance to look around the city – for obvious reasons, sightseeing after the big night isn't such a great idea. One of the most dramatic events in Edinburgh during the lead-up to Hogmanay is the torchlit procession down the historic Royal Mile on December 29. A popular family event, anyone can buy a flaming torch and join the crowd of around ten-thousand people as they walk from the Royal Mile to nearby Calton Hill, where a replica of a Viking longboat is set alight. Accompanied by drummers and other musicians, the event harks back to the pagan fire celebrations of the first Hogmanay revellers.

On the night of December 30, a procession of pipers and drummers, resplendent in kilts and tartan finery, provides a memorable opening to the "Night Afore" celebrations, a pleasantly alternative warm-up to Hogmanay that, in recent years, has featured some bizarre and visually dramatic continental street theatre. If there's a nip in the air, one way to get your circulation going is to head to the Scottish Ceilidh Stage, where you're encouraged to join in some traditional Scottish dances with names such as "Strip the Willow" and "The Dashing White Sergeant".

Elsewhere around town various special club nights, comedy acts and classical concerts take place in venues ranging from St Giles Cathedral to the honeycomb of haunted vaults under the Old Town. You'll also find an open-air ice rink, a carnival with various stomach-turning rides, and a big wheel towering over Princes Street. Alternatively, you can settle into one of the hundreds of cosy pubs around town and get into the right mood with a pint or two.

History

The **traditions** behind Scotland's attachment to partying at the end of December go back long before anyone decided there were 12 months in a year and 31 days in December. When Christianity started to reach pagan parts, savvy missionaries realized that it didn't help their cause much to upset established rituals, however heathen they might seem. So a fair amount of subtle reinvention went on, including changing the celebrations for the birth of the sun into celebrations for the birth of the Son. In this way, ancient pagan traditions got to run alongside rituals associated with the Mass for Christ, and everyone still got to party. The Protestants who controlled Scotland in the sixteenth century, however, took a dim view of this Catholic ritual, and Christmas was abolished, leaving the Scots no alternative but to revert to celebrating the more transparently secular winter solstice.

No one really knows the origin of the word **Hogmanay** (though there are plenty who can bore for Scotland with their theories), but this soon became the name of Scotland's special midwinter festival: houses were cleaned from top to bottom, debts were paid and quarrels made up, and, after the bells were rung at midnight, great store was set by welcoming good luck into your house. This still takes the form of the traditional **first-footing** – visiting your neighbours, bearing gifts. The ideal first-foot is a tall dark-haired male; women or redheads, on the other hand, bring bad luck – though no one carrying a bottle of whisky will be deemed to bring bad luck for long.

All this neighbourly greeting meant that a fair bit of partying went on, of course, and after a while no one was expected to go to work the next day, or if the party was that good, the day after that either. Even today, January 1 is a public holiday in the rest of the UK, but only in Scotland does the holiday extend to the next day as well. In fact, right up to the 1950s Christmas was a normal working day for many folk in Scotland, and Hogmanay was widely regarded as by far the more important celebration.

Hogmanay night

It's always been a common tradition for residents of a town or city in Scotland to gather around a central market cross or tollbooth on New Year's Eve, to wait for the hands of the town clock to reach midnight. At "the bells" there would be a great cheer, all the other church bells would ring, ships' foghorns would blare, everyone would greet everyone else, and bottles of whisky would be passed round (champagne, when you think about it, is woefully impractical). This is basically what still happens today – though with many, many, more people. In some years, the night of December 31 has seen a quarter of a million people (the population of Edinburgh is only 350,000) thronging the streets of the capital. In

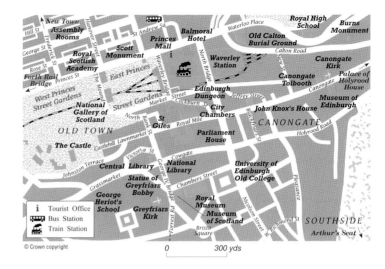

the early part of the evening the atmosphere builds, as crowds begin to gather and revellers emerge from pubs to meet up with friends or claim the best spots – either near the music stages or anywhere with a view of Edinburgh Castle – in anticipation of the midnight fireworks display. The street party officially begins at 10pm, with acts ranging from up-and-coming rock bands to big-name DJs appearing on the various music stages, while banks of screens elsewhere relay the action. You might choose to get up close to one stage, or alternatively wander from one to another to get a taste of the different styles of music – camping things up with tribute bands such as Bjorn Again, or concentrating on world music or Scottish folk, with groups like Shooglenifty introducing revellers to the local speciality of rock'n'reeling. The headline gig takes place in Princes Street Gardens with its spectacular setting under the battlements of Edinburgh Castle, though to get close to this one you'll need a separate ticket for the concert, and it's always a sellout; in recent years, UB40 and home-grown heroes Texas have done the honours.

Basically, though, the best thing to do is just hang out, drinking and dancing and making new friends as midnight approaches, when all who can still focus keep an eye on the clock face on the tower on the **Balmoral Hotel**, which dominates the east end of Princes Street. This is normally two minutes fast to help folk catch their train at nearby Waverley Station, and Hogmanay is the only day of the year it tells the right time. During the countdown to midnight, the roar of the crowd drowns out any bands still on stage, and at the first stroke of midnight, the spectacular skyline of Edinburgh is lit

Insider info Not only do the Scots have their own name for the last day of the year, but the song sung around the globe to see out the old year and usher in the new, *Auld Lang Syne*, is a traditional Scottish tune with lyrics by Robert Burns, the country's national poet.

up by eight tons of **fireworks** launched from seven hills around the city, including the most dramatic of all, the craggy volcanic outcrop supporting Edinburgh Castle. Then, all that remains is to wish 100,000 people a Happy New Year.

The music on the different stages goes on for another hour, but even after they've finished, the crowds take some time to disperse. Unless you have a ticket, invitation or are prepared to join a long queue, you'll struggle to get into most of the main clubs and venues in town. Pubs start shutting at 1am and are closed by 3am, so most people who are still standing head for a **house party**. Over the days leading up to Hogmanay you'd be unlucky if no one in your group got an invitation to one of these, and being a friend of a friend is more than enough to gain entry to most places.

New Year's Day

New Year's Day is a public holiday and should by rights be left well alone for nursing hangovers without distraction. But some people are inspired to do the strangest things (or maybe they're just still drunk). At noon at South Queensferry, underneath the Forth Rail Bridge northwest of Edinburgh, there's something called the **Loony Dook**, which involves stripping off most of your clothes and swimming in the sea. Around the same time, a triathlon takes place around Arthur's Seat, the hill that looms over Edinburgh. For everyone else, the pubs open at 11am, and quite a lot of them sell their own patented hangover cure. You can risk this if you dare, or just seek out one serving a full Scottish breakfast – porridge, followed by a plateful of bacon, sausage, egg, black pudding and fried potato scone.

eight tons of fireworks are launched from seven hills around the city, including the most dramatic of all, the craggy volcanic outcrop supporting Edinburgh Castle

Basics

Edinburgh **airport** is seven miles west of the city centre, linked by frequent buses. **Trains** arrive bang in the middle of town at Waverley Station, while **buses** arrive on the east side of St Andrews Square, just north of the station. The city centre is quite compact and easily navigated on foot, helped by numerous historical landmarks by which you can orient yourself. Should you need any advice though, the **tourist information office** is at the eastern end of Princes Street by Waverley Train Station.

Accommodation

The least expensive option is a dorm bed in one of the many backpacker **hostels** in the city, though most places now insist on a minimum stay of three or four nights. Some hostels mimic the big hotels by selling a Hogmanay package that throws in a pass for the street party and other goodies with your accommodation, but at an inflated £150–200. A small but friendly hostel worth trying is *Brodies 2*, 93 High St (☎0131/556 2223, @ www.brodieshostels.co.uk), or you could head to *Edinburgh Backpackers Hostel*, 65 Cockburn St (☎0131/220 1717, @ www.hoppo.com). Try @ www.scotlands-tophostels.com or @ www.st-christophers.co.uk for other central options.

Mid-priced **hotels** in the city centre include *Tailors Hall Hotel*, 139 Cowgate (☎0131/622 6801, @ www.festival-inns.co.uk; three-night minimum stay, £140 per room per night with breakfast, no street pass), and *Apex International Hotel*, 31–35 Grassmarket (☎0845/608 3456, @ www.apexhotels.co.uk; two-night minimum stay, £220 per room per night with breakfast, street pass included). More upmarket is the superbly situated and contemporary *Scotsman Hotel*, 20 North Bridge (☎0131/556 5565, @ www.thescotsmanhotel.co.uk; three-night minimum stay, £330 per room per night with breakfast, street pass included).

There are also hundreds of **guesthouses** and B&Bs about a mile from the centre of town. On the edge of the New Town, north of the centre, is *Ardenlee Guest House*, 9 Eyre Place (☎0131/556 2838, @ www.ardenleeguesthouse.com), while south of the centre there's *MW Guest House*, 94 Dalkeith Rd (☎0131/662 9265, @ www.mwguesthouse.co.uk). Expect a two- or three-night minimum stay, and rates of around £100 per night per room for bed and breakfast. Also worth considering if you're in a small group and staying for a few days is a **self-catering apartment**. This way you can throw your own party once everyone else has gone to bed – *Royal Garden Apartments* (@ www.royal-garden.co.uk) and *Canon Court Apartments* (@ www.canoncourt.co.uk) are two of the better-located options.

Eating and drinking

While you should have no problem finding good places **to eat** in Edinburgh in the days around Hogmanay, on the evening itself you may find many restaurants closed or only serving lavish (and expensive) special menus. Pub grub is a good fall-back option if you can find a place that isn't too crowded with drinkers, and there are plenty of fish-and-chip shops, though remember that in Scotland you can also buy what's known as a "haggis supper" – a deep-fried haggis (a dark, sausage-like mixture of meat, offal, onion, spices and oatmeal, for those not in the know) served with chips. If you're just feeling peckish, there are plenty of stalls selling hot dogs or chips, but you should try the tasty local speciality – hot stovies, a mix of chopped-up potatoes, onion and beef stock or dripping.

Edinburgh is crammed with pubs worthy of a pre-party **drink** or two, although be prepared for lengthy queues at the bar. Out on the streets, it's worth remembering that whisky and other spirits are easier to lug around than beer; note, however, that shops selling alcohol close at 10pm.

Event info

Edinburgh Hogmanay (@ www.edinburghshogmanay.org). Official site with ticket info and up-to-date information.
Hogmanay (@ www.hogmanay.net). Busy site with information on all Hogmanay events around Scotland, and bulletin boards with gossip about arrangements for the festivities.

Time zone GMT   **Country code** +44   **Currency** Pound sterling (£)

Ibiza Closing Parties

I eat when I'm hungry, I drink when I'm thirsty, I shag when I'm horny and I'll sleep when I die

Ibiza Closing Parties

Where?
Ibiza, Spain

When?
Last 3 weeks of
September

How long?
3 weeks

SPAIN

Ibiza

Notorious for its dynamic nightlife, Ibiza's summer clubbing season is an annual orgy of hedonism that reaches a messy climax during September, when the main club promoters and venues host a series of stamina-sapping closing parties to round things off and extract a few final euros from their battered punters. These end-of-season events tend to attract an older clubbing crowd, who prefer to hop over to Ibiza for a long weekend (a "cheeky one" in clubber speak) in the relative sanity of September – thus avoiding the gangs of teenage pill-monsters that descend on the island in late July and August. The British rave dinosaurs join a resident hardcore of Ibizan clubbers and an international cast of party freaks and techno geeks, all brought together by a common appetite for Class A entertainment and a devotion to dance music.

History

The origins of Ibiza's club scene can be traced back to the hippie-trippy happenings of the **1960s**, when – as a rusty ferry-ride off the road south to Marrakesh – the island was an essential pit stop for the boho bunch. The first wave of "beats" found a poor, rustic island peopled by friendly locals, who remained largely tolerant of their acid- and mushroom-fuelled excesses and general aversion to swimming costumes, combs and soap. Ibiza was already well established as an outpost for assorted opponents of the Franco regime, its residents including a substantial community of Spanish artists and lefty politicos, many of whom needed little persuasion to join the party.

Two of Ibiza's legendary clubs – *Pacha* and *Amnesia* – date back to the early **1970s**; both were originally hangouts for this international wandering class. Steadily, the simple farmhouses that formed the structural base of today's überclubs began to sprout extensions, bars and dance floors, as the venues threw bigger and bigger themed events and parties. The sheer scale and opulence of Ibiza's clubs, above all *Ku* (now *Privilege*), began to pull in the Euro jet set, plus a smattering of Hollywood faces and swinging Gulf sheikhs. Back then, the closing parties were much less commercial events, when anyone who was anyone (and plenty of nobodies) got in free, and there were cauldrons of special cocktails on the house.

The Ibiza scene remained cosmopolitan and mature – champagne flutes and cocaine spoons rather than pills 'n' thrills – until the **mid-1990s**, when increasingly rapacious British club promoters, including Cream, Manumission and the Ministry of Sound, targeted Ibiza and hosted nights in the island's clubs. Steadily, British holiday-makers began to filter into Ibiza Town and the Sant Rafel clubs from the resort of Sant Antoni (where nightclubbing had traditionally revolved around tequila-downing contests and a footie-style "'ere we go" soundtrack) to these British-promoted events.

Today's high-season club scene is unequivocally business driven, and very expensive, with twenty or so UK promoters, plus a smattering of Dutch, German and Italian clubs, scrapping it out over the summer, desperately trying to entice clubbers to their nights. The promoters organize elaborate themed parades to publicize their events, and if you spend any time in the bar area of Ibiza Town you'll see stilt walkers, spacemen and bondage-clad dancers bearing club banners as they move through the narrow portside streets dispensing flyers.

Ibiza's **mainstream club scene** revolves around seven mega *discotecas* plus a few minor venues, which, for a few weeks every year, play host to the world's finest DJs. In one season, the owners of the club *Amnesia* might hire their venue to the German techno promoters Cocoon on Mondays, the Spanish gay party La Troya on Wednesdays, Britain's Cream on Thursdays and Made in Italy on Fridays. All the Ibizan clubs adopt a similar policy of booking different promoters on different nights of the week (except *Pacha*, which has pioneered an in-house party programme in recent years). Each promoter throws a closing party sometime in September, and each club also throws its own, so if you're in Ibiza anytime after the first week of the month there's sure to be plenty going on.

What's so special about these closing parties? Well, it very much depends on the individual event – many are ridiculously over-hyped. Obviously, the bigger the club promoter, the more money goes into the night – so an organization such as the Ministry of Sound will book a really big-name DJ or two, bring in troupes of dancers and put a lot of work into decorating and lighting the venue with disco spangle and sparkle. The negative side to some of these really big closing parties is that the venue is likely to be rammed and the entrance price hiked to as much as €50 or €60.

The clubs

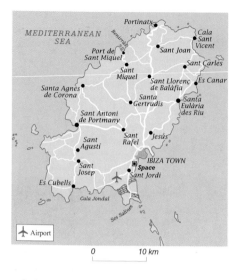

The two Sant Antoni-based clubs, **Eden** and **Es Paradis**, draw a young British rave crowd, many of them steaming after warming up in the resort's notorious West End (famed for its dozens of British pubs, raucous happy hours, wet T-shirt contests, puking and brawling). Their closing parties are always wild, with hundreds of workers who've survived the Ibiza season by waiting on tables, dishing out club flyers or dealing dodgy drugs, letting rip and joining the holidaying clubbers. At *Es Paradis*, a stunning venue topped by a pyramid, the entire dance floor is flooded just before sunrise, provoking an orgy of groping. Up in Sant Rafel, in the centre of the island, music is more the focal point of the party, especially at **Amnesia**, one of the key venues of the 1980s Acid House scene, whose final closing party in late September is another essential date. After 4am, the club usually throws open its doors and lets everyone in free, and despite official regulations, the party often continues for another twelve hours or so until the last frazzled, wobbly legged dancers are escorted away from the dance floor. Cream always puts on a mighty fine closing show as well, hiring some of the finest turntableists, and concentrating on the darker side of dance music – trance and tribal sounds – from the likes of Paul Van Dyk and Paul Oakenfold.

Over the road from *Amnesia*, it's well worth taking a look at **Privilege**, the largest club on the island, with a capacity of around ten thousand. Though the building is besmirched by an ugly roof, the vast interior is breathtaking, with a huge main dance floor, a dozen bars, and a bizarre chill-out dome-zone. You can count on Manumission to concoct an interesting theme for their closing party (though the live sex shows are no more), but no other promoters are able to fill the arena, so choose your night with care or you could be paying €50 to get in and have the floor to yourself. Since 2004, Manumission have also brought in emerging guitar bands, including Babyshambles, Maxïmo Park and the Kaiser Chiefs, to appear at Privilege's Music Box area, in a laudable effort to inject fresh energy and riffs into the Ibizan scene. Plans are afoot to further develop this idea, using more and more live acts, and there is even talk of creating a Glastonbury-style festival.

punters get down on the legendary terrace before moving inside to the vast interior, where the walls quiver to pounding progressive techno

Meanwhile, over in Ibiza Town, the club **Pacha** is unmissable. One of the most elegant venues in Europe, it started life as a *finca* on the edge of town, before being transformed into a club in 1973. It's since been extended to include a restaurant, sushi bar, and a variety of different rooms that concentrate on diverse rhythms – salsa, techno, funk and R&B – though upfront house rules the main room. Most nights are consistently good, but closing parties are very special indeed, with the cream of the world's best DJs, including Erick Morillo and Roger Sanchez, cranking up the pressure to delirious

Promoters' and clubs

Promoters

Circo Loco Ⓦwww.circolocoibiza.com
Cocoon Ⓦwww.cocoon.net
Cream Ⓦwww.cream.co.uk
La Troya Ⓦwww.latroyaasesina-ibiza.com
Made in Italy
  Ⓦwww.madeinitalyibiza.com
Manumission Ⓦwww.manumission.com
Ministry of Sound
  Ⓦwww.ministryofsound.co.uk

Clubs

Amnesia Ⓦwww.amnesia.es
Eden Ⓦwww.edenibiza.com
El Divino Ⓦwww.eldivino-ibiza.com
Es Paradis Ⓦwww.esparadis.com
Pacha Ⓦwww.pacha.com
Penelope Ⓦwww.penelopeibiza.com
Privilege Ⓦwww.privilegeibiza.com
Space Ⓦwww.space-ibiza.es

levels. Be warned, however, that the door tax is steep (€40–50) and drinks prices are outrageous (around €15 for a vodka tonic, and €10 for a small bottle of mineral water).

Ibiza Town's other main club, **El Divino**, is the smallest of the island's prime venues (capacity is around one thousand) but enjoys a stunning setting on the harbour, directly opposite the old town of Dalt Vila across the water. In recent years, it has become much more credible as a venue, with guest slots from some of the world's finest vinyl spinners (including Armand Van Helden and Little Louie Vega) helping the venue to shake off its previous reputation as party central for a dubious bunch of ageing playboys, silicon-pumped hookers, mobsters and Gulf sheikhs. A stone's throw away along the port, **Penelope** is a revamped club that has been through numerous name changes (and a long period of closure) but offers some cutting-edge German electro and minimal house nights.

One of Ibiza's most unique clubs, **Space**, 4km south of Ibiza Town, mainly operates as a day-club, opening at 8am, with punters donning shades and getting down on the legendary terrace before moving inside to the vast, crepuscular interior, where the walls quiver to pounding progressive techno. For many islanders and seasonal workers, the *Space* closing party (a whopping €50–60) was undoubtedly *the* event in the Ibiza club calendar; however, in recent years, as legal restrictions have required a roof to be constructed over the terrace and more and more "outsiders" have appeared on the scene, the vibe has suffered a little. For many, the hardcore action has shifted a couple of kilometres south to **DC10**, a no-frills club positioned virtually on the airport runway in rustic no-man's-land, with a dance floor surrounded by reeds and bullrushes. From a session ("Circo Loco") that only opened on a Monday morning with unknown DJs, the scene here has exploded in popularity, and now draws the hippest crowd (and the most incredible mullets) in Ibiza. Timo Maas has been a resident here, and guests have included Danny Tenaglia and Fat Boy Slim.

If all this sounds too commercial, there are numerous other opportunities to live it up. The venue **Underground**, a converted *finca* near Sant Rafel, hosts some terrific parties and has a bombastic sound system (and no entrance fee), while Ibiza Town has an excess of clubbers' bars. The island's once-legendary psychedelic trance scene, which centred on clandestine free parties thrown in spectacular outdoor locations, is now all but dead – killed off by police raids and hefty fines.

The morning after

On a coastline studded with sandy beaches and rocky coves, there are dozens of wonderful places to kick back and shake off the post-party comedown. **Cala Jondal**, a broad pebbly cove on the south coast, has several fine café-restaurants, including *Yemaná*, where they have sunloungers and serve a mean cava sangría. **Salinas** beach, in the extreme southeast of the island, has another good crop of chilled bars – the hippest is Sa Trincha, where DJ Jonathan Grey plays atmospheric soundscapes to a beautiful crowd. In the north of the island, **Benirràs** beach is flanked by steep wooded hills and has three modestly priced seafood restaurants.

Basics

A very regular bus network operates between Sant Antoni and Ibiza Town, including the **Discobus**, which runs hourly throughout the night; the tourist offices have full details of all bus times. To really explore the island, you'll need to rent a **moped** (from €16/day) or **car** (from €28/day) to get around. There are dozens of rental companies – try Moto Luis (☎971/340 921, ◍ www.motoluis.com) or National (☎971/395 393, ◍ www.nationalcar.com).

Accommodation

By mid-September, there's usually a reasonable selection of accommodation in Ibiza, although hardcore clubbers have little need for hotel beds, dancing all night and sleeping it off on the beach the following day; indeed, extra brownie points are awarded for serious caners, who stay up for days without seeing a bed. In the words of the don of the sleep-deprivation scene, DJ Derek Dahlarge, "I eat when I'm hungry, I drink when I'm thirsty, I shag when I'm horny and I'll sleep when I die".

Ibiza Town (Eivissa in the local Catalan dialect), the island's beautiful and historic capital, has the most diverse nightlife (including a gay-bar district) and cultural interest – most of the cheap **guesthouses** here are in the heart of town, close to the harbour, including *Casa de Huéspedes Vara de Rey*, Vara de Rey 7 (☎971/301 376, ◍ www.hibiza.com; €48–80 for a double), with attractive rooms and friendly management; and the nearby *Sol y Brisa*, Av Bartomeu Vicente Ramón 15 (☎971/310 818; €42–48 for 2 people), a popular, family-run place.

A little further from the centre, the *Apartamentos Roselló* at c/Juli Cirer i Vela (☎971/302 790; €80–96 for a double) are located close to the beach at Figueretes. Here, virtually all the light, airy one-bedroom apartments enjoy stunning sea views. For more luxury, *La Ventana* (☎971/390 857, ◍ www.laventanaibiza.com; from €160 a double) is an atmospheric, historic hotel inside Dalt Vila's walls – all rooms boast four-poster beds.

Ibiza's rural hotel sector is burgeoning, and because the island is so small it's easy enough to stay in the middle of the countryside and not be too far from the madness. Seven kilometres north of Ibiza Town, *Can Pere* (☎971/196 000, ◍ www.canpereibiza.com; from €96 a double) offers a blissfully peaceful base and has a swimming pool and extensive grounds. Or consider the splendid *Can Lluc* (☎971/198 673, ◍ www.canlluc.com; from €275 a double), 2km west of Sant Rafel, which comes close to defining Ibizan rustic chic.

Eating and drinking

Although **food** is the last thing on most clubbers' minds, there are a surprising number of decent places to eat, and some seriously swanky restaurants on the island. Traditional Ibizan cuisine is very hearty, concentrating on huge meat and fish stews and soups, of which there's a decent selection at *Restaurant Victoria*, c/Riambau 1 (☎971/310 622), a pleasingly old-fashioned dining room in the heart of Ibiza Town's buzzing port area. Close by, *Pasajeros*, at c/Vincent Soler, is a fantastic, cramped little place that serves very inexpensive, creatively prepared Spanish and European dishes, with plenty of options for vegetarians, plus good, cheap vino. For a real blowout in a wonderful setting, head up into the old walled city of Dalt Vila, where there are around a dozen excellent places to eat al fresco: *La Torreta* in the Plaça la Vila (☎971/300 411) and the restaurant attached to the *La Ventana* hotel at Sa Carrossa 13 (☎971/390 857) are superb; expect to pay around €40 a head including wine. For a snack, there are plenty of inexpensive cafés on Plaça de Parc and Vara de Rey where you can tuck into a filling *bocadillo* (sandwich). Over in Sant Antoni, some of the best nosh is at *Casa Thai*, Av Dr. Fleming 34 (☎971/344 038; around €16 a head), or for basic grub there are dozens of fast-food places around Calle Santa Agnès.

The prime **bar** action is in Ibiza Town, where a cosmopolitan straight, mixed and gay crowd live it up in the port area. Two of the most happening places are the *Base* bar on the harbourfront at Calle Garijo and the *Rock* bar next door, both a home from home for assorted dance-music industry liggers and DJs. The gay scene is centred on Calle Verge, where there are around two dozen gay bars, including the hip joint *Capricho* and the über-cool *Dôme* (just off the street in c/d'Alfons XII). In Sant Antoni, the wild streets of the "West End" are rammed with British boozers, but for a less frenetic environment, head to the Sunset Strip, where you'll find the famed *Café del Mar*, *Mambo* and the modernist *Sunsea Bar*.

Time zone GMT +1   **Country code** + 34   **Currency** euro (€)

Il Palio

*Sometimes bloody, even deadly, the Palio is
frenzied high energy all the way.*

Il Palio

Where?
Siena, Italy

When?
July 2 and August 16

How long?
2–4 days including associated festivities

Siena's legendary bareback horserace – Il Palio – is a highly charged, death-defying two-minute dash around the boundary of the city's majestic and equally famous Piazza del Campo. It's also likely to be the most rabidly partisan event you'll ever witness. Twice every summer, riders elected by each of the city's ancient districts – the contrade – compete in a bid to win the much prized palio, or banner, that gives its name to the event. Following the race, the winning jockey is feted, and the residents of his district sing, dance and celebrate his victory into the small hours.

Sound like fun? It is. But the Palio is also an utterly unique event, and one in which all of Italy's extremes are on display – the fairytale grandeur of the architecture; the colourful vibrancy of the costumes and banners; the stifling heat and packed crowds; the frenetic, desperate mood of the participants and fans; the arcanely complicated, ironclad traditions; and, not least, the shocking potential for brutality and behind-the-scenes sleaze. For the locals, this is no mere mild-mannered tourist fluff. On the two days that the Palio takes place – as well as throughout the exacting preparations – the Sienese are playing for very high stakes indeed, and, during the event, the air positively crackles

History

A **Sienese Palio** of some sort has existed for roughly a thousand years, and in its present form since the late sixteenth century. It is so critical an event to the Sienese that during all this time it has only been cancelled on a handful of occasions, and only then due to war or natural disaster. During Renaissance times it became the main annual expression of the rivalry between the different sectors of the city, taking the place of various other warlike events, which often involved hundreds of combatants and left a number of dead and wounded. The first Palio was run and celebrated on Piazza del Campo in 1597, and repeated in 1605, after which the July 2 Palio became an established annual event – being joined in 1701 by the August 16 race. Early on, the races were consecrated to the Virgin Mary and her feast days in order to atone for a soldier who had fired in rage at her image, and since 1657 her effigy has adorned the prize that goes to the race's winner – the showy banner, or *palio*.

At the heart of the Palio are the **contrade** – the districts of Siena (see box on pp.70–71). Despite the city's small size, these districts have bitter, sometimes vicious rivalries, and the Palio is essentially a competition among them. The origins of the *contrade* are lost in the mists of medieval history, but most authorities surmise that they evolved from the military organization of the citizenry – a notion that is certainly borne out by the pugnacious nature of their enmities.

with the seriousness of the business. Sometimes bloody, even deadly, the Palio is frenzied high energy all the way.

To do the Palio justice, you really need to spend several days in Siena and witness as much of the build-up as possible. Failing that, if all you can manage is the day of the race, stake your claim around lunchtime (earlier if possible) in the standing-room-only centre of the **Piazza del Campo**. Bring plenty of bottled water and something to protect you from the heat of the sun as you'll be in it for the next six to eight hours. Because of the radical slant of the Campo, it's fairly easy for everyone to see most of the goings-on, but there's no denying that a spot at the very edge of the crowd, lining the course itself, offers the best thrill. Wooden barriers, bales of hay, mattresses and the like, are set up to protect not only the horses and jockeys but also the spectators. If you're lucky enough to know someone or can blag your way in, or are willing to pay an exorbitant sum for a ticket well in advance, then you can watch the whole thing in relative comfort, either from the stands around the periphery or, better still, from one of the balconies. The seating here is pretty much the preserve of local

dignitaries but some seats are left over – contact InItaly (see p.74) for details on prices and options for tourists, but reckon on paying around €500 for a seat in the stands and up to €1000 for a place on the balcony.

During the frenetic minute-and-a-half of the **race** itself, the crowd goes wild, cursing and yelling until the thing is over, when, following the concluding ceremonious shots and drum-rolls,

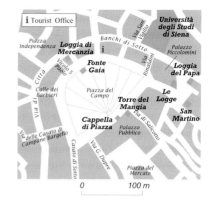

some exult and many weep. Spontaneous triumphant processions erupt, with partying into the night, and on the following day, there's another, official parade in honour of the winning *contrada*.

Bear in mind, though, that however long you're in town, you will essentially remain a tourist. The Palio is something that the Sienese do for themselves. They feel – and it is no doubt true – that only they can understand and appreciate its essential meaning. The fact is that they hold "**Palio tourists**" in some slight degree of contempt, and at best only tolerate outsiders' presence during the ritual – be prepared for certain streets to be blocked off entirely during Palio days, so that *contrade* members can celebrate with private outdoor dinners at tables groaning with the weight of feasting fare. These are definitely "members-only" affairs: respect the barricades and take a detour.

> **Insider info** Taking in one of the rehearsal races is an excellent option, meaning much lighter crowds and much more personal space

Still, there's plenty of fun to be had. For days before the race, young *contrada* members, wearing their traditional colours and clutching their favourite talisman or lucky fetish, chant and sing in packs on the street. Each *contrada* has its own, often obscene, lyrics to the same melody; you won't understand the words unless your Sienese is tip-top, but be assured that they ain't singing nursery rhymes as they try to belittle and intimidate their rivals. Everyone stays up till the early hours, strutting and swaggering around the city centre.

The build-up

Because space in the Piazza del Campo is so limited, only ten *contrade* traditionally participate in each Palio. Seven of them will not have participated in the last Palio and the other three are ceremoniously chosen by **drawing lots**. This happens on the last Sunday in May for the July Palio, and is repeated on the first or second Sunday in July for the August Palio. Both of these events command a lot of attention in the city.

As soon as the participants are known, preparations begin, starting with the selection of the horses and their riders; even at this early stage the atmosphere, the feverish hatching of strategies, plots and counter-plots can be compelling, with *contrade* who haven't won in some years particularly keen to give it their best shot. Test races are held in the surrounding Chianti countryside in order to review promising jockeys.

A few days before each race – on June 29 and August 13 – the anxious ritual of the **tratta**, the assigning of horses, takes place. Acceptable horses are presented, reviewed and tested. The ten best are selected, then matched by lots to each of the competing *contrade*, who then begin a series of trial heats so that jockey and horse can get acquainted. This is also the time for bets to be placed, and, most important of all, for shady deals, pacts and conspiracies to be proffered and sealed among the contending factions. Six **warm-up races** in all are run on the Piazza del Campo during the days leading up to the Palio – at 9am and 7.45pm – including a final, mock heat on the same morning as the real thing.

The medieval pageantry steps up a gear the day before the actual race, as the participating *contrade* officially **register** at the Palazzo Pubblico, the town hall, each procession's arrival being accompanied by ceremonious trumpets and drums, along

The banner

In Sienese, the *palio*, or banner, is affectionately referred to as the "**Rag**", and is the sole award for winning the race. There is no prize money and no other form of trophy. Every *contrada* displays the banners they've won – along with other honours they've received – in their own **museum**, all of which are open to everyone during the build-up to the Palio, and by appointment at other times.

Over the centuries, the banner has evolved considerably. In early times, it was the product of simple craftsmen, usually reflecting the conventional taste of the era. The earliest extant *palio* is from 1719 (won by the Aquila *contrada*) and depicts a typical confection of Rococo scrolling topped by a modest-looking Virgin in the clouds. In various eras, it has been politicized. For example, under Napoleonic rule it was made to show the emperor's crowned initials instead of the coats-of-arms of Sienese nobility. In the last hundred years or so, the decoration of the banner has been entrusted more and more to real artists, and has reflected real themes, for example the "Palio of Peace", at the end of World War II – which was, rather ironically, torn to shreds during the riots that followed the Drago *contrada*'s victory that year. Nowadays, the policy is to give the commission to design the *palio* to one of Italy's most prominent artists, which means that the results are always unpredictable and eagerly anticipated.

The contrade

To fully appreciate the Palio you really need to know what lies behind it all and that – in a word – is the **contrade**. Siena is traditionally divided into three main sectors, called *terzi*, or "thirds", which are then subdivided into districts known as *contrade*. To a Sienese native, his or her *contrada* remains a lifelong guiding principle, giving rise to fierce loyalties that make little sense to outsiders. For example, if a member of one *contrada* marries someone from another, the question of which *contrada* their offspring will belong to is a highly-charged issue – indeed, Sienese emigrants have been known to continue to sport the colours of their *contrada* even in their adopted countries.

Contrada	Symbol	Colours	Keyword
The City			
Aquila	Two-headed crowned eagle	Yellow bordered in black & blue	Pugnacity
Chiocciola	Snail	Yellow & red with deep-blue borders	Prudence
Onda	Crowned dolphin in waves	White and sky-blue	Joy
Pantera	Panther rampant	Red & sky-blue with white stripes	Audacity
Selva	Rhinoceros under an oak tree and sun	Green & orange with white stripes	Power
Tartuca	Tortoise in a field of daisies & true-love-knots	Yellow & blue	Steadfastness
San Martino			
Civetta	Owl on a branch	Wine-red & black with white	Shrewdness
Leocorno	Unicorn rampant	White & orange with blue borders	Purity
Nicchio	Crowned shell with coral and true-love-knots and roses	Blue with red & yellow borders	Self-restraint
Torre	Crowned elephant carrying a tower	Crimson bordered in blue & white	Fortitude
Valdimontone	Crowned ram rampant	Red & yellow with white borders	Perseverance
Camollia			
Bruco	Crowned caterpillar on a rose branch	Yellow & green with deep-blue borders	Industriousness
Drago	Crowned dragon	Red & green with yellow borders	Ardour
Giraffa	Giraffe held tethered by a Moor	Red & white	Grace & elegance
Istrice	Crowned porcupine	White with red, black & blue stripes	Sharpness
Lupa	Crowned she-wolf with twins	Black & white with orange stripes	Loyalty
Oca	Crowned goose	White & green with red stripes	Cunning

There are currently seventeen *contrade*: to the southwest, the *terzi* known as The City, has six *contrade*; to the southeast, the *terzi* of San Martino has five; and to the north the *terzi* of Camollia has six.

Each *contrada* has its own heraldic animal or other symbol, its own colours, and its own motto and keyword. It also has its own church, and traditional allies and adversaries. It's useful to know something of all this when it comes to the race – the table below gives a quick summary of the basic elements of the *contrade*. A *contrada*'s traditional **allies and enemies** can play a crucial role when it comes to the no-holds-barred clash of the race itself – as well as in all the furtive scheming that goes on in the attempt to fix the contest.

Allies	Adversary	Guild
Civetta, Drago	Pantera	Notaries
Bruco, Istrice, Pantera, Selva	Tartuca	Tanners
Nicchio, Tartuca, Valdimontone	Torre	Carpenters
Chiocciola, Civetta, Giraffa, Leocorno	Aquila	Pharmacists & chemists
Chiocciola, Tartuca	None	Weavers
Leocorno, Onda, Nicchio, Selva	Chiocciola	Masons
Aquila, Giraffa, Istrice, Pantera	Leocorno	Shoemakers, poulterers, Pursemakers, bankers
Bruco, Pantera, Tartuca	Civetta	Goldsmiths
Bruco, Onda, Tartuca	Valdimontone	Potters
Bruco	Oca and Onda	Wool beaters
Onda	Nicchio	Old-clothes dealers
Chiocciola, Istrice, Leocorno, Nicchio, Torre	None (no official relations with Oca)	Silk weavers
Aquila	None	Bankers
Civetta, Istrice, Pantera	None	Painters
Bruco, Chiocciola, Civetta, Giraffa	Lupa	Blacksmiths
None	Istrice	Bakers
None	Torre (no official relations with Bruco)	Dyers

with the introduction to the crowd of the horses and jockeys. This is all followed by a late-afternoon race that is almost as exciting as the main race itself, though admittedly in this trial run the jockeys don't push their steeds to quite the same limits.

Between 2.30pm and 3.30pm on the big day, the horses are led into the churches of their respective *contrade* to be blessed by the priest before the race – the priest says, "Little horse, go, be swift and return a winner", or something to that effect. It's considered a good omen if the beast takes a dump on the church floor during the ceremony.

The **corteo storico**, the historic parade around the Piazza del Campo, begins at about 5pm, with flag throwers – *sbandierati* – from each *contrada*, accompanied by the chimes of the bell tower, creating an undeniably dignified context for the race to come. The square is a riot of colour and activity and, at around 7pm, the "War Chariot", drawn by two pairs of white oxen, enters the Campo displaying the palio for all to admire.

The race

The race itself begins at 7.45pm on July 2 and 7pm on August 16, and the *mossa*, or **start**, can be a nerve-wracking affair in itself, with as many as twenty false starts before a drum-roll announces a valid one. Once the restraining rope is finally dropped, it takes only seventy to ninety seconds for the horses and riders to thunder around the Campo for the requisite three laps. During the chaotic, hellbent careening around the earth-covered, makeshift course, the only rule is that there are no

> *during the chaotic careening around the earth-covered, makeshift course, the only rule is that there are no rules*

real rules. Practically any sort of **violence** toward rival riders and animals is permitted, even encouraged, and anything short of directly interfering with another jockey's reins or flinging a rider to the ground is seen as fair game. Each jockey carries a special whip, called a *nerbo* – by tradition, fashioned from the skin of a bull's penis and thus thought to give a particularly deep sting, not to mention conferring super-potency on its wielder. The course is so treacherous, with its sharp turns and sloping, slippery surfaces that often fewer than half of the participants finish, although it's in fact only the horse that matters – the horse that crosses the line first (even without its rider), will be declared the winner.

Basics

Siena is in the heart of Tuscany, around 50km from Florence – the nearest international **airport** – and is well served by regular **trains** and **buses**.

The **tourist office** is on the Piazza del Campo (see below) – right in the heart of the action, so probably best visited before the event starts if possible. Given the heat and difficulty moving through the intense crowds you're better off taking **your own basic supplies** like water and snacks to the actual event, especially given that you won't be able to leave the Campo until around 8.30pm.

Accommodation

During the Palio, you must book as much as a year in advance for any **accommodation** in the moderate range. Good, cheap central options, close to the Campo, include the basic but comfortable *La Perla*, Via delle Terme 25 (☎ 0577-47-44), which has doubles for around €60, and *Centrale*, Via Cecco Angiolieri 26 (☎ 0577-280-379), slightly more expensive at about €70 for a double room, and up on the fourth floor with no elevator, but with great views over the Piazza del Campo. For more money, there's the well-furnished rooms and quieter location of *Hotel* Arcobaleno, just a short walk to the north of the historic centre at Via Fiorentina 32/40 (☎ 0557-271-092, ☻ www.hotelarcobaleno.com), where doubles cost e130. The top choice if you feel like a splurge is the magnificent resort of *Villa Scacciapensieri* at Via di Scacciapensieri 10 (☎ 0577-41-441, ☻ www.villascacciapensieri.it), whose luxurious doubles start at a more significant €200 – it's north of town, but there's a bus service to the centre every fifteen minutes. If you haven't organized anything a year in advance, you could try *Siena Hotels Promotion* (☎ 0577-288-084, ☻ www.hotelsiena.com), or, failing that, and bearing in mind this is high season all over Tuscany, neighbouring towns that won't be quite so packed, such as Volterra to the north, or Pienza or Montalcino to the south.

Eating and drinking

Most **restaurants** are extremely busy during the Palio, but there's plenty of pizza and **street food** to be had. Other fine options are the *salumeria* (delicatessen) shops and *alimentari* (grocers), where you can create your own sandwiches, choosing from local hams, cheeses and buns; try something with truffles for a real taste zing. Otherwise, with a bit more time, and considerably more money, try *Le Logge* at Via del Porrione 33 (☎ 0577-48-013; closed Sun), just southeast off the Campo, where you'll find fine regional cuisine, a traditional atmosphere and a decent wine list. Virtually opposite, at no. 28, *Nello la Taverna* is equally good, with excellent Sienese dishes. If you prefer to be right on the Campo, *Al Mangia*, at No. 42 (☎ 0577-281-121; closed Mon) is excellent, but reservations are an absolute must.

Event info

Il Palio (☻ www.ilpaliosiena.com). Lots of basic information about the Palio, much of it in English, including details on each *contrada*, and photos and results from recent *palios*.

Useful websites

InItaly (☻ www.initaly.com/ads/palio/palio.htm). A good account of Il Palio, and, for those with deep pockets, information on how to get tickets for the limited seating available.

Siena Tourist Office Piazza del Campo 56 (daily 9am–7pm; ☎ 0577-280-551, ☻ www.terresiena.it).

Time zone GMT +1   **Country code** +39   **Currency** euro (€)

La Tomatina

By midday the chant of "to-ma-te, to-ma-te" begins to ring out across the town

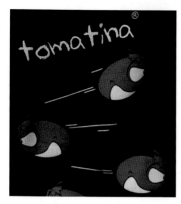

La Tomatina

Where?
Buñol, Spain

When?
The last Wednesday
in August

How long?
1 day

SPAIN

● Madrid

Buñol

La Tomatina must surely rank as one of the most bizarre and downright infantile fiestas on earth, a world-famous summer spectacular in which thirty thousand or so finger-twitching participants try to dispose of the entire EU tomato mountain by way of a massive hour-long food fight. It's an event especially appealing to repressed northern Europeans, Americans and Japanese, who swarm to the otherwise unremarkable Spanish town of Buñol each year on the last Wednesday of August, accompanied by legions of TV crews and photographers to document the carnage. Hurling 130,000 kilos of over-ripe tomatoes at each other until the streets are ankle-deep in a sea of squelching fruit is a strangely liberating experience. At the very least, it's the one fiesta where you can truly say that you've painted the town red.

History

La Tomatina is a rarity among Spanish fiestas in that its **origins** are neither religious nor political. In fact, it is very much a newcomer on the Spanish festival scene. There are three distinct versions of how it got started, although all accounts agree that it began some time during the 1940s. Take your pick from the following.

One story tells of a group of friends starting an impromptu food fight in Buñol's main square, using the tomatoes from their salads as ammunition, and drawing passers-by into the proceedings until they had so much fun that they decided to return each year to re-enact it. Another claims that an itinerant musician arrived in town, but his singing was so dire that a group of local youths started hurling insults at him. Not satisfied with the effects, they then proceeded to pelt him with tomatoes from a stall in the main square, and eventually the whole town joined in until the musician fled. A third story describes a mass brawl that broke out during the annual carnival parade, during which the participants used fruit and vegetables from a nearby stall as ammunition – again, having so much fun that they returned the following year to relive the incident.

However it started, for a while La Tomatina was outlawed as the authorities feared it was getting out of control – but the locals frequently defied the ban. In 1951, the participants were arrested and imprisoned, but the uproar amongst residents was such that the authorities were forced to set them free. In 1957, after the fiesta was banned once again, locals held "The Tomato's Funeral", a parade led by a coffin containing a giant tomato and followed by a band playing mournful funeral marches. The authorities eventually relented in 1959, but this time introduced certain restrictions on activities, which included an official start and end to the proceedings to be indicated by the firing of a rocket. From then on the fight became an institution, and by the 1980s the local town council actually had taken over its organization, with the result that it's now a well-orchestrated event that's almost too efficient, and well-attended, for its own good.

Things get going early on the morning of the fiesta, with ambulances and fire engines lining the streets (although there are hardly ever any casualties), temporary stalls selling *bocadillos* (stuffed baguettes) and commemorative T-shirts, and a steady stream of people flooding into town. As the sticky summer heat begins to build, the crowds, generously lubricated with wine and beer, begin to funnel into the narrow town square, the **Plaza del Pueblo**, while locals, young and old, are busy attaching protective plastic sheeting to their house fronts, draping them over the balconies and bolting the shutters.

When the sun eventually reaches the square the heat begins to get unbearable, and the now heaving crowd call for "*agua, agua*". Neighbours lining the balconies above respond by showering everyone with ice-cold buckets of water, while the fiesta organizers spray high-pressure hoses over the waiting throng – quite a relief if you've been jammed in there for hours. Once you've towelled off, watch out for the "*jabon de palo*" competition, which also goes on in the square, as contestants attempt to scramble up a liberally greased pole to reach a huge leg of *jamon serrano* (smoked ham). By midday, the plaza and surrounding streets are brimming with a mass of overheated humans, and the chant of "*to-ma-te, to-ma-te*" begins to ring out across the town, accompanied by rhythmic clapping and punching of the air – the Spanish equivalent of a Maori war dance.

Official rules of La Tomatina

- Throwing must start and finish on the sound of the rocket.
- Only throw tomatoes.
- Always squash the tomatoes in your hand before throwing them. In fact, after the first few minutes of the fight most of the tomatoes will have disintegrated anyway.
- Don't throw any of the rock-hard stray green tomatoes.
- Don't rip any T-shirts or clothes – a rule that is completely ignored by participants.

The tomato fight

As the church clock begins to chime **noon**, the rumble of the trucks bringing the ammunition can be heard in the distance. The sea of people begins to part, and everyone plasters themselves against the walls as the trucks edge their way into the narrow streets leading to the plaza. A rocket explodes into the sky, and scores of self-appointed helpers clamber onto the back of the trucks loaded with their cargo of ripe tomatoes and begin to pelt the waiting crowd with a volley of crimson grenades. Hostilities have commenced, and immediately the trucks disgorge the remainder of the tomatoes onto the dusty streets.

Insider info Try *Agua de Valencia* – it tastes harmless enough but this lethal cocktail based on cava and orange juice fuels the party well into the balmy Valencian night.

Then all hell breaks loose in what must be the closest most of us will ever come to all-out, no-holds-barred warfare. There are no allies, no protection, nowhere to hide; everyone – man or woman, young or old – is out for themselves; and it is, quite simply, unbelievably fantastic fun. The first five minutes is tough going: the tomatoes are surprisingly hard and they actually hurt until they have been thrown a few times. Some are fired head-on at point-blank range, others sneakily aimed from behind, and the skilled lobber might get one to splat straight onto the top of your head. Liquid oozes down your neck, seeds and skin plaster your body. The tomato targeted at the ear is a devastating experience; temporary deafness is certain until you remove the fruit remains. One in the eye leaves you blinded and, well, literally seeing red – until, that is, the sting of the mildly acidic juice wears off.

The effect of this orgy of violence is impressive, as the tomatoes spatter against white T-shirts, walls, hair and faces, leaving their blood-like trail as they explode. Ears, eyes, mouth, nose and hair are all filled with the red pulp. As flying tomatoes block out the sky, you

La Tomatina tips

- Wear something white – your battle scars will show up much better.
- Bring a spare change of clothes in a plastic bag and stash it somewhere safe before heading for the Plaza del Pueblo.
- Wear a swimsuit under your clothes – handy given the T-shirt ripping ritual that occurs during the nervous wait for the tomato trucks.
- You'll be a prime target if you look like a tourist – don't be surprised if you seem to be receiving more than your fair share of squashed tomatoes if you're sporting a baseball cap and snapping away with your camera. In fact, don't even think of getting your camera out unless you want to spend the next two months cleaning out tomato seeds.
- Bear in mind that you will also attract more attention if you have large breasts, or are wearing extra-skimpy clothing or any form of protective gear like swimming goggles.
- The real danger is not from the tomatoes, but from the lorries – keep your wits about you as they approach.
- Hone your throwing technique – the well-aimed grenade lob or the crushed tomato in the ear are infinitely more satisfying than the point-blank firing-squad shot.

begin to feel as if you're in a giant food mixer, preparing a colossal portion of tomato soup. The air is thick with the powerful aroma and the gutters begin to run red like some medieval battlefield. After what seems like an eternity the battle dies down as the tomatoes disintegrate into an unthrowable mush. The combatants slump exhausted into a dazed

the well-aimed grenade lob is infinitely more satisfying than the point-blank firing-squad shot

ecstasy, grinning inanely at one another and basking in the glory of the battle. But the armistice is short-lived, as another truck rumbles into the square to deposit its load. Battle commences once more, until the next round of ammunition is exhausted. Six trucks come and go before the final ceasefire is marked by the firing of another rocket high into the blue sky above Buñol.

The aftermath

All in all, it only lasts about an hour, but it's probably the most stupidly childish hour you'll ever enjoy as an adult. The **clean-up operation** is nothing if not efficient, though, and as you squelch through the streets extracting the remains of the pulp, seeds and skin from every conceivable orifice, an army of volunteers springs into action and starts washing down the whole town. Firemen spray high-pressure hoses over the streets, old women emerge from their homes to scrub the pavements in front of their houses, and the protective plastic sheeting is stripped away.

Most participants head to the makeshift showers in the local swimming pool and then retire to a local bar to boast about their exploits, describe their best shots and exhibit their battle scars. The majority then disappear as quickly as they arrived, but if you can, it's worth hanging around and joining in the fully blown fiesta that has grown up around La Tomatina – taking the opportunity to try some great paella cooked over a wooden fire, or the traditional local soup, *El Mojete*.

Ivrea: Battle of the Oranges

Giant fruit-fights aren't limited to Spain. **Ivrea**, a small town in the northeast of Italy, 35km from Turin, hosts one of Italy's most historic carnivals, a quirky mix of grandiose costumes, tradition and a humungous fruit-fight, this time with oranges as the missile of choice. The festival officially starts as early as Epiphany (January 6), when pipers and drummers make enough noise in the old town to wake the dead – or alert the greengrocers to stock up on their oranges.

Each Sunday afterwards sees some grand and noble custom played out by old men in feathered hats in the town square, but it can all be bypassed until the Thursday before Lent, when the cobbled streets are filled with masked partygoers romping from bar to bar, with the scent of carnival in their nostrils. On the Saturday, cloaked university students mount a series of raids on the local schools to "liberate" the kids from lessons, and later that day the organizers announce who has been chosen to play the carnival mascot, "Violetta" – who, back in the Middle Ages, refused the advances of a lecherous lord, and so forever more became the symbol of freedom from tyranny.

On the Sunday, the town fills with revellers wearing traditional floppy red bonnets who tuck into bowls of beans ladled out from giant cauldrons in the town square. Meanwhile, the Battle of the Oranges commences – several thousand people take part in a massive orange fight that lasts for a full three days. Anyone and anything is fair game here: visitors, bus drivers, ceremonial horses, buildings, the Mayor… By Shrove Tuesday, everyone is covered in fruit pulp and drenched in freshly-squeezed juice, there's nowhere to walk that's not swimming in vitamin C, and the air is full of the bitter smell of oranges. A huge procession winds its way through the streets, culminating in a celebratory bonfire in the square.

For more information on Ivrea, check out the official carnival website at Ⓦwww.carnevalediivrea.com.

Basics

Buñol is 40km west of the Mediterranean coastal city of **Valencia**, the nearest international **airport** and the best place to base yourself for the fiesta. **Trains** set off from Valencia's Estació del Nord at least every hour, making the trip to Buñol in around fifty minutes (first train from Valencia leaves around 6.30am, last train returns about 9pm). There are no **tourist offices** in Buñol, but several in Valencia – the main office is at C/Paz 48 (Mon–Fri 9am–2.30pm & 4.30–8pm; ☎+34 963 986 422, ⒲www.turisvalencia.com).

Accommodation and drinking

There's little in the way of **accommodation** in Buñol – the seven-room *Venta Pilar* at Avenida Pérez Galdós 5 by the railway station (☎962 500 923) is the only real option, so all in all you're better off staying in Valencia and making your way to Buñol early on the morning of the fiesta. Valencia has plenty of budget and small hotels, and is renowned for its **nightlife**, especially in the summer months when, at weekends, it is swamped by Madrileños, who've made the 300-km dash from the capital to the nearest beach, determined to make the most of their brief stay on the coast. Check out the "Doing Las Fallas" section of our Las Fallas coverage on p.86 for more on accommodation, places to eat and nightlife in Valencia.

| **Time zone** GMT +1 | **Country code** +34 | **Currency** euro (€) |

Las Fallas

Prepare to have your senses numbed

Las Fallas

Where?
Valencia, Spain

When?
March 12–19

How long?
7 days

SPAIN

• Madrid

Valencia •

The people of Valencia celebrate their patron saint's day and the passing of winter with a fiery party of ferocious proportions: ground-shaking fire-cracker fights, rockets booming overhead, billowing clouds of sulphurous smoke, and colossal bonfires on street corners that could cook your eyeballs from twenty metres. The main feature of Valencia's famous festival is the fallas effigies themselves, which come in all shapes and sizes, the most spectacular of them being enormous affairs. Almost four hundred are erected around the city, and as many as four hundred more in the surrounding towns and districts. Combine all this with the Spanish love of sangria, bravado and all-hours partying, and you get one hell of an early spring line-up that draws two million people from all over the world.

Festivities are centred on the **Barrio del Carmen**, a maze of narrow streets enclosed by Calle Colón, Calle Xativa and Calle Guillém de Castro (note there is some confusion in street names, as both Spanish and Catalan names are used – many local maps freely mix the two). This area is closed off to all traffic except buses and taxis, so getting around isn't too much trouble. Outside the Barrio del Carmen, stick to the **Barrio de la Turia**, between the Mercado, Plaza de la Reina and the Jardí del Turia – a beautiful, four-mile strip of gardens in the city's old riverbed, which hosts a variety of live-music events throughout Las Fallas – for the best of the festivities, day or night.

The highlights during the day make for top-quality entertainment and at night the partying presses on long and hard, but the only fixed points in your schedule are the daily **mascletà** firecracker display in the main square, Plaza del Ayuntamiento (2pm), and the **midnight firework displays** over the Jardí del Turia. Valencia has some of the most famous pyrotechnical engineers in the world and they take the bang business very seriously indeed, with advanced research into chemical reactions, computer-aided analysis and field trials that would make NASA proud.

As a tourist, you won't need any special kit for the party, just some reasonably heat-resistant clothes, and, of course, some firecrackers – available from most street stalls – so you can join in the perpetual banger-throwing along with everyone else.

History

The **origins** of Las Fallas are connected with pagan celebrations of the spring equinox. Reports of the festival date back to 1497 and relate to the custom of early craftsmen – San José is the patron saint of carpenters – who burned the wooden candelabra they had used to illuminate their workshops during winter. Later on, the candelabra were adorned with old clothes and burnt in a bonfire to accompany the night-time fiesta. Later still, a human visage was added to make a more lifelike figure, and the *ninot*, or doll-like effigy, was born, with whole groups of neighbours contributing to the display.

Las Fallas was actually **outlawed** in 1851 by the mayor of Valencia, as the huge fires were considered a threat to the city. It was revived in 1883, but a tax was slapped on each *falla*, with the result that only four *fallas* were set up. By 1886, the city had no *fallas* at all – much to the chagrin of the locals, who complained bitterly – but the following year, the tax was reduced and 21 *fallas* were built. The festival has grown in strength ever since.

Fallas and ninots

Strictly speaking, only the large central figures of each structure or effigy are the **fallas**; the smaller wooden sculptures on the same theme that surround it (as many as 75 of them) are called **ninots**. Explanatory placards – mostly written in Catalan (and occasionally Spanish), and almost always in biting or amusing verse – are placed next to each *falla*, completing the caricature embodied in the effigies themselves, which are often representative of local figures or controversial events. Over the years, *fallas* displays have grown less satirical, but recently the creations have begun to pull fewer punches – an award-winning *falla* of 2005 featured a cigar-chomping Uncle Sam seated astride a globe surrounded by Arabs grovelling in the desert. Big cheers all round when that one went up in flames.

Traditionally, *fallas* were made of papier-mâché figures placed on a wooden skeleton, but for years now painstakingly hand-painted polystyrene has been used instead. This has led to the creation of far taller and more sophisticated effigies, some of them thirty metres high, which billow acrid black smoke when they are burned. Each *falla* sculpture has its own committee, made up of a group of neighbours, who hold meetings, pay dues and seek out financing for their costly creations (in 2006, the best *falla* came in at a staggering €600,000). These amazing works of art are crafted during the preceding year – for some craftsmen and artists, this is a full-time job, with a lull in work from mid-March until late spring, and a mad rush to get them finished the following February. Still renowned as a centre of excellence, the Valencian artisans also export carnival paraphernalia to Rio de Janeiro, New Orleans and many of the other big festivals around the world.

March 15 and 16

Although Las Fallas officially starts on March 12, the serious festivities get going on March 15, the day of the **plantà**, when the *fallas* are put into place – both the towering structures and the much more modest *fallas infantiles* (children's *fallas*) – and the *ninots*, are paraded through town. After being woken by the dawn chorus of three hundred marching bands, hired just for that purpose, and accompanied by the *despertà*, the "wake-up" fireworks, you can spend the day wandering around, exploring the various *fallas* displays, mounted throughout the day by each committee, who lay on music, and, if you're really lucky, hand out free beer. All the main *fallas* are judged except the huge one on the main square, Plaza del Ayuntamiento, which crowds watch being hauled into place at midnight.

> **Insider info** Maps and official Las Fallas programmes, which show where the biggest *fallas* are positioned, are available from the tourist information office on Calle Paz.

The highlight of March 16 is the first **full-scale mascletà**. From 1pm, a vast crowd assembles in Plaza del Ayuntamiento, falling silent at 2pm, as if some great concert were about to begin. Straight away, the whooshing and whistling of the rockets split the air, which, combined with the kettledrum barrage of the firecrackers, strike up an infernal rhythm, gaining in tempo and volume as the evening progresses. The effect is mesmerizing: the sky is obscured by huge clouds of grey gunpowder and the ground shakes with the loudest explosions you'll probably ever hear. The spectacle is only about five minutes long, but your nerves will be jangling for a good few hours afterwards. Locals then organize their own *mascletaes* around town throughout much of the afternoon, so there is no let-up.

March 17 and 18

For many locals, March 17 and 18, and their **Ofrenda de Flores a la Virgen de los Desamparados**, or The Offering of Flowers to Our Lady of the Helpless, is the highlight of the festival. On Plaza de la Virgen, two disembodied heads sit atop a bare wooden frame – a half-finished monument of the Virgin Mary holding the baby Jesus. Over the two days (4–10pm each day), around one hundred thousand women from the *falla* committees process through the city in their traditional dress, carrying bouquets of flowers that they hand to the men to clothe the bare frame with. By the time the parades finish on the evening of the 18th, a veritable mountain of flowers has piled up, and everyone heads across the Jardí del Turia for the **Nit del Foc**, or Night of Fire – a fire and fireworks extravaganza that makes the explosion scenes in *Apocalypse Now* look like a picnic in the park. Grab some beers, make for the Paseo Alameda (from 1.30am) and prepare to have your senses numbed.

March 19

March 19, **El dia de San José**, is the festival's grand finale, and there's a slight feeling of sadness in the air – partly due to three-nights' aggregate hangover and partly because the festivities are almost over. The day follows much the same schedule as previous days but with a couple of final parades thrown in for good measure: the *mascletà* (the biggest and loudest of them all) is followed by the **Cabalgata del Foc**, or Fire Parade (7pm), a huge procession of firework-spluttering beasts

ground-shaking fire-cracker fights, billowing clouds of sulphurous smoke and colossal bonfires on street corners

and demons that makes its way in spectacular fashion along Calle Colón; and the dazzling **Parada Mora** (also 7pm), where people dressed in lavish Moorish costumes march down Calle Almirante Cadarso.

At midnight, all hell breaks loose with the **Gran Crema**, or Big Burn, as the effigies are stuffed with fireworks and burned in one of the most spectacular acts of pyrotechnic pandemonium you'll ever see. The first ones to go up at around 10pm (the timing is often off as the fire brigade gets into place and ensures security) are the *fallas infantiles* wrapped in explosives. At around 12.30am, the first-prize *falla* is burned, at the same time as the other major *fallas* around town, and at 1am, the *falla* in the Plaza del Ayuntamiento gets torched. As it catches, belching black smoke and shooting flames into the sky, the bands strike up the *Himno a Valencia*, and the *falla* is engulfed. As the fire grows in intensity the front rows of the crowds fall back to escape the searing heat, cheers erupt from the mob and firemen (some 450 are on *fallas* duty this night) hose down the surrounding buildings to prevent the glass panes from exploding. In squares and streets all over the city, the *fallas* succumb to the same fate as they have for nearly two centuries. After half an hour, nothing remains of the *fallas* except for their ashes, and the party is over. Well, almost, as plenty of bars fill up to the wee hours on one last hedonistic binge.

Other Las Fallas celebrations

Las Fallas is celebrated in many towns across the region of Valencia in the run-up to spring. Locals in the smaller locations often put up a *falla* during their patron saint festivities, regardless of the month in which it is held. Outside Valencia city, the towns most noted for their festivities are **Benidorm** and **Denia** (near Alicante). Both of these are essentially smaller scale versions of the Valencia festivities, with flower offerings, fireworks, and, of course, *fallas*, which, as in Valencia, are erected, admired – and finally – burnt to the ground, during the last-night *crema*.

Basics

Valencia is Spain's third-largest city and is easily reached by **plane** (the airport, 8km out of town, serves major European destinations) **train** or **bus**. Valencia has several **tourist offices** – the best is on Calle Paz (aka Carrer Pau; ☎96/398 6422, ⊛www.turisvalencia.com).

Accommodation

The official **youth hostel** in Valencia is at Calle Balmes 17 (☎96/392 51 00; €13–16), but *Hôme Backpackers* on Calle Santa Cristina (☎96/391 3797, ⊛www.likeathome.net; €14–16) is nicer, with a roof terrace and the option of private rooms if you can't stand dorm living. The closest **campsite** is the *El Salér*, on the beach of the same name, 10km south of the city. A regular (hourly) bus heads there, picking up from the Gran Vía Germanicas on the corner with Calle Sueca.

There are plenty of budget **hotels** around town; the best are clustered around Plaza del Ayuntamiento and Plaza del Mercado. Try the *Hostal Antigua Morellana*, Calle En Bou 2 (☎96/391 5773, ⊛www.hostalam.com; €34–50 for a double room), the fine old *Hostal El Rincón*, Calle de la Carda 11 (☎96/391 7998; €22), or further out, the *Hotel La Pepica*, Avda Neptuno 2 (☎96/371 4111; €16–24), near the beach and with good-value rooms and a top-notch restaurant. With a bit more money, you could stay at the *Hotel Excelsior*, Barcelonina 5 (☎96/351 4612; €103–128), just off Plaza del Ayuntamiento.

Eating and drinking

The snack of choice during Las Fallas is **chocolate con churros**, long strips of dough, deep-fried and covered with sugar, and dunked in mugs of hot chocolate – good for breakfast or an instant energy buzz any time of day. Two other common versions are *buñuelos*, basically round balls of the same fried dough, and *porras*, thicker sticks. Stalls selling these are on Plaza del Ayuntamiento and Plaza del Mercado and abound elsewhere. Otherwise, **paella** is Valencia's traditional dish, served with seafood or meat. Over the course of the party, you should sample the infamous **Agua de Valencia** – a mixture of champagne, orange juice and vodka. You can get it at any upmarket bar, and prices start at €2.50 a glass.

For cheap **eats** head down Calle Roteros in the Barrio del Carmen. *Bar Pilar*, on the corner of Calle Moro Zeit, just off Plaza del Espart, is renowned for *mejillones* (mussels), while a good vegetarian option is *La Lluna*, San Ramón 23. For paella, go to either *Malvarossa's* or head for Paseo Neptuno, a waterfront road on Playa de Levante lined with great places such as *La Marcelina* and *Casa Amancio*.

Most of the midnight party action takes place to the south of the Jardín del Turia and is centred on Calle Caballeros in the Barrio del Carmen. *Johnny Maracas* and *Fox Congo* – located halfway down Calle Caballeros – are two of the busiest and most expensive designer **bars**, while one of the oldest, and well worth a visit between midnight and 2am, is *Canovas*, a pretty posh Gaudi-style place nearby. *El Negrito* on Plaza del Negrito fills with a mixed crowd in search of a beer, while *Radio City*, Calle de Santa Teresa 19 (☎96/391 68 70), is a good place for live music, including flamenco on Tuesdays. There are also loads of great little bars with no names, which you can hop between, although virtually all serve the obligatory half-litre of cold Mahou lager.

Nightlife

Valencia lays claim to some of the best nightlife in the country and during Las Fallas you'll get to see what all the fuss is about. All the **clubs** are open until well past dawn and the longest queues form at four or five in the morning. Many churn out banging Valencian *bacalao* – a local breed of fast, bouncy house music. *La Indiana*, San Vicente 200, has reinvented itself as a mainstream club for a better-dressed thirty-something crowd. It pumps out a mix of acid jazz, funk and sometimes good, old-fashioned disco numbers from 1am to 6am. The Ibiza-born club sensation, *Pacha*, San Vicente 305 (⊛www.pacha.com), has landed in Valencia, bringing the best of that island's club sounds to this mainland party town. *La Bounty*, El Saler (☎96/183 00 18), has a mix of house and other deep grooves, while *Murray Club*, Avenida Blasco Ibáñez 111 (☎96/371 65 96), pumps out anything from rock on Thursdays to house on the weekends and is popular with a student crowd. Closer to the centre, you can find more clubbing action during Las Fallas at *No Logo*, Calle Sant Miquel (⊛www.barriodelcarmen.net/nologo), which stages rowdy fallas parties throughout the nights preceding March 19.

Event info

Central Fallas Association (Junta Central Fallera) Av. Plata 117 (☎96 352 1730, ⊛www.fallas.com). The festival organizers, whose website has photos of the pyrotechnics and a detailed programme of events.

Time zone GMT+1   **Country code** +34   **Currency** euro (€)

Lewes Bonfire Night

Forget the damp squibs of mainstream displays and lame sparklers suitable for use at home – for real pyrotechnic madness, Lewes is king

Lewes Bonfire Night

Where?

Lewes, England

When?

November 5, unless this falls on a Sunday, when it moves to November 6

How long?

1 day

The first week of November hosts one of the eccentric English's most irresponsible, unruly and downright dangerous festivals – Bonfire Night. Up and down the country, human effigies are burned in back gardens and fireworks are set off at gatherings that range from small family parties to huge civic events, sending pets into hiding across the country. In the otherwise peaceful, modest market town of Lewes (pronounced "Lewis"), things are taken to extremes, however. Imagine a head-on collision of Halloween and Mardi Gras and you're well on your way to picturing Bonfire Night, Lewes-style – barrels of burning tar, processions of thousands of fiery torch-bearing maniacs, and massive bonfires and firework displays. Forget the damp squibs of mainstream displays and lame sparklers suitable for use at home – for real pyrotechnic madness, Lewes is king.

There are parties and bonfires all over Lewes on Bonfire Night, but the focus of the action is on the **High Street** and the roads leading off it. The processions parade on a pre-defined route, with each participating society ending up at their own bonfire site – just follow the group of your choice to its fiery end. The High Street leads down into the Cliffe area of town, by the River Ouse; it's here that tar barrels are rolled over the bridge and hurled into the river.

Finding a spot from which to watch the proceedings often involves a lot of jostling, as the pressure of the huge crowds lining the route can get pretty intense. Get here before 4pm and you'll have a chance of getting into the **Crown Hotel**, on the High Street, from where you have an excellent view of the **War Memorial**. Societies stop here to burn crosses and set off fireworks to honour the war dead. All of the parades can be seen from the hotel's window seats, but this these places are in high demand, especially since the *Crown* is one of the few outlets for alcohol in town; most other places are forced to close. If you want to stand streetside, or want to have something to drink later on at one of the bonfires, bring your own. It's also a good idea to bring your own bangers to chuck at the papal blessers once they mount their platform. Wait till you see the whites of their eyes – and don't forget to go to confession the next day.

History

Lewes Bonfire Night is one of many thousands of such events that are held around the country on the night of November 5, to commemorate the attempted blowing-up of Parliament in the early seventeenth century. However, the bloodthirsty **background** to Bonfire Night in Lewes began half a century before, when Queen Mary I ("Bloody Mary") launched a furious backlash against the Protestant Church established under her father, Henry VIII, by barbecuing seventeen Sussex heretics in 1556. A monument to the Protestant Martyrs, lit at night, is visible on the hill to the north of the town.

Following the hardline reign of the Protestant Elizabeth I, England's Catholics had hoped for a relaxation of some of the restrictions that had been placed upon them, and had high expectations for James I, Mary's son, on his accession to the throne. But when these hopes were dashed, conspiracies aimed at the restoration of the old church began to grow in Catholic enclaves throughout the country. In 1605, **Guy Fawkes** and a gang of well-connected conspirators managed to smuggle enough gunpowder into a cellar at Westminster to blow the Houses of Parliament to pieces. Discovered and captured in the nick of time, Fawkes and his fellow conspirators were horribly tortured before finally being put – rather unpleasantly – to death.

Establishment propaganda in the aftermath of the so-called **Gunpowder Plot** ensured that Fawkes' name was forever associated with treason and treachery, and that "bone fires" – featuring burnings effigies of villains of the day (a tradition that Lewes is careful to maintain) – became linked inextricably with his name. The strong anti-Catholic feeling conjured by Fawkes, and fanned by the Protestant establishment, continued to be seen at the East Sussex bone fires for many years, with effigies of Pope Paul V – who took over as pontiff in the year of the Gunpowder Plot – being regular victims of the flames.

Nowadays, of course, if anyone proposed starting a regular annual festival along the lines of the Lewes Bonfire Night, they'd be ridiculed. No local authority could seriously consider cramming tens of thousands of people, many of them drunk, onto the narrow streets of Lewes, much less having them mingle with processions carrying flaming torches. Indeed, during the eighteenth century, the "bonfire boys" often ran so out of control, throwing fireworks, and rolling flaming tar barrels down the narrow lanes (oddly enough, much as they do to this day), that the army had to be called in to restore order on more than one occasion. The first bonfire societies – corresponding to different areas of the town – came into being in the late 1840s in an attempt to bring a degree of manageability to the proceedings. Since then, there have been regular attempts by the powers that be to ban or reduce the scale of Bonfire Night, but all to no avail.

Many of today's bonfire activities in Lewes, particularly those of the Cliffe Bonfire Society, remember the Protestant Martyrs of 1556, with "No Popery" banners still highly visible, hanging from windows or carried in procession. Rumour has it that black magic is also at play, especially among the five bonfire societies, whose membership is presided over by closed, traditional processes; see p.91. However, most of the religious fervour has been dropped from the goings-on, and, although there are some locals who continue to favour a sectarian approach, they are outnumbered a thousand-to-one by those who neither know nor care much about the origins of what has to be one of the strangest free nights out in the country.

The processions and bonfires

Throughout the night, smoke fills the Lewes air, giving the steep and narrow streets an eerie, almost medieval feel. From about 6.30pm onwards, the rowdy torch-lit **processions** make their way through the streets to the War Memorial at the top of the High Street, pausing to hurl burning barrels of tar into the River Ouse before dispersing to their own part of town to stoke up their bonfires.

The parades are a sight in themselves, with marching bands followed by Roman soldiers in full uniform, pirates, Zulu warriors, Vikings, Civil War soldiers, cowboys, clowns,

Insider info If you want to attend the Cliffe Society bonfire – which is the biggest and by far the best – you need to buy a ticket from the tourist office in advance (see p.92).

monks and a whole host of disreputable-looking clerical types marching through town, to the bemusement of the thousands of visitors. In short, anything goes. The streets echo with the explosions of hundreds of fireworks, thrown, like prehistoric handguns, as the local youth, fuelled with booze and sheer excitement, work on bringing a night of apparent anarchy to a climax.

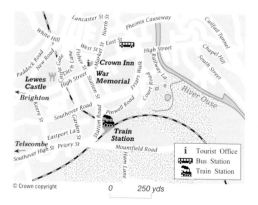

The Bonfire Societies

The anarchic antics are orchestrated by five **bonfire societies** from different parts of the town – the Cliffe and Borough (the first to be formed), and Waterloo, Commercial Square and South Street – all steeped in rivalry and competing to provide the most spectacular display each year. Officially sanctioned since 1858, they work all year round to prepare costumes and raise money to finance the yearly festivities – the buckets rattled by the various societies as they parade along the streets are just one of the ways they do this. Children and adults take part, and on the big night each society wears a different-coloured, hooped jersey and a Wee-Willie-Winkie-style hat.

As the bonfire societies and their parades leave town, each is trailed by a huge, **papier-mâché effigy** of a despised figure of the day (the prime minister is a perennial favourite, though a twenty-foot model of Home Secretary Charles Clarke – carrying the scales of justice in one hand, and an ID Stamp in the other – was the processional highlight in 2005), hauled on a cart. As the effigies are usually crammed full of fireworks themselves and are intended to provide the climax to the society's firework display, they are defended by a number of "prelates", who fearlessly bat the fireworks thrown at them by members of rival societies back into the crowd.

To the untrained eye, it might appear that there is no rhyme or reason to the torches, the fireworks and the barrels of burning tar – not to mention the American Indians with gazelle horns. But the entire affair is more structured than it looks, and revolves around three themes: Guy Fawkes, the Sussex Martyrs and remembrance of the war dead. Various effigies of Guy Fawkes are pulled through the streets and taken to colossal bonfires to be burned, most extravagantly at the Cliffe Bonfire. Fawkes goes up in a fit of fireworks that blow out of his head, body, arms and legs. In addition, effigies of unhappy, gouty popes are also dragged through the streets in revenge for Queen Mary I's actions in the sixteenth century – a favourite chant of the night is; "A rope, a rope, to hang the Pope, and piece of cheese to toast him".

smoke fills the air, giving the steep and narrow streets an eerie medieval feel

But that's hardly the end of the fun for the pope and his cardinals. After the parades, at around 8.30pm, thousands flood the **bonfire areas** of the societies for some good, old-fashioned Catholic bashing, fireworks and all-night drinking. At the Cliffe bonfire, five "cardinals" ascend a platform to bless the mobs, who in return launch fireworks at them – a bizarre spectacle, and certainly the high point of the evening. Although they're dressed in non-flammable robes and protective goggles, there's no guarantee that they won't catch a rocket in the crown jewels. The effigies of the pope, on the other hand, go up in glorious flames in much the same manner as Guy Fawkes, to huge roars of approval from the crowds.

Basics

About sixty thousand people descend on Lewes each year, and the town effectively closes to traffic mid-afternoon on the day of the fireworks, although there's **limited parking** available on the approaches to town if you don't mind a ten- to fifteen-minute walk into the centre. Public transport usually provides a far smoother ride to the heart of the action, with the station being well-served with hourly **trains** from London Victoria (1hr) and more frequently from its neighbours along the coast: Brighton (15min) – a short train journey from London Gatwick, the closest international **airport** – Hastings (45min) and Eastbourne (20min). The town's tourist office is at 187 High St (☏ 01273 483448 ⓔ lewestic@lewes.gov.uk).

Leaving town after the fireworks can be a long, slow process, with the station with people overflowing and hundreds of cars trying to out-manoeuvre one another onto the main roads. The last train for London leaves at 11.15pm.

Accommodation

To make as much of the day as possible, you'd do well to stay in **Brighton**, just eight miles from Lewes on the coast, as most of the shops and restaurants in Lewes close early on the big day. There are loads of **B&Bs** in Brighton: ones to look out for include the *Ainsley House Hotel*, 29 New Steine (☏ 01273 605310), a small, well-maintained Regency townhouse hotel that charges £30–45 per person per night for a double; and *Topps*, on Regency Square (☏ 01273 729334, ⓔ toppshotel@aol.com), which is a cut above and charges accordingly – around £80 a night for a double room with breakfast. In **Lewes** itself, *The White Hart*, a sixteenth-century coaching inn on the High Street (☏ 01273 476694), charges around £60 for a double, or there's the slightly cheaper *Crown*, also on the High Street (☏ 01273 480670). You'll need to book some way in advance for both these places, but they're great spots for watching the action in comfort. There's an official youth hostel down by the sea at **Telscombe** (☏ 01273 301357 or 0870 7708868), reachable from Lewes on bus #123.

Eating and drinking

There's little more than burgers, hot dogs and fish and chips available in Lewes itself on Bonfire Night, although Brighton is packed with **restaurants**, including a decent Italian, *Al Duomo*, 7 Pavilion Buildings (☏ 01273 326741), and a fine veggie place, *Food for Friends*, 17 Prince Albert St (t01273 202310). In Lewes, *Si*, 197 High St (☏ 01273 487766), serves pizza and pasta.

Event info

Cliffe Bonfire Society (ⓦ www.cliffebonfire.co.uk). Photos of bonfires present and archives of bonfires past.
Lewes Bonfire Council (ⓦ www.lewesbonfirecouncil.org.uk). General information on the role and history of all the bonfire societies.

Time zone GMT   **Country code** +44   **Currency** Pound sterling (£)

Love
Parade

It's an absolute ball

Love Parade

Where?
Berlin, Germany

When?
Second or third Saturday
in July

How long?
1 day

Berlin •

GERMANY

Every year, over a million people head for the steaming techno music fest that is Berlin's Love Parade, which has grown to become one of the world's largest free music festivals. Everything about the event is of epic proportions. It thumps to the beat of over €15 million worth of sound systems, creates more than 260 tons of rubbish, and must surely hold the world record for the most people simultaneously shagging in a public park. In short, it's an absolute ball. Everywhere you look there's loved-up people – on the streets and pavements, in phone boxes, bus shelters and mobile toilets, hanging from traffic lights – and, much to the annoyance of the city's authorities and horticulturists – all over the shrubbery of Berlin's sprawling Tiergarten park.

History

It all started modestly enough. In July 1989, a local DJ, Dr Motte, gathered a hundred raver friends to celebrate his birthday. A couple of VW buses blasted out techno to a few shoppers on the Kurfürstendamm, who stood bemused at the motley group dancing under the banner "Friede, Freude, Eirkuchen" ("Peace, Joy, Pancakes"). It was good timing – just four months later the Berlin Wall came down, reuniting East and West Berlin after forty years of separation, and waking the city from its Cold War malaise. In July 1990, two thousand people assembled under the Love Parade flag, marginally outnumbering the Saturday shoppers this time and dancing all day and all night under the banner, "The Future is Ours!". After the formal reunification a few months later, the event was declared an official demonstration, allowing the six thousand ravers to parade through the city under the motto "Worldwide Party People Weekend".

By 1995, attendance was up to three hundred thousand, and, in temperatures soaring above 30°C, the small streets around Kurfürstendam were gridlocked for 48 hours. The organizers negotiated a different route for the following year, passing by the Brandenburg Gate and ending up in the **Tiergarten**, Berlin's largest park, where the 750,000-strong crowd turned the immaculate lawns and shrubberies into a Glastonbury-style mud heap – and the Love Parade into the largest free assembly of young people worldwide. From 2001, however, things got trickier. The Love Parade lost its status as a demonstration, which meant the organizers had to find a way to cover the costs of preparing for, staging and cleaning up after the booze 'n' beats-fuelled love-in each year. Cue the search for sponsors and corporate backing, which began to change the event and move it away from the original spirit of an impromptu party, and which – according to many – has spoiled the event for good. (Dr Motte himself didn't attend in 2006 in protest at its commercialization.)

The Love Parade was **cancelled** in 2004 and 2005, and pretty much every year starts with the rumour that it'll be called off again. Indeed, the Berlin authorities have been trying to ban it almost since its inception – and if you look at the devastation it leaves in its wake, you can understand why. The organizers have worked hard to minimize the impact the event has on the Tiergarten, resulting in large sections of it now being fenced off, as well as a ban on unlicensed vendors in the park. So long as it can attract sponsors, however, the Berlin event should blast on. But whatever your take is on selling out to the corporate euro, when you're in the middle of the Tiergarten, wired out of your box and dancing like a maniac, none of this seems to matter.

Love Parade "activities" take place across the city from Friday night right through to Monday morning. Imagine you can do whatever you want for the weekend and you won't go far wrong. First off, there are the hottest, most banging tunes on the planet, played at supersonic volume; then there's a lot of drinking and pill-popping; and finally, very generous helpings of sexual activity. Weather permitting, people are generally scantily dressed and the further you penetrate into the Tiergarten, the wilder the action gets. Away from the Parade, there's really no set thing to do, so if you're there for the dancing and the drugs, you might want to pick a float and a stay with it for the whole day. If you want to be in the centre of the action, head to the **Siegessäule** (Victory Column), the focal point for the full-on party crowd, where a huge number congregate to lose it to the tunes. The majestic **Brandenburg Gate** on the eastern edge of the park serves as a popular entry and gawping point for those who have accidentally stumbled upon the party, while the **Englischer Garten** in the northern part of the park is the must beautiful and relatively relaxed spot. In 2006, several fixed stages were strung along the western end of **Strasse de 17 Juni**, with a variety of acts (some very loosely dance-related) performing throughout the day, but the sheer size of the crowds will curtail any plans for hopping between here and the moving floats.

The Parade

The highlight is the **Parade** itself, which kicks off at 2pm on Saturday. It lasts throughout the evening as the procession of floats, bands, mobile sound systems, dancers, skinheads, ravers and DJ trucks, blasting out their techno beats, move along the Strasse des 17 Juni, which roughly bisects the massive Tiergarten park, slowly making a circuit between the Siegessäule, at the centre of the huge Großer Stern roundabout in the heart of the park, and the Brandenburg Gate at its eastern end. The trucks are sponsored by clubs from Berlin and other major German cities, plus an increasing number of European mega-clubs, and each one carries three or four top-name DJs, cranking out big beats, drum 'n' bass, house and techno. The route is so packed with partygoers – a million-plus people getting their rocks off at the same time and in the same place means things can get pretty congested – that the trucks can only go a few miles per hour and are often forced to stop for minutes at a time. At midnight, the trucks leave the Siegessäule and set up shop in (and in front of) the dozens of clubs around the city.

After the Parade

There's a limit to the tolerance of the non-raving locals of Berlin, and, come midnight, virtually all of the park's sound systems are forced to shut down. There then follows a mass exodus to squeeze into the city's twenty-odd **dance clubs** that keep the beats pumping all night. If you're really smart, you'll have reserved tickets in advance (see p.98) and can avoid the half-mile queues. The obvious recommendation is to go wherever Paul van Dyk is playing – well worth seeing on home turf – or Sven

the hottest, most banging tunes on the planet, and very generous helpings of sexual activity

Väth, if you're into the harder stuff. If you don't make it inside a club, don't despair – some clubs park their parade floats outside and carry on right there. Even at six in the morning, so long as it's not raining, you're likely to have just as many people dancing outside a club as in it.

Christopher Street Day

Although very much a gay-friendly party, the Love Parade isn't by any means a gay festival. It does usually, however, take place at the beginning of Berlin's Gay Pride week, which culminates in **Christopher Street Day** (CSD) on the Saturday after the Love Parade. The parade takes its name from New York's Christopher Street where, in June 1969, police raids on the *Stonewall* bar led to anti-gay riots. Similar celebrations of gay pride are held all over the world – Berlin's version started as a small affair in 1979, but after the fall of the Wall has grown steadily into today's street parade-cum-carnival. Its promenade of trucks transports elegant drag queens and fetishistic queers along the Ku'damm through Schöenberg and Kreutzberg and back past Potsdammer Platz, before heading through the Brandenburg gate and finishing up at the Siegessäule. Unlike the Love Parade, CSD still maintains its status as a demonstration, so the sponsorship and corporate backing that frustrates many Love Parade regulars isn't an issue. The music is diverse, and usually provides something for all tastes; in fact, many of the Berliners who choose to leave town over Love Parade weekend head back for the CSD parade. For more **information**, see ⓦwww.csd-berlin.de.

Love Parade Inc.

The Love Parade has proved such a winning formula that copycat versions have been licensed around the globe, including Cape Town, San Francisco, Mexico City and Leeds, which all have the raw, turn-up-and-dance feel that was the Berlin Love Parade of old. In particular, the **Tel Aviv Love Parade**, held since 1998, is viewed very much as a political statement of love and tolerance by organizers and participants, as well as an excuse to get trashed listening to some top tunes. More than a quarter of a million clubbers now join in the fun every October, in an echo of the original Berlin demonstration of unity in the face of a divided country, with floats and booming sound systems blasting out across the promenades, parks and beaches of the Israeli city. The authorities are also much more sympathetic to the concept compared with modern-day Berlin, with the Love Parade weekend declared as the "Weekend of Love". For more **information**, see ⓦwww.layla.co.il/loveparade.

Doing Love Parade

Basics

Berlin's **airport** is 5km north of the centre. Germany's capital is a big, sprawling city, but there are plenty of overground (S-Bahn) and subway (U-Bahn) trains to whisk you into the vicinity of the Tiergarten. The **U-Bahn** stations of Ernst Reuterplatz and Zoologischer Garten are on the southwest edge of the park, with Unter den Linden, Mohren Strasse and Französische Strasse providing access from the east. The central **train station**, Bahnhof Zoo, sits in the southwest corner of the Tiergarten and is rammed solid throughout the weekend – best avoid it if you can. There are two **tourist offices** close to the Tiergarten: one at the southwestern edge of the park in the Europa Center on Budapester Strasse (Mon–Sat 9am–7pm, Sun 10am–6pm), and one in the Brandenburg Gate (daily 9.30am–6pm).

Accommodation

Your first step for **accommodation** should be to check out the online search and booking service offered on the Berlin Tourist Office's website (see below). Once you've secured somewhere, most of the hotels are used to the idea that they'll end up with more than two people in a double room, so you can just pack 'em in. If you've left finding something until a few days before the big day, it's worth checking out the official festival website (see below), which has an accommodation search facility. Although it lists only the high-end options, you'll be guaranteed the cream of what's left.

The following places are worth a try. On the eastern side of the city, there's the *Circus Hostel*, Weinbergsweg 1A, 10119 Berlin-Mitte (☎030/2839 1433, 🌐www.circus-berlin.de), which has accommodation ranging from an eight-bed dorm (€17/person) to double rooms (€60/room). The funky *Artist Hotel Pension Die Loge*, Friedrichstr. 115, 10117 Berlin-Mitte (☎030/280 7513, 📧die-loge@t-online.de), has seven rooms from €35 per person; while the *Hotel Transit*, Hagelberger Str. 53–54, 10965 Berlin-Kreuzberg (☎030/789 0470), is a favourite among budget travellers, with beds in a sixty-bed mixed dorm for €17 and rooms from €54 for a double. The *Hotel Bogota*, Schlüterstr. 45/Ecke, Kurfürstendamm, 10707 Berlin-Charlottenburg (☎030/881 5001, 🌐www.bogota.de), is a popular backpacker spot, with doubles from €64 and extra beds for €21.

If you've money to burn, you could join the illustrious list of international DJs and party promoters staying at the glorious five-star *Grand Hotel Esplanade*, Lützowufer 15, 10785 Berlin-Tiergarten (☎030/254 780, 🌐www.esplanade.de), by the Landwehr canal close to the Tiergarten, where rooms start at €115, or the luxurious *Hotel Intercontinental*, Budapester Str. 2, 10787 Berlin-Tiergarten (☎030/26020, 🌐www.berlin.intercontinental.com), where €187 buys you a sumptuous room and 24-hour pampering.

Eating

For **food**, you'll be fine so long as you like sausages – a couple of million bratwurst hot dogs are devoured over the weekend. Vegetarians ("*Ich bin vegetarier*") have a tougher time, but you should easily be able to locate a veggie burger stall if you wander around the park a bit.

For something a bit more substantial, head through the trees to *Café am Neuen See* by the lake in the southwest corner of the park. This Bavarian snack bar boasts a huge beer garden where a plate of pasta costs around €5. If you're here for the whole weekend and want to try something more exciting than a hot dog, head for the districts of Kreutzberg, Prenzlauer Berg or around Hackescher Markt, where numerous restaurants and cafés attract a largely local, young, alternative crowd; there's everything from Italian to Russian, Chinese to Egyptian. Try *Monsieur Wong*, Alte Schönhauser Str. 46 for fast, filling and reasonably priced Chinese; or *Good Times*, Chausseestr. 1, for authentic Thai food that's definitely worth the wait; both are near Hackescher Markt. For curry fans, there's *Shanti*, on Oranienstrasse, in Kreutzberg, which also serves a variety of cut-price cocktails.

Berlin's favourite Sunday pastime is eating **Sunday brunch**, and there's no better antidote to the night before than taking advantage of some of the all-you-can-eat deals on offer. Almost all the cafés open on a Sunday will offer a wide selection of food from 10am until 4pm for as little as €7.

Nightlife

Berlin's clubbing scene changes rapidly and nights are rarely advertised more than a day or two in advance. The following **clubs**, however, are usually a good bet and can be worth getting yourself on the guestlist for over the Love Parade weekend: *90 Grad*, Dennewitzstr. 37 (🌐www.90-grad.com), an über-cool and stylish club for those who know their Armani from their Versace; *E-Werk*, Wilhelmstr. 43 (🌐www.e-werk.net), a former electrical station that hosts a variety of dance nights; *Sage Club* (🌐www.sage-club.de), a huge superclub that dedicates Love Parade weekend to non-stop dance from Saturday through to late Sunday evening; and *Icon* (🌐www.iconberlin.de), which hosts the best drum 'n' bass in the city and houses a couple of intimate chill-out rooms and a cocktail bar as well as a large dance floor. Check out Berlin 030 (🌐www.berlin030.de) and Berlin at Night (🌐www.berlinatnight.de) for more party listings.

Event info

Love Parade (🌐www.loveparade.de). The festival's official website, providing info on floats, performers, safety issues and links to a whole host of related sites.

Time zone GMT+1   **Country code** +49   **Currency** euro (€)

Monaco Grand Prix

Monaco is more than a motor race – it's a three-day playboy's paradise

Monaco Grand Prix

Where?
The Principality of
Monaco

When?
May

How long?
3 days

FRANCE

Monaco

Set amongst the winding streets of the world's second smallest and most densely populated principality, the Monaco Grand Prix has, since its inception in 1929, grown to become the most glamorous and high-profile date on the Formula One calendar. Attracting a global television audience of millions, the prestigious race sees cars roar their way around a city-centre circuit at four times the speed it was originally designed for. The Monaco crown is still the most sought-after in motor-racing circles, though today's event is as much a showcase for the richest men and women on the planet as it is for the world's most talented racing drivers. From the hotel-sized yachts in the harbour to the celebrity-filled Casino, this is more than a motor race – it's a three-day playboy's paradise.

Watching the race

Although Monaco is patently elite, its grand prix caters for all budgets, whether you've arrived by yacht, helicopter or train or have shuffled into town on foot. Clearly, your Monaco experience will largely depend on your view of the circuit – which, in turn, depends on the depth of your pockets or the time you can get here to claim your spot.

Grandstands are erected around the circuit for the duration of the event, and these vary enormously in cost and quality of view. At the top end of the scale, race-day tickets for the grandstand at **Virage St Devote** – the first corner on the

History

Monaco's **first Grand Prix-style race** took place on April 14, 1929, organized by local resident and founder of the Automobile Club de Monaco, Anthony Noges. The circuit's reputation for speed over safety was established from the word go – the inaugural race was won by William Grover-Williams in a Bugatti 35B, averaging a comparatively impressive 50mph over 100 laps, with hugely inadequate brakes. The winning car's designer, Ettore Bugatti, said at the time, "I build my cars to go, not stop."

Over the many years and races that followed only minor amendments were made to the course, most notably the addition of various chicanes and a slight redirection of the circuit around the port in 1973. Today, the circuit measures 2.08 miles (3.37km) and is blessed with some of the most historic and memorable corners in motor racing: St Devote, Mirabeau, La Rascasse, Casino and, of course, the Tunnel to name a few.

Part of Monaco's appeal is its renowned **difficulty**. Three-times Formula 1 World Champion, Nelson Piquet, once described tackling the circuit as like, "riding a bicycle around your living room." The late, great Ayrton Senna boasts the most wins – six in all, five in consecutive years from 1989 to 1993 – although in the last six years the Grand Prix has been won by six different drivers, with Spain's Fernando Alonso topping the podium in 2006.

circuit – cost around €420, while a seat in the **Piscine** stand on the edge of the harbour, or at **Place du Casino**, will set you back a similar amount. A cheaper alternative, which offer equally dramatic views, are the stands at **Virage du Portier**, for which tickets cost around €250. Here, spectators can follow the cars round Portier – one of the few possible, but unlikely,

Insider info When the streets reopen after the race, you can stroll around the circuit and pick up an excellent free souvenir in the process: "marbles" (small bits of rubber that come off the tyres as they heat up and the cars turn), which speckle the sides of the track.

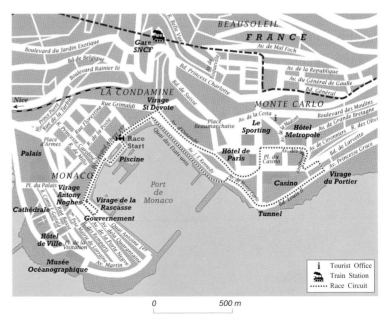

overtaking points on the course – before they disappear into the Tunnel.

The best bargains to be had, however, are the general-admission tickets to the **Secteur Rocher**, a grassy area on a hill above the penultimate corner – Virage de la Rascasse – at the circuit's

The red lights go out, and the cars scream away from the starting grid, braking hard at the first corner and then accelerating away as they set out on the first of the race's 78 laps.

western end. Race-day tickets to this section cost just €60 (tickets for qualifying Saturday cost €30) and, as well as offering finer views than the €400 stand below, place you amongst more passionate F1 supporters, arguably giving you a much better racing experience. There's no seating in Secteur Rocher, so you'll need to get there as early as possible to stake your claim; for one of the best spots – directly overlooking La Rascasse – hop over the wall to your left at the first opportunity as you walk up the Rocher road.

The Monaco Grand Prix schedule

Friday
11am–noon: Practice session 1
2–3pm: Practice session 2
The cars take to the track for two hour-long practice sessions that, although timed, do not contribute to the grid positions for the race. The sessions are designed to give drivers and team's enough lap-time to prepare for tomorrow's qualifying.

Saturday
11am–noon: Practice session 3
2pm: Qualifying
After a final hour of practice, all 22 cars take to the track for the first of three fifteen-minute timed knockout qualifiers. The six slowest cars in the first session fill the back of the grid, followed by a further six at the end of the second session, with the ten fastest cars competing for pole position in the third and final session.

Sunday
2pm: The race
The red lights go out, and the cars scream away from the starting grid, braking hard at the first corner and then accelerating away as they set out on the first of the race's 78 laps.

Basics

The nearest **airport** is in Nice, a fifteen-minute train ride away. The roads over race weekend are likely to be extremely busy, and parking in Monaco limited, so if you're staying outside the principality, then it's better to arrive by **train** – Monaco's busy railway station, Gare SNCF, is on avenue Prince Pierre and is well served by regular trains from Cannes, Nice, Menton and Antibes. The **tourist office** is at 2A Boulevard des Moulins (☎ 92 166166, ⊛ www.monaco-tourisme.com).

Accommodation

If you want to do the Grand Prix in real Côte d'Azur style, then there's only one hotel in **Monaco** to head for: owned by racing driver David Coulthard, the *Columbus Hotel*, a short walk from the circuit on 23 Avenue des Papalins (☎ 95 059000, ⊛ www.columbushotels.com), is one of the funkiest pads in town and is a favourite with the F1 teams themselves. A six-night minimum stay in a suite over race weekend will set you back a cool €10,500. However, most race enthusiasts head to nearby **Nice**, where good choices include the *Palais de la Mediterranée*, an Art Deco hotel on the beachfront Promenade des Anglais (☎ 04 92 14 7700, ⊛ www.concordehotels.com), where €340 will bag you an elegant double room; and the much cheaper *Regence Hotel*, centrally located at 21 Rue Massena, with double rooms for €75.

Eating and drinking

Unsurprisingly, **eating** out in Monaco is prohibitively expensive, unless you stick to the pizza-and-pasta fare served up in places such as *Le Pinocchio*, at 30 Rue Comte F. Gastaldi, and *Pizza Pino*, 7 Place d'Armes – simple pasta dishes at both start at €10.

The **bar** in the *Hôtel de Paris* is at its busiest after the end of the race itself and a glass of champagne here, amidst the celebs and millionaires, is a must, as long as you're prepared to pay for the privilege. *Jimmy'z*, in the luxurious *Le Sporting* complex near the Casino, is another popular bar/club where you can celeb spot and sip cocktails at €30 a go.

Event info

Monaco Grand Prix (⊛ www.visualseat.com). Run by the Automobile Club de Monaco, this is the official site for purchasing tickets for the Grand Prix. There's a full breakdown of ticket prices, and an interactive map with photographs clearly shows what the views are like around the circuit.

Formula One (⊛ www.f1.com). Official Formula One website, with details of races, drivers, circuits and statistics.

Time zone GMT +1   **Country code** +377 (Monaco) +33 (France)   **Currency** euro (€)

Notting Hill Carnival

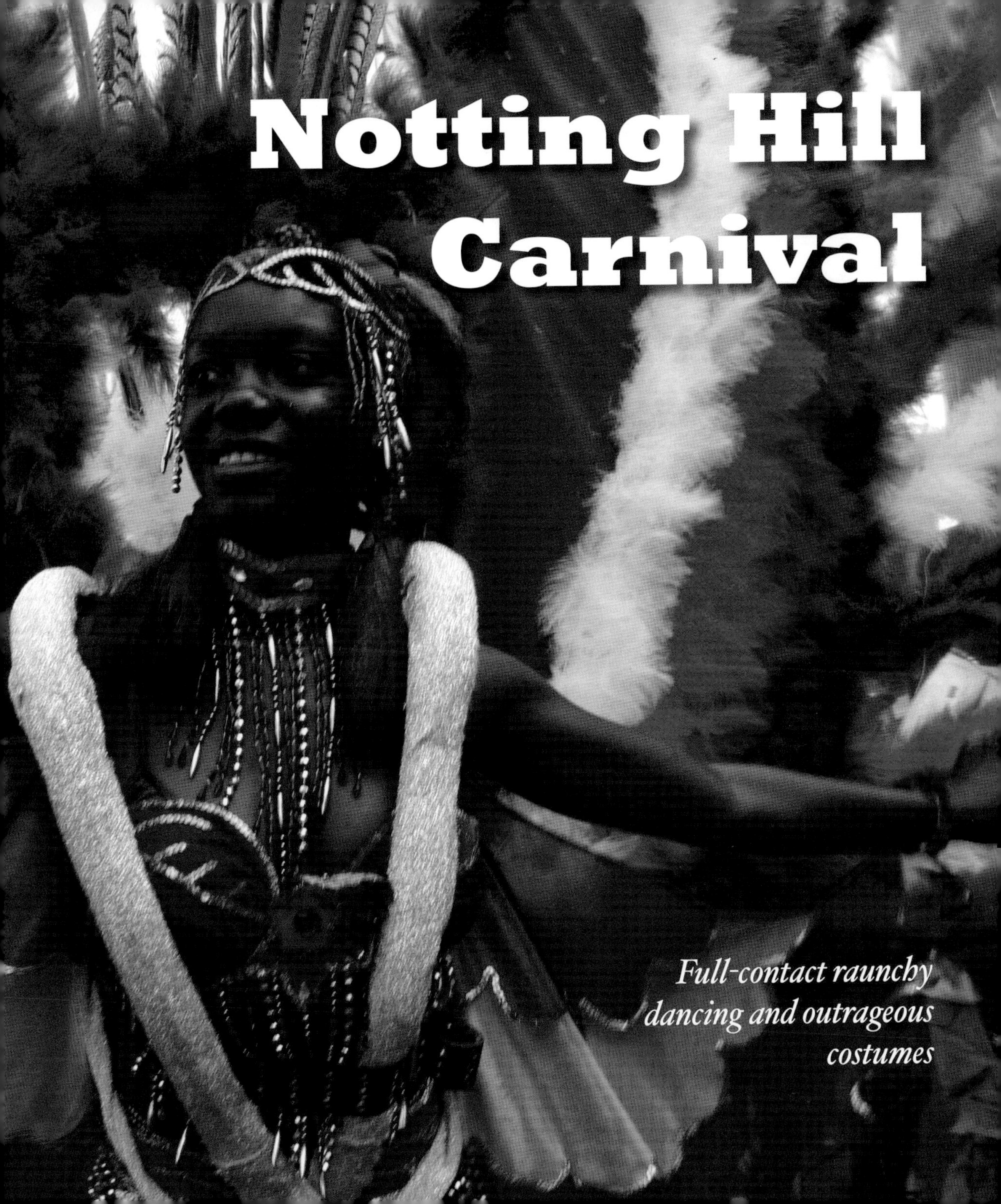

*Full-contact raunchy
dancing and outrageous
costumes*

Notting Hill Carnival

Where?
London, England

When?
Sunday and Monday of the August Bank Holiday weekend

How long?
2 days

UK
London •

Over the last weekend in August, the streets of Notting Hill shrug off their chi-chi trendiness to make way for London's biggest, best and most deliciously anarchic street festival. The splash of coloured costumes, the sound of soca, the smell of jerk chicken and the noise of a million people partying in the occasional sunshine mean it's carnival time again – and if you like Red Stripe, coma-inducing ganja and ground-shakingly deep bass lines, then this is the place to be. If the weather's good and the sound crews are on form, the Notting Hill Carnival can serve up one of the best party times you'll ever experience. Dress in your best, buy yourself a whistle from any street vendor and head into the throbbing crowds in search of that perfect tune.

History

Notting Hill Carnival's **roots** lie in an event held in St Pancras Town Hall, in 1959, when the West Indian Gazette editor, Claudia Jones, organized an event to showcase the musical talents of the local black community. This music festival was both sporadic and nomadic, but finally settled in the Notting Hill area under the stewardship of social worker Rhaune Laslett from 1964 onwards. Carnival has been taking place on the last weekend of August since that time, serving as a focal point for local black immigrants from the Caribbean, particularly Trinidad, as well as bringing together the people of Notting Hill. Believe it or not, this plush neighbourhood was one of the poorest districts in London then, and racism was rife, so the idea of a street carnival at which blacks and whites would celebrate together freely, eating, drinking and dancing to some great tunes, was nothing short of a social revolution.

Carnival bounced along as pretty much a local affair for ten years until Jamaican-style **sound systems** were introduced in the 1970s, attracting record levels of young people and swelling the weekend crowds to half a million. The increase in numbers quickly led to trouble, and the 1976 event ended in a full-scale riot. Following the Brixton riots in 1981, thirteen thousand officers were deployed at Carnival, and violence dogged the event throughout the 1980s.

Various committees have taken over the organization over the past decade, the most recent being the London Notting Hill Carnival organization, who have run the show since 2003. The **procession route** has been redefined several times, but despite pressure from the police and local authorities for a more significant change, away from the cramped streets of Notting Hill, including proposals to finish the parade in Hyde Park or relocate the event entirely to somewhere else in North London, no one's been able to move the main event. However, 2005 saw London Mayor Ken Livingstone stage a parallel "Caribbean Showcase" in Hyde Park on Carnival Monday, a family-oriented event with food stalls, live music and displays on Caribbean arts and culture. Though not a roaring success, it looks like becoming an annual addition to the main festival.

The main criticism of the Carnival nowadays is that it has lost its roots and serves merely as fertile marketing ground for multinationals gunning for a young white audience. Where once Afro-Caribbean locals cheered on their loved ones in the mas bands, now twenty-something investment bankers, gyrating self-consciously on the balconies of their half-million-pound flats, nervously eye their BMW parked outside. But though Carnival, like Notting Hill itself, has succumbed to a level of gentrification, the last few years have also seen it open up into a unique celebration of London's **diversity**, with Trinidad-style costume bands sharing the route with Brazilian samba schools and North Indian dance groups, while reggae sound systems run by middle-aged white guys draw in crowds of hardened dancehall fans. And the free and easy Carnival mentality, most usually illustrated by the image of a costumed black woman dancing with a smiling police officer, serves as a welcome excuse for Londoners to suspend their cool reserve for a couple of days and just let the party take over.

Getting your bearings

One of the first things you need to get your hands on before disappearing into the swarming masses is a **festival map**, which, apart from showing the route, details the location of the sound systems, any roads that have been blocked off for emergency vehicles and, perhaps most crucially of all, toilets. *Time Out* magazine usually publishes one of these, or you can print it off the My Notting Hill website (see p.112). Bear in mind that with up to a million partygoers out on the streets over the weekend, the crowds can be horrendous, so unless you're into spending Carnival feeling like a sheep on market day, find yourselves a good spot and stick to it. Failure to do this can lead to a bad case of

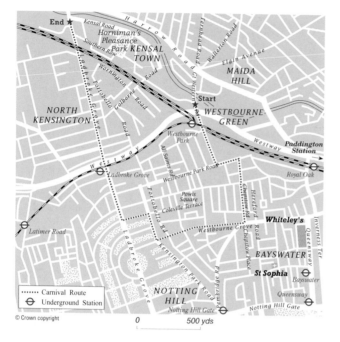

Map legend:
- ······ Carnival Route
- ⊖ Underground Station

© Crown copyright

0   500 yds

"Carnival Aimless Syndrome" – that restless feeling you get when you've walked for miles, haven't seen a thing and are starting to get seriously pissed off with the onslaught of shuffling people.

Fortunately, Carnival offers the perfect antidote to these negative vibes in terms of ice-cold beer, good mellow weed, and some of the finest jerk chicken to be found in the Northern Hemisphere. Ten minutes chilling out or chowing down and you'll feel fighting fit once more. A good site for some down time is the supermarket car park by Kensal Road, at the north end of the carnival, where one of the original sound systems, Mastermind, set up; around the corner, the small Horniman's Pleasance park is another good spot to take a break, and as there's a good playground, it's an excellent option if you're doing Carnival with kids in tow. There's also a special child-friendly area at the playground in Powis Square, too.

A much less strenuous way to enjoy the parade is from a **balcony party** held in the hundreds of flats that line the route. If you're not fortunate enough to know someone who lives along here, your best chance of getting in is to wave a handful of beers and get the best-looking, least wasted person in your group to plead to join the party.

Carnival schedule

Most locals warm up to Carnival proper by heading to Horniman's Pleasance on Saturday night to take in the **Panorama Competition**, in which steel, or pan, bands from all over the country play their hearts out in the hope of winning the coveted Band of the Year title. The action starts at around 7pm, and as the area by the judging point is always fiercely packed, you'll have a better chance of hearing some music if you walk up and down Kensal Road, where the bands line up and practice their tunes. Behind the judging point, in Horniman's Pleasance itself, there's a big screen displaying the action, and vendors sell food and drinks in the surrounding streets. The biggest cheers go to the two local bands, Ebony and Mangrove, but whether you're a pan aficionado or not, Panorama is an excellent way to get some after-dark Carnival flavour – and there are always parties in the panyards, too; just ask around.

Midday Sunday is the **official start** of the Carnival, when the floats and costumed bands start snaking their way around the route. Sunday is Children's Day, so you'll see more kids in the parade, but otherwise it's just a slightly less busy version of Monday, and a better day to go if you want to avoid the crowds. The route of the main parade has become quite controversial in recent years, with many adjustments to try

Jouvert

If you're really dedicated to Carnival, you might also want to take part in Notting Hill's version of **Jouvert**, the no-holds-barred opener to Trinidad's Carnival (see p.256), in which revellers parade around the streets covered in mud and body paint. Notting Hill Jouvert, starts at around 6am on Sunday; if you want to play "dirty mas", as it's called, during the day on Sunday, you can join up with bands such as Pure Lime. For details, check out the Notting Hill Mas Bands website (see p.112).

and quell health and safety fears in terms of crowd crushes on the sometimes narrow streets, but basically it follows a south-pointing U-shape bounded by Ladbroke Grove on the west, Great Western Road to the east, and Westbourne Grove half a mile to the south (see map), within which you find the fifty or so sound systems pumping out the tunes. The parade shakes its way clockwise, with the biggest buzz at the judging point on Great Western Road. The whole area is absolutely heaving by 2pm; 7pm is the official cut-off time for the street party, and this is vigorously enforced by the police. Once the plugs are pulled on the last of the sounds, and the trucks have left the area, the various pubs and bars take over pumping out the decibels.

dance your way through Carnival with a couple of hundred people behind a float pumping out the sunny sounds of soca

On Monday, Carnival starts again at midday, though this time it's the raunchier, fleshier, and generally better-attended **adult parade**. Again, though, it shuts down at 7pm, with many post-Carnival parties continuing in various locations around Notting Hill (see box on p.111); the only way to extend your Carnival after the cut-off is to find one of the bands or pan trucks and follow them as they wind their way towards base – following Mangrove steel band to their All Saints Road HQ is a particularly good bet. By Tuesday, the clean up has pretty much been completed, hangovers are being slept off and those who unwisely didn't take an extra day's holiday have to return to work.

Mas bands

To properly experience Carnival you've got to take in some of the mas bands that form the float parade, particularly during the "adults' day" on Monday. Mas is short for "masquerade" and these costumed players are the cultural and historical backbone of Carnival. Their roots are firmly fixed in the Trinidad Carnival (see p.252), and they are what uniquely prevent Notting Hill from turning into just another commercial street party.

The sound systems may occupy the central streets, but soca, calypso and pan are best experienced as the mas bands dance their way along the carnival's route. The dancing is full-contact raunchy, the costumes are outrageous – feathered headgear, silver thongs and gold lamé capes predominate – and there's more flesh on display than you'll see in a month on the Côte d'Azur, particularly within the Brazilian samba bands. Every year, hundreds of hours and thousands of pounds go into the creation of ever more elaborate and colourful **costumes**, and the competition for best Mas on the Road is fiercely contested. The winners are decided at the judging point on Great Western Road on the Monday. Connoisseurs will tell you that the mas bands must be seen in motion – the best way to watch the parades is to pick out a spot on one of the main runs, such as Ladbroke Grove, Kensal Road or Westbourne Grove. And though mas is definitely a wonderful spectacle to watch, the real spirit of Carnival is to participate rather than observe from the sidelines. Dancing your way through Carnival with a couple of hundred people behind

Insider info Some pubs charge an outrageous £1 to use their toilets, but there are several public facilities on the route. The underground ones on the junction of Portobello Road and Tavistock Road are the best option – miraculously, they hardly ever seem to have queues.

a float pumping out the sunny sounds of soca is an awesome way to spend the afternoon, and being in a band also means you avoid the crush on the pavements. If you don't fancy donning an elaborate costume, you can shell out a tenner or so and join a T-shirt section of one of the bigger bands, which enables you to party with them all along the route without having to get to Notting Hill clad only in a spangly bikini and a pair of butterfly wings. The best of the T-shirt sections are run by Cocoyea and Poison UK, the latter teaming up with the radio station BBC 1Xtra.

Sound systems and live stages

The whirling costumes of the mas bands are just one part of Carnival – a lot of people go as much for the **sound systems**, or sounds, as for the parade. This all-Jamaican concept was introduced some twenty years ago, and there are now about fifty official sounds packed in and around the parade route – *Time Out* gives a rundown of playlists in their Carnival issue. They're pretty easy to find. First you hear the distant sound of a pumping bass line; as you get nearer, this is joined by shouts and whistles, and soon your insides start to vibrate as the monstrously deep bass frequencies shake the foundations of the nearby buildings.

There's virtually no limit to the **music** that the sounds play; you can hear reggae, dancehall, dub, soca, soul, R&B, rap, hip-hop, uplifting house, hard house, disco, calypso and samba pumping out from the mountainous piles of speakers. Indeed, there are so many that agreeing which one to hang out at can be the biggest problem. Although sometimes painfully packed, All Saints Road has a great selection and a central location and it's also within easy reach of St Luke's Road and Powis Square, where you'll find even more. House music lovers should head for Wornington Road, off Goldborne Road, where the KCC crew rams the place solid all weekend, while the coolest kids hang out at Rampage, which strings across the canyon-like Colville Terrace and plays across-the-board black music, with a big helping of jungle and drum 'n' bass. One of the longest running and most popular sounds is Norman Jay's Good Times, which sets up at Southern Row, at the junction with Middle Row, off Kensal Road, playing rare groove, house and reggae for a very sunny, very huge crowd.

Note that the massive **live-music stages**, one of the high points of Carnival in previous years, were phased out in 2001 following "incidents" at the hip-hop stage. A smaller-scale "World Music" stage was reintroduced in 2003 at Powis Square, but it's not exactly a buzzing scene.

After-Carnival clubbing

There's a whole slew of Carnival **party nights** at clubs and venues in Notting Hill and all over the capital; look out for flyers and posters around the area. Due to the early shut down of Carnival, clubs generally open from 7pm and shut between 3am and 6am. Tickets cost between £10 and £20 and almost always sell out in advance; if you don't have a ticket, you may get into somewhere if you're prepared to queue long enough. Among local places, *Neighbourhood*, 12 Acklam Rd (℡020/7532 7979, ⊛www.neighbourhoodclub.net), always has some Carnival-themed antics going on – as do, across London, the *Scala*, 275 Pentonville Rd, N1 (℡020/7833 2022, ⊛www.scala-london.co.uk), the *Hammersmith Palais*, 242 Shepherds Bush Rd (℡020/8600 2300, ⊛www.hammersmithpalais.com), and the *Ministry of Sound*, near London Bridge on Newington Causeway (℡0870/060 0010, ⊛www.ministryofsound.com). Notting Hill also resounds with house parties on Sunday night, some of which charge a small entry fee – if you don't have an invitation, keep your ear to the ground.

Basics

London is served by four international **airports** – Stansted, Luton, Gatwick and Heathrow, the last of which is nearest to Notting Hill. There are several **Underground** stations in the area; the best thing to do is to get off at Queensway (Central Line), Bayswater (Circle and District Line) or Latimer Road/Royal Oak (Hammersmith and City Line) stations and walk – it's not far. Notting Hill Gate and Westbourne Park stations are both "exit only" and horrendously congested, while Ladbroke Grove station is closed for Carnival. The parade routes and immediate area are **closed to traffic** on both days. The main **tourist office** in London is the London Visitor Centre at 1 Regent St (Mon 9.30am–6.30pm, Tues–Fri 9am–6.30pm, Sat 9am–5pm, Sun 10am–4pm; ℗ www.visitbritain. com), and you can get up-to-date information on the transport situation at ℗ www.tfl.gov.uk.

Accommodation

There are plenty of small **hotels** and **B&Bs** in this part of London but expect to pay around £60 for a double with a shared bathroom, and in excess of £70 for an en-suite room. You may be able to get deals by visiting websites such as ℗ www.londontown.com. A couple of recommendations are the *Garden Court*, 30 Kensington Garden Sq (℗ 020/7229 2553, ℗ www.gardencourthotel.co.uk), which is very well placed and cheap; and the *St David's Hotel*, 16 Norfolk Sq (℗ 020/7723 4963, ℗ www.stdavidshotels.com) – better if you want slightly quieter surroundings. The *Portobello Gold* pub (℗ 020/7460 4300, ℗ www.portobellogold.com) has a range of rooms in the heart of the action, from very cheap backpacker-type units to a cool six-person apartment on the roof. Right by Notting Hill Gate station is the *Notting Hill Hotel*, 2 Pembridge Sq (℗ 020/7727 1216), which has thirty rooms. If you've money to burn, the *Hempel*, 31–35 Craven Hill Gdns (℗ 020/7289 9000, ℗ www.the-hempel.co.uk), is a sleek, super-trendy boutique hotel frequented by the beautiful people, whose all-white minimalist rooms have every conceivable mod-con. If you need to ask how much it is, you can't afford it.

Eating and drinking

Eating good **food** in large quantities is one of the pleasures of Carnival. Hundreds of mini-kitchens and food stalls tempt participants in need of a pit-stop; Caribbean food dominates, from spicy fried fish to jerk chicken, curry goat, ackee and saltfish or Jamaican patties, but you'll also see Thai, Spanish, Portuguese, African and Mexican cuisine. Good spots to fill up include Powis Square and its surrounds, and Oxford Gardens and the top part of Portobello Road north of here, all of which have concentrations of food stalls. If these don't tempt you, then keep yourself going with corn-on-the-cob, sugar cane, Caribbean fruits or water coconuts, all of which are widely available.

As you'd expect at a street celebration attended by one million people, the pubs and bars get pretty busy. Many pubs shut their doors and serve **beer** through the windows or put up makeshift bars on the street, though every other house seems to have a trash can filled with £3 cans of Red Stripe – a premium price, but a bearable one, and they're always cold. If you're fuelling your Carnival with **rum**, it's a good idea to buy a bottle beforehand, or decant mixed drinks into plastic soda bottles. You might also try a couple of glasses of home-made rum punch to get you in the party mood, though it's best to buy off a vendor who looks like they could at least pinpoint the Caribbean on a map. Don't forget to stock up with cigarettes and papers beforehand, as many shops are shut or just sold out.

Staying safe and out of trouble

It's a long time since Carnival hit the news as a crime fest, and these days you are quite **safe** to go wherever you want in the Carnival area. You may well encounter pickpockets or groups of kids with an attitude problem, but be ready to walk away from any negative vibes and you should be fine. Having said that, Carnival is a time when old feuds sometimes come to a head, and the fact that two men were murdered at the event in August 2000 is a clear reminder that there are always some really nasty characters around. The **police presence** is enormous – but passive – during Carnival. Hash and weed are sold reasonably openly in the heart of the festival, but if you're too blatant about skinning up you could well be arrested.

Event info

London Notting Hill Carnival (℗ www.lnhc.org.uk). Organizers' website featuring event details, route map and Carnival links.

Useful websites

Notting Hill Mas Band Association (℗ www.nhmba.com/main.html). Contacts for most of the mas bands on the road at Carnival.
My Notting Hill (℗ www.mynottinghill.co.uk). Plenty of background on Carnival, as well as the area in general, from bars to shops to hotels.

Time zone GMT   **Country code** +44   **Currency** Pound sterling (£)

Oktoberfest

Within two steins you'll be laughing with your neighbours like long-lost buddies, and banging the table in time with the oompah bands

Oktoberfest

Where?
Munich, Germany

When?
Mid-September to early October

How long?
2 weeks

GERMANY

Munich •

Officially the world's largest public festival, the Munich Beer Festival, or Oktoberfest, kicks off on the third Saturday in September and keeps pumping day after day for a full-on alcohol-soaked fortnight. Known locally as the "Wies'n", the name of the sprawling park in which it takes place, the first Oktoberfest was held in the early nineteenth century to celebrate a wedding amongst the local royalty. Like all of the best parties, however, the Oktoberfest has grown to forget how and why it started, and is now an unadulterated celebration of beer, Bavarian life and bacchanalia, attracting seven million visitors who guzzle their way through more than four million litres of beer. In case you're wondering, even at ten pints a day, it would take one person 2465 years to polish off that lot.

Getting your bearings

At the heart of the festival, spread around Wies'n park, are nine enormous **beer tents** where the boisterous crowds sit at long benches, elbow to elbow, draining one huge litre glass, or "stein", after another. If you're up for annihilation, head to the Hofbräu tent at a weekend during the festival, go for the ten-stein challenge and join the thousands of young-bloods braying for beer, naked flesh and projectile vomiting. If you actually want some recollection of your time in Munich, or to encounter some real Germans, pitch up midweek and take in two or three of the other beer tents. Whenever and wherever you go, one thing will stay the same – within two steins you'll be laughing with your neighbours like long-lost buddies, banging the table in time with the oompah bands and thinking about trying one of those suddenly oh-so-tasty-looking pork-knuckle sandwiches. Just try not to end up as a *bierleichen*, or beer corpse, as the locals delicately refer to the comatose victims who obviously knocked back far more steins than they could handle.

History

The **first Oktoberfest** was actually a rather exclusive affair, held to celebrate the marriage of Prince Ludwig of Bavaria to Princess Therese of Saxony in October 1810. The main entertainment was provided by horse races on a newly created circular green course on the edge of the city called the Theresienwiese (Theresa's Fields), shortened to Wies'n, and proved so popular that it was decreed an annual event. However, it wasn't until 1818 that the first showmen and brewers were allowed to erect their own booths and tents next to the royal marquee, and the beerfest proper was born. Despite the marriage of Ludwig and Therese ending in acrimony, the festival attracted the interest of Munich's foremost breweries and businesses, who were keen to be associated with what was at the time a unique event. Many famous characters have been involved with the festival since – none more so than Albert Einstein, who devised the first illumination for the tents in 1901. Now, that's definitely something worth raising a stein to.

The first weekend

Regarded as the best, loudest and noisiest time to visit the festival, the first weekend of Oktoberfest sees several traditional parades, and some unparalleled drinking displays. At 11am on Saturday, the "**Grand Entry of the Oktoberfest Landlords and Breweries**" is held, and is a great introduction to the traditions and scale of the event, involving around one thousand participants attired in Bavarian finery (lederhosen, basically), decorated carriages, curvaceous waitresses on horse-drawn floats and booming brass bands from each of the beer tents. The parade starts in the city centre and wends its way to the Wies'n, by which time several thousand thirsty locals and international partiers have joined in hot pursuit. The Lord Mayor

The beer

To make things as easy as possible, there's only one type of beer on offer in each major tent at the festival: the breweries own, specially brewed "**Oktoberfest-Bier**", usually a delicious pilsner with a hearty 5.7 percent alcohol content. The effects after three steins? Well, according to the official Oktoberfest programme, "after the third glass the drinker is transposed into a state of relaxed conviviality which can only develop and flourish in a Wies'n tent with at least ninety decibels of brass music". In other words, you'll be so drunk you'll be singing at the top of your voice, hugging everyone around you and soon attempting the cancan on the table. And it will only get worse. At around €8 a throw, the beers ain't cheap, but you get plenty of bang for your buck.

Map labels:
Schwanthaler Höhe · Hauptbahnhof · Karlsplatz · Westendstr. · Bayerstr. · Hauptbahnhof · Schwanthalerstr. · Marienplatz · Schwanthalerstr. · St Paul · Ludwigsvorstadt · Landwehrstr. · Hippodrom · Theresienwiese · Armbrustschützen · Pettenkoferstr. · Hofbräu · Sendlinger Tor · Schwanthaler-Hacker · Nussbaumstr. · Sendlinger höne · Tor-Platz · Schottenhamel · Augustiner · Bavaria · Löwenbräu · Matthias-Pschorr-Str. · Goetheplatz · Theresienwiese · Lindwurmstr.

Legend:
- i Tourist Office
- Train Station
- Beer Tent
- U U-Bahn stop
- S S-Bahn stop

0   500m

officially **opens the festival** at noon by tapping the first barrel of Oktoberfest beer in the Schottenhamel tent by the park's entrance. He declares "O'zapft is", which literally means "It's open", but translates more accurately as "Why doesn't everybody get as wasted as possible in my town for the next two weeks and don't worry about the mess because we'll clear up?"

The mayor's cry is met by huge cheers from the crowds, and marks the start of the mad dash to the cavernous beer tents to grab a seat before they are all taken; in all tents other than the Hofbräu, you will only be served if seated. As most of the seats on the first day are reserved, you may find yourself in the odd position of being in the middle of the largest beer festival on earth without being able to get your hands on any ale for over an hour. To avoid this, either skip the parade (there's a similar, but smaller one on Sunday) and grab a seat before noon, or mess around at the fairground for an hour or so until seats start to free up as the first of many casualties are carried out.

The Big Six

Augustiner

For traditionalists – the oldest brewery in Munich, established by Augustinian monks in 1328. This remains the only tent in which beer is poured from giant two-hundred-litre wooden barrels rather than the pressurized steel tanks with fake barrel frontages used in the other areas. Its tent (@www.augustiner-braeu.de) holds family-friendly "kids' days" on each Tuesday of the festival.

Hacker

Also known as Hacker-Pschorr, this young upstart was created when Joseph Pschorr married into the Hacker brewery in 1793. It has been rated one of the best brewers in Munich since the introduction of ultramodern equipment after its main factory was bombed during World War II. Its tent (@www.hacker-festzelt.de) hosts a big, friendly local crowd, with a massive 13,000-square-foot mural painted by artist Rudolf Reinstadler in 2004, depicting Munich landmarks and Oktoberfest revellery.

Hofbräu

Home to the rowdiest and most outrageous behaviour, and a Mecca for Kiwis, Saffas and Aussies on the road. The screaming and streaking tourists vastly outnumber the locals: its tent (@www.hb-festzelt.de) has a capacity of 4500 and is the only one in which you don't have to be sitting down to be served. The brewery was founded in 1589 to supply the royal court of Wilhelm V, and the extra-strength beer has proved a hit ever since.

Lowenbräu

The most famous Munich beer, exported to and brewed under licence in many countries following its enormous success in the USA at the start of the twentieth century. Brewed from 1524, the trademark golden lion is visible throughout Munich and a five-metre-tall version hangs over the tent entrance. Its huge tent (@www.loewenbraeu-festzelt.info) serves excellent beer and is constantly full.

Paulaner

First brewed in 1634 in the Au monastery, perched in the hills overlooking Munich. Paulaner was one of the first breweries to introduce pilsner beer (in 1895) as opposed to the traditional dark ale, much to the shock of the Munich citizens, but this early move has helped to make it the largest brewer in Bavaria. Its tent Armbrustschuetzen (@www.armbrustschuetzenzelt.de) is a favourite of Munich families.

Spaten

Traced back through tax records to 1397, although apparently the beer never amounted to much until 1807, when the business was bought by a royal brewery expert with a yearning for global domination. Its characteristic spade trademark adorns its two beer tents, Hippodrom (@www.hippodrom-oktoberfest.de), popular with a more youthful crowd, and Schottenhamel (@www.festzelt.schottenhamel.de), which has a ten-thousand-seater capacity and has served as the venue for the tapping of the first beer barrel by the mayor since 1950.

Beer tents

The beer tents are what Oktoberfest is all about. In all, there are fourteen enormous circus tents erected for the festival. Nine are run by **Munich breweries**, huge traditional companies that still produce beer according to the strict Munich purity regulations of 1487, and are the size of aircraft hangars, multi-floored, and seat over eight thousand people each. The "Big Six" Munich breweries – Lowenbräu, Spatenbräu, Augustiner, Hofbräu, Paulaner and Hackerbräu – all have their own immense marquees, decked out with brewery paraphernalia dating back over the years and really are the only German words you need to know for the duration of the festival. The other tents sell a variety of wines and food and are relatively peaceful havens from the relentless beer-chugging.

Inside, everyone sits at long **trestle tables** laid out around the bandstands. Orders are taken by buxom, corseted waitresses who have a remarkable ability to lug around up to a dozen foaming steins at a time, apparently without tiring. All you

need to do is indicate how many steins you require and the beers will be brought to your table within minutes – cold, frothy and ready to go. Tips are always appreciated and generally bring even more attentive service. To show how culturally integral the beerfest is to the local economy, most of the natives actually pay for their beer with cardboard tokens, which are given out by local companies to their employees as bonuses in the preceding weeks. Better still, Munich's senior citizens actually receive beer coupons as part of their pension each year.

Insider info If you're in a large group, you can reserve your seats in advance – very handy on the opening day beer scramble; contact an individual tent via the website links on p.120.

All of the tents are constantly heaving with people. Münchens (as the residents of Munich are called) stride or sometimes stagger around in their **traditional Bavarian costumes**. The men wear black lederhosen – sturdy leather shorts held up with shoulder straps, also popular in certain New York nightclubs – thick woollen socks and massive brown boots; real traditionalists complete the ensemble with huge handlebar moustaches. Women dress in flowing skirts and laced bodices, which have a dramatic push-up effect that reveals more cleavage than a whole season of Baywatch.

Cannstatt Volksfest

Looking for a German beerfest where tourists don't outnumber locals? Then head to the city of Bad Cannstatt, near Stuttgart, for the **Cannstatt Volksfest**, an event that is only marginally smaller than its Munich counterpart, but offers just as much beer-swilling, thigh-slapping, lederhosen-wearing fun – without the hordes of Antipodeans. The mayor taps a virgin barrel on the first day to open the festival, and there's a big parade on the first Sunday of the event. Otherwise, just check into the huge beer tents for several steins of foaming beer and then try out the huge rollercoaster and other rides next door. It's held at roughly the same time (usually last week of September, first of October) as Oktoberfest, so you can check out both if you're up for the journey – better still, it's free. For more **information**, contact the Stuttgart tourist office (☎0711/22 28 240, ⓦwww.cannstatter-volksfest.de).

Beer-tent action tends to happen in two **sessions** – lunchtime (noon–3pm) and evening (7–11pm) – but the atmosphere stays rowdy pretty much throughout the weekend. The tents open at 10am to serve breakfast – and yes, you can have beer with your cornflakes. At night, the tents close at 11pm to allow what's left of the crowds to slowly stagger home. If you really haven't had your fill by closing time, head to the "Hippodrom" tent, to the right of the park entrance, where Spaten beer is served until midnight to partygoers who can barely stand or speak.

The amusement park

Sharing the Wies'n park with the beer tents is a huge collection of rollercoaster rides, go-carts and fun fair entertainments which are absolutely fantastic after the third or fourth stein. Highlights most definitely include vomiting from the Ferris wheel, dive-bombing on the bouncy castle and re-creating Mad Max scenes with your mates on the dodgems. Things have come a long way since entertainments were first introduced in the 1820s, but some of the old rides and booths are still around. Check out Teufelsrad (Devil's Wheel), the wooden toboggan rides, or the flea circus for a bit of Oktoberfest nostalgia. Other old attractions that didn't manage to stick around were very much of the freak show variety, when, after a dozen or so steins, you got to admire a 22-metre-long fish, and meet Lionel, the world's only lion-woman. Those were the days…

Basics

Theresienwiese is about 1km southwest from the Hauptbahnhof, or main **train** station. The most hassle-free way of getting around Munich is the **U-Bahn**, which is the underground, or the **S-Bahn** railway, which is overground. The nearest U-Bahn stations are Theresienwiese, Schwanthalerhöhe or Goetheplatz, all of which lead into the grounds at different points; although heavily congested, festivalgoers are still whisked away with remarkable speed. The nearest **tourist office** is on the east side of the train station, at Bahnhofplatz 2 (☎089/233 0300, ✉tourismus@ems.muenchen.de).

Accommodation

There are a couple of large **hostels** on the outskirts of the city: *DJH München Neuhausen*, Wendl-Dietrich-Str. 20, Neuhausen (☎089/131 156), and *DJH München Thalkirchen*, Miesingstr. 4, Thalkirchen (☎089/723 6550). Both have dorm beds from €20 and are bookable online at ⊕ www.djh.de. There's also the smaller but more central *Euro Youth Hotel*, Senefelderstr 5 (☎089/599 08811, ⊕ www.euro-youth-hotel.de), which has a mixture of bunk-bed dorms, doubles, and rooms for three to five people – all simply but nicely furnished, and with prices ranging from €15 to €30 per person. Of the regular **hotels**, *Hotel Helvetia*, Schillerstr. 6 (☎089/590 6850, ⊕ www.munich-info.de/hotels/hotel-helvetia), is cheap and not far from the main train station, with decent doubles from €40 to €90; *St Paul*, St Paul Str. 7 (☎089/544 07800, ⊕ www.hotel-stpaul.de), is within staggering distance of the Theresienwiese and has (non-Oktoberfest) prices from around €90 for a good-sized double with private bath, including an excellent breakfast to set you up for the day.

If you haven't got anything sorted for the opening weekend six months in advance, then it's arguably not even worth trying. Munich's tourist office (see above) can provide you with a list of hotels and hostels to phone (you may just get lucky), while some of the larger business hotels may have rooms on offer during what is inevitably a seriously non-businessey couple of weeks. Otherwise, your best bet is to take a sleeping bag and/or tent and hope to get a spot in the massive *München-Thalkirchen* campsite, Zentrallandstr. 49, 4km from town (☎089/723 1707).

Eating and drinking

German **food** is ideal for beer-filled days. Snackwise, a festival treat is a *brezen*, a large salt-encrusted pretzel that goes amazingly well with a beer. Waitresses walk around with baskets full of them all day. For a heartier selection, you'll be able to sniff out the food stands in the beer gardens that surround every tent, which serve everything from *schweinebraten* (roast pork) and *weisswurst* (veal sausage) to the delicious *schweinbratwurst* (spiced roast-pork sausage). Alternatively, try *eisbein* (roasted pork knuckle), a tasty, if somewhat primitive, alternative. As you may have already gathered, your options are restricted if you're a vegetarian; most tents serve a vegetarian dish or two but even if you specify no meat you can end up picking bits of pork out of your soup (dead pig doesn't seem to count as meat here for some reason).

If you'd rather enjoy your pork in more salubrious surroundings, head for one of the traditional eateries serving hearty Bavarian fare that dot the city. A good, easy-to-find place – just head for the copper domes of the Frauenkirche – is *Nürnberger Bratwurst Glökl* on Frauenplatz 9, a beer hall that serves up a higher class of sausage. A walk around Marienplatz will turn up further options, including the popular *Spockmeier* on Rosenstrasse (just off Marienplatz), a huge place that is famous for its *weissewurst* or white sausage and its big noodle soup with pork.

Drinkwise, if you simply can't face another beer, try a *radlemass*, which is half-beer, half-lemonade – there's nothing wrong with a secret shandy. Or visit Munich's oldest wine bar, *Weinhaus Nuener*, Herzogspitalstr 8, which serves decent food as well as wine, in wood-panelled surroundings.

Event info

Oktoberfest (⊕ www.oktoberfest.de). The official site, and your one-stop source on the festival.

Time zone GMT+1   **Country code** +49   **Currency** euro (€)

Queen's Day

*Famed for its easy-going, fun-loving population, Amsterdam manages
to crank the party volume a few notches higher*

Queen's Day

Where?

Amsterdam, The Netherlands

When?

April 30, unless this falls on a Sunday in which case April 29

How long?

1 day

•Amsterdam

THE NETHERLANDS

If you're going to pick any European capital for a major 24-hour sleaze, drugs and alcohol binge, it may as well be Amsterdam. And Queen's Day is the wildest possible time to visit. The queen in question isn't one of the flamboyant transvestites hanging around Rembrandtplein but Holland's reigning monarch, Queen Beatrix, whose official birthday is celebrated throughout the country on April 30. The ensuing fiesta is Amsterdam's Mardi Gras and Oktoberfest all rolled into one – in a city famed for its easy-going, fun-loving population, it still manages to crank the party volume a few notches higher. Queen's Day is traditionally the one time each year when the police are forbidden to interfere with any activity, no matter how outrageous; and, of course, it's always a challenge to see where they really draw the line.

History

Queen's Day, or "Koninginnedag", was **first celebrated** on April 30, 1949, the then-Queen Juliana's birthday, when it was marked with little more than military parades, bicycle races and the consumption of orange cake slices. It has really only existed in its present, carnival form since 1980, when Queen Juliana abdicated the throne, and her daughter, **Beatrix** succeeded her. One of her first acts as queen was to declare that in future April 30 would be a national holiday, and that it would be marked by fun, rather than formality.

The Dutch didn't need any further prompting, and the present monster was unleashed. Beatrix herself was born on January 31, a day sensibly considered too cold for open-air festivities, so the date stayed; now it's only changed if it falls on a Sunday, when Koninginnedag is celebrated on the Saturday – a sensible way of placating both Dutch churchgoers and allowing extra recovery time. The festivities are held in towns and villages throughout the Netherlands, but none have the scale and energy of **Amsterdam**. The queen herself visits one or two places throughout the country, but generally stays clear of the full-scale bacchanalia underway in the capital.

The former Queen Juliana finally partied-out at the age of 94, having bequeathed a unique and much appreciated festival to her citizens. Given her mother's longevity, the present festivities are likely to keep running for some time yet – Queen Beatrix celebrated her Silver Jubilee in 2005, at the age of 67, so Queen's Day could keep going for another couple of decades, before **Prince Willem-Alexander** takes over the reins and kicks off King's Day.

Throughout this 24-hour law-free fiesta, the citizens of Amsterdam reclaim the streets, parks, squares and canals of the town from tourists, motorists and officialdom for one glorious party. Despite having carte blanche to descend into anarchy, the laid-back and responsible Dutch are of course very well adjusted to it all. This is a people's party, and everyone is going to have a good time – guys, girls, gays and grannies.

Queen's Night

The evening of April 29, Queen's Night, is nowadays the wilder of the two nights, with many people carrying on into Queen's Day itself. The general strategy is to hit Amsterdam's packed **clubs** and **bars** in the evening and lose it with a bunch of pie-eyed clubbers dancing to some of the best beats in Europe. If you aren't buckled up in the gutter by dawn, stagger out for a market-stall breakfast and hit the early morning sound systems.

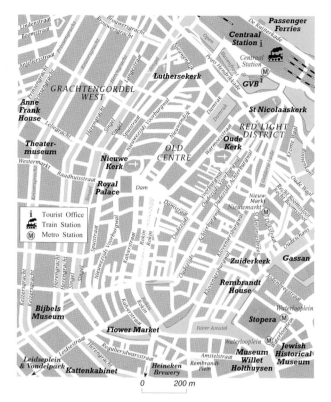

i	Tourist Office
🚂	Train Station
Ⓜ	Metro Station

0   200 m

Queen's Day

Queen's Day is a big outdoor event. It's not about the dingy hash bars or seedy sex salons so loved by mashed-up tourists. It's a day of live music and beer tents, and parties exploding onto the streets. Stages piled high with huge sound systems are set up in every available open space – the main stages are on **Rembrandtplein** and particularly **Thorbeckplein**, **Leidseplein**, **Nieuwmarkt** and **Museumplein**, where the big Amsterdam music stations hold their own mini festivals, blasting out the beats all day and night. The sheer density of people means that the streets are sealed off, and, whatever your inclination, you'll find enough beer chugging, pill-popping and red-hot partying to satisfy the most voracious of appetites. There are only two rules to observe:

- You must dress as ridiculously as possible, and this normally involves donning orange – the Dutch national colour, which adorns virtually every building, boat and body on the day.
- You must drink enough beer not to care.

Side effects, of course, include the desire to jump into canals, sing and dance like a baboon, and the misguided impression that you're attractive to everyone you meet – despite the beer and vomit stains on your T-shirt. But that's Queen's Day for you. The big danger is in peaking too soon. Amsterdam is an exhausting enough place to party any time of the year and seasoned Ibiza campaigners have been known to struggle to last the festival's full 24 hours.

barges crammed with people, crates of beer and sound systems pound their way around the canals like entrants in some disorganized aquatic carnival

Things wind down earlier on Queen's Day itself, with all music stopping around 9pm and everyone trudging off home by about 10pm, as the street cleaners move in with masterful efficiency, but you still need to take it easy if you intend on getting this far. Numerous nightclubs await the hardcore party fiends who want to carry on, though. If you last till midnight, you've made it.

Shopping for a costume

No matter who you are, or where you come from, Queen's Day is a 24-hour free market in which anything can be bought or sold. Stalls are set up everywhere, with people selling off all manner of old junk; even at 3am, you'll find Dutch kids, pensioners and teenagers strolling about and browsing as if it were a Sunday afternoon. The best thing to do is to join them late on the first night and buy an entire **party outfit**. It's obviously best if you choose each other's costumes, as long as you don't mind spending the next 24 hours in false breasts, a purple smoking jacket and a pair of crotch-less leather trousers. You'll find a huge selection of second-hand stuff just about everywhere you wander, but head for the sprawling **Waterlooplein** market in the southeast of the centre or the **Vondelpark** in the south for the best selection of orange wigs, day-glo trousers and funky clubbing gear.

Messing about on the river

The extensive and picturesque **canal system** is one of the best things about Amsterdam. There's nothing quite like taking one of the water-borne sightseeing tours and gazing at the amazing seventeenth-century gables in a hash-induced coma as the history of the city gently babbles over you in five different languages. However, Queen's Day means extra-special fun on the canals, as boating restrictions are lifted (or perhaps just ignored) and everyone goes berserk on the water – rowboats, barges and old fishing vessels crammed with people, crates of beer and sound systems pound their way around the canal system like entrants in some particularly disorganized aquatic carnival. Hang around hopefully on one of the bridges and you may get yourself on board; pick one with good tunes and people you like the look of, though, as it's hard to get off. Otherwise, just watching the boats pass by can be a lot of fun: crowds gather on the larger bridges and canal junctions to cheer on each bizarre vessel – **Prinsengracht** is a good canal for this, with Reguliersgracht and Prinsengracht a particularly chaotic and enjoyable intersection.

Chilling out

Despite the huge number of partygoers, chill-out areas are easy to find on Queen's Day. Many of the smoking bars are almost empty during the day, as the locals prefer to incapacitate themselves with Heineken rather than hash, so these serve as useful refuges. Another temporary respite from the partying can be found in the grassy relief of **Vondelpark**, where you can stretch out on the lawn for a bit of down time. For some mind-bending views, try the huge Ferris wheel set up in **Dam Square**, at the end of the main tourist drag that leads south from the train station. Or you might prefer to head for the **Planetarium**, situated next to the Artis Zoo in the east of the city centre. Here you get to lie in a reclining chair in the dark and speculate on the formation of the universe. If that doesn't rev you up for another assault on the party, nothing will.

Insider info A lot of Amsterdam's main clubs put on special Queen's Day nights; the best way to find out what's on is to pick up a copy of the freebie *Amsterdam Weekly* when you arrive.

Family ties

The **Vondelpark** is the place to head for if you have kids in tow. By tradition, it's the place for families on Queen's Day, and children bring along all their old toys and books and lay them out for sale in a giant kiddy flea market while busking the stuff they learnt at school on their favourite musical instruments. It's a great atmosphere, and a good antidote to the full-on adult partying around the rest of town, though be sure to get there early; after lunch, the Vondelpark becomes an adult-only zone much like everywhere else.

Basics

Amsterdam's Schiphol **airport** is 18km outside of the city; trains run to Centraal Station every fifteen minutes. The city itself is compact enough to navigate by **foot**; there are also excellent tram links around town, but with the heaving crowds effectively blocking up the streets on Queen's Day, you're better off walking, and a lot of trams don't run at all. The main VVV **tourist office** (ⓦ www.holland.com) is right outside the station, bang next to the GVB public transport office.

Accommodation

There's plenty of budget **accommodation** available in Amsterdam, and the VVV are experts at tracking down the last available bed for a small fee. Among low-cost places, the *Hotel Arena*, Gravesandestraat 51, near the Oosterpark just outside the city centre (☎ 020/850 2400, ⓦ www.hotelarena.nl), is a huge, very sociable place that has good, minimally furnished bright doubles (from €80), triples (from €135) and suites (around €200), a very cool restaurant and bar, and regular events and club nights in a converted chapel. The *Stayokay Vondelpark Youth Hostel*, right by the Vondel Park at Zanpad 5 (☎ 020/589 8996, ⓦ www.stayokay.com/vondelpark), is a cheaper option, and has a whole host of sleeping arrangements, from dorm beds (from €20) to double rooms (around €60). Closer to the action, the *Hans Brinker*, Kerkstraat 136–138 (☎ 020/622 0687, ⓦ www.hans-brinker.com), is a vast place with over five hundred beds, and prices per person of just €21 for a berth in a six- or eight-bed room; it's a raucous place at the best of times, and wild during Queen's Day. Among more central, regular hotels, on the edge of the Red Light District is *Winston*, Warmoesstraat 123–9 (☎ 020/623 1380, ⓦ www.winston.nl), which has doubles from €70 and quads from €120, and a self-consciously cool vibe (though they charge a slight premium over Queen's Day weekend). With a little more to spend, you could try *Misc*, on the other side of the Red Light District at Kloveniersburgwal 20 (☎ 020/330 6241, ⓦ www.hotelmisc. com) – friendly and family-run, but with only six rooms for upwards of €135, you'll need to book even further in advance. For a splurge, the *College Hotel*, Roelof Hartstraat 1 (☎ 020/571 1511, ⓦ www. thecollegehotel.com), has sleek doubles from €235 and a great location near Museumplein and Vondelpark, but is far enough away from the main party points to be a bit of a hideaway.

Eating and drinking

As many a hash-tourist will testify, Amsterdam is an absolute haven for munchie **food**. The best place to get frites is from the hole-in-the-wall *Vlaamse Friteshuis*, just off Kalverstraat at Voetboogstraat 31. For more substantial fare, try the *Keuken van 1870*, at the bottom end of Spuistraat (☎ 020/620 4018), a big, light room with long wooden tables serving up cheap Dutch nosh for just €7.50 for three courses. For a gourmet blowout, head for *Blauwe aan de Wal*, OZ Achterburgwal 99 (☎ 020/330 2257), in the Red Light District – the food is excellent.

Getting hold of a **beer** during Queen's Day is not a problem: just about every few metres you'll find someone standing over an icebox full of cold beers for sale, a lot of bars set up a counter out on the pavement, and Heineken marquees pop up on the edges of Leidseplein, Niewmarkt, Rembrandtsplein and Dam Square. Nice central bars include *In de Wildeman*, Kolksteeg 3, one of the oldest in the city, with a huge selection of beers and a traditionally dark interior that's a godsend if you're tired of bright lights and thrumming techno; and canalside *De Sluyswacht*, Jodenbreestraat 1, a lovely place to watch the boats and revellers go by.

Coffeeshops are, of course, a welcome retreat from the full-on partying. There are loads but favourites include *Abraxas*, just off NZ Voorburgwal at Jonge Roelensteeg 12; *Rusland*, just off Kloveniersburgwal at Rusland 16; *Global Chillage*, Kerkstraat 51, not far from Leidseplein; and *Siberie*, Brouwersgracht 11.

Nightlife

The long-running *Melkweg*, Lijnbaansgracht 234A, just off Leidseplein, and *Escape*, on Rembrandtplein, are both huge clubs that usually serve up something on Queen's Day night, most probably great techno and house to a buzzed-up crowd. *Jimmy Woo*, Korte Leidsedwarsstraat 18, is at the other extreme – famously selective on the door, so you'll only get in if your party gear is outrageous enough. On a smaller scale, *Bitterzoet*, Spuistraat 2, usually has a Queen's Day DJ lineup. Or you might want to just catch the "Drag Olympics" held by the Westerkerk from 5pm.

Event info

Queen's Day (ⓦ www.koninginnedag.nl). Dutch-language site detailing events taking place on Queen's Day.

Time zone GMT+1   **Country code** +31   **Currency** euro (€)

St Patrick's Day

No one does it quite like the Irish,
especially on their home turf

St Patrick's Day

Where?

Dublin, Ireland

When?

On and around March 17

How long?

5 days

Dublin •

IRELAND

There's something about the words "party" and "Ireland". In a country that turns death into a two-day piss-up (someone once observed that the only difference between an Irish wake and an Irish wedding was that there was one fewer drunk person), the national holiday just had to be something special. The official face of the festival is the street parades, but the soul of the business – the real "craic", as the Irish would say – is in the pubs of the city, where some of the antics would make Bacchus himself blanch. The parades attract street performers, puppeteers and band troupes from all over Europe, and are, like a music session in an Irish pub, about participation rather than observation. Dress up, drink up, and, as the Irish poet Patrick Kavanagh would say, "bucklep" about the streets to your heart's content.

St Patrick: fact or fiction?

"Hail glorious St Patrick, great king of our isle". So the hymn goes, and there is little doubt that the great saint is not only hailed, but also lauded, toasted, praised and toasted again, during the course of his festival. So, when you find yourself arm-in-arm with your long-lost Irish cousin, caught up in a boisterous, terrace-chant rendition of the hymn or raising a semi-drained pint of Guinness in his holy honour, you might want to turn to your new best friend and ask him just who St Patrick was? The reply will probably be that St Patrick was the greatest saint ever: he came to Ireland, converted everyone to Christianity, drove the snakes into the sea, and established the Emerald Isle as God's chosen land. Not a bad answer, but the fact is that not only was St Patrick probably not Irish at all, but he might have been... say it quietly... English, a Romanized Briton who, legend has it, first came to Ireland as a slave, escaped back to Britain, and, on hearing the Irish call him in a dream, returned to convert the country to Christianity. This makes a good story, but probably isn't quite true. What is sure, however, is that a missionary named Patrick did exist, and most probably worked in the northeast of Ireland in the sixth century. But it's unlikely he drove out snakes – Ireland never had any – and whether he converted the entire place to the ways of the Lord, who knows? But then St George probably never slew a dragon, either.

Until the mid-1990s, St Patrick's Day was a fairly arid affair in Ireland itself; indeed, the Irish took a dim view of the event, seeing it largely as an excuse for misty-eyed expats and wannabe Celts to go wild once a year in foreign climes. Dublin's St Patrick's Day Parade, in particular, was a brutal affair that passed by with all the gusto of a Soviet state funeral. Since then, though, determined not to be outdone by the rest of the world, the Irish version of the festival has perked up no end, and has become one of the country's major events – and today, of course, no one does it quite like the Irish, especially on their home turf.

Nowadays, from around the end of the **second week of March**, in the days leading up to St Patrick's Day, Dublin city centre comes alive with all manner of events and spectacles, featuring live bands and street theatre, as well as a funfair in Merrion Square and associated music concerts, stage shows, arts exhibitions, markets and various nautical displays down in the Docklands area. The festival kicks off with an evening display of street theatre, acrobatics, drumming and circus events, often headed by the Galway-based street-theatre troupe Macnas, whose outrageously flamboyant puppets and energetic performances have taken this kind of outdoor performance to a new level. Other major happenings include the annual boat race down the Liffey between crews from Trinity College and University College Dublin – a sort of Oxford/Cambridge affair but without the toffs and with *far* superior banter.

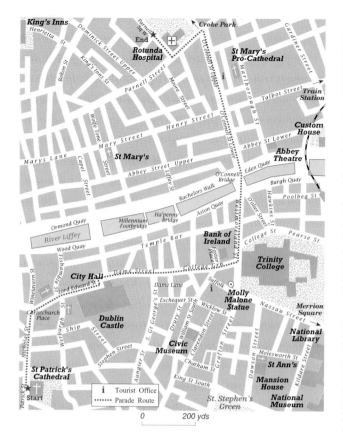

Insider info The event schedule and locations vary each year, so be sure to check the festival website (see p.132) for exact details of what's going on where.

The St Patrick's Day Parade

While the multitude of periphery events changes by the year, the St Patrick's Day Parade itself (always held on March 17) is a constant, and the backbone of the festival. As many as 700,000 green-tinged festivalgoers descend upon the city centre en masse to drink and dance the day away, and cheer on the assorted marching bands, floats and themed pageants. The parade starts at around noon at St Patrick's Cathedral on Patrick Street, but get there earlier as the warm-up street entertainment begins at 11am. The parade then heads off up Patrick Street, winding its way north through town before finishing by the Black Church near Dorset Street Upper. To get a really good view, it's best to secure a place as near to **O'Connell Bridge**, at the southern end of O'Connell Street, as early in the day as possible. If you'd rather save your legs for the Irish dancing later on, you can buy a seat for €60 in one of the various grandstand locations along the parade route in advance from the St Patrick's Day Festival office on Earlsfort Terrace (see p.132).

After the parade, most of the revellers make their way to Earlsfort Terrace, at the southeastern corner of St Stephen's Green, for the hugely popular **Céilí Mór** (literally "Great Dance Event") – a veritable orgy of Irish dance and live bands – where the alcohol-fuelled exuberance of the crowd is tempered only by the

you'll find yourself arm-in-arm with your long-lost Irish cousin, raising a semi-drained pint of Guinness in St Patrick's honour

trained dancers who try to forge some semblance of choreography from the increasingly malleable mass. Once you've spent a couple of hours looking like a reject from *Riverdance*, it's a short walk from the *Céilí* to any number of pubs, though only the music in O'Donoghue's, the traditional watering-hole of the fathers of Irish folk, The Dubliners, matches the high tempo of the earlier dancing.

Gaelic football and hurling

As well as drinking, and celebrating Irish music and dance, the St Patrick's Day Festival also showcases the traditional sports of Gaelic football and hurling. On March 17, in the country's largest sports stadium, **Croke Park**, local village teams bleed and sweat (hurlers and Gaelic footballers don't cry) for the honour of their family, village and club, and the chance of winning the **All-Ireland Senior Club Championships**. Far from the choreographed entertainment that now masquerades as team sport, this is the real deal, with the winning team being crowned champions of Ireland. The level of skill on display is breathtaking, most especially in the exhilarating stick sport of hurling, and the sense of community in the crowd gives as good a flavour of small-town rural Ireland as you're likely to get without leaving Dublin. **Tickets** for the games can be purchased at the stadium on the day without any difficulty. For more details, see the Gaelic Athletic Association's website (ⓦwww.gaa.ie).

Worldwide events

Virtually every town **in Ireland** has some form of St Patrick's Day event and there are major celebrations usually held in places associated with the saint, such as Armagh and Downpatrick, as well as in Belfast and Cork. **Outside Ireland**, expat communities fete the saint with parades and other events in places as far afield as New York City (see box below), Barcelona, Seoul, Sydney, Auckland and even the island of Montserrat. You'll also find revelry just about anywhere there's an Irish bar, be it Ballybunion, Birmingham or, as the late Pete McCarthy discovered in *McCarthy's Bar*, Budapest.

Amsterdam ⓦwww.irishclub.nl
Auckland ⓦwww.stpatrick.co.nz
Barcelona ⓦwww.elfeile.com
Belfast ⓦwww.feilebelfast.com/stpatrick
Brussels ⓦwww.irishclub.be
Copenhagen ⓦwww.stpatricksdayparade.dk
Cork ⓦwww.corkstpatricksfestival.ie
London ⓦwww.london.gov.uk/stpatricksday
Montserrat ⓦwww.visitmontserrat.com
Munich ⓦwww.toytownmunich.com/archive/st_patricks_day.html
Sydney ⓦwww.stpatricksday.org.au
Tokyo ⓦwww.inj.jp/index_e.html
Toronto ⓦwww.topatrick.com

St Patrick's Day, New York

While Dublin puts on one hell of a bash for St Patrick's Day, the chances are you'll have as much fun in **New York** (ⓦwww.ny.com/holiday/stpatricks), where 150,000 participants take to the streets of Manhattan to honour the man who brought Christianity to the Emerald Isle. Turning everything green for the day might seem a strange way to do it, but that's the expat Irish and their hangers-on for you – for one day only, it's the greatest nationality on earth, at least in New York. The signs lining the parade's route glow a shocking shade of lime, members of the parade are resplendent in their Irish livery, green ticker-tape flutters gently in the breeze, and some of the bars even manage to dye their Guinness a dubious shade of lime – just what state your insides end up after drinking it is anyone's guess.

The day starts seriously enough, with Morning Mass at St Patrick's Cathedral, after which, at about noon, the **Parade** sets off down Fifth Avenue and runs from 44th to 88th streets, led by soldiers from the Irish 165th Infantry marching bands representing Irish communities from around the world, then by delegations from various public services and local communities. It's a massive affair, and takes several hours to pass by, after which the serious partying gets going – the bars fill up and remain packed until late, as everyone spends the rest of the night drinking to Irish heritage: theirs, their forefathers', or anyone they meet who has happened to once spend a weekend in Dublin.

Basics

Dublin **airport** is 11km north of the city, while ferries from Britain dock at Dublin **port**, 3km east of the centre. The **bus** station is on Store Street, and most **trains** pull into Connolly Station – both are within walking distance of O'Connell Street. The most central **tourist information offices** are in a former church at the western end of Suffolk Street and at 14 O'Connell Street Upper.

Accommodation

Dublin has a wealth of stylish **hostels**, most of which are within walking distance of the city centre. On a tight budget, you can't get more central than the *Abbey Court Hostel*, 29 Bachelors Walk, just by O'Connell Street Bridge on the northern side of the river (☎01/878 0700, ⓦwww.abbey-court.com); or the nearby *Litton Lane Hostel*, 2–4 Litton Lane (☎01/872 8389, ⓦwww.irish-hostel.com). Alternatively, both *Isaacs Hostel*, 2–5 Frenchman's Lane (☎01/855 6125, ⓦwww.isaacs.ie), and *Jacob's Inn*, 21–28 Talbot Place (☎01/855 5660, same website), are handy for the bus and train stations. Expect to pay upwards of €20–25 for a dorm bed, and more for a private room.

For greater comfort there are decent and cheap **hotels**, many of which offer flat-rate room deals – check out the Jurys chain (ⓦwww.jurysinn.com) or the *Harding Hotel*, Fishamble street (☎01/679 6500, ⓦwww.hardinghotel.ie), for cosy rooms sleeping two to four people from around €105 per night. The other option is **B&Bs**, which offer reasonably priced rooms outside of the centre (though try to secure one either on or near a night-bus route, as hailing a taxi late at night is impossible). Some more central choices include the *Marian Guest House*, 21 Gardiner St Upper (☎01/874 4129, ⓦwww.marianguesthouse.ie; around €70 for a double), a friendly joint with en-suite rooms and good breakfasts. The *Townhouse*, 47–48 Gardiner St Lower (☎01/878 8808, ⓦwww.townhouseofdublin.com), is another good choice – a double here will cost around €115. Things get much pricier around St Stephen's Green, but you can't get any closer to the action than the *Fitzwilliam Hotel* (☎01/478 7000, ⓦwww.fitzwilliamhotel.com) or the *Stephen's Green Hotel* (☎01/607 3600, ⓦwww.ocallaghanhotels.com), both of which offer luxurious rooms overlooking the Green from around €200 for a double.

Eating and drinking

Among recommended **pubs** on or near the parade route are *The Porterhouse*, 16 Parliament St, a vibrant bar where you can sample home-brewed stouts and enjoy nightly musical entertainment. The *Palace Bar* on Fleet Street is a relaxing Victorian pub with excellent traditional-music sessions during the week, while *Mulligan's*, 8 Poolbeg St, is celebrated locally as serving the best Guinness in town. *Kehoe's*, 9 St Anne St, is an excellent bar with cosy snugs and a convivial atmosphere, though it will be full throughout the festival. *O'Donoghue's*, 15 Merrion Row, is an old-style Dublin bar renowned as the home of traditional music – commandeer a seat near the window box and you'll be sorted for the night. If *O'Donoghue's* is packed, there's another couple of bars just to the east, on Baggot Street Lower: *Doheny & Nesbitt* and *Toner's*. For something more filling than the black stuff, try the **food** at *Avoca Café* on Suffolk Street, which serves up everything from shepherd's pie to smoked salmon at reasonable prices, or *Probe*, in the Market Arcade on South Great George's Street, for filling Irish stew and fajitas. Alternatively, tuck into some of Dublin's finest fish and chips from *Leo Burdock's*, 2 Werburgh St (near the City Hall).

Event info

St Patrick's Day Festival St Stephen's Green House, Earlsfort Terrace (☎01/676 3205, ⓦwww.stpatricksday.ie). Event organizers, whose website features the festival schedule and grandstand-seating booking form.

Dublin Tourist Office (ⓦwww.visitdublin.com). Official website of the Dublin tourist office.

Time zone GMT   **Country code** +353   **Currency** euro (€)

Tenerife Carnival

Lion jumpsuits, dancing troupes, and
moustachioed men in drag

Tenerife Carnival

Where?
Santa Cruz, Tenerife, Spain

When?
The days up to and beyond Ash Wednesday

How long?
12 days

A small island two hundred miles off the African coast, Tenerife seems an unlikely spot for one of the world's largest carnivals; but with over three hundred entries on the island's annual festival calendar, it shouldn't come as a surprise that its Carnival, the biggest event of them all, is one massive, raucous jamboree. In the run-up to Lent, over a quarter of a million costumed revellers converge on the island's capital, Santa Cruz, to party so hard that they even manage to eclipse the hedonism of the holiday resorts for which the island is best known. By attracting musicians, and even partygoers, from Latin America, Tenerife Carnival captures a great deal of the passion, fervour and debauchery of the vast events from across the Atlantic, helping make it Europe's premier street party.

The real core of the celebrations take place every night in the **town centre** – along the seafront and around the city's main square, the Plaza de España – when stages are set up for bands to pump out vibrant salsa rhythms, and hundreds of kiosks lining the street host various kinds of dance music until dawn. Most islanders are experts in pacing themselves during the carnival season, and will only slowly begin to emerge around mid-afternoon, taking their time getting ready, assembling their costumes, and hanging out with friends before heading into the fray at around midnight.

Absorbed by their quest for winter sun, the bulk of the holiday-makers on the island will probably be oblivious to the goings-on in Santa Cruz, and those who do make the trip to the capital usually leave when the formal events have finished – certainly before the party really gets going. This doesn't mean that outsiders aren't welcome. On the contrary, the gregarious locals will be more than happy to party with you – as long as you're in **fancy dress**. This varies from basic tiger and lion jumpsuits to extremely elaborate get-ups, often designed to fit in with whatever the carnival's theme is that year, and you'll be well provided for by the fancy-dress stores along Santa Cruz's main pedestrian drag, Calle del Castillo.

History

Carnival of some sort has been celebrated on Tenerife **since the early years of colonization**, at the end of the fifteenth century – one of the earliest references to masquerading and public pranks on the island came in 1523 when King Carlos I passed a law prohibiting masks. However, due partly to its reputation as one of the most irreverent and subversive festivals, it has been subject to many prohibitions, and subsequent revivals, over the centuries – the flamboyant custom was revived by the debauched Felipe IV in the mid-seventeenth century, and so it continued until the early part of the twentieth century, when in 1927 the church condemned men dressing as women, a key feature of Carnival. The result was the formation of a commission of "even-tempered" men, sent to visit island houses in advance of the Carnival to verify the sex of masked participants and issue licences to be pinned on the costumes of the true women. Carnival bounced back the following year, when the ordinance was largely ignored, and, unlike carnivals elsewhere in Spain, the celebrations even managed to continue throughout most of the repressive Franco era, thinly disguised as a winter festival – mostly because Franco had a soft spot for Tenerife.

Today, due to the Canary Islands' strong links with **Latin America**, Tenerife Carnival is stronger than ever. Almost as soon as one Carnival ends, preparations for the next one begin, continuing throughout the year and attracting more column inches in island newspapers than almost any other news item. Despite originally being a religious festival – a brief indulgence before the sober period of Lent – spiritual observance has now taken a back seat to partying. Indeed, rather than ending on Ash Wednesday, like most carnivals, proceedings now extend several days into Lent itself.

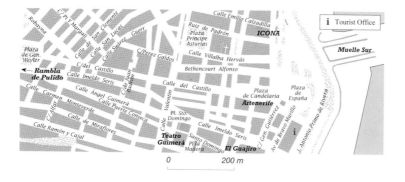

The main events

The glue that holds all this partying together is the parades and other, more-organized carnival events, which kick off with the selection of the **Carnival Queen** on the Wednesday before Shrove Tuesday, when various good-looking girls strut around in elaborate costumes in a bid to be elected. It takes the best part of a year for designers and dress-makers to produce many of these incredible, cumbersome, oversized structures, some of which require the assistance of trolleys

Cadiz Carnival

Tenerife isn't Spain's only big Carnival. The **Cadiz Carnival** celebrations are some of the best you'll find anywhere in Europe. Being Spanish, and therefore eager as ever to prolong a good party, the people of Cadiz have the usual four-day hedonistic thrash up to Shrove Tuesday, but then restart the party on Friday, keeping going throughout the following weekend with renewed fervour. The parade's organization tends to be a little rough around the edges, but the streets and alleyways are packed with up-for-it costumed revellers from dusk until dawn. For **information** on the Cadiz Carnival schedule, contact the Cadiz Carnival Committee on ☎956 211 256.

to enable the wearer to move around. The huge, heavy and precarious headdresses in particular owe more to engineering than clothing design. Beyond this, though, it's a beauty pageant like any other, and a bit of a yawn to be honest, heavily sponsored by local businesses. Indeed, things don't really pick up until the following Friday night, when an **opening parade** of bands and floats announces the start of the festivities proper and the beginning of two of the wildest nights of the Carnival.

> **Insider info** If you want to get the most out of Carnival, it's best to take a leaf out of the locals' book, and spend your day relaxing in preparation for the evening onslaught.

After everyone's recovered from the weekend, the flagship event of the official carnival is the Coso or "**Grand Procession**", which starts around 4pm on Shrove Tuesday. This is a huge, lively cavalcade of floats, bands, dancing troupes and entertainers that marches and dances its way along the dockside road, passing beside the Plaza de España, for about five hours. Again, the costumes worn by those parading (a good many of the islanders it seems) are impressively imaginative and clearly labour-intensive designs. The Grand Procession is followed by fireworks at around 9pm, which act as a starter gun for another night's partying.

The following night, on Ash Wednesday, the **Entierro de la Sardina** (Burial of the Sardine) is one of the best-attended events. Originally a parade to mark the closing of the carnival, it has now been left stranded in the middle of the festival, and has become a tongue-in-cheek event in which many dress – or more commonly cross-dress – in mourning attire. Central to the occasion is a huge wood-and-paper sardine that is paraded, at a painfully slow pace, down the Rambla de Pulido into the centre of town. The procession is accompanied by funereal music and followed by a cortege of priests, and "widows" – mostly

costumes are incredible, oversized structures, which require the assistance of trolleys to enable the wearer to move around

moustachioed men in drag – wailing miserably. A cremation, just southwest of the Plaza de España, follows, with the widows doubled over with grief and seemingly inconsolable (and usually more than a little drunk), until fireworks launch everyone back into party mode.

Still not put off by the onset of Lent, the carnival doesn't reach its climactic end until the following weekend, when some of the festival's most intense partying follows a **kids' parade** on the Saturday and a **seniors' parade** on the Sunday. While these may mark the end of festivities in Santa Cruz, this is just the beginning for many of the smaller towns around the island, who, not wishing to compete with (or miss out on) the capital's carnival, wait until the dust settles in Santa Cruz before getting stuck into their own celebrations.

Basics

Considering its relatively remote location, getting to Tenerife is a cinch, and very cheap, thanks to its popularity among northern European package tourists, as hundreds of charter planes fly into the island's **airport** every week. Getting around Tenerife is easy, too. It's well served by **buses** and, during carnival season, TITSA, the efficient public bus company, puts on regular all-night shuttles to most major island towns. This means that you can leave your rental car at home, forget about parking hassles and enjoy more than the odd drink. For timetable information, call their 24-hour information service – in both English and Spanish – on ☎ 922 531 300, or check their website, ⓦ www.titsa. com.

Accommodation

The best place to base yourself is the stylish tourist town of **Puerto de la Cruz**, less than an hour north of Santa Cruz, which a good range of resort hotels (mainly holiday-makers on pre-booked packages), and a particularly fine stock of guesthouses and inexpensive small hotels. Of several **pensions**, two of the best independent options are *Rosamary*, C/de San Felipe 14 (☎ 922 383 253), a small, friendly and immaculately kept guesthouse in the town's quaint old fishing quarter with en-suite double rooms for €28 per night; and *Los Geranios*, C/del Lomo 14 (☎ 922 382 810), also in the old fishing district, whose fantastically clean and well-kept en-suite doubles cost €27 per night.

Among **hotels**, the *Alfomar*, C/de la Peñita 6 (☎ 922 380 682), in a 1970s building also in the old fishing quarter, has en-suite double rooms (€26 per night), most with balconies, overlooking a quiet pedestrian street. The *Régulo*, C/San Felipe 6 (☎ 922 388 800), housed in a small, newly renovated house opposite the excellent Canarian restaurant of the same name, has simple rooms (good value at €35/ night for a double), and half-board deals, with dinner at the restaurant, for around €70. The *Monopol*, C/de Quintana 15 (☎ 922 384 61, ⓦ www.interbook.net/empresas/monopol), is an elegant central hotel in a traditional eighteenth-century building, complete with ornately carved wooden balconies. Its en-suite rooms are equally stylish, and cost around €72 per night for a double, including breakfast.

Finally, you could also try renting an **apartment**. The *Florasol*, Camino del Coche 7 (☎ 922 389 848, ⓦ www.aparthotelflorasol. com), is a new apartment complex with excellently equipped, tastefully decorated and very generously sized apartments – many with views over Mount Teide on clear days. Communal facilities include a restaurant, pool and tennis courts. Apartments sleep up to four; a two-person apartment costs around €400 per week.

Eating and drinking

The festival staples of hot dogs, burgers and fries are luckily not the only **food** on offer at the carnival. Thanks to South American and Iberian influences, it's also easy to get hold of tasty alternatives such as *arepas* (deep-fried crispy pockets of cornmeal dough stuffed with fillings including chicken, cheese or ham), and the famed cornerstone of all Spanish bar fare, *tapas* – freshly made and laid out under a glass counter, and available in the many bars around the centre that remain open throughout the night. These bars also supplement the vast numbers of small kiosks scattered along the seafront road and around the central pedestrian area, which serve **drink** – beer, wine and some harder stuff, too – all at pretty reasonable prices.

Event info

Tenerife Carnival (ⓦ www.carnavaltenerife.com). The rather dull official website but good for an overview of exact times and dates.

Useful websites

Living Tenerife (ⓦ www.livingtenerife.com). Excellent and useful website of the island's English expat magazine.
Sun 4 Free (ⓦ www.sun4free.com). Well-organized online guide to Tenerife, with detail on all aspects of the island, including Carnival.

Time zone GMT+1   **Country code** +34   **Currency** euro (€)

Venice Carnival

Super-saturated colours and melodramatic flourishes from a theatre of the imagination

Venice Carnival

Where?
Venice, Italy

When?
February

How long?
10 days

• Venice

Rome •

ITALY

As a setting for a carnival, Venice is unique. The city's location, built across several islands in a lagoon bordering the Adriatic Sea, means that here carnival floats do literally that, gliding along on the water itself rather than chugging down the road on the back of a truck. The maze of narrow pedestrian streets and interlaced canals are a source of discovery at every turn – all the more so if you're kitted out in a fancy costume or, at the least, a mask – and Venice as a whole is an authentic backdrop for the theatrical celebrations that form the basis of the festival. Ultimately, the sheer visual delight of the city, and the tangible feeling that somehow you are adrift on an island in some parallel universe, are what make Carnival an experience like no other.

Carnival starts ten days before Shrove Tuesday, and finishes at the strike of midnight on Shrove Tuesday itself. During this time, exploring Venice's intimate back alleys and canals is well rewarded, mainly because wherever you wander there's almost always something going on.

Apart from the two weekends of Carnival there are two particularly frenetic evenings, those of the second Thursday, **Giovedi Grasso** (Fat Thursday), and the last day, **Martedi Grasso** (Shrove Tuesday), both significant days immediately preceding Lent, and therefore the days of greatest excess. Both nights boast live-music dance spectaculars in Piazza San Marco, with Tuesday's always being the *Notte de la Taranta*, the wild, intoxicated dance of

History

The **origins** of Carnival go back to around 1162, when it was bestowing a celebration of battle victories and honour on the Doge (the ruler of Venice), but it took 134 years before the city senate declared it official. From the fifteenth century, Carnival gathered momentum, reaching its zenith in the eighteenth century but effectively ending with the conquest of the city by Napoleon in 1797. It wasn't until 1979 that Carnival rediscovered the inspiration and energy that is so apparent today. Reinvented to draw tourists to the city at what used to be (by Venetian standards) a relatively dead time of year, it pretty much took up where it left off in the late 1800s: it's this eighteenth-century posturing that makes it so different from other European carnivals.

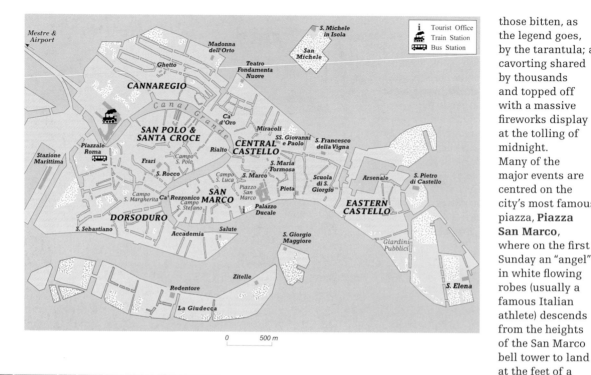

those bitten, as the legend goes, by the tarantula; a cavorting shared by thousands and topped off with a massive fireworks display at the tolling of midnight.

Many of the major events are centred on the city's most famous piazza, **Piazza San Marco**, where on the first Sunday an "angel" in white flowing robes (usually a famous Italian athlete) descends from the heights of the San Marco bell tower to land at the feet of a host of historically attired dignitaries. The piazza is usually packed with a seething crowd of thousands, many of whom are togged up in flamboyant costumes that range from closely detailed traditional dress to post-Casanova kitsch: the super-saturated colours and melodramatic flourishes from a theatre of the imagination.

Away from the epicentre of Piazza San Marco, Carnival experience disperses itself among the labyrinthine streets and small, atmospheric squares, overflowing with street performers and clusters of (always friendly) exuberance. **Piazzetta San Marco** is home to performances of Baroque music and Commedia dell'Arte – a

Theatre Carnival

Each year the carnival establishes an underlying theme and this forms the inspiration behind the concurrent Theatre Carnival; 2006's was "The Lion and the Dragon", which set the tone for a diverse cycle of shows including international collaborations. Performances take place in a variety of venues, including the Teatro Goldoni, Teatro Malibran and Teatro La Fenice, all three of which have spectacular auditoriums well worth the visit alone. A must-see, however, is the **Teatro Fondamenta Nuove**, an understated, old converted building on the north edge of the city renowned for providing the best in fringe theatre.

Masks

A key element of carnival disguise is the *maschera* or **mask**, the wearing of which was already well established by the mid fifteenth century and reached its peak in the eighteenth century. (It also went through a period of prohibition when the city senate feared that carnival fever, the "permitted madness", would overflow into the rest of the year.) Masks allowed the city dwellers to adopt alter-egos and to engage in activities without the usual constraints – which, in a way, they still do. There are a huge variety of masks on display, ranging from the minimalist pure white *Volto*, through ones with a Commedia dell'Arte influence (the Harlequin), to those of pure fantasy: mythical creatures, cosmic shapes and masks where extravagant decoration is an expression of glamorous anonymity. Wearing a mask is a fun and easy alternative if you don't fancy the full costume option, and you can either make your own or buy one from a multitude of shops selling everything from cheap but effective plastic masks (around €10) right up to beautifully crafted artisan creations – feather-plumed partial masks start at €25, beautiful leather ones cost around €50, and elaborate, often gold-leaved, full face masks will set you back up to €150.

Mask shops
Blue Moon Mask Dorsoduro 2312, (☎041-715-175, ⊚www.bluemoonmask.com).
Tragicoma Calle dei Nomboli, San Polo (☎041-721-102, ⊚www.tragicomica.it).

form of theatre with its origins way back in the heyday of the original Carnival – while left-field acolytes can seek out little **Campo San Luca**, offering more edgy live music and maybe some over-confident natives climbing flagpoles freestyle, or a spontaneous DJ set near the Ponte Rialto, where you may find yourself whisked away for a dance with a giant penguin who won't say no.

flamboyant costumes range from closely detailed traditional dress to post-Casanova kitsch

Larger squares such as **Campo Santa Margherita** are other focal points, the setting for stages for live music (bizarrely, often reflecting the modern Italian passion for ska and reggae), though probably you will have passed a quartet playing Baroque music in a street only minutes before. There is more focused nightlife around the **Stazione Marittima**, which forms the venue for dance-orientated diversions, while another of the city's larger squares, **Campo San Polo**, has plenty on offer for young children during the day – play areas, music, and small theatre productions.

On the water itself, small flotillas of decorated gondolas periodically sweep through the **canals**, to the cheers of revellers who crowd the bridges for a spectacular "aerial" view.

Insider info With so many events on offer, it's a good idea to check out some of the online programme details prior to arrival, particularly the Venice Carnival and Venice Council websites (see p.144).

Basics

Budget airlines serve Mestre **airport**, a twenty-minute bus or train journey from Venice. If you tire of walking or wish to see the city from a watery vantage point then a **water bus** (*vaporetto*) is a good option for getting around; for routes and information, visit the operators, ACTV, at their main office in the Venice bus station in Piazzale Roma.

Accommodation

Venice, unsurprisingly, is full of **hotels** and those in the central historical areas are more expensive; a typical double room in a three-star will cost between €95 and €200 per night. If you opt to stay in mainland Mestre, twenty minutes from the city, you can save at least €30 per night on your hotel costs, but your Carnival experience will inevitably be diluted by not being in Venice itself.

There are an increasing number of cheaper **guesthouses** in Venice, of which the *Corte 1321*, San Polo 1321 (☎ 041-522-4923, ☻ www.corte1321.com), run by a couple of Americans, has very comfortable rooms, a beautiful courtyard, and is only fifteen minutes' walk from Piazza San Marco. A double room with breakfast is €100 per night. Alternatively, *Casa Mimma*, Santa Croce 1412/C (☎ 041-522-2264), has en-suite doubles for €120 per night with breakfast, while a double room with shared bathroom in the *Abis Maria*, Dosodoro 611/A (☎ 041-522-3512), costs €30–62 per night. **Hostels** provide more economic options and are often located in historical buildings; a bed in the hostel *Santa Fosca*, Cannaregio 2372 (☎ 041-715-775, ☻ www.santafosca.com) costs around €22 per night, with similar prices at *Foresteria Valdese*, near Piazza San Marco (☎ 041-528-6797, ☻ www.diaconiavaldese.org/venezia/). Advance booking is, of course, essential everywhere during Carnival. If you would rather save a few pounds by staying outside Venice, the *Antica Locanda Ai Veterani* at Piazzetta Da Re 5 (☎ 041-971-912) is a comfortable hotel in a good location, with double rooms for €90 per night with breakfast.

Eating and drinking

There is a tremendous array of places to eat and drink in Venice, and the best advice is to wander off the main tourist drag a little to discover the most atmospheric, authentic (and least expensive) haunts. It is a must to sample the bar **food**, called *cicheti* (equivalent to a Spanish *tapa*), and coming in many varieties, especially seafood, costing an average of €5 a dish. Fish is particularly good in Venice, and sardines with sweet onion and polenta, *sarde in saor*, is a must. One particularly authentic bar is *Alla Vedova*, Calle del Pistor 3912, near Rialto, where a glass of good wine and a single *polpette* (a very moreish, refined kind of meatball) will knock you back about €1.50. *Paradiso Perduto*, Cannaregio 2540, Fondamenta de la Misericordia, is a larger bar, much loved by natives and visitors alike for its *cicheti*, and its live music some evenings. *Osteria alla Botte*, Calle de la Bissa 5482, also near Rialto, is a small, authentic bar and a popular meeting place all year round and very reasonably priced. On the sweeter side, customary Carnival cakes are the delicious *frittelle* and the *galani*, to be found in any *pasticceria*.

A traditional Venetian early evening apéritif is a *Spritz*, an orangey mix of white wine, water and Aperol (similar to Campari) – a lively, refreshing and sociable **drink**. The rest of the time is best spent sampling the red wines (the quality of red wines is much more reliable than white, and a more popular choice in the winter). In bars, there are often blackboards displaying the best selections of the day, and the Italian pride in wine means you can trust these implicitly.

Event info

Venice Carnival (☻ www.carnivalofvenice.com). General Carnival listings, including details of lots of expensive private parties to gatecrash.
Venice Council (☻ www.comune.venezia.it). City-council site, with links to hotel sites and the Carnival programme.
Venice Tourist Office (☻ www.turismovenezia.it). Official accommodation website of the Venice tourist office.
Hello Venezia (☻ www.hellovenezia.it). Useful site with plenty of tourist information, and ticket sales for cultural events.

Time zone GMT+1   **Country code** +39   **Currency** euro (€)

Europe

The best of the rest

Anastenaria

Where? **Serres and Thessalonkiki, Greece**
When? **May 21–23**
How long? **3 days**

Every year on the feast days of Saint Constantine and Saint Eleni (his mother), the villagers at Ayia Elleni near Serres, and Langada near Thessaloniki, dance across hot coals. The "fire dance" is of unknown origin. Legend has it dating back to Byzantine times, when locals risked their lives to save icons of the two saints from a burning church, emerging with the icons – and themselves – miraculously unscathed; though, given that these saints weren't recognized before 1833, it seems more probable that the Anastenaria is a pagan ritual. A bonfire is lit during the day and at nightfall the participants (mainly women) take off their shoes, hold images of the two saints to their chests, and "dance" – in reality, more of a run – over red-hot coals without burning their feet, sometimes even kneeling to rub hot ash into their hands. During the first two days of Anastenaria, visitors are welcome to observe the ritual, indeed seating is provided for that very purpose, but the last day is a private one.

Apokriatika

Where? **Patras, Greece**
When? **February**
How long? **3 weeks**

As the birthplace of Dionysos, the ancient god of wine, Greece takes carnival excess to heart, and although the occasion is celebrated all over the country, the most energetic partying is done in Patras in the Peloponnese, Greece's third-largest city. Traditionally, the first week is devoted to slaughtering fattened-up pigs; the second to feasting on meats of all kinds; and the third to scoffing belly-busting quantities of cheese. Everything reaches a peak on the Sunday before "Clean Monday", which marks the start of Orthodox Lent, when up to fifty-thousand participants and three-hundred-thousand revellers join in as the Carnival King and Queen preside over *bourboulia* dances, in which women are hooded and masked in black to allow them to flirt anonymously.

Elsewhere in Greece, activities range from flinging bags of flour at everyone and everything (Galaxidi) to dressing up as goats (Skiros), but one of the oddest celebrations are the ritual "executions" in Messini; after the ceremony on the morning of Ash Monday, locals and visitors step up to the gallows one by one to be "despatched" by the hooded "executioners". Weird stuff.

Avignon Festival

Where? **Avignon, France**
When? **July**
How long? **3 weeks**

Avignon's immaculately preserved medieval buildings provide a magnificent backdrop for its prestigious festival (Ⓦ www.festival-avignon.com), a feast of culture that draws performers and art enthusiasts from around the world. Non-commercial in outlook, and reliant on public subsidy, the festival is the annual shop-window on French cultural life, particularly contemporary performing arts, attracting some two-hundred-thousand visitors each year. At its best, it meets all expectations, with theatrical forays that are remarkable in both scale and artistic experimentation. At its worst, however, it can be downright pretentious – in 2005, theatre-goers shouted abuse at the performers, and critics savaged the organizers, accusing them of displaying contempt for mainstream audiences and making the event culturally irrelevant. Nonetheless, the sheer number of events means that it is impossible, even in a "bad" year, not to find something to suit every taste, and in any case some of the venues are fantastic, utilizing the town's squares and spectacular architecture, not least the magnificent Palais des Papes (Pope's Palace).

Avignon Festival

Look out, also, for the fringe Festival Off (Ⓦwww. avignon-off.org), which uses dozens of different venues for performances that range from the comic to the obscure.

Basel Carnival

Where? **Basel, Switzerland**
When? **February or March**
How long? **3 days**

One of Europe's better carnivals, Basel's is known as Fasnacht, and starts, unusually, on the Monday *after* Mardi Gras – thought to be a snub by Protestant Basel to the Catholic idea of giving up things for Lent. These days, about 12,000 people take part in the festivities, and, this being Switzerland, everything is extremely well organized, with participants divided into so-called *Cliques*, presided over by an all-powerful Carnival Committee, though once Fasnacht approaches, the Swiss desire for order goes out of the window. On the Sunday night after Mardi Gras, celebrations kick off at the nearby town of Liestal, where a huge and spectacular bonfire parade known as Chienbesen fills the narrow medieval cobbled streets. After midnight, everyone heads back to Basel for the famous Morgestraich, a magical parade of huge lanterns through the city centre that begins at 4am sharp and continues through the day, with the various Cliques parading through the city in their giant cartoonish papier-mâché masks and jester-like costumes to the accompaniment of fife-and-drum bands. The city's squares fill up with impromptu *guggemusig* sessions of absurdly comical oompah music played on old, dented trumpets and trombones, and the partying continues in Basel's bars and cafés until Wednesday night.

Bayreuth Festival

Where? **Bayreuth, Germany**
When? **July–August**
How long? **1 month**

Unlike any other festival, Bayreuth (Ⓦwww.bayreuther-festspiele.de) is dedicated to the work of one composer, Richard Wagner, whose various works are performed at the purpose-built Festspielhaus between the end of July and end of August each year. The rub is that tickets are almost impossible to come by unless you're super-organized – most have gone by October of the previous year, and in any case there's a waiting list so you may well have to wait years before your application is accepted. As for the music, the organizers aim to stage a new production of Wagner's *Ring Cycle* every five years, along with three other operas. When no *Ring* is performed, then five operas in all are staged.

Benicàssim Festival

Where? **Benicàssim, Spain**
When? **July**
How long? **4 days**

Held just north of Valencia, Benicàssim is in its thirteenth year, and is now one of the most established music festivals on the European circuit: Glastonbury, without the mud. Each year the event plays host to some big-name headliners – Oasis, Kasabian, Franz Ferdinand and Pixies have starred recently – but most festivalgoers come to rave all night in one of a number of dance tents that stay open till the early hours. If crawling back to your pre-heated tent at ten o'clock in the morning for a couple of hours' kip before heading down to the beach for paella and Frisbee sounds like fun then this is the festival for you. Tickets cost around €70 a day.

Brighton Festival

Where? **Brighton, England**
When? **May**
How long? **3 weeks**

Drenching Britain's raffish capital of coastal cool with vivid colour, this is the biggest arts festival in England, with a main programme of music, dance, theatre and talks that features a healthy mix of the conventional and the Avant Garde. As with so many arts festivals, it's the fringe events that give Brighton (Ⓦwww.brighton-festival.org.uk) its unique flavour. Stroll through the city centre on Streets of Brighton day and you'll happen upon impromptu performances from torch-song divas dressed as nuns, gangs of giant seafood and other masters of the surreal. And every weekend, artists all over the city turn their homes and studios into public galleries, showing original work by themselves and their colleagues in extremely convivial surroundings.

Bastille Day

A combination of pomp and circumstance, street parties and a general letting down of hair

Bastille Day

Where? Paris and across France
When? July 14
How long? 1 day

France celebrates its national holiday (*la fête nationale*) with a combination of pomp and circumstance, street parties and a general letting down of hair. Declared a holiday for all French men and women only in 1880, in recent years it has lost some of its popular appeal – partly because Bastille Day falls in the middle of the very month when most French people take their sacrosanct four-week vacation by the seaside – but the party-like ambience, particularly in the capital, can make for a joyful time in a city where people often seem afraid to laugh in case it gives them wrinkles.

The Bastille, a grim fourteenth-century fortress serving as a state prison and long despised as a symbol of despotism, used to guard the insalubrious eastern reaches of Paris. In July 1789, after months of anti-royal unrest and food riots, an angry mob got wind that the place was being used to stamp out opposition, and decided to storm the fortress. Two days after the Bastille was taken, the National Assembly ordered that it be razed to the ground – all that remains of the fortress is a few lumps of masonry, some of which are visible in the Bastille metro station. The event is now seen as the first step in the French Revolution – within four years, the king, queen and more than 1300 aristocrats had been beheaded.

The Fall of the Bastille came to represent the triumph of the people over tyranny and oppression, which is why a radical government, at the start of the Third Republic, declared its anniversary the national day of celebrations, in 1880. Today, on the morning of July 14, military parades take place all over the country, showing off the products of France's thriving arms industry. Obviously, the centrepiece is the *défilé* that trundles along the avenue des Champs-Elysées in Paris, where the President of the Republic surveys his troops, of which he is supreme commander. New members of France's highest honour, the Légion d'Honneur, receive their medals, and government members, other politicians and all kinds of VIPs sit in the grandstand, pretending to look interested in columns of policemen, the Foreign Legion and the *gendarmerie*. There are fly-pasts by the French Airforce, demonstrations of the latest fighter helicopters, Mirage jets and bombers. Tanks, troop carriers and all manner of artillery pass by as the defiant notes of *La Marseillaise* played by military brass bands ring out. In the past – that is, straight after World War II, when a triumphant General de Gaulle led the parade to celebrate liberation and a bright new future – all of this made sense, but it can now strike the outsider as somewhat bizarre.

one of the best and the biggest firemen's balls is in the Marais Fire Station in Paris' rue de Sévigné – ask around or enquire at the tourist office for other good bashes

Believe it or not, far more interesting times are to be had at the local fire station, which give you a real taste of the *fête populaire*, or working-class party. Since the 1930s, the *bals des pompiers*, or firemen's balls, have been the traditional venues for the most enjoyable night out on Bastille Day. One of the best and the biggest firemen's balls is in the Marais Fire Station in Paris' rue de Sévigné – ask around or enquire at the tourist office for other good bashes; recommended stations are those on rue Blanche (9th *arrondissement*, near Montmartre) and rue des Vieux-Colombiers (6th, near St-Sulpice). The less chic outer districts of the capital, to the north and east (13th–15th and 18th–20th *arrondissements*), tend to be more fun. Things don't really get started until late evening but the fire stations are full to the roof by midnight. And, who knows, if you ask nicely, you might even get a chance to slide down the pole.

Binche Carnival

Where? **Binche, Belgium**
When? **February or March**
How long? **3 days**

This four-hundred-year-old Belgian festival features the spectacular March of the Gilles, a parade of six hundred peculiarly and identically dressed men, and a pitched battle involving blood oranges as ammunition that rivals Spain's La Tomatina (see p.75) as Europe's largest food-fight. Anyone who has ever been to Belgium will know that the Belgians take their beer very seriously, and Binche's carnival (ⓦwww.carnavaldebinche.be) is a magic combination of this national preoccupation – outdoor beer tents are stacked high with a huge variety of Belgian brews – and a bizarre tradition that dates back to the Middle Ages. Why is it so bizarre? Well, mainly because the Gilles, the strange giant-like figures who dominate this event, all wear the same wax masks with green glasses and moustaches – apparently, if incredibly, in the style of Napoleon III.

The action starts weeks before Shrove Tuesday, when groups of drummers, or *tamboureurs*, roam the streets each Sunday evening, culminating in the Sunday before Mardi Gras; the first revellers appear at about 8am, and from then on the streets of Binche are packed with people of all ages, sizes and shapes, some in fancy dress, others

> *the Gilles, the strange giant-like figures who dominate this event, all wear the same wax masks with green glasses and moustaches*

with masks and painted faces. Confetti covers the streets at every turn, but the real focus of the scene is the never-ending rhythmic beat of the drummers. Processions over, the focus of the party changes from the streets to the bars and restaurants, where the Binchois take a long lunchtime pit stop before the evening's bar-hopping and street-partying begins. The next day is predominantly a family day, when children and young people gather in the main square in the afternoon; there are fireworks and a fairground in the evening – and yet more drifting from bar to bar.

The next day, Mardi Gras itself, groups of Gilles gather in the Grand-Place to dance around in a huge circle, or *rondeau*, holding hands and tapping their wooden-clogged feet in time to the beat of the drum. The *tamboureurs* are situated in the middle of the circle, as are a smaller *rondeau* of *petits gilles*. Get inside the circles if you can, as you're then ideally placed to get dragged in amongst the Gilles as they are beckoned into the town hall to ritually remove their masks. Later on, at about 3pm, the Gilles emerge to lead the Grand Parade, sporting tall hats elaborately adorned with ostrich feathers, and clutching wooden baskets filled with oranges, which they throw with gusto into the crowd, covering everyone in blood-red juice and pulp. Be warned, though, that this is a one-sided affair – it's not done to throw them back.

*This four-hundred-year-old Belgian festival
features the spectacular March of the Gilles*

Binche Carnival

British Summer Festivals

Where? England, Scotland and Wales
When? June–August
How long? 1-3 days

Whatever you think about summer music festivals, there's no denying their explosion across Britain over the last few years. Glastonbury set the standard, and the vibe, and now barely a week goes by over the main summer months when there isn't some sort of out outdoor shindig going on. The big names – Reading and Leeds (now depressingly known as the Carling Weekend), and relative newcomers such as Scotland's T in the Park and the two V events – tend to draw the largest crowds and most currently favoured acts, while other mid-sized newbies such as the revived Isle of Wight Festival and its late-season Isle of Wight brother, Bestival, fill in the gaps. August's The Big Chill is, as you might expect, a more laid-back, family-orientated affair, as is the previous month's Guilfest, which tends to draw popular old favourites rather than cutting-edge acts. Then there's the niche and specialist events, including Reading's well-established world-music extravaganza, Womad (which over recent years has replicated itself in other locations around the world, Adelaide, Taormina, Gran Canaria and Singapore among them), and the notoriously hard-to-get-tickets-to Cambridge Folk Festival, both held in July; others include Monsters of Rock – metalheads only; Creamfields – house and diehard dance fans only; and the Brecon Jazz Festival – cool jazz aficionados only. Weather permitting, you could have a great summer.

Bestival Robin Hill Country Park, Newport, Wales; ⓦ www.bestival.net
Brecon Jazz Festival Brecon, Powys, Wales; ⓦ www.breconjazz.co.uk
Cambridge Folk Festival Cherry Hinton Hall Grounds, Cambridge, England; ⓦ www.camridgefolkfestival.com
Carling Weekend Reading Rivermead Leisure Complex, Reading, England; Leeds Bramham Park, Leeds, England; ⓦ www.meanfiddler.com
Creamfields Daresbury Easte, Halton, Cheshire, England; ⓦ www.creamfields.com
Guilfest Guildford Stoke Park, Guildford, England; ⓦ www.guilfest.co.uk
Isle of Wight Festival Seaclose Park, Newport, Wales; ⓦ www.isleofwightfestival.com
Monsters of Rock Milton Keynes National Bowl, Milton Keynes, England; ⓦ www.monstersofrock.co.uk
T in the Park Balado, near Kinross, Scotland; ⓦ www.tinthepark.com
The Big Chill Eastnor Castle, Ledbury, England; ⓦ www.bigchill.net
V Hylands Park, Chelmsford, England; Weston Park, Staffordshire, England; ⓦ www.vfestival.com
Womad Rivermead Leisure Complex, Reading, England; ⓦ www.womad.org

Reading Festival

Cannabis Cup

Where? **Amsterdam, The Netherlands**
When? **July 14**
How long? **4 days**

As if Amsterdam weren't depraved enough, *High Times* magazine dreamed up the annual Cannabis Cup (ⓦwww.cannabiscup.com/ht/cancup) fourteen years ago and it's since grown into a major international event. For four days, potheads, hash connoisseurs, hemp entrepreneurs, and other Rizler freaks gather to fill their minds, bodies and souls with the Holy Herb and eat their way through a mountain of junk food. Oh yeah, and they try to get it together to award the Cannabis Cup to the best grass and hash around. All the toking and voting action takes place in the Pax Party House on Ferdinand Bolstraat. This is where you'll find several hundred of the world's finest stoneheads sprawled around the room passing spliffs and trying to remember what on earth it was they were meant to be doing there in the first place. If you want, you can register as a judge – this is free, and grants you access to an armoury of the most powerful types of weed known to man. They also give lectures (methods to grow the best bud in the world, avoid legal troubles, etc), show and sell hemp products, hold meetings to decide the best coffee shops, and put on some great gigs and DJ-ed events, often hosting big names. If you like a bit of a toke yourself, there's no better place to be in the world. As *High Times* puts it, it's a "Spaced Odyssey".

Cannabis Cup

Canelli under Attack

Where? **Canelli, Italy**
When? **June**
How long? **2 days**

The Siege of Canelli, in the northwestern Italian region of Piemonte, took place in 1613, and is still remembered every third weekend of June with a reconstruction of how the townspeople heroically held out against the troops of the Duke of Mantua. The entire town – and most of its people – is decked out in the manner of the times, troops repel the attacks of the "invaders", monks perform torchlight processions, and bars and restaurants stay open continuously and serve "period" food and drink – culminating in the Victory Lunch, served on the Sunday, when the Mantuan forces have been sent packing and everyone can relax. Which they do with a vengeance. Music, juggling, drumming, and street performances all go on till late, finishing up with a firework display.

Cartier International Polo

Where? **Windsor, England**
When? **July**
How long? **1 day**

The sponsor's the main giveaway, isn't it? Polo may not be the "Sport of Kings", but you have to have money to play it, and thus it has its own international circuit – known well to the glitterati who follow the sport but a mystery to the rest of us – of which the Cartier International day is a special highlight. It's one match between the England polo team and an international side, and it takes place at the end of July at the impeccably appointed Guards Club in Windsor Great Park, just west of London. Naturally, the Queen is the guest of honour, and although there are many who take the result – and the game – seriously, the real point is to be seen at this prestigious society event. The grassy car parks host outdoor feasts around mahogany picnic tables, with silver cutlery and top-notch champagne drained from fancy glasses, while lesser mortals (yes guys, you are admitted) make do with plastic cups and wander around eyeing up the nobs. Grandstand tickets cost £20–40 and are available from the ticket office. Don't forget to wear your Class War T-shirt.

Cologne Carnival

Where? **Cologne, Germany**
When? **February or March**
How long? **5 days**

Don't be taken in by the stereotype – Germany can party with the best of them, and Cologne Carnival, starting on the Thursday before Mardi Gras, is one of Europe's wildest. The first night, Weiberfasnacht, or Women's Carnival, sets the tone, as drunken dames rush around the city's streets grabbing anything in trousers for a hefty snog. Street parties and the kind of binge drinking that made a legend out of Oktoberfest fill the city's Altstadt, or Old Town, with the bars and beerhalls packed all weekend. Rosenmontag, on the Monday, features a gigantic costumed parade, five miles long, that has been altered little from its origins half a millennium ago, and still features jesters, plenty of impromptu and organized street-dancing, floats and carnival bands. Truly one of the best carnival experiences to be had in Europe – and about as abandoned as the streets of Cologne ever get.

Combat des Reines

Where? **Martigny, Switzerland**
When? **October**
How long? **1 day**

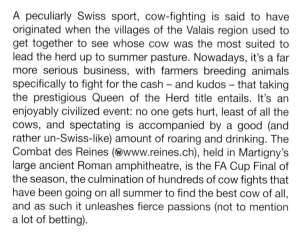

A peculiarly Swiss sport, cow-fighting is said to have originated when the villages of the Valais region used to get together to see whose cow was the most suited to lead the herd up to summer pasture. Nowadays, it's a far more serious business, with farmers breeding animals specifically to fight for the cash – and kudos – that taking the prestigious Queen of the Herd title entails. It's an enjoyably civilized event: no one gets hurt, least of all the cows, and spectating is accompanied by a good (and rather un-Swiss-like) amount of roaring and drinking. The Combat des Reines (ⓦwww.reines.ch), held in Martigny's large ancient Roman amphitheatre, is the FA Cup Final of the season, the culmination of hundreds of cow fights that have been going on all summer to find the best cow of all, and as such it unleashes fierce passions (not to mention a lot of betting).

Cooper's Hill Cheese-Rolling

Cooper's Hill Cheese-Rolling

Where? **Cooper's Hill, England**
When? **May**
How long? **1 day**

An organized bout of chasing cheese down a hill in Gloucestershire has become one of Britain's best-known festivals – a totem, somehow, of a country of eccentric and long-established events. Held on the Bank Holiday Monday at the end of May, Cooper's Hill Cheese-Rolling (ⓦwww.cheese-rolling.co.uk) is certainly in the best spirit of British amateurism: anyone can enter, and all they have to do is fling themselves down the hill after a wheel of cheese – the first one to reach it wins. Needless to say, it attracts all manner of drink-fuelled daredevils. It kicks off at noon, and there are several races, including a women-only event, before it all ends at 1pm and everyone goes off to get even more drunk, often nursing the odd bruise or two.

Copenhagen Jazz Festival

Where? **Copenhagen, Denmark**
When? **July**
How long? **10 days**

The Danes aren't exactly known for their jazz, but the Copenhagen Jazz Festival (ⓦwww.jazzfestival.dk), beginning early morning and ending late at night, is one of Europe's best such events, a chilled-out festival featuring over six hundred concerts held beside Copenhagen's rivers and canals and in its concert halls, piazzas, parks, bars, cafés and clubs. It's a great time to visit the city; many of the concerts are free, and the headline gigs are reasonably priced by Danish standards. Street parades are held in the early afternoons and the beat goes on throughout the night. Scandinavian artists are a particular forte of the festival, but there are big international names, too, offering everything from New Orleans jazz to swing, fusion and new experimental stuff. Copenhagen's best known jazz club *The Jazzhouse*, and the old Circus building or the Tivoli Gardens, host the big names.

Corsa dei Ceri

Where? **Gubbio, Italy**
When? **May**
How long? **1 day**

The Corsa dei Ceri (Ⓦ www.festadeiceri.it), or Race of the Candles, is one of Italy's more bizarre spectacles, in which three teams in bright costumes race around Gubbio's medieval lanes and squares, each of them shouldering a five-metre-high, four-hundred-kilo wooden candle. It's held in honour of St Ubaldo, patron saint of masons, and is a typical fusion of the pagan and Catholic. Having been roused at dawn by drummers, the three teams, each consisting of about twenty men dressed in colourful silk shirts, assemble at Piazza Grande where the candles – huge wooden constructions, octagonal in shape, fixed to a hand-barrow, and up to seven metres in height – are doused in water for good luck and then briefly raced around the square. A parade follows – with that most important of Italian traditions, a couple of hours' break for lunch – and then, at 6pm, the teams hoist their candles. The candles are blessed, and with a roar from the crowds the race begins. There are a couple more high-speed circuits of Gubbio's piazzas, then a stop for the teams to draw breath before they leg it uphill to the finishing line at the basilica of St Ubaldo. Interestingly, as overtaking is forbidden, the winning team is decided by the spectators on the greatest style shown during the race – a truly Italian way to win. Afterwards, the candles are left at the basilica, and everyone heads back to town, to hit the bars and relive the day over a drink or two.

Cowes Week

Where? **Cowes, England**
When? **August**
How long? **8 days**

Around eight thousand competitors and one thousand boats descend on Cowes on the Isle of Wight for this eight-day event, the biggest sailing regatta in the world (Ⓦ www.skandiacowesweek.co.uk). Whether you're a yachtie or not, it's a good time to be in this provincial little port, with lots of live music, outdoor parties – and lots and lots of drinking.

Dead Rat's Ball

Where? **Ostend, Belgium**
When? **March**
How long? **3 days**

The annual Dead Rat's Ball (Ⓦ www.ratmort.be) was conceived earlier this century by the artist James Ensor after a visit to a Paris cabaret bar, and is a very popular event with the locals, forming as it does part of the town's carnival celebrations. In true Belgian style, this, of course, includes lots of drinking, starting with a pub-crawl on the first Friday in March and the burning of the *Tjannie Carbon*. There's also a clog-throwing event in the main square on the Saturday afternoon, and a carnival parade on the Sunday. The ball itself is a predictably decadent affair: a costumed event held in the casino on the seafront that attracts a varied crowd, among them a large contingent of seriously dolled-up transvestites. Starting at 9pm, it builds slowly throughout the night; there are usually five bands, and you'd do well to arrive late and leave late, as the partying only really gets going in the small hours, by which time there's around five thousand people in attendance, and some truly dramatic attire, the best of which are awarded prizes, and have to been seen to be believed. It's about as close as the north coast of Belgium gets to the spirit of Rio.

Dragacevo Trumpet Festival

Where? Dragacevo, Serbia and Montenegro
When? August
How long? 7 days

Who can resist the "largest trumpet event on the planet", held in Dragacevo, the home of Serbian trumpet playing, for nearly fifty years? People pick up a trumpet to serenade almost any event around these parts – weddings, baptisms, deaths, fights, the harvest – you name it. And this is reflected in the variety of acts and styles on show in Dragacevo (ⓦ www.guca.co.yu). Lots of music, lots and lots of dancing, and associated art and cultural events all make the trip to this relatively unvisited part of western Serbia well worth making.

Düsseldorf Carnival

Where? Düsseldorf, Germany
When? February or March
How long? 1 day

As with its near-neighbour Cologne, Düsseldorf's pre-Lenten carnival is a riotous, beer-soaked affair, and quite the best reason for visiting the city. The Thursday before Mardi Gras is dubbed Alt Weiberstag, or Old Hag's Day, when women roam the streets, snipping off men's ties and generally harassing them until they submit to the granting of at least a kiss. The drunken antics of the weekend are only a prelude for the Rosenmontag parade on the Monday, featuring half-a-million revellers packing the streets.

Edinburgh Festival

Where? Edinburgh, Scotland
When? August
How long? 3 weeks

The Edinburgh Festival (ⓦ www.eif.co.uk) is the largest arts festival in the world, three weeks of music, opera, dance and theatre in a fantastic array of locations across the city. Actually, it's two festivals in one, because the so-called Edinburgh Fringe (ⓦ www.edfringe.com), which goes on simultaneously, attracts at least as many people, and specializes in less highbrow, more experimental stuff – the events that get all the publicity basically. There's no better thing to do than spend a week or so up there, wandering around town and soaking up as much culture as you can stomach.

Edirne Oil Wrestling Championships

Where? Edirne, Turkey
When? July
How long? 3 days

Enjoy watching groups of grown men dressed in leather and doused in olive oil grappling with each other? Well, oiled wrestling has been a national sport in Turkey since at least 1360, and you'll see the best of it at the Wrestling Championships at the Sarayiçi Stadium on mid-river Kirkpinar island, just outside the ancient border city of Edirne, where it has been held since 1924. It's a great event, whether you're into the wrestling or not: the grounds are gripped in a medieval fairground atmosphere, with gypsy bands, dancing bears, and wandering kebab-sellers entertaining the crowds. Over a thousand wrestlers take part in the tournament, divided between the main "open" category and a smaller one for youngsters, many of whom are barely into their teens. The wrestlers wear tight leather shorts called *kisbet*, made of water-buffalo leather, and the worst offence that a wrestler can commit

Edinburgh Festival

– one that merits instant disqualification – is to pull off an opponent's *kisbet*. Competitors are covered with specially produced olive oil just before a match, with more oil applied during the fight itself – with over five hundred litres used during the tournament, it's a wonder that either man can grab the other at all. Fights last up to 45 minutes; a few nastier holds are barred but winners have to pin their opponent's shoulders down or prise out a verbal submission. With victory comes prize money, nationwide fame and the title "Champion of Turkey". To train for this you either have to be naturally talented or work out a programme along the lines of legendary champion Koca Yusuf, who was apparently strong enough to shift a 450kg boulder around. Tickets are sold as three-day passes, enabling fans to see all the matches during the festival.

Exit Festival

Where? Serbia and Montenegro
When? July
How long? 4 days

This event has only been going a few years, and it's no accident that its vibrancy is in inverse proportion to the grim realities of life in Serbia over the last decade or so. It's appropriate that as the country begins to rejoin the rest of Europe the Exit Festival (ⓦwww.exitfest.org) goes from strength to strength, attracting around 150,000 people to its dramatic fortress setting in Novi Sad, just north of Belgrade, and a host of world-class bands and DJs – the White Stripes, Fatboy Slim, Franz Ferdinand have appeared at recent events.

Fastnachtsmontag

Where? Switzerland
When? July 14
How long? 1 day

Just south of Zurich, the town of Zug is home to the peculiar female carnival figure of Greth Schell, who on the Monday before Mardi Gras parades through the streets of the city accompanied by seven fools in ludicrous costumes. At midnight, she proceeds to carry her husband home in a basket after he has had too much to drink at the inn – a centuries' old custom has faithfully served as the perfect excuse for the towns mensfolk to get absolutely bladdered in the name of tradition.

Feast of St George

Where? Skiros, Greece
When? April 23
How long? 3 days

The English are far too reserved to make a fuss about their patron saint's day, but the Greeks go absolutely mad for it. In Greece, St George – Ayios Yioryios – is the patron saint of shepherds, and he has also been adopted as the special protector of the tiny north Aegean island of Skiros, where the saint's day celebrations last three days. They fire up with a bagpipe-led parade and service in St George's honour, followed by the bizarre "Old Mens' Race", in which Skiros' male geriatrics take each other on in a steep hillside scramble. The rest of the festival sees the island's younger athletes in wrestling and other competitions, while the whole population helps out with heavy doses of dancing and feasting, joined by an ever-swelling number of visitors who boat in to take part.

Festa de Noantri

Where? Rome, Italy
When? July
How long? 8 days

As Romans begin their annual summer migration to the hills and seaside, the locals of the Trastevere district, just across the river from the ancient centre, are warming up for the Festa de Noantri, a religious procession commemorating a sixteenth-century group of fishermen on the Tiber who supposedly caught a statue of a Madonna in their nets. Amazed by its beauty, they took it to their local church, Sant'Agata, where it became an object of veneration. Nowadays, it's just a neighbourhood party, the name deriving from "*noi altri*", literally "we others", a reference to the traditionally detached nature of Trastevere. On the first Saturday after 16 July, the statue of the Madonna is taken from Sant'Agata; carried by about ten men and led by the local bishop dressed in his finery, it is paraded through the packed and narrow streets to the church of San Crisogno, where it remains on display for eight days. In the days before and after this event are much less formal festivities – street theatre, dances and music – making it a great time to be in town.

Feria de Abril

Where? **Seville, Spain**
When? **April or May**
How long? **6 days**

The Feria de Abril, or Spring Fair, is the kind of big, raunchy party that the Spanish do so well – a heady mix of tradition, drinking and dancing that's held two weeks after the country's more solemn but equally tiring Semana Santa (Holy Week) activities. Similar spring festivals are held around Andalucía, but none match Seville's for the intensity of colour, pageant and sheer party energy.

In the months leading up to the *feria*, a vast area on the west bank of the Guadalquivir river – about a half-hour walk southwest of the city centre – is taken over by a temporary mini-city of hundreds of *casetas* (brightly festooned tents), set up behind an elaborate *portada*, or gate. The only way to visit these is if accompanied by a local with an invite; otherwise, head for the handful of public "open" tents (*casetas de los distritos municipales*), which burst with good-natured festivity.

The fun starts at midnight on the Monday, when the *portada* is lit up in all its glory and the party kicks off with all-night eating, drinking and – a stipulation for Seville – dancing. The following days all follow much the same pattern. *Sevillanos* in traditional Andalucían finery – short waistcoat and flat hat for the men, frilled and flouncy gypsy-style *faralaes* (flamenco dresses) for the women – parade around the fairground on horseback or in elegant horse-drawn carriages. Locals generally stop working at 2pm during the week of the *feria*, and as the afternoon wears on, the

the music blares out, saucy couples frolic in the shadows, and you are free to stagger from one party to another until dawn

focus shifts to the Plaza de Toros de Maestranza, north of the river, where the daily bullfights are some of the best of the season. In the early evening, things quieten down – the calm before the nocturnal storm. Be aware that you pay a high price for generally mediocre food in the *feria* grounds so your best bet is to dine in town and do what the locals do: start the evening with a round or two of drinks in the city-centre bars before making the trip (walk or shuttle bus from Prado de San Sebastián) out to the grounds around midnight. Here, you'll see girls (and some men) dancing *sevillanas* (a dance similar to flamenco) in their bright polka-dotted *farales*. As you tank up on the sherry, you'll soon find yourself dancing, too, although you should probably leave the *sevillanas* to the locals, who look like they've been dancing it since birth. The music blares out, saucy couples frolic in the shadows, and you are free to stagger from one party to another until dawn – it's impossible to sit on the sidelines, and even if you're on your own, you won't be for long.

The *feria* reaches a crescendo on Friday and Saturday nights, when the grounds are full to bursting, and the whole party comes to an end with a bang on Sunday night, with a deafening fireworks display.

Feria de Abril

A heady mix of tradition, drinking and dancing

Festa del Redentore

Where? **Venice, Italy**
When? **July**
How long? **2 days**

Venice's Festa del Redentore – the Festival of the Redeemer – is a high point of the city's summer, both for tourists and locals, and a superb maritime event. Originally conceived to give thanks for Venice's recovery from a devastating sixteenth-century plague, which killed more than a third of the city's inhabitants, it takes place very year on the third weekend of July. On Saturday, St Mark's basin fills with as many as two thousand boats – festooned with flowers, lanterns and balloons, their occupants eating and drinking as they eagerly await the now traditional spectacular evening fireworks. At around 11.30pm, the display begins and the lagoon becomes one of the most atmospheric stages in the world, fireworks illuminating the silhouetted spires, domes and bell towers of the city. Afterwards, the feasting on the boats continues, although the youth of Venice have started a new tradition, retreating to the Lido to party on the beach until dawn. On Sunday, a pontoon of decorated gondolas and other boats is strung across the Giudecca canal to allow the faithful to walk to the Church of the Redentore. Mass is held in the presence of the Patriarch of Venice, a reminder that the *festa* has a solemn side.

Festa do São António

Where? **Portugal**
When? **June 12**
How long? **1 day**

Lisbon's favourite saint, São António (St Anthony), was born in the city's Alfama district, and his feast day traditionally kicks off a bout of saint-inspired partying that continues throughout June, in celebration not just of St Anthony but of John (João) and Peter (Pedro), whose feast days take place later in the month (though St John is celebrated more up in Porto; see p.27). During this time, streets are decorated with coloured lanterns, and there's plenty of music, dancing and street parties – all over the city but particularly in Alfama – and a big evening parade, down the Avenida da Liberdade, after which everyone gets their rocks off into the small hours. There's a romantic element too: António is the patron saint of matchmakers and this is traditionally the time for unattached folk to find a mate.

Fiesta de San Isidro

Where? **Madrid, Spain**
When? **May**
How long? **10 days**

Madrilenos need little excuse to stay up all night and enjoy themselves, so it has to be something pretty special for them to go even more wild than usual. But the feast day of the city's patron saint more than fits the bill. Each neighbourhood stages its own celebration, and there are jazz concerts, flamenco and other events taking place in every available open space. The partying goes on for around ten days either side of May 15 – a date that also traditionally marks the start of the bullfighting season in Spain, with the country's best fighters performing at the city's huge and prestigious Plaza de Ventas.

Festival du Vent

Where? **Calvi, France**
When? **October**
How long? **3 days**

Fancy a ride in a home-made balloon with a French dude who's clearly on something stronger than onion soup? Or getting the adrenaline pumping with high-speed kite-driven skate-boarding, or chilling out in the world's first wind-powered Jacuzzi? Well, this may be the festival for you. Adhering to the mantra of "the universal language of the wind opens your mind", some forty thousand visitors of all ages descend on the beautiful, ancient seaside town of Calvi to participate in the Festival du Vent, or Festival of the Wind (www.lefestivalduvent.com), which conveniently coincides with the arrival of the dry Mistral wind that sweeps down from northwest Europe to cross Corsica and the central Mediterranean. Over the course of the long weekend there are dozens of diverse events, from wind-related water and aerial activities to high-brow political and cultural debates (all, of course, in French) taking place each day from 10am until dawn the following morning. Should you tire of the impassioned debates on climate change, human rights or globalization, walk along the beach and view the installations laid out on the sand or attend creative workshops or concerts held both outside and in around town. Alternatively, just wander through the old town to be entertained by mime and circus artists, watch agitprop or more esoteric forms of street theatre.

Children are estimated to represent almost a quarter of the festival participants, the primary attraction being the Fête en l'Air, where dozens of fun and educational workshops are offered on art, music and eco-technology, with at least a vague wind-related theme blowing through all the activities.

Fiesta de Sant Joan

Where? **Ciutadella, Spain**
When? **June 24**
How long? **1 day**

Celebrating both midsummer and the saint's day of Sant Joan (St John), this amazing equestrian event takes over the centre of the Menorcan town of Ciutadella. With thousands of people, and cavalcades of riders on black stallions racing and jousting their way through the narrow streets, this massive midsummer party culminates in fireworks and partying right through the night. Somehow, it's not what you expect from this relatively sedate resort island – and it's all the better for it.

Gäuboden Volksfest

Where? **Straubing, Germany**
When? **August**
How long? **10 days**

Although technically the country's second largest beer festival after Munich's Oktoberfest (see p.113), with in excess of one million visitors, the excellent Gäuboden Volksfest in rural Straubing is much, much, less well-known outside Germany. Named after the area of Bavaria surrounding the town, the festival originated in the early nineteenth century as a gathering of farmers doing business together, but has developed over the last hundred years or so into a chance for everyone to let their hair down and clash steins with each other. A mini-city of tents, band stages, fairground rides and food stalls offering every type of sausage imaginable is set up in the centre of this elegant town near the Czech border, and revelling officially begins with the raucous Bierprobe parade on the first Friday, after which the aim of most visitors is to remain pleasantly schlossed until Sunday week. Above all, the nice thing about this festival is that, unlike Munich, there are loads more Germans in attendance than tourists. Just get your lederhosen on and get drinking.

Fiesta de Sant Joan

Giants of Douai

Where? **Douai, France**
When? **July**
How long? **1 day**

Many towns in northeast France and Belgium hold festivals involving giants made of wood or papier-mâché. But the one in Douai is the oldest, the biggest and the best. Built – or at least repaired and maintained – by local clubs that are the successors to the city's medieval craft guilds, over a hundred of these enormous effigies – some over eight metres tall and requiring six men to carry – are paraded through the city streets on the first Sunday after July 6. The effigies represent characters from local legends, who are received as guests of honour at celebrations throughout the town; some of them hark back to the sixteenth century, commemorating a group of local knights who protected the town from attack, others are of more recent provenance. The entire town goes crazy over the giants as they are carried down the street accompanied by music and dancing – though a lot of the kids are scared half to death.

Giostra del Saracino

Where? **Arezzo, Italy**
When? **September 3**
How long? **1 day**

Early September sees the beautiful Tuscan town of Arezzo burst into colour and life with the Giostra del Saracino, or Joust of the Saracen (ⓦww.lagiostradelsaracino.it), a no-holds-barred jousting competition that continues the traditional festivities started by Siena's Il Palio (see p.65) in July. Taking place on the day of San Donato, Arezzo's patron saint, it's basically a contest between the four main districts of the town, and each neighbourhood has its own colours displayed in the standards and costumes of the competing jousters and their supporters. The event kicks-off in the morning with a parade of hundreds of people dressed in fourteenth-century garb, followed by a blessing on the steps of the Duomo, performed by the bishop.

The jousting itself takes place in the afternoon, after the procession enters Piazza Grande. First there's a display of the *sbandieratori* (flag wavers), and then the jousters gallop into the piazza's competition ground. Then comes the jousting itself, each lance-armed knight charging at a wooden target attached to a carving of a Saracen king. The pair of knights who accumulate the most points by hitting the Saracen's shield wins the Golden Lance, the tournament's trophy.

Gotland Medieval Week

Where? **Gotland, Sweden**
When? **August**
How long? **1 week**

Commemorating a mid-fourteenth century battle with the Danish when the Gotland capital of Visby was an important

Gotland Medieval Week

Hanseatic port, and which saw the town valiantly, but comprehensively, defeated, this is a week of music and dance, medieval markets – and, not surprisingly, a jousting tournament. And it all culminates with a great medieval banquet, complete with jugglers and fire-eaters, on the main square on the closing Sunday. It's all terrifically bogus, but the atmosphere is great, as everyone gets into their roles, and the ancient town of Visby makes a great backdrop.

Independence Day

Where? **Reykjavik, Iceland**
When? **June 17**
How long? **1 day**

Most holidays in Iceland are taken as good excuses to party, and this one – nominally to celebrate the shaking off of seven hundred years' of Danish rule in 1944 – is no exception. Parades of children in colourful clothing fill the streets through the morning, at which there's much patriotic waving of the red, white and blue Icelandic flag. As always, outdoor hot pools become the social focus afterwards, with an evening of hard drinking to follow. Then it's time to experience the Nordic spirit in full swing, as bands play through the night, and the action at Reykjavik's legendary bars and clubs spills out into the streets, where plenty of locals are bent on drinking themselves into a coma, aided by copious quantities of the national fire water, *brennevin*.

Inter-Celtic Festival

Where? **Lorient, France**
When? **August**
How long? **10 days**

One of the largest Celtic gatherings in the world, the Inter-Celtic Festival (ⓦwww.festival-interceltique.com) draws crowds of around 350,000 to this small Breton town from the first Friday to the second Sunday of every August. Set up as part of the resurgence of interest in the Celtic roots of the region, it has been going strong since 1971, and features around 4500 musicians, singers, dancers, artists and film-makers from Celtic communities around the world. Prominent professors give lectures about Celtic culture, and more formal courses of study are available, but above all, this is a music festival, with loads of organized gigs taking place at venues dotted around town, and any number of impromptu jam sessions in Lorient's streets and bars – bringing your own instrument along and joining in is positively encouraged. One to avoid if you hate the sound of bagpipes.

Kulmbach Bierfest

Where? **Kulmbach, Germany**
When? **July**
How long? **9 days**

Tucked away in a quiet corner of Bavaria, on the edge of the Thuringian forest, the town of Kulmbach is traditionally known for its beer – indeed, in medieval times every inhabitant had the right to brew his own here – and it remains a major brewing centre, with an astonishing variety of ales. Most of these are on offer at the town's beer festival (ⓦwww.bierfest.de), where you can sample the local brews to your heart's content and to an oompah band soundtrack. Two to look out for are Schwarzbier, a fine, full-bodied dark beer, and the head-spinning Kulminator 28, one of the strongest beers in the world.

La Tamborrada

Where? **San Sebastian, Spain**
When? **January 20**
How long? **1 day**

Without doubt, La Tamborrada, or Drum Festival, is one of the noisiest events you will ever come across. Held in honour of San Sebastian, the town's eponymous patron saint, several thousand specially suited and booted drummers – done up like toy Napoleonic soldiers – march around town for 24 hours with the sole objective of making as much of a racket as possible. The action kicks off at the Plaza de la Constitution at around midnight as rival armies of drum and barrel bashers make their way through the streets of the old town to be joined by noisy, drunken locals as they pass from bar to bar. There's a massive children's drumming session in the afternoon, and the darlings make the most of their annual chance to make some serious noise and not get shouted at. One for the Duracell bunny.

Lajkonik Festival

Where? Krakow, Poland
When? June 1
How long? 1 day

This procession celebrates a famous defeat of the Mongols, who were repelled from the gates of the city back in the thirteenth century. Basically, everyone follows a "Mongol warrior" on a hobby horse around the streets for three hours until they get to the main square, where they wander off to get drunk in one of the city's many cosy bars.

Landskronakarnevalen

Where? Landskrona, Sweden
When? July
How long? 4 days

Designed to let off summer steam and raise the town's profile, Landskrona's carnival (Ⓦwww.landskrona karnevalen.se) inevitably suffers by comparison to other, more traditional European carnivals, and it obviously has no indigenous roots, but there's usually a great selection of imported Caribbean calypso and local bands, samba processions, some kicking sound systems, and big street parties throughout the weekend. The best time to be there is on the Friday and Saturday nights, when the music pumps out non-stop before winding down to the so-called Family Day on Sunday.

Midsummer Celebrations

Where? Finland
When? June
How long? 2 days

There's something about those long hours of summer daylight that set the normally sober Scandinavians partying, and nowhere is this more so in Finland than during the weekend before the midsummer solstice on June 21. Nominally in honour of St John, Juhannus Eve festivities start with a good clean-out of the home, which is then decorated with birch sprigs, before dragging all manner of scrap wood outside to build giant conical piles known as *kokko*. Later there are lively parties, at which everyone eats themselves insensible and the local brew *Koskenkorva* is enthusiastically downed, after which the *kokko* are set alight and great bouts of folksinging and dancing ensue around the flames. Saunas and rivers are on hand if you need to clear your head, after which you can befuddle it again with beer and more spirits.

Midsummer Celebrations

Where? Sweden
When? June
How long? 2 days

The weekend closest to midsummer solstice is a national holiday in Sweden, and there's a tradition of making merry that dates back to Viking fertility festivities designed to ensure a fruitful harvest. This perhaps explains the slightly phallic-looking "maypole", which is tightly garlanded with greenery and flowers and raised as the focus of the event. Morning dances around the pole give way to time-honoured family meals of potatoes and herring, and if this sounds a bit bland for the occasion, your spirits will be restored after washing it down with some good (Danish) beer. Traditional singing and dancing fills the rest of the day, with more hard-core partying well into the light summer night.

Midsummer Celebrations/ Jaanipäev

Where? Tallinn, Estonia
When? June 21–24
How long? 4 days

In Estonia, the midsummer festivities traditionally continue for a couple of days afterwards, running into Jaanipäev (St John's Day) on June 24, resulting in a full four days of partying and celebrations. The fun rages nationwide, but is particularly good in Tallinn, where as part of the so-called Grillfest there are plenty of bands playing and other events around the city, and huge quantities of chargrilled pork on offer at open-air barbecues. On Jaanipäev Eve, it's traditional to light a huge bonfire and then jump over the flames for good luck in the coming year – followed by some serious drinking, singing and dancing, to take you through the few short hours of darkness.

Mondial du Snowboard

Where? **Les Deux Alpes, France**
When? **October**
How long? **3 days**

The French Alpine town of Les Deux Alpes kicks the snow season off a bit earlier than its near neighbours with the mammoth Mondial du Snowboard (ⓦwww.mondialdusnow.com), the wildest snowboarding gig in Europe. Now in its eleventh year, the event remains at the cutting edge of snowboarding and is used as a showcase for numerous board manufacturers to reveal their latest designs, as well as laying on a world-class competition. Around thirty thousand boarders party it up in the breathtaking alpine scenery while laying down tracks across the two-thousand-acre snow-covered glacier. Non-boarders can take in skateboarding and BMX biking expos as well as the infamous nocturnal music, partying and clubbing scene.

Montreux Jazz Festival

Where? **Montreux, Switzerland**
When? **July**
How long? **15 days**

Even if you don't know anything about jazz, the chances are you'll have heard of the Montreux Jazz Festival (ⓦwww.montreuxjazz.com), one of Europe's most prestigious music events, and guaranteed to pull in the biggest international names. It's not just what you might call jazz either – everything from hip-hop to acid jazz, gospel, techno, reggae and African jazz get an airing, and for added fun you can groove the days away on themed samba and salsa boats that head out on to the town's lake every afternoon. Now in its 35th year, the festival continues to expand and diversify, with a bewildering range of workshops, and it prides itself on showcasing emerging talents as well as established stars. Herbie Hancock and John McLaughlin are but two of the more regularly featured artists from a cast of around two thousand. There's also Festival OFF, featuring over three hundred free concerts in just about every open space around town. For specific concerts, book early; otherwise, just show up and wander around looking for the tunes that suit you.

Montreux Jazz Festival

Nava Cider Festival

Where? **Nava, Spain**
When? **July**
How long? **1 week**

You may not think so, but cider is a big deal in northern Spain, and every year Nava, in the province of Asturias, throws a party to celebrate the town's greatest product. Like their Galician neighbours, the Asturians aren't your typical castanet-clacking, flamenco-wailing Spaniards, and their local customs include the playing of the bagpipes and the drinking of lots and lots of cider. Nava's festival features dozens of different types of cider to sample – if you can stand the alcoholic pace. There are tastings, competitions for the best brew, and even for the best pouring technique – it's supposed to be done with as much height as possible between the bottle and the glass – but really it's an excuse to drink lots of stuff, which everyone does with huge abandon on the main Saturday of the festival.

North Sea Jazz Festival

Where? **Rotterdam, The Netherlands**
When? **July**
How long? **3 days**

Held over a weekend in the middle of July, the North Sea Jazz Festival (Ⓦwww.northseajazz.nl) has attracted high-level names to its multiple stages since 1976. Now held in Rotterdam, it's a big event, pulling in around a hundred thousand festivalgoers and hosting not just names from the world of jazz but crossing into other, related genres, too – recent performers have included Al Green, Chaka Khan, Chick Corea, Robert Cray and Archie Shepp, for example.

Pageant of the Juni

Where? **Braşov, Romania**
When? **May**
How long? **1 day**

Lacking the Dracula connections of its near neighbours, Braşov, an atmospheric medieval town in deepest Transylvania, has to rely on more accurate historical events for its folklore traditions. One such festival is the Pageant of the Juni, a horseback parade that celebrates the only day of the year – the first Sunday in May – that, traditionally, Romanians could freely enter the Saxon city. Dressing up in elaborate costumes, young townsfolk ride through the streets of the historic quarter – with the married men, or "Old Juni" trailing behind – before heading out into the surrounding hills. Here they break off into groups to perform the rhythmic *horăs* (round dances), which are stamina sapping for both performers and spectators alike.

Pageant of the Juni

Paleo Festival

Where? Nyon, Switzerland
When? July
How long? 6 days

This is one of Europe's best-established open-air music festivals, usually with a wide and deliberately eclectic line-up, and held in a great setting close to the town of Nyon. Originally a folk event, the philosophy is to embrace all musical styles in a truly festive atmosphere – both things that Paleo (Ⓦwww.paleo.ch) manages extremely well. There are two main stages, a world music stage, and smaller venues for up-and-coming (and Swiss!) bands, as well as street theatre, circus performers, and stand-ups. Around 225,000 people attend the whole event – not far off forty thousand a day – and you need to book early if you want to be sure of getting in on your chosen day.

Palio of Asti

Where? Asti, Italy
When? September
How long? 1 day

Less well known than the Siena *palio* (see p.65), Asti's bareback horse race (Ⓦwww.palio.asti.it) dates back to the thirteenth century but was only revived in 1967, since when it has been held annually on the third Sunday in September. It's very similar to the Siena event in lots of ways: the 21 entries represent the different neighbourhoods of the city; it's held on the city's main square – in this case the triangular Piazza Alfieri; and there's a big, drawn-out build-up, during which the rival teams attempt to undermine their adversaries in every possible way. The day starts with a procession, which is a big deal in itself with thousands in costume, including the *sbandieratori*, or flag-wavers, who are competing for their own *palio*, or banner. After the parade, the race itself is run, the prize a velvet cloth decorated by a local painter, the booby prize a humiliating pauper's meal of anchovy and lettuce. A great time to be in Asti, and a less crowded – and cheaper – alternative to Siena.

Pink Pop Festival

Where? Landgraaf, The Netherlands
When? May
How long? 3 days

One of Europe's biggies as far as rock festivals go, Pinkpop (Ⓦwww.pinkpop.nl), as it's known, has been going since 1970 and always attracts the biggest names. Held over the last weekend in May, it draws around sixty thousand to its site in Landgraaf, just outside Heerlen down in the southern Dutch province of Limburg. But make sure you book early – it's usually sold out well in advance.

Polo World Cup on Snow/ White Turf, Switzerland

Where? St Moritz, Switzerland
When? January–February
How long? 7 days

The last weekend of January, and three successive Sundays in February, are red-circled dates in every international jet-setter's diary, home as they are to two events that pull in aristocratic punters from all over Europe to sip champagne in tents and meet and greet their brethren. Now in its seventeenth year, the annual Polo World Cup on Snow (Ⓦwww.polostmoritz.com) is the major cheese among polo tournaments. This four-day tournament takes place on the frozen lake of St Moritz, with the world's top four teams battling it out for the coveted championship title and the Cartier trophy, not to mention the accompanying prestige. It's organized by the renowned St Moritz Polo Club, whose team last year took on rivals from Buenos Aires, Veytay and Dallas. It's giddy stuff: competition is ferocious, and the players hurl themselves and their steeds into some spectacular duels. Between games, everyone hits the trough, with suitably elegant eating opportunities in specially erected tents.

The first three Sundays of February see the staging of the unique century-old event of White Turf (Ⓦwww. whiteturf.ch), in which thoroughbred horses compete on a frozen lake in a series of equestrian events: straight racing, "chariot" races, and "skijoring", in which the "rider" is pulled along on skis. It's a glamorous location, and a glamorous event.

Queima das Fitas

Where? **Coimbra, Portugal**
When? **May**
How long? **8 days**

Founded in the thirteenth century, the University of Coimbra is one of the oldest in Europe, and they must drive their students hard judging by the way they celebrate the end of the academic year. Putting their formal black gowns in mothballs for the summer, the students take over the town over for a week of boisterous non-stop hedonism (ⓦwww.queimadasfitas.net) punctuated by concerts, surf competitions, and evenings spent drinking and performing Fado de Coimbra – soulful melodies sung to guitar accompaniment. The only formal event is when the students parade through the streets on Tuesday afternoon, ending when those entering their final year burn graduation ribbons in a big bonfire in one of the university's forecourts – *queima das fitas* means literally "the burning of the ribbons".

Regatta of the Four Maritime Republics

Where? **Amalfi, Genoa, Pisa, Venice, Italy**
When? **May or June**
How long? **1 day**

Sort of an Italian university boat race, this annual rowing regatta gives the four maritime republics of Italy – Amalfi, Genoa, Pisa and, of course, Venice – the chance to celebrate their past greatness and rivalries with a pageant and boat race. It alternates between the four locations, and so is both a sea-based and river-based event, but the principle is basically the same each time: four vessels, eight metres long and with four sets of oars, compete over a straight two-thousand-metre course. It's been taking place since the 1950s and draws big crowds, not only for the race but also for the parade that's held beforehand – lots of folk dressed up in period costumes and astride horses, commemorating a different historic event in each town. As for the racing, Venice has always been the strongest team, but recently Pisa and Amalfi have also done well.

Roskilde Festival

Where? **Roskilde, Denmark**
When? **July**
How long? **4 days**

With over ninety thousand people turning up each year to hear big-name punk, rock and metal bands from Scandinavia and beyond, Roskilde (ⓦwww.roskilde-festival.dk) is one of the biggest events of its kind in Europe – second only to Glastonbury – and also one of the best organized, although the 2000 event was marred by the tragic deaths of some of the festivalgoers.

Roskilde Festival

Romeria del Rocio

Where? El Rocio, Spain
When? May or June
How long? 3 days

By far the most spectacular of Andalucían holy pilgrimages, the Romeria del Rocio is held over the Pentecost weekend, when a million people from all over southern Spain gather to pay homage to a statue of the Nuestra Señora del Rocio, or Virgin of the Dew. They've been doing this since the thirteenth century, and many pilgrims still arrive as they would have then, wearing their silver medals and either riding in on horseback or trundling in aboard brightly decorated ox-carts to set up camp in the Guadalquivir marshes around the tiny village. A fairground atmosphere ensues, with much friendly partying, singing and dancing, especially on the Saturday night. On the Sunday, everyone attends mass and then converges on the local church where the statue of the Virgin is kept, to watch her being brought out at dawn on a float; church bells ring and firecrackers are hurled around as the crowd hauls the statue aloft and passes it around, everyone trying to touch it for good luck. The action continues until Monday afternoon, when the statue is returned to the church and everyone begins to pack up for the journey home.

Sa Sartiglia

Where? Oristano, Sardinia
When? February or March
How long? 3 days

The town of Oristano hosts one of Italy's most extravagant costumed spectacles every year at carnival time. Infused with the mystique of medieval knights, and perhaps with its origins in the crusades, Sa Sartiglia is a series of equestrian events, judged by a mysterious, androgynous masked figure known as the King of Sartiglia or Su Cumpoidori, and culminating in a high-speed joust to pierce the centre of a silver star – *sartiglia* – which dangles by a ribbon on the central Piazza Eleonora, where the proceedings take place. It's a magnificent sight: Oristano isn't somewhere you would normally linger for long, but this is worth a pretty hefty detour if you get the chance.

Salzburg Festival

Where? Salzburg, Austria
When? July and August
How long? 5 weeks

One of Europe's biggest and best arts shindigs, Salzburg's festival (www.salzburgfestival.at) inevitably concentrates pretty heavily on the work of its favourite son, Mozart, but there's plenty of other music besides, including cutting-edge modern stuff, and a sprinkling of theatre productions, too.

Schützenfest

Where? Hannover, Germany
When? June
How long? 10 days

The Schützenfest (www.schuetzenfest-hannover.de) is northern Germany's largest and most spectacular municipal fair, with every part of the pleasant city of Hannover chipping in to the general feeling of well-being. There's something for everyone, from a wide range of kids' activities through to processions with fancily decorated floats, firework extravaganzas, oompah bands and huge marquees, where a good proportion of the adult population quaff frothing pints of ale. Everyone gets legless, of course, but all in a very German, civilized fashion. The Schützenfest originated as a medieval marksmen's competition, but the closest anyone comes to demanding hand-to-eye co-ordination these days is trying to put a beer glass to their mouth.

Semana Santa

Where? Seville, Spain
When? March or April
How long? 7 days

Every year a million or more Spanish and foreign tourists flock to Seville to witness the spectacular processions of Holy Week (Semana Santa), one of Europe's most affecting and unforgettable events, and worth experiencing whether you're a Christian or not. Sweeping up the population in the story of Christ's passion, death and resurrection, the processions have centuries of history in much of Spain, and indeed other parts of the Spanish-speaking world, but are most extravagantly staged in Seville.

The first of the processions begin on Palm Sunday, as the city springs out of its winter torpor, and each day different brotherhoods parade through the streets, building to the highlight of the week, the Madrugá, from midnight on Holy Thursday until well into Good Friday. As many as sixty thousand brothers from 57 *cofradías* or *hermandades* (religious brotherhoods attached to a particular parish church) participate in the processions, and they can take hours to complete. In most cases, each *cofradía* parades two elaborate floats, the first bearing a sculpted image of Christ depicting a scene

the sombre drum and brass notes of a marching band set the pace, as the enormous floats emerge, borne by a team of thirty or so men, hidden from view

from *The Passion*, the second one of the Virgin Mary in generous finery, usually portrayed mourning for her son. The procession starts at the parish church, where the floats are flanked by long lines of Nazarenos (so-called Nazarenes) dressed in the hood and pointed conical hat that you may have seen in pictures; they march slowly, some holding huge candles, accompanied by Penitentes (penitents), who don't wear the pointed hats but bear a cross instead, and often parade barefoot to

Semana Santa

*One of Europe's most affecting
and unforgettable events*

increase their penance. The sombre drum and brass notes of a marching band set the pace, as the enormous floats emerge, borne by a team of thirty or so men, hidden from view. They move rhythmically, making the float sway gently from side to side as it advances, under the orders of a "foreman", who marches ahead and tells them when to rest and when to start moving again. Each procession takes a different route but all aim for the Cathedral, converging on the final stretch, from Plaza del Duque de la Victoria, along Calle de Sierpes, Plaza de San Francisco and Avenida de la Constitución – known as the Carrera Oficial (Official Route). After reaching the Cathedral, each procession then heads off, generally by a different route, back to their church for the formal *entrada* (entrance, or return).

The first procession on Thursday is the black-clothed parade of El Silencio. As their name suggests, they march without noise, unaccompanied by a band and imposing their eerie silence on bystanders. They are followed by the Cofradía del Señor del Gran Poder, also dressed in black, and later, one of the most spectacular processions, La Macarena, which reaches the Cathedral at about 4.30am. More than three thousand Nazarenos and Penitentes march in La Maracana, and you can be waiting well over an hour before sighting the Virgen de la Macarena, the most beloved of the floats. At midnight, is the climatic Madrugá, when the most important of the city's brotherhoods parade to the Cathedral and back all night – the last don't return to their starting points until 2pm the following day.

Spoleto Festival

Where? **Spoleto, Italy**
When? **July**
How long? **2 weeks**

Spoleto is a deliberately broad-based event, with theatre, cinema and visual arts events, although the focus is very much on music and dance (Ⓦwww.spoletofestival.it). Even if you're not attracted to anything special, the inaugural and closing concerts, held *al fresco* on the main town square, are a wonderful spectacle.

Up-Helly Aa

Where? **Lerwick, Scotland**
When? **January**
How long? **1 day**

Around a thousand people, many of them costumed Vikings, complete with winged helmets, axes and shields and flaming torches, take to the streets of Lerwick in the Shetlands on the last Tuesday of January to drag a Viking galley through the town. It's set up on the seafront, and then everyone hurls their torches on board and it's razed to the ground, at which point everyone disappears off to the pub or to one of many invitation-only events around town – there's definitely no chance of gate-crashing these, as it's very much a local celebration.

Viareggio Carnival

Where? **Viareggio, Italy**
When? **January and February**
How long? **4 days**

Ever since 1873, the Tuscan coastal town of Viareggio has been hosting one of Italy's liveliest carnivals. For the four consecutive Sundays leading up to Lent there's an amazing parade of floats that would pass muster in some of the best Brazilian affairs. The floats carry as many as two hundred people in costume, as well as – the main feature, and the thing that makes Viareggio unique – the so-called *carri*: colossal, lavishly designed papier-mâché models of politicians and celebrities, (many of whom come especially to Viareggio to see how the float designers have depicted them). Each of the *carri* have up to ten people inside them, to manoeuvre the weights and levers that prevent them from toppling over. Each parade ends with a huge firework display, and Viareggio's bars and restaurants buzz for some time after, often with hip Pisans and Florentines who have made the short journey for Viareggio's dance clubs. For the rest of the year, the *carri* reside in huge seaside hangars, and in the town's carnival museum, where they are on display to the public.

Vogel Gryff

Where? Basel, Switzerland
When? January
How long? 1 day

This is a very strange and very Swiss festival that dates back to the sixteenth century and involves the mascots of the three Basel neighbourhoods – a dancing lion, a tree-carrying bushman and the Vogel Gryff itself, a griffin that bears an uncanny resemblance to Sesame Street's Big Bird. These three creatures first have to make their way down the Rhine on a makeshift raft before disembarking at Basel's main bridge. They then lead the huge assembled crowd through the streets of the town in what is best described as conga-line dance meets pub-crawl, the pace of which doesn't let up until well after midnight.

White Nights

Where? St Petersburg, Russia
When? June–July
How long? 3 weeks

Russia's most cultured city gets an added dimension through midsummer – it's so far north that for a month it never gets dark enough to fire up the street lights, with the normal night-time darkness replaced by a pearly twilight that lasts until the sun rises again around 2am. Dostoyevsky found the atmosphere so alluring he wrote *White Nights*, or *Beliye Nochi*, his homage to the city, and for the last century this has been marked by a festival of the same name, with nightly programmes of concerts, theatre and ballet at the Mariinsky Theatre. Downtown cafés, bars and restaurants stay open, and the streets, with their magnificent architecture, stay full of life. There's a splendidly romantic mood, which draws couples to promenade along the riverbank, where each sunrise is greeted with amateur firework displays and roars of approval from the champagne- and vodka-soaked crowds.

Wife-Carrying Championship

Where? Sonkajärvi, Finland
When? July
How long? 1 day

Apparently, it was once common practice in central Finland to steal women from neighbouring villages, and a local brigand used this, among other things, to test the manliness of his recruits. This gave birth to the peculiar but fiercely competitive Wife-Carrying Championship, whereby men attempt to be the fastest to carry a woman down a 250-metre-long track, wading through water and clambering over fences and other obstacles. You don't have to be married to the woman you're carrying, and neither do you have to be Finnish; in fact, couples come from far and wide to compete, and recent years have been dominated by the Estonians, winning in times of just under one minute. Other events take place at around the same time: there's a Wife-Carrying Triathlon, and a team competition, in which groups of three men take turns to carry a long-suffering "wife". There are some strict rules to be observed, most importantly that no wife should weigh under 49kg (if they do, they have to wear a heavy rucksack as a handicap). In some ways, the heavier the wife the better – the winners receive their passenger's weight in beer.

Westmann Islands' Festival

Where? Heimaey, Westmann Islands, Iceland
When? August
How long? 3 days

If you're searching for an offbeat party destination, then the Westmann Islands' Festival – Þjódhátíð-Vestmannaeyjar – is just the ticket. Held on a three-mile wide volcanic outcrop off the south coast of Iceland, this music fest (Ⓦwww.eyjar.is/thjodhatid) has it all: smoking volcanoes, immense bonfires, tent-busting shagathons, enough booze to keep the entire Russian armed forces zonked out for a month, and some great music – even though, hailing as it does mainly from Iceland, Greenland and the Faroes, you won't necessarily be familiar with much of it.

The festival commemorates the signing of Iceland's first constitution on July 1, 1874, which granted it semi-independence from Denmark. The story goes that foul weather prevented the Westmann islanders from reaching the celebrations on the mainland, so they held their own a few weeks later on the six-kilometre island of Heimaey, and the Þjódhátíð was born. Vestiges of the traditional festival can be seen in the grassy crater of the extinct Herjólfsdalur volcano, where one hundred identical white tents, all owned by the locals, are laid out in a grid with wooden pallets serving as walkways between them. Each is immaculately appointed and contains heaters, carpeting, lights and a cosy Heimaey family.

the weekend passes in almost perpetual daylight – everyone is very, very drunk, and jumping around the pools with complete abandon

It is likely to be cold, wet and miserable, so buckle down your tent and wrap up well. Some people just wear huge fishermen's luminous orange oilskins, although most Icelandic partygoers turn up in very un-waterproof fancy dress – Hawaiian hula dancers, snowmen, superheroes and the like. More essential items, however, are plenty of warm clothes, booze (you can't buy any alcohol on site, and Heimaey's liquor store and pubs are extremely expensive) and, if you run out of booze, money – at around £10 for a beer in a bar you won't be surprised that in 2006 Iceland was voted the world's most expensive country.

After shelling out the hefty £80 ticket price for what amounts to three days of sitting in a wet field, everyone is understandably intent on making the most of it. The entertainment kicks off in earnest about 3pm on Friday, but things only really get going from midnight onwards, with music blasting out till 5am. Friday night at midnight sharp, a huge, volcano-sized, bonfire is lit on a small hill at the edge of the camp, the heat from which warms the whole place for the next three or four hours and makes the party a whole lot happier. Saturday night gets going at midnight with a pretty awesome fireworks display followed by the headline bands. Sunday night is more communal, with the whole crowd joining in traditional Icelandic songs, sitting around small bonfires and finishing the last of the booze through until 6am. Shuttle flights run all day back to Reykjavik, weather permitting, and the campsite is cleared out by late Monday afternoon.

Throughout the weekend, activities are focused on a unique kind of Icelandic triathlon, which involves participants running from bar to volcanic hot-pool to freezing sea and back to the bar again. By the time the hour of darkness arrives that marks night – due to the extreme northern setting, the weekend passes in almost perpetual daylight – everyone is very, very drunk, and jumping around the pools with complete abandon – usually naked, and usually still necking vodka shots. It's a sight that will stay with you for a long time.

Westmann Islands Festival

*most Icelandic partygoers turn up
in very un-waterproof fancy dress
– Hawaiian hula dancers, snowmen,
superheroes and the like*

Wine War

The object is perfectly straightforward: to squirt, hose, blast or throw some 25,000 litres of what is presumably not vintage vino tinto over everyone else

Wine War

Where? **Haro, Spain**
When? **June 29**
How long? **1 day**

One of the truly great events of the summer in Spain, the Wine War (Batallo de Vino) is the modern-day remnant of ancient feuds between the wine town of Haro and its Riojan neighbours, and basically boils down to a massive wine-fight on a hillside overlooking Haro's beautiful medieval centre. The first wine battle took place in 1710, but the event became popularized in the 1950s, and from the mid-1960s started to draw crowds from outside the immediate area, attracted by the fact that La Rioja is one of Spain's – and Europe's – foremost wine-producing regions.

The festival begins at around 7am with what must be one of the most bizarre religious processions anywhere: the congregation – as many as five thousand people, mostly dressed in white – comes armed not with Bibles, crucifixes and rosary beads but with an ingenious array of weapons ranging from buckets, water pistols and *bota* bags (or wine-skin bottles) to agricultural spraying equipment. This motley crew makes its way from Haro to a shrine 15km away in the Riscos de Bilibio, to pay homage to San Juan, San Pedro and the Virgin of Valvanera. Mass is said, and then on the route back to town wine is distributed free of charge by the city council. After this, battle commences and the warring factions start drenching each other with Rioja. In theory, the townsfolk of Haro are battling it out with those of neighbouring Miranda de Ebro, but in the good-humoured but frantic battle that rages, there are no obvious sides, and no winners or losers. Instead, the object is perfectly straightforward: to squirt, hose, blast or throw some 25,000 litres of what is presumably not vintage *vino tinto* over everyone else, in particular aiming at the previously unscathed.

you won't be spared as a spectator, so you may as well join in

You won't be spared as a spectator, so you may as well join in. At the very least, come armed with a water pistol, though be warned that the locals have perfected the art of the portable water cannon, and can practically blast you off your feet from five metres. Whatever you use, you'll finish the day a stinking, soggy mess, so don't don your Sunday best for this one. White outfits are preferred; all the better to display your battle wounds. As noon approaches, the stragglers quickly return to town and the bars around the Plaza de la Paz to finish of the vats of wine that are left. Just to round things off as you're staggering homewards, they let out steers into the plaza that are then sent running towards the bullring – not quite Pamplona, but enough to get the heart racing and to make you spend the rest of the evening having the odd stiff drink or two.

The Americas and The Caribbean

The Americas and The Caribbean

Burning Man
Crop Over
Day of the Dead
Fantasy Fest
Fiesta de Merengue
Halloween Parade
Junkanoo
Mardi Gras
Reggae Sumfest
Rio Carnival
Trinidad Carnival
BEST OF THE REST

Burning Man

If you've ever dreamed of driving a cupcake car or being the high priestess of a spanking temple, you're in the right place

Burning Man

Where?
Black Rock City, Nevada, USA

When?
The week before Labor Day (first Monday in September)

How long?
8 days

Picture a nudist miniature golf course, an advanced pole-dancing workshop, a motorized magic-carpet vehicle and a bunch of neon-painted bodies glowing in the night, and you may be getting close to imagining what the legendary Burning Man is all about. Every year during the last week of August, several thousand digerati geeks, pyrotechnic maniacs, death-guild Goths, crusty hippies and too-hip yuppies descend on a prehistoric dry lakebed in the Nevada desert known to insiders as Black Rock City. It's not the ideal place to consume a heady cocktail of alcohol and drugs – temperatures can exceed 100°F by day and the sun isn't happy until it has bleached your bones white – but the thousands of anarchists, deviants, mad scientists, techno-heads, trace-dancers and freakish performance artists that arrive here from all over the world every year give it their best shot.

The highlight of the week is the burning of a fifty-foot-tall effigy of a man, constructed from wood and neon and stuffed with fireworks – an event that's frankly an anticlimax after the laser-filled skies, electroluminescent wired bodysuits, fire-breathing mechanical dragons, oversized, fuel-oozing metal faces and techno tribal tunes that illuminate each and every evening. Basically, this is the most artistic, survivalist, futuristic and utterly surreal show on earth, where the strangest part of your alter ego reigns supreme. Some of Burning Man's participants see the event as a social experiment and total free-for-all, where they can shed their uptight work veneers and technological props almost as easily as many people do their clothing. But the main goals are universal. First, you're there to participate, not observe. Burning Man enables all the black sheep of the world to graze together, so the more experiential art you share, gifts you give, bizarre costume you wear, or free services you provide, the better. Second, you're there to build a temporary autonomous "city" – one that rivals some of Nevada's largest in size and leaves no trace when it disbands. Third, you're there to share and barter, as no commercial vending is permitted, with the exception of the *Center Camp Café* that spoons out $3 lattes just in case your mud-caked glittered ass needs warming up. In short, Burning Man survives – and thrives – on the gift economy.

History

In 1986, a San Francisco artist named **Larry Harvey** inadvertently sparked the first match in what would become a legacy when, as a result of a broken heart, he burned a small wooden stick figure amidst the ceremonial cheers of a handful of friends. For the next four years, he continued with this ritual back home until the cops interceded. Harvey and about one hundred friends then started to tug the now forty-foot "Man" across state lines to Nevada's Black Rock country, nearly 4000 feet above sea level and 120 miles northeast of Reno, just beyond the tiny town of Gerlach.

Black Rock country is home to an alkaline salt stretch known as the **playa**, and is so expansive it's said you can actually see the curvature of the earth. The barren, cracked-mud surroundings are the perfect tableau for the even more surreal bacchanal that is Burning Man: 36,000 people now descend on the five-square-mile encampment, making it, for just over one week a year, the fourth largest "city" in Nevada.

Black Rock City

Despite its whimsical, anything-goes appearance, Burning Man is extremely organized. Not only is there plenty of breathing space for everyone, but there is also relative assurance that you will be safe, have a decent place to pee, and that good vibes will abound. The largest work of art on the playa is arguably **Black Rock City** itself, a temporary metropolis of tents and theme camps that arcs out from the *Center Camp Café* in a large horseshoe shape, its mile-wide centre empty but for the Man in the middle. Art installations and the like are allowed in this space but people are not permitted to camp here. The city's "streets" are set out in a radial design according to the hours on a clock face, ranging from 2.00 to 10.00 – the *Center Camp Café* is always at 6.00. The concentric streets are bisected by roads with names inspired by the annual

Burning Man enables all the black sheep of the world to graze together

Dance parties

Many people come to Burning Man exclusively for the **all-night dance parties**. But what is today ubiquitous on the playa was not always so. The advent of the first DJ stages in 1995 several miles away was met with much criticism; in fact, it took a few years for the first dance music stage to be allowed into Black Rock City proper, and only then reluctantly, and for just a single night. Slowly, the old guard relented and even the "quiet side" of town began featuring phat beat parties.

Nowadays, it's difficult to believe that there was ever a time when dance music didn't feature at Burning Man – indeed, it's regarded as one of the best assemblages of American and worldwide DJs in one place, with every DJ superstar worth their salt making an appearance here in recent years, from Tiesto to Freq Nasty, Paul Oakenfold to DJ Peretz.

theme; for example, the year of "The Body" saw people taking a stroll along Sex Drive, Head Way, Gut Alley and Brain Boulevard. If you're part of an organized and listed theme camp (see p.186), your home plot is predetermined. Otherwise, you can drive in and meet up with friends wherever you choose to form your own mini trailer-trash community. The inside of the horseshoe is where much of the action resides, such as random art installations, temporary performance stages and motorized wet bar parties.

In addition to the theme camps and music stages, the hive around the **Center Camp Café** also boasts multiple medical outposts, a bike-repair shop, three radio stations, a media tent, a lost-and-found area, a bus stop that serves Gerlach, a freezer truck selling ice, an information and locator area – and Burning Man rangers to keep the peace. There's also a smattering of local cops, who have recently tightened up on drug use and possession (there have been well-founded rumours of undercover cops using theme camps to lure in people to buy drugs, and then arresting them on the spot). But it doesn't seem to inhibit anyone from having a good time.

Tickets

Tickets are available from the official **website** (see p.188) or from some **walk-in outlets** in San Francisco, Berkeley, Sacramento and Reno: they go on sale at the beginning of the year for around $200 and then get progressively more expensive as the year goes on – rising to $280 two weeks before the event. You can also buy a ticket at **the gate** for $300, as long as you arrive by the Thursday before the burning of The Man – after that, no newcomers are allowed in.

Theme camps

Art and interactivity are at the very core of the Burning Man ethos. If you've ever dreamed of creating an oversized fallopian-tube walk-in maze, swinging on 18,000-pound boulders at the Temple of Gravity, plopping a wall of rubber gloves for groping strangers in the middle of nowhere, constructing a tower of animal bones, or being the high priestess of a spanking temple, then you're in the right place. Just join a like-minded, participatory group, known as a **theme camp**, and away you go. A theme-camp group must be entirely self-reliant, with its own power source, and be able to protect its mechanisms and props against the elements, while also ensuring safety. If you fancy burning down your camp or installation upon the closing of the festival, predetermined burning platforms must be used.

If you fancy making a smaller-scale statement and having more autonomy, you can choose whatever alter ego or fantasy you desire. Leashed slaves with foot fetishes wander around offering footbaths, faceless Pythia offer advice in oracle booths, flying zebras circle, caged men in ape suits pounce, and motorized lobster cars tool about. Just pack your politically correct non-feathered boas, body paint and imagination, and you're all set.

Decompression Street Fair

In the weeks following Burning Man, many participants speak of disquiet and restlessness. Some become downright depressed. Recognizing their anguish, and also wishing to continue their concept throughout the year, the founders of Burning Man came up with the **Decompression Street Fair**, a one-day event that takes place on the second Sunday in October, six weeks after Burning Man goes up in flames. Performance artists and flamboyant theme campers relive the playa for one day in San Francisco's Esprit Park, with five fun-filled blocks of entertainment, along with daytime and night-time art installations, and even the homeless take a break from panhandling and mingle with recently returned Burners, or those wannabes who missed the real deal.

> **Insider info** If none of the theme camps quite float your boat, you can set up your own on the Burning Man website (see p.188) and publicize your planned theme-camp events online.

There are several Decompression parties in other cities, too, including Los Angeles, Seattle and New York City, while smaller Regional Burns are starting to emerge across the country – the Seattle Burning Man community, for example, holds a four-day camping event, where amplified music is played and art installations torched. Like Burning Man proper, the Regional Burns promote respect, courtesy, self-control, and a pledge not to interfere with anyone else's experience; and, if Larry Harvey and others have their way, they may even eclipse Burning Man altogether.

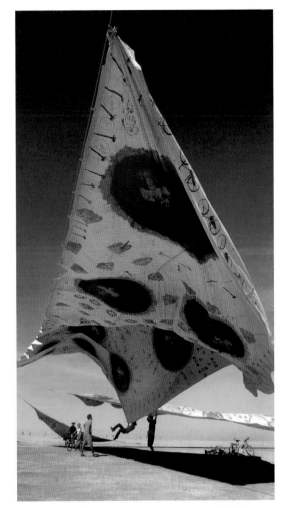

Die yuppie scum?

You can definitely depend on a more consistently intelligent, accomplished and eclectic group of people at Burning Man than at many other American festivals, where straight-out partying is the main order of every day. Part of this is due to the fact that this carnival attracts an **older demographic**: 37 percent of the festgoers are between 31 and 40 years old, and 28 percent are older than 41. On one hand, this makes for constantly stimulating and quirky spectacles; on the other hand, the median age points to the fact that older people have the deep wallets and planning chutzpah to attend such an event. In fact, there's some controversy about just how sold out Burning Man is getting. High ticket prices, a lack of people of colour, rave camps taking over, and art becoming too politicized are the new dynamics of the modern Burning Man. There's no doubt that struggling artists and ramshackle dwellings are being joined by fancy RVs, overnight-millionaire brats, and corporate bods sent here for "team-player" training. But whatever you think about this, Larry Harvey's social experiment in Utopia undoubtedly now serves as a model that is being shared with prospective festival planners throughout the US and Europe.

Basics

The planning required to get to Burning Man, and the weather Mother Nature doles out once you're here, automatically weeds out the weaklings from the diehards. But it makes the pleasurable carrots that dangle here taste even sweeter. Reno, 120 miles to the southwest, is the nearest **airport** – but whichever direction you're coming from you need to head for the town of Gerlach, 12 miles south of Black Rock City. From Gerlach, head northwest on Hwy 447 for one mile. At the fork, take the right (Hwy 34) – from here it's 11 miles to the Burning Man entrance. More detailed directions starting from further afield can be obtained from the Burning Man website (see below).

You can **rent an RV**, car and/or camping equipment in Reno, Sacramento or San Francisco (driving distances: 2, 5 and 7hr respectively); on the way, keep an eye out for "Honk if you Burn" signs – the vibe heats up miles before the desert in a moving tailgate party. Around Black Rock City, bicycles are the festival transport of choice, since driving is prohibited on the playa (except for special art cars), and pedalling around will increase your odds of seeing more of the festival spread.

Accommodation and eating

Whether you come for a long weekend, the entire week, or join the veterans who arrive a week or two early, the festival requires that you **bring all your own provisions**, every bit of shelter, food, water and other accoutrements that you will need – the closest grocery store is in the town of Empire, 3 miles from Gerlach. And when you're packing, be aware that the desert elements are volatile and spontaneous – high winds, rain, dust storms, scorching sun and cold nights are all apt to make an appearance. Also, don't forget to refuel your vehicle before leaving "civilization."

Once here, **dwellings** run the gamut, from authentic Bedouin tents to home-grown pyramids to modest tents with just enough room for you and whoever you've elected to warm your bones at night. If you don't plan on being one of the higher-profile theme campers, you're probably best off with an RV or tent.

Event info

Burning Man (ⓦwww.burningman.com). The official site, with ticket info, directions, great photos and a helpful "First-Timers' Guide." Also contains info on the Decompression Street Fair and Regional Burns.

Time zone GMT-8   **Country code** +1   **Currency** US dollar ($)

Crop Over

*Parades, calypso concerts and jump-ups – rum-fuelled block parties
that shake the entire island*

Crop Over

Where?
Bridgetown, Barbados

When?
From the second Saturday in July to the first Monday in August

How long?
24 days

BARBADOS

• Bridgetown

The yell of "Crop Over!", traditionally marking the end of Barbados' back-breaking sugar harvest, is the gleeful signal for the start of one of the Caribbean's most extravagant summer carnivals. For most of its history, sugar cane has pretty much defined the island and, although it's not as important as it once was, the delivery of the last crop still prompts a prolonged party. During the carnival, the whole of this beautiful Caribbean island explodes into a festival of parades, calypso concerts, and jump-ups – rum-fuelled block parties that shake the entire island. Colourful costumes are brought out of storage, a legion of musical instruments get dusted off, and the rum starts to flow more liberally than ever.

The three weeks or so leading up to Grand Kadooment is a mellow time in Barbados, with a cool, laid-back party atmosphere that, as the day approaches, slowly cranks up to the max. The island is less crowded, accommodation is easier to find, and it's a good opportunity to hang out with the carnival bands and catch a real variety of parties and shows. Proceedings normally begin in Bridgetown, the island's capital, in mid-July, with a noisy **parade** of brightly decorated carts, floats and the occasional bicycle ending at the National Stadium – just north of Bridgetown – where there's an exuberant gala opening with the crowning of the festival's king and queen (the season's record cane-cutters). The ceremonial delivery of the last canes of the harvest sparks an all-night party, with competing stages hosting events such as African drummers, Scottish dancing, Latin merengue and gospel singers, and dozens of stalls selling food and drink to keep you energized into the early hours.

History

Started more than two hundred years ago, when Barbados was an important sugar producer, the annual Crop Over carnival celebrated the end of months of exhausting work for the field-labourers on the patchwork of sugar estates that once covered the island. Like many nations' carnivals that immediately precede a period of fasting, Crop Over was marked by an atmosphere of frenzied abandonment, as workers combined their relief at ending work with the bitter knowledge that earnings would now be minimal until the next crop. Inevitably, as sugar has been overtaken by tourism as the country's main money-spinner, some of the traditions of Crop Over have been lost. However, it remains the most important annual festival on the island, and a great excuse – if one were needed – for an extended party.

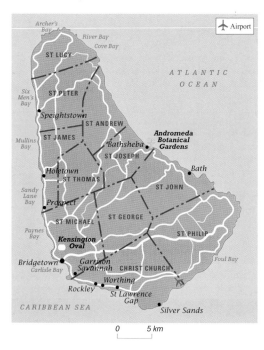

For the next three weeks, Barbados hosts a series of **street markets**, **craft fairs** and **cook-outs**, while the musicians' tents start warming up, as the bands prepare to battle it out for the season's top honours. As in the nearby Trinidad Carnival (see p.249), the music spans a wide range and is invariably great for dancing: there are traditional tuk bands, based around a banjo, a drum and a tin whistle; poetical and politicized calypso songs; hypnotic steel-pan drummers and more upbeat soca and ringbang bands.

The final weekend

The final weekend, which always concludes on the first Monday in August, is the jewel in the Crop Over crown. Friday has the **Pic-o-de-Crop** finals at the National Stadium, at which the best calypsonsians take it in turns to play through the evening, fighting it out for the top spot. Afterwards, there's a massive jump-up that lasts through to dawn on Saturday, which tends to be a quieter day as folks take a short

The music scene

The music scene in Barbados has been dominated for several decades by its **calypsonians**, particularly Mighty Gabby and Red Plastic Bag, who have both been voted Calypso Monarch at Crop Over numerous times in the last thirty years. Biting and satirical (Gabby was once sued by the Prime Minister for ridiculing government policy), they are still inspirational to the new generation of island bands.

Grynner – the Bajan Pied Piper – is king of the Road March, while more high-energy stuff comes from the soca stars Square One and Krosfyah, whose music you'll catch around the island, particularly in the bars and clubs on the south coast. If you're nursing a sore head, look for the lighter tones of Arturo Tappin, Barbados' own jazz hero, whose sax sounds are ideal for a balmy night under the stars.

break from partying. Sunday night hosts **Cohobblopot**, another huge show at the National Stadium where the top calypsonians and performances by the winners of the Party Monarch (best show) and Road March Monarch (the artist whose songs are played most often by the music trucks on the various parades). With the whole island rocking, don't count on much sleep during the weekend – at least not during the hours of darkness – though you can join the recovering hordes draped along the beach during the day.

Insider info Try to hit the celebrations as they climax on the first Monday in August with Grand Kadooment, a massive carnival of music, dance and drink in Bridgetown.

Tempting as it might be to retire to the beach at this stage, make sure you set your alarm so you don't miss the best party of all – Monday's **Grand Kadooment** (from the Bajan vernacular "to-do-ment" meaning "big fuss"). Starting around 9am, dozens of bands, some of them with hundreds of colourfully dressed groupies, parade around the National Stadium before embarking on a long road march to the capital that ends up in a drunken spree along the Spring Garden highway, which runs parallel to the beach just north of Bridgetown. Crowd participation is encouraged (at times, it's insisted on), and you'd be well advised to join the throng as they snake their way through the streets. Make an effort with your costume and whistle and you'll be invited to top up your glass from the iced rum punch generously hosed out of the nearest float.

The morning after

Given the small size of Barbados, your involvement in Crop Over shouldn't stop you from experiencing the island's other highlights. The wild northeast, where the surf lashes in at the **Bathsheba** "soup bowl", offers stunning scenery as well as some of the Caribbean's most spectacular flora at the **Andromeda Botanical Gardens**. Along with the rolling sugar-cane fields that give Crop Over its *raison d'être*, the island's interior has patches of jungle, spectacular caves and some great views. Close to the beaches on the south coast, the **Garrison Savannah** was where the British military maintained its headquarters until the early twentieth century: the fabulous colonial buildings now house the excellent Barbados Museum, while horse racing takes place on the surrounding grassland.

top up your glass from the iced rum punch generously hosed out of the nearest float

Basics

Book your **flights** well in advance and bear in mind that, with some of the best beaches in the world, recovering from party excess on Barbados is as delightful as the jump-up itself. Getting around the island is easy: cheap **buses** run to every nook and cranny, while renting a **car** for a day or two gives you more freedom to roam.

Accommodation

Though most of the action is in and around Bridgetown, there's no accommodation in the capital itself. The **south coast** has the best-value accommodation, all within fifteen minutes by bus from town: the *Pirate's Inn* in Hastings (☎ 426 6273), a quiet and friendly place close to one of the island's busiest beaches, has double rooms from $90; while just to the east of here, in the small resort of Worthing, *Beachhouse Cleverdale* (☎ 428 1035; around $30) and *Crystal Waters* (☎ 435 7514; same price) are two of the island's best guesthouses; both are just metres from the beach. The **west coast**, reputed for its gorgeous sunsets, is more upscale, with some truly excellent hotels. *Treasure Beach* in Paynes Bay (☎ 432 0817) has double rooms for $265, or if you'd prefer self-catering, the nearby *St James* (☎ 432 0489) has modern, well-equipped units by the beach from $170.

Eating and drinking

Eating well – and eating cheap – is never a problem during Crop Over. Vendors sell jerk chicken, *rotis* and other tasty morsels on street corners and around the principal venues during the main events; at other times, plenty of restaurants on both the south and west coasts offer a staggering range of food for all budgets. Cheaper places include the *Carib Beach Bar*, right on the beach in Worthing (☎ 435 8540), and the numerous stalls selling tasty grilled fish at *Oistins Market* in Oistins, just to the east. The *Waterfront Café* in Bridgetown (☎ 427 0093) serves authentic Bajan food in an attractive setting facing a marina known as the Careenage, while, for a splurge, try *The Tides* in Holetown on the west coast (☎ 432 8356) or *Josef's* in St Lawrence Gap (☎ 420 7638).

Most of the **nightlife** in Barbados is centred around St Lawrence Gap. In the Gap itself, The *Ship Inn* and *McBride's* are two popular pubs that offer live music most nights; while *Club Xtreme*, close to the Gap on the main road in Worthing, is the place to go for flashing lights, thumping music and gyrating hips. In Bridgetown, *The Boatyard* and *Harbour Lights*, both by the beach, are famous for their all-you-can-drink parties.

Event info

Crop Over (ⓦ www.cropoverfestival.bb). Official site of Crop Over, containing all you need to know about the festival.
Barbados Tourism Authority (ⓦ www.barbados.org). Info on events, accommodation, restaurants and tours.

Time zone GMT-4	**Country code** +1 246	**Currency** Barbados dollar ($)

Day of the Dead

It's not every day you get to party with the dead

Day of the Dead

Where?
Mexico

When?
November 1 and
November 2

How long?
2 days

MEXICO

Mexico City
Veracruz
Pátzcuaro •
Oaxaca •

It's not every day you get to party with the dead, but on the first two days in November, all of Mexico does just that, as everything stops for the most distinctive festival on the calendar, a nationwide communion with the departed, known as the Día de los Muertos, or Day of the Dead. Sound a touch morbid? It's actually a more joyful occasion than you might expect, as it's both a time for the remembrance of loved ones and a celebration of the eternal cycle of life – a carnival of welcome, if you like, for the spiritual return of the dead. For days in advance, favourite dishes are prepared and placed on flower-bedecked altars, along with a beloved tequila. Come nightfall, graveyards quickly start to resemble Mexican roadside restaurants, as picnic tables and chairs are set around graves, tortillas are fried, and substantial quantities of tequila are consumed in memory of the deceased.

History

The Day of the Dead may not be a depressing occasion, but it is certainly rather Gothic, an intriguing synthesis of Aztec ritual and Spanish Catholic tradition. The peoples of Mesoamerica traded, warred, conquered and progressively handed down their traditions from one ruling civilization to another until 1519, when Spanish conquistador Hernan Cortés arrived to spoil the party. The principal guardians of the Mesoamerican heritage were the **Aztecs**, who had adopted the beliefs of the Otomí, Nahua, Purepecha and Totonac tribes, which held that the departed weren't dead, they were just residing in *Mictlan*, a dark waiting-room where they could bide their time before returning to visit their loved ones – who couldn't see them but could sense their presence. At the end of the harvest season, in mid-August, deceased children were remembered in a festival known as Miccailhuitolntli (Little Feast for the Dead). This was immediately followed by Hueymiccaihuitl (Great Feast of the Dead), during which living relatives could help the dead make a more pleasant journey back to the land of the living by strewing aromatic flowers all about to guide them to a banquet prepared as temptation.

The **Spanish** brought a different tradition, ostensibly Christian, but with roots in European paganism that may date back 25 centuries to the Irish Celts. One version has early Celtic peoples marking the end of summer on October 31, when the spirits of those who had died during the previous year would return in search of a living body to inhabit for the following year. The living tried to discourage the dead from taking over their bodies with noisy processions and ghoulish costumes. Aided by the Romans, the tradition found its way to southern Europe, where, by the seventh century, Christians were celebrating All Saints' Day (also known as All Hallows Eve), in honour of all saints and martyrs without their own saint's days. This was followed by All Souls' Day, when people would pray to speed their deceased relatives' passage through purgatory. To gain acceptance for Christian teachings, Pope Gregory IV set the date of All Souls' Day to coincide with the Celtic pagan festival, encouraging an early synthesis of pagan and Christian traditions.

Spanish military conquest went hand in hand with religious dominion, and the clash of cultures was devastating, forcing pragmatic priests to seek only a partial conversion. Heathen Aztec practices were tolerated as long as they could be subsumed into the new religion and their gods made to conform to the Catholic pantheon of saints. Their indigenous celebrations of the dead fitted neatly with European All Saints' and All Souls' days, and so Miccailhuitolntli and Hueymiccaihuitl were shifted a couple of months back to November – a pseudo-Christian Halloween that became inextricably entwined with Aztec spirituality, and quickly took on a uniquely Mexican identity.

Many of Mexico's fiestas are raucous occasions – anything from a religious procession with music and chanting to all-out street-warfare with rotten fruit, and usually with a good deal of tequila-fuelled carousing. But the Day of the Dead is principally a **family affair**, with the rites enacted in the home and in the cemetery. Open doorways – left ajar in case the spirits should lose their way – reveal dimly-lit front rooms where photos of a deceased husband or daughter reflect the candlelight from makeshift altars, and extend a welcome to neighbours who often pop in to help add the final touches to the fireside

altar. Built from plywood (or perhaps an old beer crate), they're always beautifully turned out: decorated with flowers and laden with gifts – typically food in clay pots. It may be just a few snacks, or a complete meal of chicken in spicy chocolate sauce accompanied by a stack of tortillas, with hunks of pumpkin boiled in brown sugar syrup. But there will always be *Pan de Muerto* (Bread of the Dead), a sweet dough shaped into human forms known as *ánimas* (souls). Meanwhile, at the local cemetery, mausoleum-style graves get gussied up and old men in overalls go around daubing their ancestral plot with blue or white paint. Paths are weeded and everything is draped in flowers. Anything bright and blowsy will do, but marigolds – the Aztec flower offering for the dead, known as *zempasuchitl* – work best.

On the days leading up to the Day of the Dead, marigold petals pave the streets in a kind of paperchase from people's houses to the cemeteries, and market stalls all over Mexico groan with ghoulish reminders of mortality, many of them edible. Everywhere, you'll see the painted sugar-candy skulls – traditionally seen as a symbol of life rather than death – often ranked in metre-high pyramids ready to be hauled off to decorate the home altar, alongside skeletons (*calaveras*; see box opposite) made of cardboard, clay or, most often, papier-mâché; dressed like the deceased – musicians, brides, lawyers, even beer-swilling *borachos*, or drunks – they're a kind of *danse macabre* with a wry twist of Mexican black humour.

Where to go

All of Mexico celebrates the Day of the Dead, but ardent festival hounds will want to make a special journey to one of the towns and villages famed for the authenticity of their events. Most of these are in the southern half of the country, where the indigenous culture is strongest; however, if you're planning on being in one of the more popular towns, you might want to get there a day or two beforehand to soak up the atmosphere before the hordes arrive, and to secure a hotel room. Many of the smaller places are tiny villages that will be hard to find on small-scale maps, but asking in the nearest large town should set you on the right track.

Around Mexico City, otherwise known as Distrito Federal, or DF for short, the suburbs of San Lucas Xochimanca (DF) and Nativitas (DF) are particularly popular, as is the small town of Mixquic (DF), 20km southeast of Mexico City,

which is known as "The City of the Dead" for its funereal procession that calls at shrines to the dead around town. East towards the Caribbean coast, there are colourful festivities at Naolinco (Veracruz), 90km northwest of Veracruz city, and, further south, San Gabriel Chilac (Puebla), near Tehuacán.

Perhaps the most fruitful hunting ground of all is the city of **Oaxaca**, in the south, where the concentration of events enables you to experience the widest range of Day of the Dead proceedings in a single visit. Here, the local council organizes activities (including a "Best Altar" competition) at the San Miguel cemetery, and there are even commercial tours around the top sites: check times and dates with the tourist office (see p.200). Tours include trips to Xoxocotlán, on October 31, and, later that same evening, Santa María Atzomp. The next

painted sugar-candy skulls are often ranked in metre-high pyramids

day, there are activities around the city, especially at San Miguel cemetery, and on the afternoon of November 2, people flock to San Antonino and, subsequently, San Felipe del Agua. Another place in the area worth checking out is the tiny village of Nopala (Oaxaca), up in the mountains, where the celebrations are as authentic as anything you'll find in Mexico.

If you're in the north, head to the central interior, where some of the country's most alluring Day of the Dead festivities take place in lakeside **Pátzcuaro** (Michoacán), 250km west of Mexico City. Here, the main activity centres on Lago de Pátzcuaro, and particularly its small island, Isla Janitzio, where, on the late evening of November 1, an incredible flotilla of flower-festooned canoes, paddled by local Purépecha, converge on the island, each with a candle burning on its prow. One of the highlights of the country's Day of the Dead celebrations, this marks the beginning of an all-night vigil with hypnotic chanting and traditional dances.

Lastly, along the **Pacific Coast** make a bee-line for the small village of Atoyac de Álvarez (Guerrero), 60km west of Acapulco, scene of particularly colourful celebrations.

Skeletons

The papier-mâché skeletons that dominate street stalls during the Day of the Dead have evolved into an art form of their own, thanks in no small part to nineteenth-century engraver **José Guadalupe Posada**, whose most famous cartoons all depict the main characters as skeletons. Muralist **Diego Rivera** picked up the reins a few decades later, using Posada's La Calavera Catrina as the central character in his monumental mural *Dream of a Sunday Afternoon in Alameda Park* in Mexico City – images you'll see recycled over and over again throughout the country during the Day of the Dead.

Basics

Most flights to Mexico land at the **airport** in Mexico City; Oaxaca and Pátzcuaro are within easy reach of the capital. Mexico is a large country and distances can be daunting, but the **bus system** is tremendous, with services to just about every village – though obviously less frequent (and less comfortable) the more remote you get. There are **tourist offices** in both Oaxaca (Palacio Municipal; daily 8am–8pm; ☏ 951/516-0123) and Pátzcuaro (Plaza Vasco de Quiroga (Mon–Sat 9am–2pm & 4–8pm, Sun 9am–2pm; ☏ 434/342-1214).

Accommodation

Mexicans travel to be with their family during the Day of the Dead – if people can only visit their family once a year, this will be the time. Consequently hotels can fill up quickly, even in Mexico City, particularly when local demand is coupled with an influx of tourists, so it's best to book accommodation as far in advance as you can.

The wave of backpacker hostels sweeping through Mexico has hit **Oaxaca**, one of the best being *Hostal Paulina*, Trujano 321 (☏ 951/516-2005, ⊛ www.paulinahostel.com; dorm US$11, double room US$27). For something smarter, try *Casa de la Bugambilias*, Reforma 402 (☏ 951/516-1165, ⊛ www.mexonline.com/bugambil.htm; US$75–85), where you can participate in the owner's Day of the Dead celebrations.

In **Pátzcuaro**, budget options cluster around the Plaza Bocanegra, and have the advantage of being very close to bus stops for the lake. The *Concordia* at the southeast end of the plaza (☏ 434/342-0003; US$30–40 for a double) is a good modest place; or there's the more expensive *Fiesta Plaza* (☏ 434/342-2515; US$60-80 for a double), on the north side of the plaza. Both are fairly large so might have spaces left if you haven't booked ahead.

Eating and drinking

For Mexicans, **eating** on the Day of the Dead revolves around family meals, tucking into *tamales* or some of the specialities, especially bread, mentioned earlier. Restaurants stay open throughout, with the typical range of Mexican dishes, usually simpler and less rich variations on what you might expect at your local Mexican restaurant back home. And of course there's plenty to **drink** – beer, tequila – more or less anything is consumed in honour of the dead.

Event info

Day of the Dead (⊛ www.go2mexico.com/article/dayofdead). Cultural background and rituals of Day of the Dead.

Useful websites

Mexico Online (⊛ www.mexonline.com). Lots of good, and frequently updated content.
Mexico Tourist Board (⊛ www.visitmexico.com). Official tourist-board site that makes a pretty useful starting point.

Time zone GMT-6　　　　**Country code** +52　　　　**Currency** Mexican peso ($)

Fantasy Fest

One of the wildest fancy-dress free-for-alls on earth

Fantasy Fest

Where?
Key West, Florida, USA

When?
From the penultimate Friday to the last Sunday in October

How long?
10 days

USA

Key West

At the end of October, Key West, the last in the string of islands that stretches south from Florida, plays host to one of the wildest fancy-dress free-for-alls on earth. Fantasy Fest is a music- and rum-fuelled party marathon that reaches its zenith with a massive themed costumed parade – something along the lines of "Fright Night on Bone Island" and "Delirious Dreams and Hilarious Screams" if past years are anything to go by. It's a camp affair all right, but is by no means limited to gays and lesbians – organizers estimate that half of the attendees are straight, and as Key West grows more and more wealthy, its once predominantly gay atmosphere is becoming more inclusive by the year. Still, the open, let-it-all-hang-out vibes are endlessly cruisey for everyone, whatever your sexual orientation, and the mood so exuberant, so candid, that it's hard not to get drawn in.

Key West is a tiny, rather remote place, and most things happen in the Old Town, in the well-named **Fantasy Zone**, which stretches along Duval Street from Front to South streets and across the intersecting roads to Simonton and Whitehead. There's a well-publicized official programme of events, these days heavily sponsored and fairly slickly organized, but there are also plenty of impromptu goings-on all the time, and whenever Halloween falls just after the grand finale weekend, the festivities continue on beyond the allotted ten days.

The build-up

The proceedings kick off at the **Goombay Celebration** (noon to midnight throughout the festival) in Bahama Village on Petronia Street, with Caribbean sights, tastes, sounds and entertainment. However, the Fest only really gets going after the coronation of the Fantasy Fest King and Queen on the Friday night, and things hot up as the week goes on. On Tuesday, there's the **Headdress Ball**, featuring toppers of every imaginable description, some up to ten feet high. Wednesday sees the outrageous **Beach Party** at the *Hog's Breath Saloon*, with its infamous home-made-bikini contest, as well as the **Pet Masquerade and Parade**, featuring cross-dressing animals and their look-alike owners. Head for the fancy-dress party at the *Green Parrot Bar* on Thursday evening, where you can get your arse painted (amongst other things) at the body-painting competition. Also on Thursday, check out – or enter – the Fest's most flamboyant costume competition, **Pretenders in Paradise**, boasting designers from across the nation, and thousands of dollars in cash prizes. There's also the notorious **Toga Party** at *Sloppy Joe's Bar*, where you'll see some of the skimpiest togas ever worn and witness the presiding Roman Emperor order his amply proportioned female entourage to strip anyone not sporting traditional dress. On Friday, the **Caribbean Street Fair** bursts onto the scene, transmogrifying Duval Street into a tropical marketplace, with feathered masks and tons of frivolous exotica on offer, along with spicy edibles and cooling libations. Just before sunset on Friday, the **Fairvilla Megastore Masquerade March** winds its way through the Fair, with the emphasis on – what else? – fantasy.

> **Insider info** If all the accommodation in Key West is booked up, you can stay in Miami, from where Party Tours' Fantasy Fest bus leaves at 9am on the day of the main parade, returning at 1am (☎ 305/553-2099; $80).

History

Key West was a rather run-down and cheap backwater in the 1970s that was quick to welcome the influx of hippies and gays that hit the town at the start of the decade – outcast groups who swiftly established themselves in this traditionally live-and-let-live haven. The hippie flavour faded for the most part, but the hedonism didn't, and gays and lesbians stayed on and soon made Key West their own. In 1979, a group of imaginative islanders came up with the idea of an **autumn celebration**, mostly as a ploy to drum up business during the rather dead season between late subtropical summer and Christmas. Halloween was a natural excuse for what started as a two-day bash but soon grew to ten days of all-out bacchanal. The **climate** is an essential part of the mix, and the Fest takes place after the hurricane season has (just about) ended, when the temperatures reach about 80°F and there are balmy gulf breezes and clear skies. Only in 2005 have storms disrupted the schedules somewhat, when Hurricane Wilma roared through town, but usually the weather is about as perfect as you could wish for.

The Captain Morgan Fantasy Fest Parade

The climax of Fantasy Fest, the **Captain Morgan Fantasy Fest Parade** begins at around 7pm on Saturday, at the junction of Southard and Whitehead streets, and heads north towards the Gulf of Mexico, along Front Street, before trailing all the way down the town's main drag, Duval Street, to the Atlantic side of the island. A crowd of up to seventy thousand revellers of all ages show up to watch this procession of brilliant bands, outlandish dancing groups and, of course, dazzling floats – some blaring music or breathing "fire", some sporting elaborately realized pink elephants and other creatures of fantasy. Caribbean marching bands and dance groups, decked out in feathers and eye-popping colours, along with costumed walkers, complete the parade line-up. The main activity of parade participants is the tossing of beads – the Fantasy

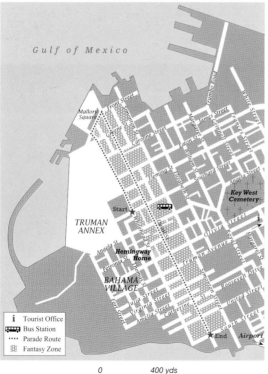

Wednesday's Pet Masquerade and Parade features cross-dressing animals and their look-alike owners

Fest "currency" – to the spirited, eager crowds lining the parade route. The fever to acquire these beads grips everyone; some will do whatever it takes to get their share, flashing the necessary parts of their anatomy to get a string of shiny glass. You can just buy the beads, but somehow it's not quite the same.

As with all great festivals, you can't help yourself from joining in with the madness, and soon you'll be jiving along with the bands, swapping drinks with your new best friends, and generally having the time of your life. The partying stays on the streets virtually throughout the night, and the bars are packed to the rafters with some of the most bizarrely dressed, or undressed, individuals you will ever come across.

The morning after

There's plenty to do once the final parade's passed by. **Snorkelling** and **diving** trips are on offer from a number of dive shops – try Captain Corner's, 125 Ann St (☏305/296-8865), Seabreeze Reef Raiders, 617 Front St (☏305/292-7745), or Southpoint Divers, 714 Duval St (☏800-891-DIVE). If the sybaritic overload of Fantasy Fest has left you feeling the need for some culture, pay a visit to Key West's biggest tourist draw, the **Ernest Hemingway Home and Museum**, at 907 Whitehead St (daily 9am–5pm; ☏305/294-1136; $10).

Best of the bars

Bull & Whistle Bar 224 Duval St. Loud and rowdy, featuring the best of the local musicians each night, and special events during Fantasy Fest.
Garden of Eden Cnr of Caroline and Duval sts. If baring it all is your thing and you don't want to risk a fine, check out the clothing-optional roof-garden bar.
Green Parrot Bar 601 Whitehead St. Enjoys a reputation for being laid-back and iconoclastic, and is a great hangout for chatting up locals. Top live bands, too.
Hog's Breath Saloon 400 Front St. Lots of heavy drinking, and their own popular Fest programmes, including the legendary Beach Party.
Sloppy Joe's 201 Duval St. Right in the midst of Fantasy Fest madness, with live music nightly.

Gay bars
Exclusively gay venues host some of the hardest partying in town – worth a visit whether you're gay or straight.
Aqua 711 Duval St. Great "Reality is a Drag" show (Tues–Sat), and karaoke every night, if you feel like getting in on the act.
Bourbon Street Pub 724 Duval St. Home of G-string-clad model boys dancing for dollars.
Eight-O-One Bar 801 Duval St. Zany drag shows upstairs, heavy cruising downstairs.

Basics

The local **airport** is four miles east of the Old Town, on South Roosevelt Boulevard. Given its small size, Key West is easily explored on **foot** or by **bike** – you can hire bikes from Adventure Scooter and Bicycle Rentals at 1910 North Roosevelt Bld (☎800/742-2044).

Accommodation

Unless you reserve months ahead, getting a room at all will be impossible, and, in any case, **accommodation** at Fantasy Fest is very expensive, running easily to $300 a night, with a three- or sometimes five-night minimum stay. Some of the best options in Key West are the guesthouses lined up along the Duval Street axis, just a few minutes' walk from the fun and games. For location, charm and comfort, *Duval House*, 815 Duval St (☎800/223-8825, ⍟www.duvalhousekeywest.com), is one of the top Fantasy Fest choices. An excellent alternative is *The Blue Parrot Inn* at 916 Elizabeth St (☎800/231-BIRD, ⍟blueparrotinn.com), a beautiful house built in 1884, with lush gardens. *La-Te-Da Hotel and Bar*, 1125 Duval St (☎877/528-3320; ⍟www.lateda.com), is a wonderful resort-within-a-resort, towards the south end of Duval. Another excellent choice, with a pool, and an array of accommodation options, all near the beach, is the *Southernmost Hotel*, 1319 Duval St (☎800/354-4455), which has a tropical atmosphere, and is a ten-minute walk from the heart of the Fest.

If you're after somewhere **exclusively gay** and male, *Island House*, 1129 Fleming St (☎800/890-6284, ⍟www.islandhousekeywest.com), is the perfect choice. This renovated Victorian mansion is a clothing-optional resort, with great pools, gym and spa facilities – and it's in a very private, peaceful location. *Pearl's Rainbow*, 525 United St (☎800-749-6696, ⍟www.pearlsrainbow.com), is a former cigar factory and Key West's sole **lesbian-only** establishment.

A cheaper option is reserving a place (for about $150 a night) at Marathon Key, one hour up the coast, on the eastern end of the Seven-Mile Bridge, from where there's a special shuttle to the festivities.

The Flamingo Inn, MM59 at Grassy Key (☎305/289-1478, ⍟www.theflamingoinn.com) and *Seaward Resort Motel*, 8700 Overseas Hwy (☎305/743-5711), are comfortable, reasonably priced options, and both have pools. Parking lots on Key West aren't expensive (about $10 for 24hr) and are within easy walking distance of all the action.

Eating and drinking

Good restaurants and bars abound in Key West, but in many of them you can run up sizeable tabs. In any case, most of the time you'll be **eating** on the street, at the stalls on the side streets just off Duval Street, which offer great barbecued chicken, ribs and beer. For something quick and cheap, try local favourite Five Brothers Grocery, at the intersection of Southard and Grinnell streets, which serves up strong Cuban coffee and cheap sandwiches. *El Siboney*, 900 Catherine St, also specializes in traditional Cuban cuisine. *Duffy's Steak & Lobster House*, 1007 Simonton St, is another top choice, with good food at nice prices, while *BO's Fish Wagon*, 801 Caroline St, is a cheap seafood option, offering great fish 'n chips and conch fritters.

Event info

Fantasy Fest (⍟www.fantasyfest.net). Official all-singing, all-dancing site providing details on the theme of the year; also has photos, a live webcam, and an event schedule.

Useful websites

Key West Information Center 1601 North Roosevelt Boulevard (☎888/222-5148, ⍟www.keywestinfo.com). Local information, accommodation listings and other useful details.
Florida Keys (☎800/FLA-KEYS, ⍟www.fla-keys.com). Official tourist-board site, with information on the whole region.

Time zone GMT-5   **Country code** +1   **Currency** US dollar ($)

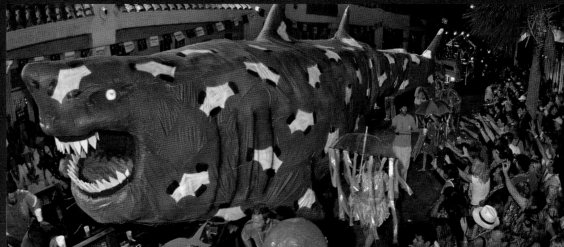

Fiesta de Merengue

*The ultimate rum-drenched
tropical blast-out*

Fiesta de Merengue

Where?
Santo Domingo,
Dominican Republic

When?
Last week of July

How long?
1 week

DOMINICAN REPUBLIC

Santo
Domingo

For one week every summer since 1967, the three-million-plus denizens of Santo Domingo have converged on the Malecón, a seven-kilometre strand of palm-lined Caribbean boulevard that runs along the southern side of the Zona Colonial, for the Dominican Republic's biggest event of the year. The Fiesta de Merengue is the ultimate rum-drenched tropical blast-out, with twenty different bandstands belting out live music from Dominican stars past, present and future – including the city's former mayor, hip-swivelling singing legend Johnny Ventura. The atmosphere and location are unbeatable – an expansive ribbon of turquoise sea stretches out into the distance, and headline acts such as Juan Luis Guerra, Toño Rosario and Los Toros Band play under the spectacular limestone palace of Christopher Columbus and the ruins of the walled city he built five centuries ago.

History

Banned during the nineteenth century as "a cause of depravity among the people of this island who perform it, and a scandalous sight to all who view it", the Fiesta de Merengue has matured into a Dominican national obsession, and the music has lost none of its essential raunchiness – a hard-driving, hyped-up dance music whose signature rhythmic pattern is a relentless on-the-beat thump. The standard **merengue rhythm section** is made up of a lap drum called the *tambora*, a metal scraper, and a thrumming metal box known as the African thumb piano, and produces a music that's as rhythmically nuanced as the most complex Latin pop but extremely easy to dance to.

All the indications are that merengue itself grew out of **religious music** that originated in west and southern Africa, and was brought over by the hundreds of thousands of slaves that worked the sugar plantations both here and on the other side of the island, in what is now Haiti. If you head out into the far northern suburbs during one of the country's many religious festivals, you can still hear the traditional music of *vodù dominicana*, called *palos*. Even in its original religious context of call-and-response choruses backed up by a series of enormous drums carved whole from hollowed-out tree trunks, this is serious party music. Over the centuries, the music of merengue has moved away from its religious roots. However, it was still regarded as suspect by the Europe-leaning elite in Santo Domingo, at least until the era of notorious Dominican dictator Rafael Trujillo, who really loved merengue, and had a top-notch band following him around on campaign stops and state-radio stations blasting out favourite tunes between edicts. Trujillo was also partially responsible for the development of a more stately form of the dance, called "**ballroom merengue**".

The Fiesta de Merengue is a time for street dancing, swinging in hotel ballrooms and terraces, and partying on the beaches throughout balmy Caribbean summer nights. It's an overwhelming experience travelling the length of the **Malecón**, at Avenida Máximo Gómez, a never-ending labyrinth of jam-packed venues blaring high-octane Latin hits that stretches from one end of the city's coast to the other, leading the *Guinness Book of World Records* to dub it the "world's largest disco". Another main area of activity is at the atmospheric colonial-era Puerta San Diego, at the far eastern end of the same seaside boardwalk, where bands gather, competing for the partygoers' attention. All along the seafront, though, you'll find amateur DJs setting up sound systems, and the major beer and rum companies selling their wares beneath. The dance fever is

intense: the thumb piano has been ditched in favour of electric bass, synthesizers and strong, salsa-influenced horn sections stuttering pyrotechnic riffs, as the singers engage in wickedly quick dance routines, and scantily clad back-up vocalists strut their stuff as the wall-to-wall crowds go berserk.

As always at such events, the **crowd** is more than half the fun. Phalanxes of drunken youths bump up against white-haired old folks cutting quick, graceful moves across the asphalt; beaming teenage girls in formal, powder-pink dresses converge at the fringes

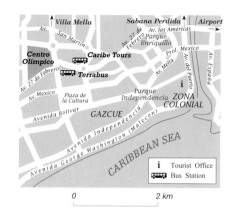

the Malecón is a never-ending labyrinth of jam-packed venues blaring high-octane Latin hits and giggle in rhythm as they bob up and down; candy-striped vendors weave through the masses hawking everything from sugar cane and boiled corn to condoms and Clorets; former Mayor Johnny Ventura – a legendary merengue singer himself – ploughs across the promenade at midnight in a horse-drawn carriage, shaking his thing in a tailored three-piece suit as he waves to his fans. Local politicians get in on the act, too, as pickup trucks driven by blatantly tipsy party members slowly cruise the major city streets, blaring out merengue jingos full of political slogans as they go.

Juan Luis Guerra

Cuban son

If you start longing for a little variety from the non-stop outdoor festivities, it's worth checking out that other great Santo Domingo musical tradition, **Cuban son**; Dominicans in the capital have been playing *son* for a couple of centuries, and some even claim it was born here.

A number of local **clubs** specialize in *son*, none of them much frequented by tourists. For unmatchable opulence, try the *Mauna Loa* at Calle Héroes de Luperón on the Malecón (☎533-2151), a super-suave Art Deco-style nightclub straight out of the Roaring Twenties, featuring nightly shows with legendary old-timers Francisco Santana and Antony Ríos. A more down-home experience can be had at *Vieja Havana*, on Avenida Máximo Gómez in Villa Mella, a no-frills outdoor dancehall that features eye-popping dance contests on Thursday and Sunday nights. Or try *Monumento del Son* on Avenida Charles de Gaulle in Sabana Perdida (☎590-3666), at the far eastern end of town, which has a steady stream of top local acts and a lot of great corny old vaudeville touches, such as a ventriloquist MC.

Basics

The **airport** is 13km east of Santo Domingo. The city's **public transport system** is informal to say the least, but it works and you can get anywhere in Santo Domingo either by *carros públicos* (shared private cars) or *guaguas* (privately operated vans) – just don't expect a timetable or designated stops. To get where you want, stand on the corner of a main street, wave animatedly at the first car or van you see with a taxi sign, state your destination, and then smile and nod politely as you squeeze in with the passengers already on board. Private **taxis** are largely booked up during the Fiesta de Merengue, so you'll need to order one at least an hour in advance; try Apolo (☎ 537-0000) or Tropical (☎ 540-4446).

Accommodation

There's no shortage of **hotels** in Santo Domingo; even around festival time you should have little problem finding somewhere to bed down for the week. Those wanting to be as close as possible to the action can opt for the affable *Napolitano* at Malecón 51 (☎ 687-1131; $30–40 for a double room). If you want to go to sleep before 3am, though, you're best off heading further inland to the residential Gazcue district and its clutch of low-budget *pensiones*, including the somewhat overbilled *La Grand Mansión* at Danae 26 (☎ 689-8758; $12–18 for a double). If the sky's the limit, crash out amid the relative splendour of a pricey seafront high-rise such as the *Melia Santo Domingo*, Malecón 365 (☎ 688-8531; $140–200), where you can watch the festivities from on high.

Eating and drinking

The **food** carts hawking meals along the Malecón encompass a wide variety of cheap, indeterminate meats. Instead, you may want to load up at *Charlie's*, Llúberes 9, just north of the Malecón, an unpretentious spot specializing in large portions of grilled pork chops, chicken, steak and rabbit. For all-night eating, *El Provocón*, set in a large open courtyard at Santiago and Cervantes, serves delicious grilled chicken and rice 24 hours a day. For the best seafood, head to nearby *La Mezquita*, at Independencia 407, an outstanding restaurant with a cosy dining room, a loyal local following, and an out-of-this-world Creole sea bass.

There are several different brands of Dominican **beer** on sale from mobile carts all along the Malecón; the most popular and by far the best is *Presidente*, which comes in both regular and surreally huge bottles. Dominicans are obsessed with getting it as cold as possible – if you don't want it to turn into a block of ice when you open it, rub your hand under the bottom of the bottle before popping the cap. Also available in thumb-sized plastic cups are the good, inexpensive local **rums** – *Brugal*, *Barceló* and *Bermúdez*. Of these, the last is the best, but the dark, aged versions made by all three are pretty good. If you sit down at one of the many outdoor bars along the north end of the street, ask for a *Cuba libre servicio* – a bottle of rum, two Cokes and a bucket of ice. Keep an eye out also for a potent local concoction called *Mama Juana*, a tough-on-the-stomach cloudy brew made from local wines, rum, honey and the leaves and bark of various indigenous shrubs – locals claim that it prolongs both sexual potency and lifespan. After hearing them go on (and on) about its miraculous properties, you may want to try it at least once. Traditionally, it's supposed to be buried underground for three months and laid out in the sun for another three, so it's best to proceed with caution.

Useful websites

Santo Domingo Tourist Office Isabela 103, Santo Domingo (☎ 686-3858 ext. 1321).

809K (🌐 www.809k.com). Spanish-language nightlife-listings site for Santo Domingo, with info on all festival-related events as well as local raves and "open bars", where you pay an entry fee then dance and drink as much as you like.

Dominican Republic One (🌐 www.dr1.com). Rather formal site giving general info on the Dominican Republic – news, business, events.

Time zone GMT-4   **Country code** +1 809   **Currency** Dominican peso (RD$)

Halloween

Put on a costume and take to the streets

Halloween

Where?
New York City, New York, USA

When?
October 31

How long?
1 day

USA
New York City

Halloween is a big event in America, and nowhere more so than in New York, where a massive parade takes over much of downtown Manhattan – from the bottom of SoHo to the top of Chelsea – making it the biggest Halloween celebration on the planet and the only major night parade in the US. It's a totally over-the-top, costumed street party, at which it's impossible not to have a good time. Like its counterpart in San Francisco, New York's Halloween has become something of a gay event in recent years, although everyone, gay or straight, young or old, uses it as the last pre-winter excuse to go nuts in the streets while wearing just about anything from a Frankenstein mask to a clingfilm wrap bridal gown – maybe at the same time.

History

Halloween **started** as a pagan festival, when Irish Celts tried to ward off evil spirits with noisy processions and ghoulish costumes, but it was America that made it into a national institution. Across the USA, there are few kids of any cultural background that haven't slipped on some kind of crazy garb on October 31 in an effort to score some candy. What makes New York special is that the majority of "kids" dressing up in the streets have day jobs, and most of them are after another kind of treat.

The other unique feature of New York's Halloween is that it's centred on a puppet parade, a tradition that couldn't have more wholesome roots. On October 31, 1973, a puppeteer named Ralph Lee went from house to house in Greenwich Village, putting on his puppet show for the neighbourhood kids. Today, both the crowds and the puppets have grown substantially in size, but the event is still basically run by one person and relies entirely on the participation of volunteers. Jeanne Fleming took over Ralph Lee's role as parade director in 1982, and still spends most of the year coordinating the activities of more than a hundred volunteers, who design and assemble the parade's oversized papier-mâché monsters.

In 2001, the Halloween Parade was the first major event in New York City to take place after the tragic events of **September 11**, with the theme that year being "Phoenix Rising" and the star puppet a new-born bird rising out of the city's ashes. In 2005, the phoenix rose out of the waters that swamped New Orleans in the wake of **Hurricane Katrina** and was carried by evacuees from the sunken city living in New York, once again reinforcing the annual event's ability to unite and inspire.

Insider info Halloween has been broadcast live on television every year since 2000, and it can now be seen on the NY1 channel.

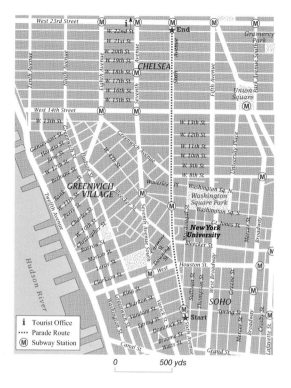

The Halloween Parade runs up **Sixth Avenue** from just south of Spring Street in SoHo to 23rd Street in Chelsea. Nearly two million spectators descend on downtown Manhattan to check out the costumed paraders each year, so getting an unobstructed kerbside spot from which to view proceedings requires getting there well before the starting time of 7pm – try two hours earlier and you might be OK. It's worth it, though, as there's nothing to beat the views of the tremendous skeletal puppets that loom overhead against the black sky, pointing their bony, foot-long fingers towards the crowd. The parade usually runs about two to three hours from start to finish; if you stay in one spot, you can see the whole thing pass in around an hour. After the parade is over, the more serious revellers show off their costumes along **Christopher Street** in Greenwich Village, which is usually blocked off completely into the early hours; if you plan to join them, try to catch the parade in the nearby vicinity, ideally between 14th Street and Bleecker Street.

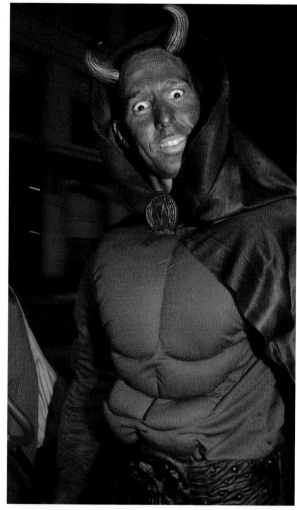

Superior Concept Monsters

Over the years, the huge papier-mâché creatures – or **"Superior Concept Monsters"**, as the group that designs the parade's largest and most original puppets call them – have grown to become the size of buildings, requiring nearly a thousand people in total to manipulate. Known as "sweepers" for their rapid, broad movements, these massive, sculpted creatures are constructed on steel-rod skeletons, and symbolically "sweep the negative energy from the streets" for the year to come.

Watching the parade is all very well, but if you're really going to do Halloween in New York, you need to **put on a costume** and take to the streets. This is community theatre on a grand scale, with tens of thousands of participants, and if you want to understand what it's all about, you've really got to get involved. You could opt for the classic scary – witches, vampires, etc – and non-scary – French maid, King Arthur, Winnie the Pooh – look, or dress up as an "overnight wonder" from popular recent movies or current events, such as Kenny from South Park (big orange Eskimo Parka, mumbled speech) and Michael Moore (pillow gut under shirt, beard, cap, camera always rolling). You could go down the conceptual-costume route (don a pig-nose mask and wave a Canadian flag and you're Canadian Bacon) or raise the outfit ante with a really scary number, the kind that's done so convincingly that no one's even sure it's a costume at all. And then there's always the option of going in drag – scary in a whole other way and not really a costume for some. But whatever you choose to go as, go the whole hog, and remember that, above all, it's the costume that will determine what sort of night you have – and who you end up spending it with.

skeletal puppets loom overhead against the black sky, pointing their bony, foot-long fingers towards the crowd

Halloween in San Francisco

Given the way that Halloween has developed in recent years, it's not surprising that it's also a big deal in **San Francisco**, the gay capital of America. Second only to Pride in the city's gay and lesbian festival calendar, Halloween is a more sanitized – and organized – affair than it used to be, when it took over San Francisco's original gay village of the Castro in a riot of singing, dancing and parading drag queens. It became so popular, however, that it could no longer be contained in the Castro's crowded streets, and the city authorities decided to relocate it to the more self-contained area of Civic Center, closer to downtown San Francisco. Here, it's inevitably as much an event for tourists as for San Fran's gay revellers, but it's still a riotous affair, well worth attending even if you're not gay. If you are, though, you may well want to continue the party later on back in the Castro.

For more information, contact the San Francisco Visitor Information Center, 900 Market St (☎415/391-2000, ☻www.sfvisitor.org).

Basics

New York has three **airports**: JFK out in Queens, and Newark across the Hudson in New Jersey, are served by both international and domestic flights; and La Guardia in Queens is domestic only. Once in the city, New York is easy to get around – the **subway** and **bus network** works well, operates all night, and is relatively cheap (one-way ride $2, unlimited daily pass $7) and easy to use. For short distances, the omnipresent **taxis** are relatively affordable.

Accommodation

A few budget **accommodation** options near the parade route are the *Chelsea International Hostel*, 251 West 20th St (☎ 212/647-0010, ⓦ www.chelseahostel.com), which couldn't be more conveniently located, and charges just $28 for a bed and $70 for a private room; and the *Chelsea Pines Inn*, 317 West 14th St (☎ 212/929-1023, ⓦ www.chelseapinesinn.org), a gay hotel with double rooms ranging from $139 to $219. Expect both of these places to be sold out almost a year in advance for Halloween night, though. Otherwise, try *Colby International* (ⓦ www.colbyintl.com), an agent who rents out good-value bed-and-breakfast rooms and apartments all over Manhattan; the *Washington Square Hotel*, 103 Waverly Place (☎ 212/777-9515, ⓦ www.wshotel.com), perhaps Greenwich Village's best-value alternative at upwards of $160 for a double; or, with a lot more money, the *W New York* at Union Square, 201 Park Avenue South (☎ 888/625-5144, ⓦ www.whotels.com).

Eating and drinking

New York City offers the most diverse selection of cuisine on the planet, and the Halloween Parade cuts through three of the city's best eating neighbourhoods – SoHo, Greenwich Village and Chelsea. The problem is that it's almost impossible to get around in these areas while the parade is on, and in any case you probably won't want to be tied down by reservations or time-consuming formal dining on a night as crazy as this. Your best bet for food is to grab a slice of real New York pizza along the route. *Ray's* – the best pizza joint in the city – happens to be smack in the centre of the action on the northwest corner of Sixth Avenue and 11th Street: despite the claims of other *Ray's* pizza parlours around town, this one is the true original, serving up fat slices dripping with real mozzarella. Across the street, on the southwest corner of the same intersection, is *Sammy's Noodle Shop*, home to some of the freshest Chinese food in town. *Cucina Stagionale*, 289 Bleecker St, serves great Italian food at unbelievable prices, and the equally inexpensive *Benny's Burritos*, 113 Greenwich Ave, has huge portions of NY-Mex food, and good margaritas. There's a *Benny's-to-Go* right across the street from the dine-in restaurant if you prefer to stuff your face as you watch the parade pass.

New York's **club** scene changes faster than some people change their underwear, so any guess as to what's going to be hot next season – gay or straight – is futile. If you want to dive deeply into the club scene, check out either the *Village Voice* or *Time Out New York*. In any case, Halloween in New York is all about taking to the street. Any of the **bars** that line the parade route will be packed with people who've come for the event, regardless of the venue's usual clientele. If you find that you need a drink, just poke your head into a few of the joints along the way or, for some respite from the insanity of the streets, you could sneak into the *Chelsea Commons*, 242 10th Ave, and warm yourself in front of their cosy fireplace. Or drop by *Chumley's*, 86 Bedford St, the legendary pub where James Joyce is said to have dotted the i's on his *Ulysses* manuscript. For another cocktail with a history chaser, be sure to visit *Stonewall*, at 53 Christopher St on Sheridan Square, for a glimpse of the place where the Stonewall riots kicked off the Gay Rights Movement. Still on the gay front, across the street is the *Monster*, while *Marie's Crisis* is a cosy forgotten-in-time cabaret/piano bar, just around the corner at 59 Grove St.

Event info

Halloween (ⓦ www.halloween-nyc.com). Loads of great photos, and info on the event.
NYC & Company Visitor Information Center, 810 7th Ave, between 52nd and 53rd streets (☎ 212/484-1222, ⓦ www.nycvisit.com).

Time zone GMT-5   **Country code** +1   **Currency** US dollar ($)

Junkanoo

The first cowbells are heard around 2am.
Everyone swigs from bottles of rum, and
fireworks crackle in the sky. It's Junkanoo.

Junkanoo

Where?
Nassau, New Providence Island, The Bahamas

When?
Early hours of December 26 and again on New Year's Day

How long?
Two all-night parties, a week apart

Nassau

BAHAMAS

The Bahamas' most important and spectacular party, Junkanoo is a blast to the senses. Parades flood the streets of Nassau in a whirling, reeling mass of singing and dancing chaos, as competing groups or "crews" rush out to meet the dawn, moving toward one another from all directions rather than following each other in the semi-organized fashion of the modern parade. Various groups and societies compete to be the biggest and loudest floats, which means you'll see stilt-dancers, clowns, acrobats, go-go girls, goatskin-drum players, and conch and cowbell ringers, all blaring out their tunes in an awesome celebration of life that can only have originated in the Caribbean.

You can attend one of the smaller Junkanoo celebrations on the islands of Grand Bahama, Bimini, Green Turtle Cay in the Abacos, or Eleuthera, but Junkanoo in **Nassau**, on New Providence Island, is the granddaddy of them all, a truly once-in-a-lifetime celebration not to be missed. On each side of Bay Street in downtown Nassau bleacher-type seating is constructed – you can try to get tickets ($5–100) for these through the Junkanoo ticket agency (see p.224) or the Ministry of Tourism in Nassau (☎302-2000), though most are sold to local VIPs – but it's far more fun to be free to whoop it up with the rest of the revellers. Bring a bottle of rum or two to keep warm in the chilly night air, and perhaps an umbrella if rain threatens (as it often does at this time of year), and prepare to participate.

The parades

The first parade takes place in the early hours of December 26, starting off from the *British Colonial Hilton Hotel* at around 2am – weather and crews permitting (check Channel 13 ZNS for updates) – when upwards of forty thousand people assemble on Nassau's historic **Bay Street** to witness the first Junkanoo crew pass by. The distant beats of Goombay drums indicate that the paraders are shifting into formation, and is your cue to get yourself down there

Insider info

For an overview of the history of Junkanoo, head to Educulture at 31 West Street North (Mon–Fri 9am–5pm, Sat & Sun by appointment only; $5; ☎328-3786, ℮educulture@coralwave. com), a community-run museum that displays some of the more elaborate costumes from past parades and holds Junkanoo workshops – including a hands-on session in costume construction – which can be arranged for groups of two or more if you call in advance ($25, $12 for children).

History

Junkanoo **began** in the late sixteenth and early seventeenth centuries, during plantation times, when the slave owners in Jamaica, the Bahamas and southern states of the US traditionally gave their chattels three days off at Christmas to see family and friends and generally let off steam, mainly as a way of preparing them for another year of hard work.

The word "**Junkanoo**" is thought to have either derived from the French phrase *gens inconnus* ("unknown people"), an appropriate term for the anonymous slaves who first donned grotesque masks and paraded on stilts during these holidays, or from the name "John Canoe", who, depending on historical interpretation, was either a West African slave trader responsible for selling many of his compatriots into bondage, a slave revered for rebelling against his master, or a mythical West African "Everyman" who encapsulated the slave experience as a Christian movement grew to suppress the festival as dangerous and pagan.

Following the abolition of slavery, the festival survived only in the Bahamas, and even there there have been attempts to put an end to the celebration on many occasions – during World War II, the British authorities, aghast at the Burma Road riots, which saw black construction workers demonstrate for equal wages, banned it altogether. Since then, however, Junkanoo has made a comeback, and is more popular than ever – both as a joyous Christmas and New Year's celebration, and a political expression of independence and freedom.

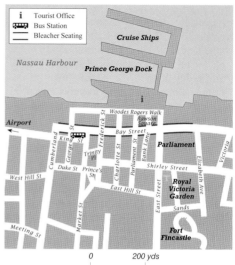

i	Tourist Office
🚌	Bus Station
▭	Bleacher Seating

Cruise Ships

Nassau Harbour

Prince George Dock

Airport

Woodes Rogers Walk
Rawson Square
Bay Street
Frederick St
Cumberland
King St
George St
Trinity Pl
Charlotte St
Parliament St
Bank Lane
Parliament
Duke St
Prince's St
Shirley Street
Elizabeth Ave
Victoria
West Hill St
East Hill St
East Street
Royal Victoria Garden
Sands
Market St
Meeting St
Fort Fincastle

0   200 yds

Crews

Junkanoo features dozens of **"crews"**, extended families or community groups of a thousand or so members that are organized into cadres of dancers, musicians and revellers, young and old, men and women. Crews are corporate-sponsored, and during the year their members hole up in their base camps, or "shacks", where they spend months working towards the two nights of Junkanoo, creating huge fantastical crêpe-paper costumes – which tower as much as ten feet above each member's head – constructing elaborate floats to illustrate a central theme, orchestrating their own music played on traditional instruments, and choreographing intricate weaves of dances to go with it.

Conducted by legendary Junkanoo leaders such as "Emperor Gus" of the Valley Boys, crews compete for substantial money prizes awarded by judges who carefully examine every float, costume and mask, though the top spots invariably go to one of the "Big Five": the Saxon Superstars, the Valley Boys (ⓦwww.valleyboys.com), the Prodigal Sons, Roots (ⓦwww.rootsjunkanoo.com) and One Family (ⓦwww.onefamilyjunkanoo.org).

and join the spectators jockeying for the best views, climbing trees and spilling onto balconies and the verandas of stores, hotels and houses. Under the Christmas lights, the crowds reach a frenzy of anticipation. The first cowbells are heard soon after, everyone swigs from bottles of rum, and fireworks crackle in the sky. Behind, in Nassau harbour, the looming cruise ships form an almost surreal counterpoint to the phantasmagoric crowds, who are now stamping and clamouring in time to the music. Then, as if from everywhere and nowhere, Junkanoo crews – some numbering a thousand – flood the streets in a swirling, kaleidoscopic mass of singing and dancing.

Dancers wearing multicoloured costumes – made of crêpe paper, satin and sparkly beads – with wide shoulder yokes that can be moved in unison with remarkable dexterity, like the fins of a school of fish, spin and weave around huge monster creations. In past parades, giant donkeys, cows and goats reflected crew **themes** such as "Let's Feed the Nation"; the paraders from "Let Freedom Ring" depicted enormous likenesses of Nelson Mandela, Mahatma Gandhi and Martin Luther King; a mammoth lobster celebrated the bounty of the sea; while pirates had a go at a ten-foot Captain Bluebeard.

The crew's musicians are draped in costumes, too, and their hypnotic drumbeats and bold brass provide the main fuel for the fire, while howling conch shells, bicycle bells, whistles

Junkanoo crews flood the streets in a swirling, kaleidoscopic mass of singing and dancing

and cowbells add their out-of-control nuances. The crews keep on coming by for hours, until at least 4am – but, if anything, the crowds grow larger and louder than ever, chanting, cheering and stamping their feet as the dancers gyrate wildly, in time and in step. And dawn is still two hours away.

Standing in the throng, it's hard to imagine that barely one week later another, even larger and more elaborate Junkanoo parade will attract more than sixty thousand islanders – over half Nassau's population – who will jam the city's main shopping street in a pitch of excitement and fervour. It's Junkanoo.

Junkanoo music

Junkanoo music is a West African blend of Goombay – traditional Bahamian folk music – and more ancient sounds. The African slaves who performed the first Junkanoo made music from improvised instruments – tin cans, goatskin drums, mouth whistles and home–made "rum bottle" horns. Crews now incorporate these elements, especially the goatskin drum, but add brass instruments such as tubas, trumpets and trombones. Despite the addition of brass, however, Junkanoo music is still driven by primal African drumming. Even today, modern Junkanoo drummers tune their drums the old way, by holding a lighted candle under the skins until the right pitch is attained.

Basics

All flights into the Bahamas land at Nassau **airport**, 12km outside the capital. At 34km by 11km, New Providence Island can be explored by **car** or **bus** in just a few days, while downtown Nassau itself is easy to navigate on **foot** – Bay Street, on which most of the city's sights are located, is the heart of the Old Town and runs parallel to the harbour.

Accommodation

There is a number of basic but comfortable downtown **hotels** close to the action: the scrupulously clean *Mignon Guest House*, 12 Market Street (☎322-4771), where a double room with shared bath is $56; the *Buena Vista Hotel* on Delancy Street (☎322-2811/2, ☜www.buenavista-restaurant.com), a slightly shabby but still grand old-fashioned place overlooking the city, with doubles for $100; and the *El Greco Hotel*, on West Bay Street (☎325-1121), which has inviting Spanish-style decor and a small pool – doubles here are $110 including continental breakfast. A short bus or taxi ride from downtown, the *Red Carpet Inn*, East Bay Street (☎393-7981, ☜www.redcarpetinnbahamas.com), is also a decent budget option, charging around $110 for a double.

If you have the cash for a more expensive resort-style hotel, two are uniquely worth it: the *British Colonial Hilton Hotel* (☎322-3301, ☜www.nassau.hilton.com), on Bay Street, at one end of the parade route, pampers its visitors in old-school luxury with lots of brass and plush carpeting (doubles cost around $270 per night for a minimum three-night stay during Junkanoo); while further uphill, the fabulous *Graycliff* on West Hill Street (☎322-2796, ☜www.graycliff.com), where Ian Fleming stayed when he visited the island, is a Victorian dream-world of cupolas and gargoyles, with double rooms starting at about $375. It also happens to have one of the finest restaurants in town.

For something a little different, try either the *Orange Hill Beach Inn* (☎327-7157, ☜www.orangehill.com), a relaxed, seaside hotel fifteen minutes' bus ride west of the city centre (doubles from $145); or *Dillet's Guest House* (☎325-1133, ☜www.islandeaze.com), a gem of a place set in an acre of gardens, in a residential west Nassau neighbourhood, which rents out spacious one-bedroom suites with kitchen and private bathroom by the week ($800) or month ($1400).

Eating and drinking

Although many restaurants and bars close during the holidays, there are still plenty of options, and everything is within a four-block-square area in the city centre. Right on Bay Street, the Pasta Market at the *El Greco Hotel* proves a good choice for **food**, while nearby on Bay, *Imperial Take Away* is a local favourite for greasy fried chicken and even greasier Chinese fare. The popular if spartan *Bahamian Kitchen* on Trinity Place, about three blocks uphill from Bay Street, serves authentic Bahamian meals, as do the dozen or so waterfront seafood restaurants in Arawak Cay, a short bus-ride west of town. For a wonderful French bistro meal in casually elegant surroundings, go to *Café Matisse* in Bank Lane (closed Mon).

For a **drink**, take a water taxi over to the relaxed, open-air *Green Parrot Bar* at Hurricane Hole Marina, or hop on a bus to the *Traveller's Rest* overlooking the beach west of town, which has live music some weekends. For the **clubbing**, try *Club Waterloo* on East Bay or the *Fluid Lounge* on Bay Street, both open until dawn.

Event info

Junkanoo (☎324-1714, ☜www.junkanoo.com).
Info about attending Junkanoo and how to get hold of tickets.

Useful websites

Nassau Paradise Island Tourism Board (☎936-9371, ☜www.nassauparadiseisland.com). A good source of Nassau info.
Bahamas Tourism (☜www.bahamas.com, ☎302-2000). The official tourist-board site for the whole of the islands.

Time zone GMT -5   **Country code** +1 242   **Currency** Bahamian dollar (B$)

Mardi Gras

Masked locals, bead-strung tourists, tit-flashing teens, strutting drag divas, and banner-carrying Baptists preaching hellfire and damnation

Mardi Gras

Where?
New Orleans, USA

When?
February or March

How long?
Around 6 weeks

New Orleans has one of the most original, weird, accessible and mind-blowing carnivals of them all. Though the name refers to the entire season, Mardi Gras itself – French for "Fat Tuesday" – is simply the culmination of a whirl of parades, parties, bohemian street revels and secret masked balls, all tied up with the city's Byzantine social, racial and political structures. Much of official Carnival revolves around members-only "krewes", who, as well as organizing the public parades, hold elite, invitation-only, costume balls. Visitors are more likely to be sucked into unofficial Carnival: shindigs thrown by "alternative" krewes, spontaneous carousing in the narrow old streets of the French Quarter and the neighbouring Faubourg Marigny, and always, everywhere, the city's famed live music – the best jazz, R&B, funk and wild brass bands you'll ever dance to.

History

Mardi Gras, brought by French colonists to New Orleans in the 1700s, has its **origins** in medieval European carnival. The colony always had a significant black population, however, and gradually the pre-Lenten bacchanal got mixed up with African and Caribbean festival traditions – drumming, street parades and wild costumes. Then, in 1857, a mysterious torch-lit procession, calling itself, bafflingly, the "Mistick Krewe of Comus", took to the streets, with a parade that was more elaborate than anything yet seen – and very different from the earlier, rowdy street processions, when revellers hurled flour, mud and bricks. The concept of the "krewe", a secret carnival club, was taken up by New Orleans' Anglo elite; each krewe elected their own annual king and queen – usually an older business man and a debutante – who, costumed, masked and attended by a make-believe court, reigned over a themed parade and a secret tableau ball.

Weird stuff. But it gets weirder. In 1872, out of the blue, newspapers published a portentous announcement heralding the arrival of "**Rex, King of Carnival**", and ordering that the city be closed down for the day and handed over to him. On Mardi Gras morning, the masked Rex arrived by riverboat and went on to lead a brilliant parade. Official Carnival wasn't all good clean fun, however: in post-Civil War New Orleans, the krewes were the realm of white supremacists, and the role of blacks in their grand parades was limited to that of torch carrier, float hauler or band member. In the 1880s, though, groups of black men began to lead their own processions through local neighbourhoods. **Zulu**, the first official black krewe, appeared in 1909, when, so the story goes, a black man mocked Rex by dancing behind him wearing a tin-can crown. Today, Zulu is one of New Orleans' biggest krewes, and its parade of black-faced savages in grass skirts is among the most popular of the season.

In 1941, the **Krewe of Venus** was the first female krewe to parade. The 1950s saw the first gay Carnival ball, which was raided by the police, and in 1969 a very different kind of krewe, **Bacchus**, emerged, with the biggest floats ever, a celebrity king (Danny Kaye), and, in place of the hush-hush ball, a public extravaganza open to anyone who could afford the ticket. So began the era of the **super krewes**, with members drawn from New Orleans' new wealth – barred from the gentlemen's-club network of the old-guard krewes – and parades characterized by expensive, flashy floats. Other super krewes include Orpheus, set up by Harry Connick Jr, whose parade always boasts the 120-foot-long "Leviathan", with its blinding fibre-optic lights.

Carnival is, however, still tangled up with the city's complex **race relations**. In 1992, the city government insisted that, in order to be granted a parade licence, all parading krewes confirm their organizations to be open to anyone, regardless of race or religion. While Rex and most of the other krewes agreed, Comus, along with Momus and Proteus, refused, insisting that their membership be kept secret. Though Proteus has since agreed to the statute, neither Momus nor Comus has paraded since 1992, though they continue to stage their elaborate balls – as exclusive and all-white as ever.

More recently, the devastating effects that **Hurricane Katrina** (see box on p.231) had on the city almost caused the 2006 Mardi Gras to be cancelled, and there are those who would have preferred that it was. But the spirit of New Orleans shone through, and the event went ahead, a symbol – if one were needed – that the city was alive and very much kicking.

The build up

More than sixty krewes organize official **parades** during Carnival, most of them over the two weekends before Mardi Gras itself. Though they're held all over the city, the biggest ones head downtown and attract hundreds of thousands of people. Following routes of up to seven miles, they can take three hours to pass, their multi-tiered floats joined by the city's famed high-school marching bands, whose ear-splitting blast of brass and drums can be heard for miles, along with weirdly masked horsemen, stilt-walkers and, of course, second liners – dancers and passers-by who informally join the procession.

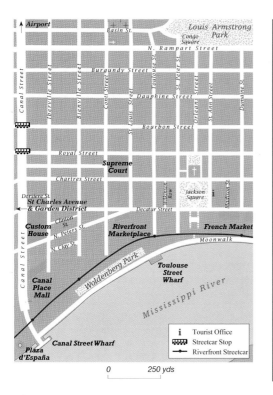

Mardi Gras Indians

New Orleans' **Mardi Gras Indians** are low-income black men who organize themselves into Indian tribes, or gangs, each with a chief, a spy boy, a flag boy and the like. The tradition of "masking Indian" is said to have started in the 1880s. Some say it harks back to New Orleans' earliest days, when local tribes made links with African slaves; others that it developed in response to the hugely popular traveling Buffalo Bill Wild West show. The first Indians dressed simply and fought gang wars on "battlefronts". More recently, however, they've competed for the best songs, dances and costumes. The last, hand-sewn by the gangs, can weigh up to a hundred pounds, their tunics, leggings and enormous feather-headdresses heavy with beads, rhinestones and sequins.

Gangs set out early on Mardi Gras morning, greeting each other with gestures, percussion rattling and improvised calls-and-responses. Traditionally, they paraded through local black neighbourhoods, where tourists, although tolerated, weren't particularly welcome. Since the post-Katrina flooding, however, many of those neighbourhoods have been lost, and the tribes have diminished in number. The remaining Indians are determined to continue their traditions, but how they will do this is not yet clear. If you want to catch some of their **music**, however – an extraordinary, chest-thumping blend of funk, African beats and New Orleans carnival tunes – scan the music listings for gigs by the Wild Magnolias, a fantastic Indian band that shouldn't be missed.

Marvelling at the best floats and bitching about the lame ones is part of the fun, but most people are here to do more than just watch: everyone is here to catch "**throws**" – strings of plastic beads, fluffy toys, beakers, knickers, tin coins, CDs, whatever, hurled by the towering float-riders into the crowd. Competition is fierce, and the float-riders milk the crowd for all it's worth, taunting and jeering back at them. Throws vary in worth: bright, cheap strings of beads are the most common, while the customized coconuts thrown by the Zulu krewe are the most prized. You'll haul most booty at the excessive super-krewe parades, when plastic-bagfuls of fat, shiny beads and a rainstorm of gifts shower the streets.

Visitors who don't fancy scrabbling on the sidewalk for plastic medallions can pay for

one of the most original, weird, accessible and mind-blowing carnivals of them all

places on stands, often linked to a hotel or restaurant, where $10 or so gets you good views and a prime throw-catching position. In the less crowded areas outside downtown, families colonize the sidewalk with picnic boxes, folding chairs and stepladders. Good

viewing areas include Canal Street, which sees the densest crowds, and St Charles Avenue, where there's more of a local, family scene. Remember when staking your place that parades always set off late – sometimes by as much as two hours. While the free-flowing beer and cocktails (New Orleans is the one city in the US where it's legal to drink on the streets) help pass the time, be warned: public toilets don't exist, and during Carnival local bars and restaurants charge non-customers to use theirs.

After the parades have rumbled past, throw-fever continues citywide – among tourists, anyway – in a ritual whereby complete strangers, already weighed down with beads, stagger through the streets and attempt to get what they can from necklace-laden fellow revellers – showing their tits, dropping their trousers, whatever it takes to get another string of beads. The most frenzied action takes place on **Bourbon Street** – a tacky strip at the best of times, and sheer mayhem during Mardi Gras – where girls on packed-out balconies tease the baying street mobs below into a frenzy. It's Carnival at its raunchiest, basest, worst and best. Though the police make half-hearted attempts every now and again to clamp down on these antics, no one can be bothered to get very worked up about it. New Orleanians, of course, who rarely venture into Bourbon Street in any case, leave this stuff to the tourists.

Insider info Official events and parades are advertised in the press: check the city's daily paper, the *Times Picayune*; pick up the free monthly music paper, *Offbeat*, and the free weekly, *Gambit*, from local bars and cafés; and tune in to WWOZ (90.7FM), the superb local radio station, for news of the best gigs and parties.

Alternative krewes

Chief among the city's alternative krewes is the anarchic **Krewe du Vieux** (from Vieux Carré, another name for the French Quarter), whose irreverent "ball" – basically a wild party, open to all – is the first of the season, starting with a parade through the French Quarter. Ragtag costumes and mini-floats satirize current local affairs and scandals, while the funkiest brass bands blast the roofs off. As usual in New Orleans, anyone's welcome to join in, passers-by and spectators leaping in to form a rowdy, dancing "second line". Uptown, the **Krewe of OAK**'s parade (read: bar crawl) climaxes at the *Maple Leaf* – one of the best bars in the city, where OAK (Outrageous And Kinky) costumes reveal as much flesh as possible. But, for the ultimate in camp, check out the **Mystic Krewe of Barkus** parade, when a thousand or so dogs – all spiffed up on some spurious theme – trot through the French Quarter before ending up, with owners and onlookers, at *Good Friends*, one of the city's liveliest gay bars.

Lundi Gras

It's Monday morning, the day before Mardi Gras. You're staggering under the weight of beads, and though a small voice tells you that you've lost it, mostly you believe that you look really cool. You've yelled yourself hoarse at the parades, danced till dawn for nights on end to the best live music on earth, swigged too many local cocktails and stuffed yourself on crawfish and gumbo. You're secretly yearning for some rest before the big day. But as any partygoer worth their salt knows, the fun is only just beginning – Lundi Gras is one of the most feverish days of the season.

From mid-morning, the city's top musicians, most of whom will have been gigging till daybreak for the past fortnight, play at **Zulu's free party** on the banks of the Mississippi. At last you can lie down for a bit, close your eyes in the sun and doze off to some down-home R&B, blues and jazz. Grab a plate of fried chicken and a cold beer, and you'll find that life doesn't get any better. At 5pm, it's time to leap up again and rush off to see Zulu's king and queen arrive by boat, at the Canal Street Wharf. Don't ask why you have to do this; you just do. When they've safely disembarked and waved at you, their subjects, everyone heads around the corner to the **Plaza d'España**, where, in a formal ceremony, unchanged since Rex first flounced onto the scene more than a century ago, the mayor

hands the city to the "King of Carnival". The ensuing party – whiter than Zulu's, with more families and tourists – continues with music and fireworks, after which people head off to the Orpheus parade or to yet another evening of live music.

Mardi Gras

The fun starts early on Mardi Gras itself: walking clubs, made up of local musicians, writers and sundry lowlife, stride through uptown on ritualized bar crawls. Meanwhile, the Mardi Gras Indians prepare for their afternoon standoffs. The Zulu parade, scheduled to set off at 8.30am but usually starting much later, heads from uptown to Canal Street, the float-riders daubed in war paint and dressed in grass skirts. The Rex parade, dominated since its debut by the "Boeuf Gras", a colossal, blue, papier-mâché bull, hits Canal Street in the afternoon. Ironically, by the time Rex arrives, most people are through with the official parades. The wildest parties are going on in the **French Quarter** – which is teeming with masked locals, bead-strung tourists, tit-flashing teens, strutting drag divas, and banner-carrying Baptists preaching hellfire and damnation – and the **Faubourg Marigny**, where the artists and creatives dance (literally) to a different drum.

Though it's best to do as most people do, and drift spontaneously through the maelstrom, there are a couple of high points to know about. The **Krewe of St Anne walking parade**, a surreal procession of the most extraordinary costumes, sets off from the Marigny, a low-rent, arty area downriver from the French Quarter, weaves through the Faubourg Marigny and arrives in the Quarter at about noon. Anyone is welcome to prance through the streets with them; you'll fit in best if your costume is risqué, fancy or creative. Meanwhile, the flamboyant gay costume competition known as the **Bourbon Street Awards** gets going at noon. This is one for the spectators, really, unless you're a drag queen who has just happened to wander by in a twenty-foot-high sequinned ensemble.

Late afternoon, everyone heads to the **Faubourg Marigny Street Party**, which is ablaze with costumed dancers and drummers in a scene as irreverent and skewed as you can imagine. The fun continues throughout the streets and bars until midnight, when mounted police sweep through Bourbon Street declaring through megaphones that Mardi Gras is over. Don't think they're joking. Many bars do stay open later, but most people, masks askew, are drifting off home by 1am. Like all good Catholic cities, New Orleans takes Carnival very seriously. Midnight marks the imminence of Lent, and repentance must begin.

Mardi Gras post-Katrina

Following the catastrophic flooding that **Hurricane Katrina** brought to New Orleans, many believed that Mardi Gras would, or should, be cancelled in 2006. Few of the naysayers, however, truly understood the importance that the Carnival holds in the city's heart – far more than just a party, or a show for tourists, in many ways Mardi Gras *is* New Orleans, combining its strong awareness of history, community and family with its unique mix of spirituality, decadence and fun. After some six months of rebuilding, New Orleans needed something positive, and a sign for itself, and for the rest of the world, that the city was coming back. It also needed to share its sorrow and lick its wounds. Like some massive jazz funeral, **Mardi Gras 2006** was a place as much to mourn as to celebrate.

Naturally, there were changes. The parade season was shorter, as were the parades themselves, as some streets were still too difficult to pass – while the French Quarter, Faubourg Marigny and Garden Districts remained relatively physically unscathed by the hurricane and the flooding, it was the poorer, black-dominated neighbourhoods that suffered irreparable damage. The krewes that did parade approached the limitations with gusto, however, patching up and redoing old floats, even pairing up where possible. In the unofficial parades, masqueraders fashioned weird and wonderful couture from the bright blue tarps that had swathed so much of the city since the storm, or simply wore plain rags blighted by a high brown tide-mark.

It remains too early to say how New Orleans' tourist infrastructure will shape up for **Mardi Gras** in the years to come, and what effect that will have on the future of Carnival as a tourist attraction. It also remains hard to imagine how the disappearance of so many low-income neighbourhoods, and of the people who lived there – the musicians and the hospitality industry workers and the school kids and the schoolteachers – will impact the city, let alone its carnival. For now, the message that this unique culture refuses to go down without a fight is loud and clear. It may even be that Mardi Gras, the battered city's heartbeat, will ultimately prove to be New Orleans's saving grace.

Basics

New Orleans **airport** is northwest of the city centre – a twenty-minute taxi ride. If you're arriving by **bus** (Greyhound) or **train** (Amtrak), note that the area where these stations are located, near the Superdome, isn't safe to walk around at night – it's best to get a taxi to your hotel. United Cars (☎504/522-9771) is by far the best and most reliable **taxi** firm. You'll need to do some planning and get oriented to make the most of Mardi Gras – a good place for maps and general **information** is the New Orleans Welcome Center at 529 St Ann St, on Jackson Square, in the heart of the French Quarter (daily 9am–5pm; ☎504/566-5031).

Accommodation

Room rates in New Orleans, never low – there's nothing half decent for less than $95 – might increase by as much as two hundred percent during Mardi Gras, and you should book well in advance. Ideally, you'll stay in the **French Quarter**, right in the heart of things. Guesthouses here, in atmospheric old Creole cottages, range from shabbily decadent to romantic hideaways. The *Biscuit Palace*, 730 Dumaine St (☎504/525-9949, ⊛ www.biscuitpalace.com), is a well-run, friendly and brilliantly located guesthouse named for the old biscuit ad painted on its outside wall. It's housed in an 1820s mansion, with a pretty courtyard, and characterful suites from around $100. Another popular option is the simple *Villa Convento*, 616 Ursulines St (☎504/522-1793, ⊛ www.villaconvento.com), which has basic rooms from $80. If that just doesn't work, check out the cheaper options in the funky – and occasionally dodgy – Lower Garden District, or the good-value B&Bs in hip **Faubourg Marigny**. In the latter, the *Royal Street Inn*, 1431 Royal St (☎504/ 948-7499, ⊛ www.royalstreetinn.com), has just five simple rooms above one of the funkiest bars in the Faubourg. Residents get two free drinks a night included for their $90 or so.

Eating and drinking

Creole **food** is delicious, cheap and usually spicy. As well as the fantastic seafood – raw oysters, crawfish, softshell crab – you can't go home without stuffing yourself silly on gumbo, a thick soup-cum-stew made with seafood, chicken, vegetables or sausage, and po-boys, huge French-bread sandwiches crammed with almost anything you can think of. For your first New Orleans gumbo you can't do better than the *Gumbo Shop*, a convivial Creole restaurant in the French Quarter at 630 St Peter St, while the nearby *Johnny's Po-Boys*, 511 St Louis St, is a New Orleans institution, heaving at lunchtime with local workers and in-the-know tourists. For seafood, the *Acme Oyster House*, a couple of blocks away at 724 Iberville St, has been the French Quarter hangout for raw oysters for nearly one hundred years. If you're after a fry-up or a post bar-crawl breakfast, however, head for *Clover Grill*, 900 Bourbon St, a lively, camp-as-Christmas all-night diner.

   Drinking can be a big part of Carnival evenings, though on Mardi Gras day itself most people find themselves on a natural enough high without alcohol. To avoid a killer hangover, steer clear of the

"Hurricane", a lethal combination of rum, fruit juice and sackfuls of sugar. Far less naff, and far more delicious, is the "Ramos Gin Fizz", a frothy swirl of gin, lemon, egg white and orange-flower water invented here early last century, or the "Sazerac", another New Orleans original, a golden mix of rye whisky, bitters, lemon and ice. Try them at the atmospheric old *Napoleon House*, a classic French Quarter bar at 500 Chartres St. With its crumbling walls, ancient oil paintings and old, well-stocked wooden bar, this charming place exudes a stylish, relaxed New Orleans elegance. Also in the French Quarter, *Molly's at the Market*, 1107 Decatur St, is an Irish bar – famed for staying open throughout Katrina and refusing to join in the evacuation – that pulls in a happy mix of locals, rowdy tourists, service-industry workers and street punks. Nearby, in the Faubourg Marigny, the *R-Bar*, 1431 Royal St, is a friendly, attitude-free place with quirky, thrift-store decor and a pool table. Heading uptown, on swanky St Charles Avenue, the *Columns Hotel*, at no. 3811, is a stunning old mansion with a louche Victorian bar and a huge columned veranda that overlooks the St Charles parade route – perfect for posing with a cocktail or two.

Live music

On the fringes of the French Quarter, *Donna's*, 800 North Rampart St, features the best brass bands and trad jazz in a down-home barbecue joint. *One-Eyed Jack's*, 615 Toulouse, is a decadent cabaret-type place that flings together an offbeat mix of music and styles, and appeals to the pierced and tattooed set. In the Faubourg Marigny, Frenchmen Street is lined with bars and clubs: there's always something happening at *Café Brasil*, on the corner of Frenchmen and Chartres streets, while for a mellower vibe you can head for the *Blue Nile*, 532 Frenchmen St. Best bets uptown include the legendary *Tipitina's*, 501 Napoleon Ave – named after a Professor Longhair song, and usually with a great funk, R&B, brass and reggae line-up. The friendly, old *Maple Leaf Bar*, 8316 Oak St, offers fantastic traditional piano, brass bands and blues every night.

Event info

Mardi Gras New Orleans (⊛ www.mardigrasneworleans.com). Video clips, accommodation options, parade schedules, articles on the krewes and the Mardi Gras Indians, and tips on where to stand to get the best view of the parades.

Useful websites

New Orleans Convention and Visitors Bureau (☎800/672-6124, ⊛ www.neworleanscvb.com). Multi-faceted site offering tourist info and online accommodation booking.
Gambit (⊛ www.bestofneworleans.com). The website of New Orleans's fantastic free weekly, *Gambit*, which has feature articles, listings and local news.
Offbeat (⊛ www.offbeat.com). Web version of the city's music monthly, a must for local listings, musician interviews, articles and news.
WWOZ (⊛ www.wwoz.org). Listen to New Orleans' excellent non-profit radio station online.

Reggae Sumfest

One of the best reggae shows in the world - period

Reggae Sumfest

Where?
Montego Bay, Jamaica

When?
Mid- to late July

How long?
3 days, plus several warm-up events in the preceding week

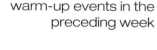

As you might expect from what has become Jamaica's flagship music festival, Sumfest is one of the best reggae shows in the world. If you're expecting a bacchanalian free-for-all of campfires on the sand, you'll be sorely disappointed – it's a series of concerts preceded by sound-system jams and beach parties – but if you're interested in seeing the hottest names in Jamaican music past and present, with a few international R&B or hip-hop acts thrown in for good measure, then you're in for a serious treat. The island's stage shows start late, carry on until dawn and involve some serious audience participation – or lack of it, if a performer fails to please the famously fickle local crowd. And it's doubtful you'll find a better high than standing under the stars in a grassy bowl by the Caribbean with the music echoing out over the bay.

It's best to arrive in Montego Bay a week or so before the event and head for the beach (there are several fine strips of sand in town) in order to rid yourself of that fresh-off-the-plane pallor, and to attend pre-festival events. These tend to change annually (check the Sumfest website – see p.238 – for details of what's on), but there's usually a "**Blast Off Beach Party**" on the Sunday before the festival starts, with music supplied by some of the best sound systems and DJs in the business (the 2006 event had Black Chiney, Renaissance, Coppershot and Tony Matterhorn), as well as fashion shows, food stalls, and unlimited Red Stripe included in the admission. The next day sees the free "**Mad Monday**" street party, a take on the outdoor jams that have become the liveliest thing in the Kingston nightlife scene in recent years – music is supplied by DJs from the best of the Kingston parties: Fire Links from Hot Mondays, Stone Love from Weddy Weddy Wednesdays, and Swatch from Passa Passa. The main Sumfest shows – Top Ranking, Storm Front, Ignition and The Summit – still take place right in Montego Bay, at the Pier One club and the Catherine Hall Entertainment Centre on Howard Cooke Boulevard.

History

In 1993, as Jamaica's original reggae festival, Sunsplash, collapsed (for more on which, see p.237), a group of Montego Bay-based businessmen hit upon the idea of reviving a reggae festival in the town, and staged the **first Sumfest** in the town's Catherine Hall Entertainment Centre, then a nothing plot of chalky marl by the sea at the scraggy end of the downtown area. Their slicker, more concert-like Sumfest was an immediate winner, boasting smooth organization and great lineups but lacking, some said, the proper "festival-like" atmosphere of its predecessor. Nonetheless, the show went from strength to strength, attracting the great and the good – and the bad – of the reggae pantheon, alongside a string of international performers. Sumfest was somewhat marred in 2005, when the use of obscenities and homophobic lyrics led to a (short-lived) ban on Beenie Man and other Jamaican artists that remain supremely popular with the local crowd, while in the eyes of some Jamaicans, the event has become somewhat sanitized in its quest to be as appealing to foreigners as it is to the locals. Nevertheless, it continues to attract some brilliant lineups, and with nearly 55,000 tickets sold each year, it remains an unmissable and hugely popular event.

Top Ranking

Recently reintroduced after the organizers realized the lunacy of dropping their original Vintage Night (it wasn't seen to draw a big enough crowd to fill the main venue), Wednesday night's **Top Ranking** kicks off Sumfest proper, attracting a crowd of serious reggae aficionados. Its setting at the smaller, oceanside Pier One is arguably prettier and certainly more intimate than the Catherine Hall Entertainment Centre, which hosts the other three major events – you'll get closer to the performers and it'll be a night to remember while singing along to the classics of the reggae canon.

Storm Front

On Thursday, the newly renamed **Storm Front**, a showcase for the current biggest names in the dancehall scene and with a more raw feel than the Friday and Saturday nights, is often the busiest night of the festival, with a mostly local crowd packed right to the edges of the circular arena. Jamaican audiences know their music and are notoriously hard to please; people waste no time demonstrating their appreciation – showering firecrackers or setting light to a stream of hairspray, some cardboard or anything else combustible – or otherwise, with some blistering heckling and, occasionally, a hail of bottles. By the time Beenie Man or Sizzla take to the stage in the early hours, the atmosphere is truly electric. Things are almost always good-natured, despite the rivalry up on stage; as well as the lyrics and the posturing, you'll also be treated to some of the rudest dancing in the world courtesy of the "dancehall queens" who take to the stage between acts.

you won't find a better high than standing under the stars by the Caribbean with the music echoing out over the bay

Getting tickets

Though you can pay on the gates, the most popular nights often sell out, so it's wise to **buy tickets in advance**. They're available from Jamaica Tourist Board offices at the airport and islandwide, in Montego Bay bars, or from tour desks in larger hotel lobbies in town; check the Sumfest website (see p.238) for details. Ticket prices are posted online nearer to the time – expect to pay around US$10 for the Blast Off Beach Party, US$15 for Top Ranking, around US$30 for the Storm Front dancehall night (Thurs), and US$45 for the Ignition and Summit international nights (Fri & Sat). You can also buy a season ticket (around US$145), which covers entry to all the main nights, and a VIP version (around US$170), which gives access to the backstage and front of stage areas as well, though the latter isn't really worth bothering with unless you're an autograph-hunter or want to stand between the stage and the barrier that separates it from the main crowd – a great spot to take pictures. Friday and Saturday passes are also available for around US$85 (VIPs around US$110).

Reggae Sunsplash

Though Sumfest has ruled the roost for some ten years now, Jamaica's original reggae festival was **Reggae Sunsplash**, first put on in 1978 in Montego Bay's Jarrett Park cricket ground. The tone was set by the legendary shows of the late 1970s, in which Bob Marley and the Wailers headlined alongside reggae legends such as Burning Spear, Culture, and Toots and the Maytals. By the mid-1980s, Sunsplash was huge, attracting some 30,000 people and ensuring that flights and hotel rooms were booked up months in advance. However, a series of venue changes (including a move to the more volatile location of Kingston) combined with legal wrangles amongst the original promoters saw the festival go downhill; journalists and tourists were scared off by tales of gang warfare in the capital, and audience numbers went into decline. A miserable, half-empty 1999 festival at Chukka Cove was the last straw, and with Sumfest muscling in on the act down the coast in Montego Bay, Sunsplash was brought to its knees.

However, given the upward skyrocket of all things Jamaican on the global "coolness" scale, be it in the success of Damian Marley and Sean Paul or the propensity of teenagers everywhere to chat patois and worship ganja, it was only a matter of time before Sunsplash would rise from the ashes, and in late 2005 it was announced that **August 2006** would see the first Sunsplash in seven years. Backed by some of the island's wealthiest men, and with some heavyweight corporate sponsorship, too, the four-day Sunsplash 2006 was staged in the middle of Jamaica's north coast, right by the sea at the two-hundred-acre Richmond Estate. This grassy venue can accommodate 150,000 people and, thankfully (given that getting there and away is often the bane of Jamaican festivals), space for twenty thousand cars to park. Two stages put an end to the lengthy band changes that have long led to restless crowds at Sumfest, while multiple screens ensured that everyone got a good view of the stage. And the lineup wasn't bad, either: over the four nights – Dancehall, Worldbeat, International and Singers – Beenie Man, Bounty Killer, Buju Banton, Macka Diamond, Vybes Kartel, Elephant Man and Wayne Marshall played from the dancehall side of things, alongside Morgan Heritage, Culture, Freddie McGregor, Toots and the Maytals, Bob Andy and Gregory Isaacs from the reggae old school. Rubbing shoulders with them all were international acts including Steel Pulse, UB40, Maxi Priest and Wyclef Jean.

For more **information**, visit ⊛www.reggaesunsplashja .com.

Ignition and The Summit

Friday and Saturday nights see a more international lineup, as well as a higher tourist presence and brisk sales at the T-shirt stands. The new generation of roots reggae artists add a cultural flavour, and grizzled old dreads advertise their wares by waving enormous sticks of ganja in the air. (Sumfest probably isn't the place to get the deal of your life, though, and if you intend indulging in a few spliffs, you should be careful when buying and discreet when smoking.) The seaside setting, brilliant lineups and a fabulous PA that bounces all your favourite tunes into the hills surrounding the town can be a heady combination.

Lofty lineups

Sumfest is Nirvana for reggae fanatics, with sets from huge names such as **Damian "Junior Gong" Marley** or **Sean Paul** as well as more rootsy headliners like **Morgan Heritage**, and fiery deliveries from all the hottest dancehall kings and queens, from **Sizzla** and **Capleton** to **Lady Saw** and **Macka Diamond**. It also offers the chance to catch rare performances from stalwart reggae acts who rarely take to the stage these days; 2005 saw sets from **Josey Wales, Charley Chaplin** and **Pinchers**, as well as **Ini Kamoze, Toots and the Maytals** and **Alton Ellis**. And Sumfest has also been able to attract some huge international stars, from **Destiny's Child** and **Kanye West** to **Alicia Keys** and **50 Cent**.

Basics

Jamaica is a pretty popular holiday destination and there are plenty of charter **flights** from the UK to Montego Bay, while Air Jamaica flies daily to Montego Bay from the UK. Air Jamaica and American Airlines also offer regular scheduled flights to Montego Bay from major US cities. The Jamaica **Tourist Board office** in Montego Bay (☎ 952 4425) can provide basic information on accommodation, tickets and transport.

Accommodation

Montego Bay is one of Jamaica's main resorts, and there is a good variety of **accommodation** choices. The downtown area is closest to the site, though walking back at the end of the night isn't advisable and you'll be away from the beaches by day. *Gibbs' Chateau*, 54 Jarrett Terrace, Barnett View Gardens (☎ 979 7861), has basic but comfortable rooms at knockdown rates. The "tourist strip", where most of the hotels are slung along the best beaches, is a five-minute drive north from the Catherine Hall Entertainment Centre – inexpensive choices here include *Beach View Apartments*, Gloucester Ave (☎ 971 3859, ⓦ www.marzouka.com); *Bayshore Inn*, 27 Gloucester Ave (☎ 952 1046); *Caribic House*, 69 Gloucester Ave (☎ 979 6073, ⓦ www.caribicvacations.com); and *Hotel Gloriana*, 1–2 Sunset Blvd (☎ 979 0669, ⓦ www.hotelgloriana.com). Double rooms at all of these places are US$45–70. For a bit more luxury, try *Doctor's Cave Beach Hotel* (☎ 952 4355, ⓦ www.doctorscave.com), where doubles start at US$110.

Eating and drinking

The legions of **food** stalls that form a perimeter ring around the main festival area offer everything from fried fish to traditional Jamaican hot dinners – jerk chicken, curry goat, oxtail with butter beans, ackee and saltfish, or stewed chicken with rice and peas – and vegetarian cuisine at the "ital" outlets; look out for veggie stews and patties filled with gunga peas and tofu, or ackee and callaloo. The ultimate party fuel is soup, particularly "mannish water" – a spicy, filling goat-based concoction that's sold by the cup from huge cauldrons balanced on rickety push-carts that set up around the main gates. Another delicious soup option is fish tea – a fish and veg broth that's a lot nicer than it sounds.

Given the Caribbean horror of appearing drunk in public, Sumfest isn't really a time to get too smashed, but if you are going to be **drinking**, the ubiquitous Red Stripe beer is always delicious, as are the strong local Guinness and Dragon stouts. Jamaican rum is some of the best in the world – Appleton Estate or twelve-year-old Appleton VX are the smoothest. Wray and Nephew Overproof white rum packs the heaviest punch; it's normally drunk with water or Ting, a grapefruit soda.

Event info

Raggae Sumfest (ⓦ www.reggaesumfest.com). Official festival site with details of the lineup, ticket prices and photos.

Useful websites

Montego Bay (ⓦ www.montego-bay-jamaica.com). Good info on the city, plus maps and links to relevant websites.
Jamaica Tourist Board (ⓦ www.visitjamaica.com). Very slick with lots of general travel info.
Jamaicans.com (ⓦ www.jamaicans.com). US-based site on all things Jamaican.
Reggae Times (ⓦ www.reggaetimes.com). Website of the excellent US-based magazine, with the lowdown on all the latest happenings on the reggae scene.
Jah Works (ⓦ www.jahworks.org). Reggae website with a cultural flavour.
Dancehall Reggae (ⓦ www.dancehallreggae.com). Everything you ever needed to know about dancehall, and regularly updated to boot.

Time zone GMT-5   **Country code** +1 876   **Currency** Jamaican dollar (JS$)

Rio Carnival

The world's best
party - period

Rio Carnival

Where?
Rio de Janeiro, Brazil

When?
February/March – from the Friday of Carnival weekend to Shrove Tuesday

How long?
5 days

BRAZIL

Rio de Janeiro •

Carnival celebrations are hardly unique to Rio de Janeiro, but, without doubt, the city boasts the world's wildest, glitziest and largest carnival of them all. Drawing people from all over the globe to participate, this is the world's best party- period. Local reaction varies – some *cariocas* (the inhabitants of Rio) hate Carnival, and flee the city over the long weekend to stay at their mountain or beachside second homes, though most simply see it as one long, citywide party. And partying at the Rio Carnival is something you definitely won't forget. Boasting the largest gathering of transvestites in the world, the event is infamous for its "I-went-to-bed-with-a-woman-and-woke-up-with-a-man" style incidents. Leave your inhibitions at the airport.

History

Rio's Carnival is rooted in the **entrudo**, or mock-battle, imported to Brazil by Portuguese immigrants in the seventeenth century. A riotous outburst preceding the abstinence of Lent, the *entrudo* was a brutal four-day festivity where soot, flour and the foulest liquids imaginable were thrown on passers-by who dared venture onto the streets. So out of control were Rio's *entrudos* that they were formally abolished by the city authorities in 1843, by which time the modern-day forms of Carnival expression had started to evolve.

In the late eighteenth century, Rio's wealthier citizens began to seek means of enjoyably participating in Carnival. The first **float parade** was organized in 1786, and masked balls, long popular in Italy, were introduced at about the same time. By the mid-nineteenth century, Rio's elite were holding European-style carnival celebrations in private clubs, many of which were linked to civic groups. At the same time, the city's poor had organized their own celebrations with Zé Pereira bands, named after the Portuguese *tambour* that provided the basic musical beat. Migration to Rio from Bahia – a state in the northeast of the country – in the 1870s introduced African influences to Carnival, and gradually the two strands combined to create an event that became an expression of a growing Brazilian nationalism.

From these beginnings, Rio's *escolas de samba* (**samba schools**) emerged. The first, Deixa Falar, was established in 1928 in a *favela* (shanty town) just north of the city centre, and for the next twenty years, more samba schools sprung up in other *favelas* and working-class neighbourhoods of the city, each developing its own strong individual identity. As Carnival became an ever more elaborate spectacle, visitors from around the world started to attend the festivities – not least inspired by the absurdly costumed figure of Carmen Miranda, the Broadway and Hollywood star who was to become the patron saint of Rio's Carnival transvestites. Paradoxically, the laid-back sounds of bossa nova – introduced to North American and European audiences in the late 1950s and early 1960s by artistes such as Tom Jobim, Astrud Gilberto and Stan Getz – brought yet more international attention to Rio. The fashion of "flying down to Rio" for Carnival was briefly interrupted by the military's seizure of power in 1964, but in the years since, the event has firmly re-established itself on the world-party circuit.

Rio Carnival exists somewhere in everybody's imagination. When foreigners think of it, the images that usually spring to mind are of a colourful parade, loud music and pounding drums, extravagant costumes, lots of near-naked flesh – and unbridled hedonism. However, it's worth knowing that nowadays Carnival is a highly organized – and commercialized – event, and despite its reputation, the casual visitor to Rio during Carnival could easily leave Brazil wondering what all the fuss is about. This is partly because, with some ten million inhabitants, Rio often enjoys its Carnival far off the tourist track and behind closed doors. To enjoy it, either as an observer bent on soaking up the atmosphere or by actively joining in, you need to know where to go.

The Zona Sul suburbs of **Copacabana**, **Ipanema** and **Leblon** are the places to see the best Carnival bands and sound systems. Each evening during Carnival, towers of speakers line the Copacabana seafront promenade along Avenida Atlântica, which swells with a mixture of hookers, tourists and people who've had a hard day looking sexy on the beach or recovering from the night before. The whole area is bathed in bright gaudy lights from beach bars and food stalls, which provide an excellent pit-stop before you throw yourself deeper into the mêlée. The rest of the partying rages in the downtown area, either on **Rio Branco**, where the unofficial parades take place, or at **Praça Onze**; both places are packed every night until at least 2am. Praça Onze is located next door to the **Sambódromo**, into which the samba schools and dance ensembles pour as part of the Carnival Parade itself. Getting a seat in one of the makeshift spectator stands here is a good move; you can eat and drink yourself stupid in comfort while watching the paraders marching by.

Samba and the samba schools

Although **samba** is heard throughout the year and all over Brazil, it actually emerged in Rio and is synonymous with the city's Carnival. The *batucada* – the continuous, hypnotic rhythm that is the basis of samba – flows through the city's veins, and as Carnival approaches, the sound increasingly replaces even Rio's traffic as the city's background noise. Spontaneously created on the streets, beaches and buses, the *batucada* is produced by simply beating or tapping whatever is at hand – tin cans, tables, pans, your legs – and it's always amazing how many people happen to have a drum or other percussion instrument with them. The simplest of bars is, in many ways, as good as anywhere to enjoy the *batucada*, but no visit to Rio is complete without experiencing a samba-school performance – either a rehearsal (see box), or, better still, during Carnival itself.

Each **samba school** has its own devoted followers, flags and colours, and is linked to an individual neighbourhood, often a particular *favela*, from where it draws its most fervent supporters and participants; competition is an important part of Carnival, and the rivalry between Rio's samba schools is fierce. There are five samba-school divisions – *grupos* A, B, C and D, and the elite "Grupo Especial" – and promotion and relegation can take place between these divisions; only the Grupo Especial and schools from *grupos* A and B are allowed to parade in the Sambódromo on Carnival weekend (see box, opposite).

Serious **preparations** for Carnival don't get underway until August, when a samba school's theme – usually based on an event or a notable individual from Brazilian history – for the next Carnival is announced. From then until October each school holds a public competition between composers, and a different *samba de enredo* (theme song) is eliminated each week until the winning one is chosen. Meanwhile, the business of designing and making the costumes and the huge floats gets underway – to maintain an element of secrecy, costumes are only issued to participants a few days before Carnival.

Visiting a samba school

To get the best sense of what all good **samba schools** aspire to, a visit to one of the fourteen schools that make up the Grupo Especial is an essential Rio experience. The schools are based and rehearse in a *quadra*, generally located at the edge of a *favela*. Depending on the wealth of the particular school, this may be a large building or it may simply be a space beneath an overpass of an inner-city highway. All the schools welcome visitors from outside of the *favela*, in part to fund the school – through entrance charges, and the sale of drinks, CDs and T-shirts – but also because they're keen to improve the image of *favelas* to the outside world. That said, *favela* crime is a harsh reality of life: it's best to take a taxi there and back, or take a tour arranged through a hotel or local travel agent (see p.248).

Grupo Especial **rehearsals** (*ensaios*) take place Monday to Saturday evenings and on Sunday afternoons. The Saturday-night rehearsal is more of a money-making event than anything, with an admission charge and more recorded than live music – it's far more enjoyable and interesting to attend one of the other days' rehearsals, when the local community dominates events and the real Carnival *batucada* is being pounded out by the massed *baterias* (percussion ensembles).

Several of the samba schools are easy to reach from Zona Sul: *Mangueira*, Rua Visconde de Niterói 1072, Mangueira (☎ 21/3872-6786), is one of the oldest and most traditional, while *Salgueiro*, Rua Silva Tellas 104, Tijuca (☎ 21/2288-3065), attracts a large white, middle-class following that's especially gay-friendly. Other schools worth checking out include *Império Serrano*, *Imperatriz Leopoldinense* and *Unidos da Tijuca*.

Samba shows

If venturing to a samba school's *quadra* doesn't attract you, an alternative option is to take in a so-called **samba show**. Most are extremely tacky events, totally geared to foreign tourists, but one exception is *Asa Branca*, Avenida Mem de Sá 17, Lapa (☎ 21/2232-5704), which offers an enjoyable and authentic samba experience that attracts locals, Brazilians and foreign visitors alike. Featuring some of the best Mangueira musicians and dancers, the club remains open after the show for guests to dance to samba and other local sounds.

Cidade do Samba

The **Cidade do Samba** (City of Samba) is an enormous complex that combines workshops of aircraft-hangar proportions for each of the Grupo Especial's fourteen schools – as Carnival approaches, though, secrecy mounts, and sections of the workshops are cordoned off from prying eyes – with a central display area where samba dance moves are demonstrated and drum rhythms pounded out. Each of the schools sells T-shirts and other souvenirs, and offers information on rehearsal times and places. The Cidade do Samba is on Avenida Rodrigues Alves, across from Armazéns 10 and 11, in the port neighbourhood of Gamboa; the surrounding area is considered dangerous, so it's best to take a taxi there and back.

Street Carnival: blocos and bandas

Even though the Rio Carnival has become incredibly commercialized, the street carnival side of things hasn't vanished altogether, and can make a cheaper and in a way more authentic alternative to the Sambódromo events. For two weeks preceding Carnival, and during Carnival weekend itself, you're sure to stumble across numerous *blocos* (small groups of percussion players) and *bandas* (larger, better-organized and more riotous groups) all over the city – the chances are that you'll just get dragged along, whether you like it or not. And don't worry that you can't dance samba in the sexy, shuffling way the locals do; there are worse things in life than being taught how to samba by a sexy Brazilian with her arms and hands guiding the movements of your hips.

Bandas to look out for include the **Banda de Ipanema**, which performs to an excited crowd at the Praça General Osorio, in

the heart of the wealthy beach suburb of Ipanema, and the **Simpatia é Quase Amor**, which starts at the same square. Otherwise, Santa Clara, Rua Bolivar and Rua Duvivier – all in Copacabana – are also good places to find *bandas*. For a more impromptu, neighbourhood feel, make for the hilly, Bohemian district of Santa Teresa, where the **Carmelitas de Santa Teresa**, their members dressed as nuns, attract a light-hearted following that winds its way through the neighbourhood's narrow streets and small squares.

Getting into the Sambódromo

You need to buy a **ticket** – ranging from US$30 to well over US$500 to see the Grupo Especial – to get into the Sambódromo; if you haven't come to Rio on a package holiday with the tickets included, your best chance of getting hold of one is through Riotur, the city's tourist office (see p.248). You can also usually get tickets through hotels and travel agents, though expect to pay much more for these.

If you haven't got hold of a ticket in advance, you can buy one from a **tout** on the streets before or during the parade. Touts hang around by the entrances to each of the sectors: the east side of the Sambódromo (sectors 1, 5, 7, 9, 11, 13) has more stands and therefore more options for tickets; the west side (sectors 2, 4, 6) is decidedly dodgier. If you want to see the whole thing, turn up around mid- to late afternoon; if you're only interested in the main parades, then you can leave it later and party in the meantime – as a rule of thumb, the later you leave it, the cheaper the tickets. Try not to take tickets for sectors 6 and 13 unless you're desperate, and be sure to shop around. Once you've agreed on a price, ask to see the ticket before you hand over the money: it should be a credit-card-sized piece of plastic with a magnetic strip on the back. There should be a sector number, the location and the date, and the ticket colour should correspond to the appropriate day. There should also be a paper ticket that validates the plastic ticket. Although it is possible to get in with just the plastic ticket, you really need both. And don't even think about paying just for the paper ticket because it won't get you anywhere.

Finally, if you really can't afford to buy a ticket, then you can see some of what goes on inside the Sambódromo for **free**. Behind the east side of the complex is a flyover that rises to create a perfect vantage point into part of the stadium. The crowd here is brilliant, and the partying almost as good as if they were in the parade itself.

The Carnival Parade

When people talk about the Carnival Parade, they're thinking of the samba schools of the Grupo Especial that perform – or compete – in the **Sambódromo**, a purpose-built concrete structure seating over sixty thousand and designed by the great Brazilian architect, Oscar Niemeyer. The Grupo Especial parades on the Sunday and Monday (seven schools each night), with the lower ranking Grupo A performing on the Saturday night and Grupo B on the Tuesday night. The parades start at about 7pm and continue until around 6am. Unless there's a particular school that you're following, don't bother to turn up until after 10pm – after a few hours the spectacle can grow somewhat monotonous for all but the most devoted of samba-school fans. You can get to the Sambódromo by metrô, but you'll have to return to your hotel by taxi, as the metrô doesn't run through the night.

The competing samba schools have as many as five thousand members each, and their performances last between sixty and eighty minutes per school. The *baterias* – each made up of two hundred to four hundred drummers – set the beat, and the solo vocalist (*aspuxador*) repeats the hopefully catchy *samba de enredo* until almost hoarse, joined by the entire school as a backing group. The most spectacular feature of every school are their **floats** (*carros alegóricos*), each illustrating a part of the chosen theme, but there are other entrancing formations, too: the Baianas section, made up of women in colourful, colonial-style dresses; the Velha Guarda, senior samba-school members (always men) who march in white suits and Panama hats; the children's wing and the enormous groups of

Batucada – the continuous, hypnotic rhythm that is the basis of samba – flows through the city's veins

Joining the parade

If you're itching to be more than just a spectator, with a bit of advance planning you can be **part of the Carnival Parade**, something that a growing number of foreign visitors have been doing in recent years. Despite mounting concern that foreigners have lowered the standard of the parades, as they don't adequately learn the words of the songs and their samba dance steps are clumsy at best, some schools – most notably Mangueira (see box on p.242) – continue to welcome tourists. If you want to join in, you'll need to arrive in Rio a couple of weeks in advance to identify a school, join their rehearsals, and, when you're ready, purchase the most glamorous costume you can find.

ordinary supporters of the school, who are rated more for their enthusiasm than their dancing skills. Costumes range from flowing dresses or African robes to glitter applied to an otherwise naked body (complete nudity is banned). A commission of **judges** awards schools points for each of these areas, as well as for timing, the overall theme and whether the entire show comes together as one. Unless you're a Carnival expert, you won't have a clue how one school is selected over the others as a winner, but the winning school is honoured throughout Brazil with appropriate fervour.

As a show, there's nothing to beat the Sambódromo extravaganza. But if you can't get in, don't worry – if it's dancing and hanging out with people that you're really after, you'll be far better off joining a street event, or, better still, attending one of the many Carnival balls (see p.246). Furthermore, the twenty-minute walk down **Avenida Presidente Vargas**, which connects Rio Branco with the Sambódromo, is perhaps the real highlight of the whole weekend. The floats queue up here before they take their turn in the parade, and you can hang around, chat or have a drink with the hundreds of richly costumed paraders nervously waiting their turn. The square by the paraders' entrance to the Sambódromo is packed with makeshift bars whose TVs show what's going on inside and play the never-ending anthems from each samba school while you munch on sausages, *empañadas*, kebabs, corn and plates of rice. These places are generally surrounded by costumed revellers sating their thirst, accompanied by groups of people singing and dancing and banging out a samba rhythm on drums. Above the cacophony, music rises from the stage set up in nearby Praça Onze. Knock back a *caipirinha*, and join the writhing, wriggling masses at the front who tend to dance until dawn.

Carnival balls

Carnival balls are an important element of the weekend events, although they are, in fact, now only faintly reminiscent of the high-society gatherings of the nineteenth century. Each year hundreds of balls – typically featuring two live bands and very, very loud percussion – are organized, with the best held on Carnival Friday, Saturday and Tuesday. Although many are entirely private affairs at exclusive members-only clubs, a fair few are open to anyone able to meet the sometimes-steep entry charges. Most of the biggest balls are held in hotels or in the nightclubs of the well-heeled Zona Sul, often with as many tourists as locals; indeed, the most reliable traditional ball open to the paying public takes place on the Saturday at the *Copacabana Palace Hotel*, Avenida Atlântica 1702 (☎ 21/255-7070), a glorious Art Deco pile that's considered to be one of the best hotels in the world. Attended by local socialites and the rich and famous from around the world, tickets cost well over US$500 (available from the hotel itself) and always sell out in advance. Black tie or some sort of very glamorous costume is obligatory. Most balls, however, are far less expensive (expect to pay US$30–80 for admission) and have no set dress code; you can also usually just turn up on the night to buy a ticket, although if you want a table you'll need to book a few days in advance.

Even though pretty well all balls are **gay-friendly**, there are a few that are very much considered high points of Rio's gay social calendar. The most traditional is the Gala Gay, held on the Tuesday at the elegant *Teatro Scala*, Avenida Afrânio de Melo Franco 296, Leblon (☎ 21/2239-4448). Guests – straight, gay, transvestite – turn up in some of the most outrageous costumes that you're likely to see anywhere, although fancy dress is by no means compulsory. There's no need to actually participate in the ball to get a sense of its style – there are always hundreds of people milling around outside to watch and photograph the extravagantly dressed partygoers arriving – though you'd be passing up a pretty unforgettable experience if you did get no further than the door; it's well worth the US$80 entrance price, with amazing costumes, stunning women, and a glistening knot of near-naked bodies on the dance floor getting down to the non-stop samba.

Gala Gay is nowadays a fairly mainstream event, televised live to a massive audience and with photos splashed across magazines and newspapers after Carnival. For more gritty, gay-oriented balls, find out what's happening on Saturday and Tuesday at *the Fundação Progresso*, Rua dos Arcos 24, Lapa (☎ 21/2220-5070), a huge dance space in a renovated downtown factory that attracts a younger, trendier and slightly less exhibitionist crowd.

> **Insider info** There's so much going on during Carnival that you'll need to work out a timetable of where to be and what to do. On arrival, buy copies of the newspaper *O Globo* and the magazine *Veja* – their listings sections give the exact times, prices and venues for all of the party hot-spots.

The morning after

One of Rio's most obvious attractions is its **beaches**, the two most popular of which are, of course, **Copacabana** and **Ipanema**, two huge stretches of sand that are more like city parks than anything else. Copacabana beach is always the more crowded of the two, drawing tourists from the beachside hotels as well as *cariocas* from every section of Rio society. Ipanema is slightly less frenetic, and the beachgoers like to think of themselves as more of an elite. Different sections of the beaches – marked by identifying posts, or *postos* – attract markedly different social groups. For example, the stretch of sand east from Rua Farme de Amoedo to Rua Teixeira de Melo is where gay men congregate, while artists and intellectuals relax shoulder-to-shoulder around *posto* 9. Watch out for red flags placed on the beaches not only to signify heavy seas (even at the best of times, there's a strong undercurrent) but also some plentiful pollution. If the sand's not packed solid, there's probably a very good reason why.

Apart from the beaches, taking the cable car to the top of **Sugar Loaf Mountain** is a fine way to wind down, as is experiencing the view from the famous statue of **Christ the Redeemer** on the Corcovado hill. The tram ride from the city centre to Santa Teresa is a must, especially the breathtaking section that takes you across the mid-eighteenth-century Arcos da Lapa, an impressive Roman-style aqueduct. In Santa Teresa itself, you can wander the narrow streets, admire the once grand hillside houses and linger in one of the district's many bars and restaurants.

Salvador: a rival for Rio?

These days, Rio has a challenger for the title of Carnival Capital of the World. Arguably the coolest party in the Americas, and rivalling Rio for its hedonism, atmosphere and sheer unstoppable beat, takes place in **Salvador**, the capital city of the state of Bahia, on Brazil's tropical northeast coast. Salvador was once the biggest slave city on the continent – people of African origin are still in a huge majority here and Salvadoreans take their partying seriously. More than two hundred groups keep the carnival beat going over five days of continuous mayhem, as a million party people (the vast majority from Salvador and elsewhere in Bahia) sweat, shake and shimmy their way to oblivion – or at least until the morning of Ash Wednesday. Some five million litres of beer are downed against a backdrop of the hottest sounds in Brazil – Gilberto Gil, Timbalada and Carlinhos Brown, to name a few, play here each year.

Even if you don't catch one of the big names, you can't miss the awesome sound systems that trundle their way round the blocked-off streets that form the carnival circuit. Each one of these things, called a *trio elétrico*, is a two-storey-high stack of speakers mounted on the back of a truck, with a live band, or *bloco*, on top – most often playing Salvador's homegrown African *axé* music (pronounced "aa-hay"), and surrounded by dancing girls. The *blocos* have specific days and times when they parade through the streets. You can join them by buying a shirt or uniform, called an *abadá*, which entitles you to enter a cordoned-off section as the *bloco* dances its way through the Campo Grande, and the neighbourhoods of Barra, Ondina and Pelourinho – where the pace is more relaxed and the celebrations, held among a stunning array of colonial architecture, more traditional.

For more **information**, contact Bahiatursa, the Bahia Tourist Authority, at Rua das Laranjeiras 12, Pelourinho, Salvador (☎ 71/321-2133, ⦿www. bahiatursa.ba.gov.br).

Basics

Rio's Tom Jobin **airport** is on Ilha do Governador in Guanabara Bay, 20km north of the city. All major intercity **bus** services arrive at the Novo Rio Rodovária, 3km north of the centre, in São Cristoão. Riotur is the best source of **tourist information** (see below).

Rio is divided into a Zona Norte and the more affluent Zona Sul, where most of the Carnival action takes place and where pretty well all hotels are located, in Flamengo, Copacabana, Ipanema and Leblon. You can easily reach – by taxi, bus or metrô – the best Carnival spots from each of these neighbourhoods.

Accommodation

Despite Rio's abundance of hotel beds, you'd be foolish to arrive in the city during Carnival without having first arranged a **place to stay**. Predictably, rates shoot up around this time, with many hotels and hostels only accepting reservations for the entire five-night period and charging twice as much as normal. Expect to pay at least US$70–100 per night for a double room in a basic two-star hotel, rising to well over US$500 per night for luxury accommodation.

For those on a tight budget, Rio's numerous **hostels** – charging around US$40 per person – are by far the best option. The *Chave do Rio Hostel*, Rua General Dionísio 63 (☏ 21/2286-0303, ⊕www.riohostel.com.br), in Botafogo, and the *Copacabana Chalet Hostel*, Rua Pompeu Loureiro 99 (☏ 21/2236-0047), a few blocks back from the beach in Copacabana, are long-established and popular places, while *Hostel Ipanema* (☏ 21/2268-0565, ⊕justfly@justfly.com.br) is a friendly, laid-back choice in the classy suburb of the same name.

For a real insiders' experience of Carnival, *Cama e Café* (☏ 21/2224-5689, ⊕www.camaecafe.com.br) offer a range of **bed and breakfast places** (US$100–200 for a double) in Santa Teresa, a pretty Bohemian neighbourhood in the hills overlooking the city centre – most of the hosts are great sources of local knowledge.

Of Rio's cheaper **hotels**, it's worth checking out *Turístico*, Ladeira da Glória 30 (☏ 21/2558-9388), located in Glória, roughly midway between the city centre and the Zona Sul beaches, which is always popular with foreign backpackers, and the simple *Hotel Santa Teresa*, Rua Almirante Alexandrino 30 (☏ 21/2242-0007), the only hotel in Santa Teresa. Both charge US$70 or more per night for a double room at Carnival. With more money (around US$120), you could upgrade to the *Hotel Acapulco Copacabana*, Rua Gustavo Sampaio 854 (☏ 21/2275-0022, ⊕www.acapulcocopacabanahotel.com.br), set in a quiet location moments from Leme beach, which merges into Copacabana, or the very friendly *Arpoador Inn*, Rua Francisco Otaviano 177 (☏ 21/2523-0060) – about the least expensive option in fashionable Ipanema. If money is less of an issue, the *Grandville Ouro Verde*, Avenida Atlântica 1800 (☏ 21/2543-4123; around US$250), might be more your style; while unremarkable-looking, it offers comfort and style faintly reminiscent of a European grand hotel. If you can manage upwards of US$600 per night, the luxurious *Copacabana Palace Hotel*, Avenida Atlântica 1702, Copacabana (☏ 21/2548-7070, ⊕www.copacabanapalace.com.br), is really the ultimate Carnival place to stay.

Eating and drinking

Brazilian beer is the summertime **drink** in Rio; it's always drunk ice-cold and is a watery, rather tasteless brew that's easy to drink as a thirst-quencher – and, as such, easy to down in huge quantities. Antarctica and Brahma are the brands to go for. Ask for a *chope* – pronounced "shoppie" – when you are in a bar and you'll get a smallish glass of draught beer. For something a little stronger, Brazil's most famous cocktail, the *caipirinha*, makes for a wonderfully simple drink of lime, cachaça (rum) and sugar. As a liquid antidote to excessive partying, try the hugely popular *guaraná*, a sweet fizzy drink with an Amazonian berry as its key ingredient, or some of the wonderful *sucos* (juices) and *vitaminas* (juices made with a milk-base rather than water) that are freshly made at juice bars on seemingly every block of the city. One of the best of these is *BB Lanches*, at Rua Aristides Espinola 64-A in Leblon – *açaí*, the juice of Amazon palm fruit, is the locals' choice of refreshment.

Restaurants and **bars** are as varied as you'd expect in a city the size of Rio. Santa Teresa and Botafogo are particularly good neighbourhoods for restaurants – in the former, *Bar do Arnaudo*, Rua Almirante Alexandrino 316, is a landmark hangout that does excellent food from the Brazilian northeast. If you want to splash out, try the nearby *Aprazível*, Rua Aprazível 62, which serves superb Franco-Brazilian dishes on a terrace overlooking the city. There are lots of choices in Botafogo, too, with one of the best being *Yorubá*, Rua Visconde de Pirajá 128, serving distinctive Afro-Bahian dishes.

Health and safety

Rio de Janeiro has a poor reputation for **personal safety**, but much of the violence is drug-related, and tourists are rarely affected. Nevertheless, a few common-sense precautions should be taken: don't carry too much money or your only credit cards with you; always be sure to carry some readily available cash if threatened by a mugger; and don't be stupid enough to take anyone on – they're likely to be armed with a knife or even a gun. If you need help, or need to report a theft, go to the helpful Tourist Police, Avenida Afrânio de Melo Franco, across from the Teatro Casa Grande in Leblon.

It's wise to bring a good supply of **mosquito repellent**, as Rio has been struck before by dengue fever, a viral disease spread by mosquito bites. Early symptoms include severe aches and pains and a blinding headache so, unless you're absolutely sure these symptoms are just the result of a hard night's dancing and drinking, get yourself to a hospital.

One other thing: despite the high level of HIV and AIDS awareness in Brazil, the quality of Brazilian **condoms** is poor. If you think that there's even the slightest possibility that you'll be in need of some, be sure to bring them with you.

Event info

Rio Carnival (⊕ www.rio-carnival.net). One of the best sources of information about Carnival, and a reliable means of purchasing tickets to the Sambódromo.

Useful websites

Riotur Rua da Assembleia, Centro (☏ 21/2217-7552; Mon–Fri 9am–6pm), and Av. Princesa Isabel 183, Copacabana (☏ 21/2541-7522; same hours). Rio's city tourist information office can tell you most things you need to know.

Love Rio (⊕ www.love-rio.com/samba). Great details on Rio's samba schools.

Time zone GMT-3   **Country code** +55   **Currency:** Real (R$)

Trinidad Carnival

moko jumby, jamettes, pissenlits, sailors and jab jabs

Trinidad Carnival

Where?

Port of Spain and smaller towns, Trinidad and Tobago

When?

February or March

How long?

2 days

Port of Spain

TRINIDAD

A huge, joyful, rum-soaked celebration, Trinidad's carnival – by far the biggest in the Caribbean – consumes almost the entire country. The two days of Carnival itself are not a national holiday, but shops and offices islandwide close their doors, and general business comes to a respectful halt in favour of partying. In the days – indeed months – leading up to the event, almost every aspect of Trini life has some connection with pre-Carnival activities, from corporate calypso competitions to fundraising fetes (fete being the usual term for a huge outdoor party). Carnival is nothing short of a national obsession, a fixation that stems from the fact that in Trinidad, perhaps more than anywhere else, it is an overwhelmingly participatory event. It's not something you watch, but something you're part of – a festival that belongs to everybody.

History

Originallly a three-day splurge before Ash Wednesday, the Trinidad Carnival was **first celebrated** in the late eighteenth century by white French planters, who paraded in costumes that parodied their slaves. Men played *negres jardines* (field labourers), and women *mulattresses* as a means of escaping the so-called responsibilities of power and respectability. Following emancipation in 1834, freed Africans took to the streets as well, satirizing their former masters' affectations and idiosyncrasies with Carnival characters such as the Dame Lorraine, a salacious, huge-bottomed planter woman, or drawing on West African cultural traditions to create characters such as the stilt-walking, ten-foot tall *moko jumby*, and mischievous devils known as *jab jabs*. Music came courtesy of makeshift percussion instruments, while atmosphere was added by *canboulay* – flaming flambeaux that symbolized the Africans' freedom from the dangerous task of putting out burning cane fields.

All this exuberance was viewed with displeasure by the white ruling class, who took exception to what they saw as desecration of the Sabbath on the first day of Carnival. In 1843, it was decreed that Carnival could not begin until Monday, but as no specific time was given, carnivalgoers began to celebrate on the stroke of midnight, and **Jouvert** (a corruption of the French *jour ouvert*, or "the beginning of the day"), the no-holds-barred early-hours opener to Carnival that still takes place today, was born. Carnival continued to act as an outlet for irreverence and satire, with new characters such as *jamettes* (prostitutes), cross-dressing *pissenlits* (literally, bed-wetters) and sailors (outrageous parodies of the British naval officers stationed in Trinidad), while revellers moved to the beat of drumming bands and entertained themselves with *kalenda*, or stickfighting, competitions. Again, the British administration (Trinidad had by now been ceded to England) saw Carnival as a threat to its authority, and took steps to subdue the event. Riots ensued when a group of masqueraders were apprehended in 1881, but the Brits went on to prohibit *jamettes* and *pissenlits* on the grounds of lewdness, and ban African-style drumming, *canboulay* and *kalenda*.

Carnival wasn't about to go quietly, though, and while the celebration was subsequently toned down, it never disappeared completely. Masqueraders continued to parade the streets, and received a boost in the 1890s by the introduction of a competition for the best costume band. During the early twentieth century, practically every aspect of Carnival was turned into a competitive event, and in 1921, calypsonian Chieftain Douglas established Trinidad's first **calypso tent**, where performers showcased their compositions for the forthcoming Carnival in front of audiences, who were (and remain) as generous with their booing and heckling as with their applause. Many more tents sprung up around the city, and the tradition became firmly established, the canvas giving way to today's permanent structures.

After a break during World War II, Carnival returned with a vengeance, this time swinging to the sweet tones of the newly invented **steel pan**. The event's growing cultural significance was officially recognized in the late 1950s with the establishment of the **National Carnival Commission**. The masquerade (usually shortened to "mas") bands became ever larger, with trucks pumping out live music alongside the steelbands marching the streets, and traditional costumes giving way to more contemporary and sometimes political themes. Costumes also became more brief and, these days, it's bikinis rather than traditional mas that rule the road. There are some who bemoan the fact that Carnival traditions are being swept away, but the changes in tone of the bands' presentations have at least kept people on the streets – particularly women, who make up the majority of the masqueraders – and you can still see all the traditional characters on parade at Victoria Square on Carnival Sunday.

Trinidad's obsession with Carnival doesn't only take over the nation for the two days of the party itself – preparations for Carnival start in autumn of the previous year, when mas bands start to hold launches of their chosen theme, and potential players are invited to sign up. The carnival calendar is determined by whenever Lent is, but things always move up a gear by late January, with the atmosphere building at the opening of the calypso tents, where the steelbands rehearse their pan performances in anticipation of the Panorama Finals. By the time Jouvert, the official start to Carnival, arrives you might feel like you've done it all already – it pays to pace yourself and save your best for last.

Mas bands and costume hunting

As mops and buckets are employed to contend with the last of the summer rains, Trinidad's most dedicated carnivalists are already hard at work. Mas-makers – creative, hardworking souls who dedicate months of free time to making the costumes worn in the mas bands – are hunched over chicken wire, fibreglass and innumerable glittery substances producing prototypes of the final designs.

From October onwards, the various bands present their designs to the public by way of a **launch** – basically, a huge party, with free-flowing rum and blaring soca music only just taking second place to the designs on display. The largest bands have a variety of "sections" as each design is known. Everyone wants to "play mas" with their friends – and for US$100–150 you can buy a costume and play mas, too – so there's much deliberation over which section of which band to choose. Wearability is a key element, along the lines of "Will these beads become trapped in my groin while I dance?" and, "Can I really get away with a thong, a bikini top and some feathers?" – but unless you choose to play with a more creative band such as MacFarlane or Minshall's Callaloo (with whom you'll get some thought behind the theme, and considerably more fabric over your body), you'll be faced with much of a muchness. These days, what's known as **pretty mas** rules the streets, and though the colours and themes may differ, the bands are fairly indistinguishable

Insider info If you're not around to attend the launches, you can still buy a costume by visiting the mas camp of your band of choice, where the designs are on show until they sell out (visitors are often welcome to view production as well); or buy online via the bands' websites (see box).

from each other – basically, embellished bikinis for women, fancy shorts and a waistcoat or chestpiece for men, both topped by an elaborate headdress and garnished with bits to attach to the legs and arms. Flags and standards come with most costumes, and you'll usually get a small bag to hold your rum and your "rag" (an essential anti-sweat tool, also used to wave in the air in appreciation of the tunes you like). Bands vary in terms of the facilities they supply for revellers; all bands will have music trucks, while some offer everything from moving bars, breakfast and lunch, to "wee-wee trucks" (flatbeds topped with a row of portaloos), security guards, or misting stations, where overdanced players get a cooling spray of water. If you're a soca aficionado, it's also worth checking out who's DJing on the music trucks, and which local acts will be performing live during the course of the parades.

Getting each and every costume complete and ready for collection before Carnival weekend is a serious business – all around the city, the camps become a whirl of activity, as mas-makers work through the night to meet the deadline. These places are more like factories than workshops (imagine being the person responsible for ensuring that the thousand-odd costumes in a section all have exactly seven strings of beads attached to them, or just the right amount of sequins on a bra-top), and it's difficult not to get excited by the buzz of industry that suffuses the air as fingers deftly sew, glue, nail and prod the costumes into shape.

Mas bands

All the addresses below are in and around Port of Spain. Note that at the time of writing, Poison, formerly T&T's largest mas band, had been disbanded, although some former organizers (including Meg Cheekes, with her Pulse 8 band) plan to bring out smaller bands in future Carnivals; for more information, check out the Carnival websites listed below.

Brian MacFarlane 7 Ariapita Ave, Woodbrook (☎623/0011, ⊛www.macfarlanecarnival.net).

Callaloo Company/Peter Minshall Building C, Western Main Rd, Chaguaramas (☎634 4491, ⊛www.callaloo.co.tt).

D'Midas Associates 15–17 Kitchener St, Woodbrook (☎622 8233).

Genesis 6 Picton St, Tragarete Rd (☎622 8060, ⊛www.genesiscarnival.com).

Harts 5 Alcazar St, St Clair (☎622 8038, ⊛www.hartscarnival.com).

Island Events 55 Luis St, St Clair (☎622 5581, ⊛www.islandevents.com).

Island People 11 Stone St, Woodbrook (☎625 1386, ⊛www.islandpeoplemas.com).

Legacy 88 Roberts St, Woodbrook (☎622 7466, ⊛www.legacycarnival.com).

Masquerade 19 DeVerteuil St, Woodbrook (☎623 2161, ⊛www.masquerade.co.tt).

Skandal-Us Cnr Alberto St & Ariapita Ave, Woodbrook (☎622 3953, ⊛www.skandalmas.com).

Trevor Wallace & Associates 2 George Cabral St, St James (☎628 4185, ⊛www.trevorwallacemas.com).

Tribe 20 Rosalino St, Woodbrook (☎625 6800, ⊛www.carnivaltribe.com).

Trini Revellers 35 Gallus St, Woodbrook (☎625 1881, ⊛www.revellers.com).

Feting

Costume choice out of the way, mas-playing Trinis set about getting their bodies into good enough shape to parade through the streets and dance for hours on end. Gyms are packed and the three-mile perimeter around the city's biggest open space, the Queen's Park Savannah, becomes a glorified jogging track in the cool early morning or twilight hours. Those with a slightly more frivolous bent, however, tone their muscles by dedicating themselves to attending each and every one of the pre-Carnival fetes that start once Christmas is over.

Hugely varied in atmosphere and character, **Carnival fetes** are staged by practically every institution in Trinidad: during one week, you can take your pick from the National Flour Mills, Blood Bank or Police fetes (the last is a surprisingly raucous affair) or more chi-chi, all-inclusive events, where tickets cover food and unlimited drink, and the more well-heeled come out to shake a leg. All the fetes, though, are a means for carnivalists to get into the party spirit. Usually held outdoors, with a stage for soca artists to showcase their Carnival tunes, they're hugely good-natured affairs, fuelled by copious amounts of rum and an unbelievably energetic party madness that's uniquely Trinidadian. Attend one and you'll inevitably be pulled into the throng and taught to "wine" (as the local elastic-waisted dancing style is known) until you stagger home at daybreak. Look out, too, for so-called "wet fetes", where power hoses are liberally employed to cool down the dancing hordes.

While some fetes are one-offs, most return each year, and the mother of them all is **Brass Fete**, held at the Queen's Park Oval cricket ground a couple of weeks before the Carnival. With several stages and a predominantly young crowd, it's also regarded as one of the rougher events, and is best attended in a group. You'll see plenty of young guys wearing bedraggled women's wigs and sock-stuffed bras, some of the dirtiest dancing on the planet, and loads of impossibly huge flags that revellers wave to demonstrate appreciation of the acts. By the end of the night, you'll have a good idea of who's who in the soca world – and very tired hips.

The panyards and the Panorama Finals

It may not seem physically possible to attend a fete every night of the week, but in the last few days before Carnival, many Trinis pride themselves on doing exactly this and still turning up for work the next day. So, it's a good idea to intersperse your feting by touring around Port of Spain's **panyards**, where the steelbands practice for the annual Panorama Finals, a giant tournament in which T&T's greatest bands do battle. It's best to reserve a whole night for panyard visiting, so that you can compare how different bands sound, and it's a good idea to visit more than once, so you can hear the tunes getting sweeter and crisper, as the heats and the final draw near. Panyards expect visitors, so there's usually chairs or bleachers to sit on while you listen, and a bar. Renegades on Charlotte Street is one of the most central yards, while Phase II Pan Groove, housed in a large, open compound in Woodbrook, a neighbourhood just west of downtown, is always good for a lime as you take in the music. High in the hills of Laventille, where the steel pan was invented, Desperadoes panyard is probably the most atmospheric, with fanatical "Despers" supporters ensuring that things are kept lively.

By far the sweetest place to hear pan, though, is at the **Panorama Finals**, staged on the Saturday before the main Carnival parades. Head down to the Savannah at dusk, by which time the grass around the main stage is packed with practicing bands, as well as stalls selling drinks and snacks to the crowd. You have three choices in terms of where to be. The more grass-roots crowd stick to the area around the approaches of the

stage, where bands queue up before performing; variously known as the "tracks" or the "drag", this is the place to watch practice sessions and help push the trolleys of pans and players onto the stage. If you fancy a seat, there's the rowdy North Stand, where coolers packed with rum and Carib fuel the party atmosphere, or the more genteel Grand Stand – both of these have a minimal entrance fee. (Tickets for both stands sell fast, so it's best to buy in advance). Wherever you watch from, it's essential to catch at least one of the big bands crossing the stage: most number around 150 pannists. Stand within fifty feet of the players and the music vibrates through every sinew of your body.

Calypso tents

Though they've little to do with canvas these days, **calypso tents** are one of the original components of Trini Carnival, and catching at least one performance of traditional *kaiso* (the purists' name for calypso) provides an essential introduction to – and analysis of – whatever's making the news or the gossip columns in T&T. Each year, the country's established calypsonians write two or three compositions to perform in the tents, with subject matter ranging from the price of World Cup football tickets or satirical character assassinations of politicians and public figures to serious political comment on the state of the nation. The tents provide a public platform for the favorite Trini pastime of *picong*: employing verbal dexterity so as to take the mickey, and do so very wittily. Sex – by way of none-too-subtle but inevitably hilarious allegory and double entendre – is also a hugely popular topic. However, what with the liberal use of local slang and constant allusions to recent scandals, it pays to visit a tent with someone local who has the patience to explain the more parochial jokes and references.

The main tents are now established annual institutions, attracting similar lineups each year. Most tents are open every night in the last month or so before Carnival (as well as for a couple of weeks after Carnival weekend), and some switch venues – to the Savannah Grandstand, or the Trinidad Country Club in Maraval, for example – just before Carnival in order to accommodate a bigger crowd. Most stick to pretty much the same formula: an MC marshals events, usually taking every possible oral swipe at the competitors he or she introduces, and one by one the performers take to the stage. If the first verses of their tune are greeted with applause, the calypsonian sings on; stony silences can be rectified by dextrous vocal retorts, but it's more likely that anyone that doesn't get a positive crowd response will not finish their song. Those that prove popular get to the end of their tune, and often come back with another as well.

Like everything concerned with Carnival, the tents are all about showmanship, and though traditional singers stick to a mike and some killer lyrics, performances are becoming increasingly more theatrical, with impressive costumes themed to fit the tune, and back-up from dancers, *moko jumbies* or a series of props. Newer "humorous" tents have completely changed the formula, too, creating a seamless comedy cabaret in which calypsonians' tunes are intermingled with skits – perhaps a more accessible style if you're attending for the first time. For more serious calypso, head to Kaiso House (City Hall, Knox Street), where stalwarts such as the marvellous Singing Sandra, Brother Resistance and Shadow are heckled by the brilliant local comedian Rachel Price; the tent of the late great Lord Kitchener, Calypso Revue (SWWTU Hall, Wrightson Road), draws an equally prestigious line-up and has a more traditional feel.

Panyards

The panyards below are all close to central Port of Spain.
BP Renegades 138 Charlotte St, Port of Spain (☏785 6010).
BWIA Invaders 147 Tragarete Rd, Woodbrook (☏633 2397).
Carib Tokyo 2A Plaisance Rd, East Dry River, John John (☏623 7758).
Neal & Massy Trinidad All Stars 46 Duke St, Port of Spain (☏632 8187).
Petrotrin Phase II Pan Groove 13 Hamilton St, Woodbrook (☏627 0909).
PCS Starlift 187c Tragarete Rd, Woodbrook (☏622 9308).
Scrunters Pan Groove 10 Jeffers Lne, St James (☏622 9550).
WITCO Desperadoes Upper Laventille Road, East Dry River, Laventille (☏752 2742).
Woodbrook Playboyz 24 Woodford St, Newtown (☏628 0320).

Carnival weekend

After an ever-more fete-heavy week, Carnival Friday sees the first of the full-blown Carnival fixtures, the **Soca Monarch** competition, usually held on the hallowed turf of the Oval cricket ground. Featuring all the big-name soca acts in the Caribbean, it's a similar, if slightly more orderly, scene to Brass Fete – lots of flag- and rag-waving, wining, drinking and crowd response; if you see chamberpots placed on the stage, or a flurry of toilet rolls aimed at a performer, you can be pretty sure they're not going to win.

Come Carnival Saturday, the city is all set and raring to go: with a mini-village of huts constructed around the edges of the Savannah, and stalls along the main streets, selling *roti*, bake-and-shark, corn soup, doubles and, of course, rum and beers. If you're not at the Savannah for the Panorama Finals, then Saturday night should see you grooving away at one of the numerous fetes or getting a decent night's sleep in preparation for the taxing few days ahead.

Jouvert is the raw side of Carnival, in which people play "dirty mas", daubing themselves from head to toe in mud, grease, body paint and chocolate

Sunday morning is best spent watching the fabulous traditional Carnival characters in Victoria Square, while the afternoon offers a pick of several last-minute fetes: TASA all-inclusive fete in the Queen's Hall car park is usually one of the most intense of the lot. However, if you've any sense, you'll be at home with your feet up, because Sunday evening should see you back at the Savannah for **Dimanche Gras**, when the huge king and queen costumes are presented to the judges. Here, calypsonians competing for the **Calypso Monarch** title give equally lavish performances, with plenty of special effects to enhance the music. Inevitably, the show drags on into the early hours so, if you can, leave yourself enough time to get out onto the streets for Jouvert, which starts at about 1am.

Jouvert

Jouvert is the raw side of Carnival – pure, unadulterated bacchanalia, in which people wear wickedly satirical home-made costumes or choose to play "dirty mas", daubing themselves from head to toe in mud, grease, body paint and chocolate and then slithering along the streets with a mass of happy, drunken, dirty humanity, anonymous enough to do pretty much anything that takes their fancy, while a steelband, sound-system truck or rhythm section (a band of percussion players) marches alongside. It's immensely joyful, and it's a good idea to dress in something old and brief – wear white, and you're guaranteed a host of filthy hugs. The crowning point of the night is an anarchic crossing of the Savannah stage in all your muddy glory.

Many people just head out onto the streets independently to play Jouvert – you'll find that it won't take long for someone to cover you in mud, and there are plenty of music trucks and wandering pan bands to which you can attach yourself. However, if you're new to Carnival it's a good idea to sign up with an organized **Jouvert band**. Names to look out for are Mudsters Inc, Mudders International, and

the band created each year by Rapso group 3-Canal, but new outfits spring up each year. As with the main costume bands, organized Jouvert bands charge a fee (from US$45), which includes a rudimentary costume, purified (and sometimes heated) mud, body-paint and drinks, as well as mobile toilets and facilities in which to shower off all the gunge before going home. Furthermore, most of the established outfits avoid the traditionally manic downtown area, and have posses of burly security men to look after their revellers – a comforting thought given that robberies and even assaults amidst all the madness are becoming increasingly common. Whether you're with a band or not, leave all jewellery at home, secrete your money away carefully, and be wary of getting too inebriated.

Carnival Monday and Tuesday

At six or seven in the morning, the Jouvert crowds start to drift home for a quick shower (those with real stamina head for Maqueripe Beach to wash off in the sea) before meeting their Carnival band at around 8am for the **Parade of the Bands**. Most start in Woodbrook, and make their way towards central Port of Spain, winding through the streets towards the Savannah, where they'll cross the stage and then head homewards. Many bands ask their revellers to wear only some of their costume (or something entirely different) on Monday, saving their best outfit for Tuesday's parade, though the sound trucks that accompany the bands are still out in force. By the evening, the best plan (if you're not already exhausted and sunburnt) is to find a steelband truck that's headed in the direction of wherever you're staying, and follow it home.

The final Carnival Tuesday sees bands out on the streets again at 8am, this time dressed in all their finery. If you're not playing mas and want to see the costumes, position yourself at any of the judging points, where the ground troops' costumes and enthusiasm are assessed, and where someone keeps track of what mas players' feet are moving to – the song that's played the most at the judging points is awarded the coveted title of "Road March". In the Savannah, the Grand Stand and North Stand provide the best views, as masqueraders summon every last ounce of energy to impress the judges as they cross the stage. Some of the larger bands, which can number several thousand people, can take hours to pass, much to the fury of security guards and the bands behind, but now that the massive Poison is no more (ten thousand revellers was too much for the organizers to handle), passage across the stage should be smoother. Standing in the tracks is perhaps a more atmospheric viewpoint, though, and you can join in the dancing anywhere on the street (though woe betide you if you try and mingle with a costume band anywhere near a judging point). The partying continues non-stop all day, with "last-lap" parades on the streets allowing the most dedicated their final dance. By midnight, it's all over – though most continue the fun the following day by heading to huge beach parties at nearby Maracas and Manzanilla, along the east coast.

Basics

Port of Spain is the capital city of Trinidad and Tobago but it's easy to orient yourself among the landmarks, and the neighbourhoods mentioned are all walkable or a few minutes' drive from downtown. **Getting there** at least two weeks before Carnival ensures that you'll be able to tour the panyards and mas camps, take in the calypso tents, attend the fetes, the Soca and Calypso monarchs and Panorama Finals, and get a bit of a tan at Maracas before the main event. BWIA **fly** to Trinidad daily from London, and offer services from several US gateways; you'll need to arrange flights well in advance – seasoned revellers book up for the following year on Ash Wednesday. If you want to play mas, you should also reserve a **costume** in good time (you can buy online; see the box on p.252), as popular sections sell out fast.

Accommodation

Accommodation is in severe demand during Carnival. Most places in Port of Spain hike their rates hugely at this time, and many insist on a five- or seven-night minimum stay, from Carnival Friday onwards. For a middle-of-the-road kind of place, expect to pay at least US$100 per double room per night. TIDCO have an exhaustive list of accommodation on their website (see below), and several of the sites listed below have details of places to stay, as well.

Some good options include *Pearl's*, 3–4 Victoria Square East (☎ 625 2158), a rambling colonial house in the heart of Carnival territory (overlooking a judging point), whose rooms are basic but perfectly adequate – although the best thing about them is the price, US$20, unheard of at Carnival time. Going up in cost, *Trinbago*, 37 Ariapita Ave, Woodbrook (☎ 627 7114, ✉ tourist@tstt.net.tt), has a fab location on the Carnival route, a tiny pool, and rooms with a/c or fan, private or shared bathroom, for US$70. *Alicia's House*, 7 Coblentz Gardens, St Ann's (☎ 623 2802, ✆ www.aliciashousetrinidad.com), is five-minutes' walk from the Savannah on a quiet cul-de-sac that offers respite from the party madness. It has a pool, restaurant, and neat rooms with a/c and TV, and breakfast is included in its five-night Carnival package of US$850 for two people in a double room. *Normandie*, 10 Nook Ave (☎ 624 1811, ✆ www.normandiett.com), on the outskirts of St Ann's, a short walk from the Savannah, is an old-timer that's still one of the best Carnival bolt-holes, with peace and quiet interrupted only by the fantastic annual concerts held here during Carnival season – king calypsonian David Rudder is a regular performer. Rooms are tasteful, with all mod cons, and there are shops, a pool and restaurant on site. The five-night Carnival package for two in a double room, including airport transfers and breakfast, is US$1390.

Eating and drinking

Carnival is a time for partying rather than gastronomic heaven. As most restaurants close during Carnival itself, you'll need to make do with **street food** most of the time – not a problem in Trinidad, as it's almost always delicious, and sold by vendors lining Western Main Road in St James, who proudly display their government-issued food-hygiene badges.

The best option to soak up the rum is a *roti*, the ultimate Trini snack; flat Indian bread folded over to hold fillings from curried chicken to pumpkin, potato or spinach. Another good filler is a plate of *pelau* – chicken, vegetables and rice cooked down in coconut milk. Otherwise, bake-and-shark, seasoned shark steaks sandwiched between a freshly made bread-like "bake" and served with tamarind sauce and salad, is freely available, though never tastes as good eaten away from Maracas beach, its traditional home. Other staple fillers are split pea-filled corn soup, with chunks of sweetcorn and coriander-like *chadon beni* herbs; doubles – chickpea (known as *channa*) curry and cucumber relish slapped between two fried *bara* breads; and *pholourie*, moreish doughballs served with sweet and spicy tamarind sauce.

Event info

National Carnival Commission Queen's Park Savannah Grandstand, Port of Spain (☎ 627 1350, ✆ www.ncctt.org).
National Carnival Bands Association Queen's Park West, Port of Spain (☎ 627 1422 or 625 9772, ✆ www.ncbatt.com)
Pan Trinbago Suite 1D, Victoria Suites, Victoria Square North, Port of Spain (☎ 623 4486, ✆ www.pantrinbago.com).
Trinbago Unified Calypsonians Organization Business Unit Office, 22 Jerningham Avenue, Belmont (☎ 6623 9660, ✆ www.tuco.co.tt).
T&T Tourist Board (TIDCO) 10–14 Phillips St, Port of Spain (☎ 623 1932 or 6022 7 623 3848, ✆ www.visittnt.com).

Useful websites

HOMEVieWTnT (✆ www.homeviewtnt.com). Slick site with live radio feeds and hoards of Trini titbits.
Trini diary (✆ www.trinidiary.com). Information site on current events in T&T; and an e-newsletter, which includes an exhaustive and regularly updated calendar of events in the run-up to Carnival.
Carnaval.com (✆ www.carnaval.com/main.htm). Excellent site with plenty of Carnival-related background info, from accommodation in Port of Spain to pan, mas and Trini music.
TnTisland (✆ www.tntisland.com); **PlayCarnival.com** (✆ www.playcarnival.com); **Trinibase** (✆ www.trinibase.com). Eclectic sites on all things Trinidadian, with plenty of Carnival information.
Trinidad and Tobago Web Directory (✆ www.search.co.tt). Directory of T&T-related links.

The Americas and the Caribbean

The best of the rest

Accompong Maroon Festival

Where? St Elizabeth, Jamaica
When? June
How long? 1 day

June 1 is the most important day of the year for Jamaican Maroons, descendants of the escaped African slaves who lived wild on the island and waged ferocious war against the British in the seventeenth and eighteenth centuries. Maroons from across Jamaica flock to commemorate the signing of the June 1, 1739, peace treaty, which ended the First Maroon War and granted their ancestors semi-independence. You have to be up early: celebrations start before dawn, with drumming, dancing and chanting at the nearby Peace Cave, followed by a procession by the elders and much blowing of horns and banging of Goombay drums. After the ceremony, the dancing, singing, feasting and drinking raves away pretty much uninterrupted all day and all night. Spectators are welcome, but outsiders need to bring a pretty robust sense of humour and a stomach for rum, as the Maroons are a pretty wild lot, not least when they celebrate their independence and warrior heritage. All are welcome, but Brits are advised to adopt American accents for the day.

Aloha Festivals

Where? Hawaii, USA
When? September and October
How long? 6 weeks

The Hawaiian islands come to a standstill each year for these awesome festivals (Ⓦwww.alohafestivals.com),

a sixty-year-old event designed to celebrate Hawaiian culture and which is in fact the only statewide festival in the entire USA. The Big Island of Hawaii hosts traditional ukelele music and hula dances against a backdrop of rain forests, vast mountains and lava deserts, while the smaller, more developed islands of Oahu and Maui boast high-octane partying. Wherever you are, try to hit a "hoolaulea" or block party. Honolulu and Waikiki Beach see the biggest celebrations, with a downtown street party attended by over a quarter of a million people.

Bay to the Breakers Festival

Where? San Francisco, USA
When? May
How long? 1 day

Held every year since 1912, Bay to the Breakers (Ⓦwww.baytobreakers.com) is one of the largest road races in the world, with around 75,000 participants. The course is 12km long, running from the Embarcadero to the ocean, with competitors ranging from serious athletes to people just along for the ride – the race starts at 8am and finishes early, so that Footstock, the accompanying music festival, can get going in Golden Gate Park. It's all rather corporate and organized these days, with lots of sponsorship and merchandise for sale, but makes a fun day out nonetheless.

Belize National Day

Where? Belize City, Belize
When? September
How long? 3 weeks

Belize's National Day festivities embody one of the great qualities of Caribbean and South American events, namely why cram a party into a day or a weekend when you can roll out the fun for almost a whole month? Just imagine Notting Hill Carnival lasting for three weeks and you get the idea. The extravagant celebrations start on the first weekend of September, with carnival parades, firework displays and all-night parties on pearl-white beaches to commemorate getting rid of the Spanish in 1798, and culminate with the mother of all jump-ups on Independence Day on September 21. Belize only gained independence from the British in 1981, and the novelty in post-colonial Belize City is a long, long way from wearing off.

Aloha Festivals

Boi Bumba

Where? Parintins, Brazil
When? June
How long? 3 days

One of South America's great parties, Boi Bumba (ⓦ www.boibumba.com) is a riot of colour, dancing, pageantry and parades on an island deep in the Amazonian jungle, and as remote as any major festival, even in Brazil, gets – it's a two-day boat journey from "nearby" Manaus. Surrounded by more than 1000km of rainforest on all sides, the isolated location is key to making the festival special. Whereas partygoers in Rio or Salvador gather for the parades and disperse into the city afterwards, in Parintins the sixty-thousand-plus crowd is contained by the Amazon itself – over the three-day frenzy, the festival becomes a private party of familiar faces and dancing bodies.

The event's origins lie in the northeastern Bumba Meu Boi festival (it was introduced into Parintins by immigrants from the state of Maranhão), telling the story of Pai Francisco, his wife Mae Catarina and their theft of a prize bull from a rich landowner. But it tells it on a huge scale, in a purpose-built forty-thousand-seater stadium called the Bumbódromo. Here, two competing teams, Caprichoso and Garantido, parade a series of vast floats made up of thirty-metre-tall serpent heads, jaguars, macaws and other rainforest creatures, which change like scenes from a play, wheeled on by troupes dressed in Indian costumes and surrounded by one-hundred-strong drum orchestras and scores of scantily clad dancers. Against this spectacular backdrop, a whole host of characters tell the story, led by the beautiful feminine spirit of the rainforest, the Cunhã-Poranga, and an Indian shaman, both of whom emerge, in a burst of fireworks, from the mouth of a serpent or jaguar on the most spectacular of the floats. Fans of each group are fiercely partisan, and roar their encouragement from the stadium stands throughout.

Bob Marley Birthday Bash

Where? **Kingston, Jamaica**
When? **February**
How long? **1 day**

The chances are that, even if you aren't a huge reggae fan, you'll still have time for Bob Marley, the Lion from Zion, whose music still plays in every bar in the country, and where he is still regarded with awe. It's hardly surprising, then, that the red-eyed Rasta curators of the unofficial Bob Marley Museum and Mausoleum in Kingston host a highly prestigious knees-up in his honour each year on the date of his birthday, February 6. Gigs – usually featuring Ziggy Marley and other stellar reggae artists – take place at a handful of locations, including Negril, the Bob Marley Museum itself, and the Bob Marley Centre at the great man's birthplace – Nine Miles, in St Ann. Nestled in the middle of ganja plantations, high up in the mountains away from the coast, Nine Miles is well off the tourist beat, but it's easy to jump in a jeep and follow the clouds of smoke to join in the homage to the island's greatest-ever musician.

Bumba Meu Boi

Where? **São Luís, Brazil**
When? **June–August**
How long? **10 weeks**

Large numbers of mostly Brazilian travellers make their way to São Luís, the crumbling old capital of the state of Maranhão in northeastern Brazil, to take part in this annual song-and-dance extravaganza. Around one hundred groups enact the legend of farmhand Pai Francisco and his wife Mae Catarina, who are sentenced to die after killing their estate-owner's bull but are saved from execution by a motley crew of shamans and healers. In June and July, the groups give nightly performances all over town – on church squares, in the old slave-market, and in the open-air Ceprama arena, until the bulls are killed in late August, and their skin, a richly decorated piece of cloth, divided among the participants for good luck. The costumes are incredible, as is the music; of all the different styles now prevalent at the festival, the sotaque de matraca is the most hypnotic of them all, with dancers, wearing disk-like ostrich feather hats, producing clacking rhythms on two simple pieces of wood and stomping their feet on the ground.

Bumbershoot

Where? **Seattle, USA**
When? **Labor Day weekend**
How long? **3 days**

The biggest end-of-summer party in the US, and one of its most eagerly awaited music festivals, Bumbershoot (ⓦ www.bumbershoot.org) attracts a very wide array of international talent. It's held at the Seattle Center park, right in the heart of the city, although its focus on different artistic media other than music makes it like a US version of Glastonbury in outlook. Ticket prices tend to be low for the park, and then extra for specific artists.

BVI Spring Regatta

Where? **British Virgin islands**
When? **April**
How long? **2 days**

Many of the Caribbean islands use Easter time as the launch pad for the start of their regatta season, and none is better than the BVI beanfeast (ⓦ www.bvispringregatta. org), held over the first weekend in April. It doesn't matter if you've never even rowed a boat across the town pond, half the fun is simply being here and watching the contestants' sails tearing through the Caribbean's crystal-clear waters. If the truth be told, the regatta itself is just an excuse for a great land party; whoever manages to win the events at sea is almost secondary. Each night sees the Mooring Marina take on a carnival atmosphere, with calypso bands letting rip, beach parties over-running the shores and the local beach shacks serving up delicious grilled fish.

Calgary Stampede

Where? **Calgary, Canada**
When? **Mid-July**
How long? **10 days**

The Stampede (ⓦ www.calgary-stampede.com) brings around a quarter of a million spectators to this likeable Canadian city every year. It's not just about chaps in chaps either; this is the real thing – a succession of seriously manly events that kicks off on the first Friday with a traditional parade, featuring the several thousand participants and their horses. Thereafter, the focus of activity is Stampede Park, a vast open area that contains an amusement park, concert and show venues, bars, restaurants and all sorts of stalls. There's a cracking World Blacksmith competition and nightly country-and-western performances, but everyone's really here to see the rodeo events, including bronco- and bull-riding, branding, steer-wrestling and cow-tackling – fiercely competitive affairs that draw the bravest and most talented cowboys from every corner of the continent. Equally compelling are the enormously dangerous chuck-wagon races, held nightly, with the top four drivers going through to the final on the last night – a fitting and exciting conclusion to the festival.

Calle Ocho

Where? **Miami, USA**
When? **March**
How long? **4 days**

Over a million people turn up to Miami's Calle Ocho (Ⓦwww.calle8.com), the largest Hispanic event anywhere in the world; and they come for a roaring street party, fed by rolling rhythms from salsa to merengue. Held over the first two weekends of March, the final two days are the most interesting, kicking off at noon on Saturday when bands take over Bayfront Park and play on into the small hours. All of this is just a warm-up for Calle Ocho itself,

on the following day, when Central and South America's best performers play around thirty stages strung along 24 blocks of downtown Miami to extremely enthusiastic audiences. In between these events, don't miss the sidewalk barbecues or the chance to pick up hand-rolled cigars and Cuban rum from street stalls. The official show winds up around 8pm, but don't worry, plenty of clubs and parties pick up the slack, while a giant conga line winds itself all through Little Havana.

Cheyenne Frontier Days

Where? **Cheyenne, USA**
When? **July**
How long? **7 days**

Calling itself the "Daddy of 'em All", this is the biggest rodeo event there is, with nine daily rodeos ($12–25, depending on where you sit) spread over the last week in July (Ⓦwww.cfdrodeo.com). But it's not just about rodeos: there are hat acts every evening, various western-themed activities, and parades through the streets of Cheyenne.

Cirio de Nazare

Where? **Belém, Brazil**
When? **October**
How long? **2 weeks**

The second largest festival in Brazil after the Rio Carnival takes place in the rambling colonial city of Belém near the mouth of the Amazon, on the country's northeast coast – and it's one of the bawdiest religious celebrations on the face of the planet. The Cirio de Nazare honours Belém's Virgin Mary, the country's most revered icon. The focus of the festival is the transfer of Her image ("Nossa Senhora de Nazara") from the city's cathedral to the Basilica de Nazare – a solemn process, which takes five hours, and during which thousands of barefoot devotees try to get as close to the Virgin as possible. Once the icon is safely installed, the huge town fiesta breaks out, with the

Calgary Stampede

kind of street partying that matches anything in Rio, and lasting virtually non-stop until the Virgin makes the return trip two weeks later. The great twist here is that the more you drink, the more you actually honour the Virgin. Don't ask why – just get here, grab a beer and join the million people dancing to syncopated Amazonian beats in the name of Christ.

Festa de Iemanja

Where? Rio de Janeiro, Brazil
When? 31st December
How long? 1 day

One of the best New Year's Eve parties you'll find anywhere, Rio ushers out the old and brings in the new with sex, sweat and samba down on Copacabana beach. It's dedicated to Iemanja, the Goddess of the Sea – and Rio's patron saint – who, as well as her aquatic connection, is known for her enjoyment of carnal pleasures. Accordingly, the only proper and fitting way to honour her is, of course, through a great deal of drinking and raunchy full-body-contact dancing.

Festival of the Assumption of the Virgin

Where? Huamantla, Mexico
When? August
How long? 2 weeks

Pamplona's famous Fiesta de San Fermín (see p.31) is actually for wimps. Real men take part in a far more lethal version in the colonial Mexican city of Huamantla, a hundred miles' bumpy bus ride southeast of Mexico City. Here, every August 16, the bulls are let loose at midday in nine separate locations, causing up to four hours of utter havoc. The event is the culmination of a two-week fiesta that leads up to the Assumption of the Virgin on August 15, which is celebrated with a procession through flower-strewn streets. Get here for this, and then take on the bulls the next day. Be warned: attempting to play matador after consuming half a dozen tequila slammers is not good for your health.

Fiesta de la Virgen de la Candelaria

Where? Copacabana, Bolivia
When? February
How long? 1 week

This huge festival is held on February 2 in honour of an effigy of the Virgin Mary, which was consecrated in 1583, and which resides at Copacabana, a small town way up in the Andes on the shores of South America's largest lake, Titicaca. The religious tone of the event – part-Christian, part-traditional – is completely swamped by the energy and euphoria of the locals, who like nothing better than to rig up open-air barbeques in the streets, and drink, dance and sing the night away: shamanic characters perform devil dances and tell fortunes, while Christian priests are on hand to bless anyone and anything (more often than not the miniature objects – houses, cars, and so on – that many people wish for in the year ahead). The rainy season is well underway in early February, with a daily downpour guaranteed, but this does nothing to dampen the spirits, and people flock to Copacabana from all over Bolivia, giving the town a bazaar-like atmosphere. Tourists aren't all that common, but are still made to feel incredibly welcome.

French Quarter Festival

Where? New Orleans, USA
When? April
How long? 3 days

As the self-proclaimed Birthplace of Jazz, New Orleans hosts three essential events in the first half of every year: the Jazz Festival, the legendary Mardi Gras and the French Quarter Festival (@www.frenchquarterfestivals.com), which is the least-known and, perhaps because of that, maybe the one to catch. The Vieux Carré, as the city's French Quarter is known, was left relatively untouched by Hurricane Katerina, and is given over to exuberant crowds intent on making the most of this huge celebration of the food, music and culture of the city. The madness is concentrated around stages along Bourbon Street, which shake to the traditional sounds of Dixieland, ragtime, Creole, and, of course, "Nawleens" jazz, while riverside Woldenberg Park stomps to more freestyle zydeco and R&B. Once the live music dies down, you can spend the rest of your time staggering from one street party to another.

Fiesta de Santo Tomas

Where? **Chichicastenango, Guatemala**

When? **December**

How long? **7 days**

The Fiesta de Santo Tomas takes place over the seven days leading up to St Thomas's Day on December 21, and is arguably one of the biggest and best annual events in Central America. Held in the relatively remote (and unpronounceable) highland town of Chichicastenango – "Chichi" to you and me - the festival combines Catholic and native Mayan traditions in a series of unique dances, processions and live music.

The central square, with the church of St Tomas on one side, forms the centre of activities each night, hosting traditional masked dancing to crowds of locals in swirls of billowing incense. It's a solemn, quasi-religious affair, but not without humour and the odd modern touch. The dancers, exotically dressed, are traditionally led by a king and queen who command the show with whistles; in years past, they have been followed by Batman and Robin, Fred Flintstone and Barney Rubble, a bumblebee couple, a few mockingly endowed "women", and a variety of others that really fit no description. In pairs, they do a sort of two-step, side-to-side jig with their arms swinging, to music that is pumped out of huge speakers mounted on a van.

After the dancing, thousands of firecrackers and firebombs are let off, after which there's a candlelit procession of the Virgin that starts at the steps of St Tomas, and proceeds to the indigenous Indian church of El Calavario, where native musicians play simple drums and flutes and an incense burner stokes yet more clouds of smoke. The procession stops at the next corner of the square, with more firecrackers and firebombs soaring into the sky, a deafening practice that is repeated at every corner throughout the three-hour parade. This is repeated every night until the festival is over, although the focus during the last couple of days shifts to the Palo Voladores, a towering twenty-metre-tall tree trunk off which inebriated daredevils fling themselves, bungee-style – much to the amusement of the gathering crowds.

Inti Raymi

Where? **Cusco, Peru**
When? **24 June**
How long? **1 day**

The winter solstice has been a big thing for the Peruvians ever since the Incas, who were so concerned that the sun might one day disappear forever that they marked it with a huge festival to honour Wiracocha, the Sun God, and entice him to return for the new year by ritually sacrificing a whole farm's worth of llamas. The event was revived in the latter part of the last century and now draws up to two hundred thousand people to the three-hour ceremony, held in the ancient Inca ruins of Sacsayhuamán, 2km outside Cusco. The re-enactment comes complete with costumes; speeches in Quechua, the Inca tongue; the parade of an Inca high priest in a golden throne; and choreographed dances. All rather cheesy, but it does give a hint of the incredible spectacle the original festivities would have presented. One thing that is missing, however, is the ritual animal slaughter – the llamas only notionally get their throats cut, and survive to spit their way through another day. The only other concession to modernity is the introduction of comfy seats for wealthy spectators, but there's plenty of standing room with the locals if you get there early enough.

La Diablada

Where? **Puno, Peru**
When? **November**
How long? **1 week**

Everyone knows that the devil has the best tunes, and they never play louder than during La Diablada, held on the shores of beautiful Lake Titicaca. The festival serves several purposes. It's a celebration of the city's liberation from the Spanish, and a way of paying homage to the ancient spirits of the lake; but, mainly, one suspects, it's an excuse to dress up in outrageous costumes and to party like old Nick himself. An extravagant parade, led by the Peruvian version of Beelzebub, winds through the town's streets to the lakeside in the afternoon of November 5.

Los Diablos Danzantes

Where? **St Francisco de Yare, Venezuela**
When? **Pentecost**
How long? **1 day**

Like many South American festivals, Pentecost in Venezuela has a mixed African heritage and a Christian front. Fired by rum, performers dressed as devils play drums, dance madly, and generally stir up merry hell in the streets from dawn to dawn, while there are also big

Los Diablos Danzantes

Mazatlán Carnival

Where? Mazatlán, Mexico
When? February
How long? 5 days

The five crazy days of Carnival in Mazatlán is the time to see the city at its very best – and worst – when this usually bustling fishing port and low-key beach resort transforms itself into a frantic maelstrom of partygoers, hawkers and bug-eyed tourists. Carnival here is an excuse to eke out the last of your sins before Lent, and in Mazatlán's wild meat market, in some of the thickest, craziest crowds you'll ever encounter, it's sometimes difficult to tell exactly whose hands are on whose body. The countdown to Mazatlán's Carnival (Ⓦwww.mazatlan.com.mx) begins five days before Ash Wednesday, but predictably the festivities are at their wildest on Saturday, Sunday and Monday, before people head home to be with their family or their church.

There are two drastically different parts to the town: Old Mazatlán, the original town centre, which is a quaint, colonial fishing port, and the Zona Dorada, otherwise known as "Gringo Hell" – a pricey, practically purpose-built resort. Don't be too put off, though – the best hotels are close to the Zona Dorada, and it's not far to go to experience some real Latin street culture. Carnival itself is one long parade along the Paseo Olas Atlas, which is sealed off for about ten blocks – a Latin-music band on the corner of each – and mobbed with security personnel. Both sides of the avenue are bursting with food and beer stands, as well as some classy restaurants, cafes and a few hotels, and in the middle, the crowds form long lines and dance from one end of Paseo Olas Atlas to the other, grinding against one another or jumping from line to line to grind with as many people as possible. This is actually a lot of fun during the more tranquil hours of Carnival, from about 8pm til midnight, but after that it gets pretty wild, as locals arrive here – Westerners seem to prefer their own parties in the bars of the Zona Dorada – to finish off their evening and party until dawn. Then, like clockwork, the crowds abruptly leave to crash out on the beach to sleep off a heavy hangover.

church services and cross-carrying parades. The point of all this is to chase away evil and so purify the community, and so the harder you party, the more effective your efforts will be. St Francisco de Yare, sixty miles southeast of Caracas, puts on one of the best shows, but it's also worth getting out to some of the smaller coastal towns or villages a few days in advance to enjoy tourist-free warm-up sessions. Either way, you'll get plenty of dance practice.

National Finals Rodeo

Where? **Las Vegas, USA**
When? **December**
How long? **1 week**

The premier championship of rodeo, held every year at the Thomas & Mack Center in Las Vegas (Ⓦwww.nfr-rodeo.com), sees competitors battle it out in saddle bronco-riding, bull-riding, bareback-riding, calf-roping, team-roping, steer-wrestling and barrel-racing in front of crowds of over 140,000. It's not the most atmospheric place to enjoy this most American of sports, nor the cheapest (ticket prices start at around $75), but it's as good an excuse to be in Vegas as any.

New Mexico State Fair

Where? **Albuquerque, USA**
When? **September**
How long? **5 days**

Getting your ass kicked by an ass is the ideal way of getting in touch with the cowboy in you. Dating back to 1938, this event has converted more people to the joys of leather chaps than all of John Wayne's films put together. Haul your butt down to New Mexico and you can take part in a Wild West scene in full cowboy gear, try your hand at riding a full-size bull or just hang with the ol' boys drinking, spinning yarns and spittin' chaw at the daily rodeo events. Tickets cost from $15 per event.

New Orleans Jazz and Heritage Festival

Where? **New Orleans, USA**
When? **April/May**
How long? **2 weekends**

Held over the last weekend of April and first weekend of May, Jazzfest (Ⓦwww.nojazzfest.com), as it's more often known, is now second only to Mardi Gras on the New Orleans calendar, and in many ways it's the preferable event, with all of the fun but none of the spring-break loutishness that Mardi Gras attracts. Acts run the gamut from Dylan to Fats Domino, and around half a million attend over the two weekends. Acts play in tents out at the city fairgrounds, and the atmosphere is great – relaxed and informal, with excellent food and wonderful music. Weekend tickets cost $30 in advance, which makes it one of the best festival bargains going.

Olinda and Recife Carnivals

Where? **Olinda and Recife, Brazil**
When? **February**
How long? **5 days**

These neighbouring carnivals have a reputation as the Brazilian carnivals that haven't sold out. In the way that

Oruro Carnival

Rio and Salvador have grown into highly commercial events, Olinda and Recife remain true to their roots, with every last neighbourhood cobbling together floats and participants, and with music and rhythms – for example, frevo, a fast, whirling beat – you won't necessarily hear anywhere else in the country. In all, the best Brazilian carnivals to choose if you're truly into participating rather than observing.

Oruro Carnival

Where? Oruro, Bolivia
When? February
How long? **3 days**

Combining Mardi Gras and the traditional devil dances for which Bolivia is famous, the festivities in this long-established mining town are, naturally enough, all about the devil's submission to Christ: participants dress in satanic costumes and masks, and dance as if gripped by the devil. On the final day, the Día del Agua, the purification or exorcism of the demons is marked by an enormous water-bomb fight in the town square, in which the devil figures get soaked, and tourists are particular targets.

Pendleton Round-Up

Where? Pendleton, USA
When? September
How long? **4 days**

Held two hundred miles east of Portland, Oregon, this is the world's largest four-day rodeo – a kind of Western-style Highland Games that is your chance to check out the pros at the wild bronco rodeo and steer-wrestling contests before trying your hand at tomahawk-throwing, greased pig-catching and buckin' bronco riding (ⓦwww.pendletonroundup.com; tickets from $10). And if you really think you might make a real cowboy, you can head over to the Happy Canyon Saloon – open till 2am – and gamble and drink like you're Clint Eastwood.

Phujllay

Where? Tarabuco, Bolivia
When? April
How long? **1 day**

"Phujllay" is a Quechua word meaning "play", and there's plenty of that going on in Tarabuco, as thousands of peasants descend on the town to celebrate their defeat of the Spanish on March 12, 1816, at the battle of Lumbati. After the necessary celebration of Mass on the Sunday, it's time to air national pride and fire up some crackers, as everyone dons traditional garb – including dancers dressed in parody of the Spanish, with huge spurs and green trousers – and drinks, wolfs down the fiery local snacks, and sings and dances the festival away.

San Marcos National Fair

Where? Aguascalientes, Mexico
When? April
How long? **3 weeks**

Mexico's oldest fair, the Feria Nacional de San Marcos (ⓦwww.feriadesanmarcos.com), pulls in thousands of revellers for three weeks of genial mayhem in the heartland town of Aguascalientes, particularly in and around the San Marcos Gardens. It's exactly what most people imagine when they think of Mexico: roaming vendors hawking everything from blankets and wooden toys to enchiladas and chocolate chicken; mariachi bands entertaining the crowds; and sideshows where you can blow your money on a cock fight or have your fortune told. For a change in pace, head for the bullfights, which are some of the best in Mexico, and pull in matadors from as far away as Spain. Evening brings on big firework displays and the urge to dance away the night while washing your tonsils in tequila, if you haven't started doing so already. You'd have to be a real diehard to stay upright for the whole shebang, so if you need to focus on one day in particular, make it the highly charged San Marcos Parade on April 25, when there's a brief reminder that all this started in 1604 as a religious event.

Semana Santa

Where? **Cusco, Peru**
When? **Palm Sunday to Easter Sunday**
How long? **7 days**

Pagan frenzy and Catholic idolatory meet during Holy Week in Cusco, held over the last week of Lent. Whatever is driving them, there's no mistaking the crowd's religious intensity, as the show kicks off with an after-dark procession of the Holy Sepulchre, the coffin carried aloft by black-robed bearers while thousands of candle-bearing worshippers follow. The subsequent days blend into a succession of church services and holy parades, in which performers recreate scenes from the crucifixion story and beyond – including a vengeful lynching of Pilate that the Bible somehow missed. There's also some wild partying after Good Friday, along with some general civic chaos seemingly spurred on by the belief that, as Christ is dead for a few days between the crucifixion and resurrection on Sunday, He isn't going to be around to judge your actions.

Spring Break

Where? **USA and Canada**
When? **March**
How long? **1 week**

Not so much an event as a cultural institution, Spring Break (Ⓦ www.springbreak.com) sees thousands of US and Canadian college kids descend on the beaches of – among other places – southern Florida for their annual weeks of raucous partying. Depending on your point of view, this is either a place to flock to for some beer-chugging madness or somewhere to avoid like the plague, as beefcake teenagers give each other high-fives and drink until they puke in the sand. In Florida, Panama City (Ⓦ www.pcb06.com) is nowadays the unofficial party HQ, attracting half-a-million college students every year. It hosts the biggest and best beach parties plus enough volleyball, limbo dancing, wet T-shirts and cold beer to keep the most red-necked Joe Sixpack happy. Outside of the USA, Cancun (Ⓦ www.springbreakcancun.com) sees the most action, with Negril and Acapulco coming up close behind.

Semana Santa

Toonik Tyme

Where? **Iqalit, Canada**
When? **April**
How long? **1 week**

Every year during the last two weeks of April, Iqalit (also known as Frobisher Bay), the tiny capital of the newly proclaimed Canadian region of Nunavut, throws off the hard Arctic winter with Toonik Tyme, a showcase of Inuit skills and northern life. Toonik is the mythical herald of spring, and as the festival gets underway, vague sightings of him are made around town – even if he does look suspiciously like a man dressed in caribou skins. Fishing and hunting sprees are central events, along with an endurance snow-mobile race over the icy plains surrounding town. If these don't appeal, try your hand at building an igloo, using only traditional knives and the odd hardware tool to shape the blocks – the winning structure has to be able to support a man standing on the roof. After this you might want to take in one of the ancient Broadway shows that come to town during Toonik Tyme, but those in search of a more authentically Inuit experience may prefer the traditional throat-singing competitions, where the singers' voices seem to bubble up from the vocal chords, bypassing the mouth completely. The winner is, of course, the singer who manages to reduce all the others to laughter.

Vendimia Festival

Where? **Mendoza, Argentina**
When? **March**
How long? **7 days**

Nowhere are the Argentinian trinity of wine, colossal quantities of barbecued beef, and singing (along with the occasional tango) better indulged than at the Vendimia Festival, which celebrates the grape harvest each March. Held since 1936 on the first full weekend of the month in the small Andean town of Mendoza, this extravaganza celebrates Argentinian wine big-time, packing the place with hundreds of thousands of the world's wine aficionados – and the occasional party-loving soak – who spend their time rollicking through the streets and doing their best to make an impression on the 1.3 billion litres of wine (mainly red, of course) that Argentina produces annually – it's the world's fifth-largest producer, and this is its principal wine-producing region. The main pageants are as commercial as they come, with a blessing of the grapes, parades of gauchos showing off their horsemanship, big flowery carnival floats, and a closing-night sound-and-light spectacular culminating in the election of the year's "Queen of Wines". But when the wine is this good, who cares?

Vendimia Festival

Winter Carnival

Where? **Québec, Canada**
When? **January and February**
How long? **2 weeks**

Held for a fortnight from the last Friday in January, this bills itself as the biggest and best Winter Carnival on the planet, and, despite strong Scandinavian (and US) competition, it generally lives up to the title, with mad ice slides, skidoo races, dyed-snowball-fight competitions and some of the most raucous après-ski you'll find anywhere (www.carnaval.qc.ca). Thousands of people take part in the fire-lit, night-time parades through the streets of Québec that more often than not turn into all-night parties. Come dawn, if you're brave enough – or just plain drunk enough – you can join in the traditional morning dip in the freezing St Lawrence river, which is guaranteed to cure any hangover. The carnival even has a mascot, a lovable snowman called "Bonhomme", and after two weeks of snow-induced hysteria you too will be sobbing into your scarf as he waves farewell for another year.

Africa and the Middle East

Africa and the Middle East

Festival in the Desert

Rustler's Valley Festivals

BEST OF THE REST

Festival in the Desert

The most remote music festival in the world

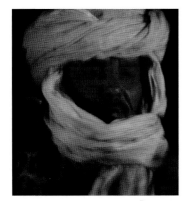

Festival in the Desert

Where?
Essakane, Mali

When?
Early January

How long?
3 days

MALI
• Essakane
• Timbuktu

Every January since 2003, growing numbers of foreigners have joined around 3000 Tuareg nomads to camp among the sand dunes of Essakane, northern Mali, for a shindig of music, dance and camel racing. By world-party standards, it's a small, even low-key affair; but the spectacle alone makes it well worth the effort of travelling all the way to Timbuktu and beyond. For the Tuareg, many of whom have ridden their camels for weeks to get there, the Festival in the Desert is as much an opportunity to get together and discuss social and economic issues as it is an annual music festival. For outsiders, the festival offers a unique chance to meet these intensely independent people and learn about their traditional way of life, to sit among them under the stars and listen to some of the most electrifying, rhythmic live music you're ever likely to hear.

History

The Festival in the Desert as it is today is a relatively recent phenomenon: the first one took place in January 2001. But its **origins** date back to pre-Islamic times when tribes of **Tuareg** nomads first gathered together in the desert to exchange news, settle disputes, race camels and entertain one another with their swordsmanship, music, singing and dance. The festival also has strong links with the Tuaregs' long struggle for freedom and basic rights. Tuaregs, or Kel Tamasheq (people who speak Tamasheq) as the tribes of the southern Sahara prefer to be known, are an independent people who for centuries lived by herding their camels and goats across the sands, trading in salt, gold and slaves from West Africa up to the Mediterranean. Theirs is a prolonged history of resistance, from the early days of French colonisation through almost four decades of brutal repression – armed fighting finally came to an end with Mali's gaining of independence in 1996 when, in a public square in Timbuktu, a crowd of ten thousand assembled to watch the symbolic burning of three thousand weapons laid down by Tamasheq rebels and the Malian army.

During the period of conflict leading up to independence – centred, mainly, on the government's ineptitude in trying to unify the country's many ethnic groups, especially the now semi-nomadic Tuareg – many rebels were forced to take refuge in neighbouring countries, some fleeing as far as Libya where they were welcomed as recruits for Ghaddafi's revolutionary training camps. It was in these camps that disaffected young men such as Ibrahim Ag Alhabibe, founder member of the award-winning band **Tinariwen**, first took up the electric guitar. By the time the peace accord was signed, Tinariwen had developed quite a following, and returned to base themselves in the Kidal region of Mali, east of Timbuktu. As they started also gaining support in Europe, a revival of the traditional gatherings in the Sahara was underway, under the auspices of a local Tuareg association, EFES; it was out of these events, encouraged by growing foreign interest in Tinariwen's compulsive "desert blues", as well as other forms of Malian music, that the idea for an international desert festival was born.

The **original festival** was attended by Mali's prime minister and many other dignitaries, an estimated two thousand Tuaregs and around eighty foreigners, most of them journalists, photographers and film-makers. The following year, a second, smaller festival near the Algerian border was disrupted by a sandstorm, but by 2003 there was enough momentum to support a highly successful three-day event on what has become a permanent site at **Essakane**, 65km north of Timbuktu. That year, Tamasheq artists such as Tinariwen and the renowned women-led group, Tartit, performed alongside some of Mali's best-known stars, including Oumou Sangare and the late great Ali Farka Toure, not to mention England's Robert Plant. Since 2005, the number of international names has perhaps diminished but the festival continues to attract the likes of Amadou and Mariam, Tinariwen and the wonderfully versatile guitarist Habib Koite, as well as lesser-known performers from neighbouring Guinea, Niger and Burkina Faso.

Afel Bocoum and band

It's not for nothing that Mali's best-known musical event is billed as the most remote music festival in the world. Set among the sparsely populated sand dunes of the southern Sahara, this musical bonanza is not easy to get to: after reaching the mythical outpost of Timbuktu (an adventure in itself), expect another three hours' gruelling off-road travel to Essakane. As you near the festival site, the landscape abruptly changes to a startling expanse of rolling white sand. It's the height of Mali's dry season at this time of year and the sky can seem as pale as the sand, with the sun hidden by a veil of dust. Against this bleached-out backdrop a single, arched gateway welcomes crowds of Tuareg tribesmen in richly coloured robes, their heads swathed in turbans, standing about chatting and laughing on camels bedecked with tassles of yellow, red and turquoise blue. Occasionally there's a yell, and a couple of riders break free of the group, swords aloft, to race away, reins and robes flapping, over the sand. All around, families have set up camp with their goats, donkeys, pots and pans – the lucky ones pitched beneath one of the few acacia trees that dot the landscape.

sit under the stars and listen to some of the most electrifying, rhythmic live music you're ever likely to hear

Inside the gate, once you've been allocated a tent in which to dump your bags, it's fairly easy to get your bearings, but making your way over the sand dunes can be hard going. Most of the daytime action takes place in and around a shallow, natural **amphitheatre** marked by an open-sided tent and brightly coloured rugs spread out on the sand. Here, if you can ignore the banks of foreign photographers, there's still a sense of this being an indigenous event, with Tamasheq musicians – using traditional instruments such as the *ngoni* (forerunner of the banjo) and the upturned calabash – and dancers performing for each other. Tall and graceful in immaculate blue, white and green robes, swiping their swords in the air, almost in slow motion, they skip and sway to the music, never seeming to put a foot wrong. Camels dance, too, though it's more of an uncomfortable shuffle as riders force them to drop to their knees and edge along in front of the cheering crowd. As with most of

the festival, it's the audience – impossibly cool tribesmen in designer-style shades, women in colourful clusters with their naked babies playing in the sand, resting camels gazing haughtily over the horizon – as much as the official performers that make this such an extraordinary event.

By night, the temperature drops dramatically and focus switches to the **main stage**, at the far edge of the site, away from all the tents, where, against all odds, the festival's main acts pump out a dazzling mix of sounds spanning traditional Kora music, wild drumming from neighbouring Burkina Faso, hypnotic singing from Tartit, and the highly popular African soul of Amadou and Mariam. Each year brings another unpredictable line-up, but you can usually catch some of Mali's greatest musicians, from the deeply resonant desert blues of Tinariwen and Afel Bocoum to the blistering guitar rifs of Baba Salah. Scattered over the dunes in front of the stage, braziers filled with burning charcoal provide flashes of light as well as welcome warmth, which slowly dies out as the desert rocks on towards dawn.

Getting tickets

Tickets, which include entry to the festival, shared tent, water, and food vouchers for three basic meals a day, cost around €300 and can be purchased in advance from the official festival website (see p.280); it should also be possible to turn up and pay on arrival at the site.

Basics

The journey from Mali's capital, Bamako, to Essakane takes stamina and, above all, time, at least four days, especially if you're travelling independently. Drawn by the security of pre-booked tickets, food and accommodation, plus back-up vehicles and guides with local knowledge, even experienced travellers sometimes opt for an **organized tour**; London-based Tim Best Travel (☎ +44 207 591 0300, ⊛ www.timbesttravel.com), who link up in Mali with the highly knowledgeable Affala Voyages Initiatives (☎ +223 285 0092, ⊛ www. affala.com), is a good choice, but be warned: in 2006, Tim Best followed British Foreign Office advice regarding the danger of Tuareg bandits north of Timbuktu and cancelled the trip. Other options are the French operator Point-Afrique (⊛ www.point-afrique.com), also good for flight-only deals from Paris, and Mali-based Saga Tours (⊛ www. sagatours.com). There are no direct **flights** to Mali from the UK.

If you've got patience, a couple of weeks to spare and a taste for adventure, **travelling independently** is a lot cheaper. Mali's erratic public transport will get you as far as Timbuktu, from where you'll find no shortage of 4WDs heading for the festival. This last leg of the journey can be done by camel with a Tuareg guide, but it takes at least three days, riding eight or nine hours a day, so don't expect to be able to walk on arrival.

Accommodation and eating

Independent travellers can bring their own camping gear; otherwise, you're likely to end up in either an open-sided goatskin **tent** or one of the big white tents that were once the property of the UN. Everyone needs a **sleeping bag**. Water and food vouchers covering three basic meals a day are included in the ticket price (see box on p.279), but there's little **food** on offer outside this system. Breakfast tends to be hard Tuareg bread, baked in a hole dug in the sand, served with jam; other meals consist mainly of meat, traditionally cooked in a sheep's stomach filled with hot coals, served with millet or rice. Vegetarians will have a hard time without their own supplies. More or less the only **alcohol** for sale is *Castel*, Mali's home-produced, perfectly drinkable beer, available from the festival's two or three basic refreshment tents.

Event info

Festival in the Desert (⊛ www.festival-au-desert.org). Official festival website with some good images of past festivals but a bit slow to provide current information.

Useful websites

Friends of Mali (⊛ www.friendsofmali-uk.org). Extremely helpful London-based group dedicated to disseminating information about Mali in the UK.
Mali Tourist Office (⊛ www.malitourisme.com) French-language site with information on Mali's major towns, including Bamato and Timbuktu, and tour operator details.

Time zone GMT   **Country code** +223   **Currency** CFA Franc (CFA)

Rustler's Valley Festivals

All good, New Agey fun

Rustler's Valley Festivals

Where?
Rustler's Valley, Free State, South Africa

When?
New Year and Easter are the big events, but there are two or three other parties held between September and April each year

How long?
3–4 days

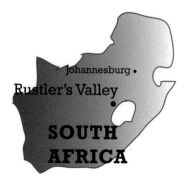

Renowned even in South Africa for its small-town conservatism, the province of Free State rarely lives up to its enticing name, but the excellent Rustler's Valley Festivals are a notable exception – the parties feel and operate like true celebrations, and the revellers are experts at getting down to fine music in a stunning location. Held on a spacious farm in Rustler's Valley, at the foot of the majestic Maluti mountains, the festivals span the summer, offering mainly DJ'd sounds interspersed with live music, a muddy dam to cool off in, tepees and sweat lodges, plus accompanying devotees, good food and even stuff for the kids to do (not to mention babysitting) – all good, New Agey fun. The parties are just big enough to make you feel you're part of a scene, but just small enough to keep it a family affair.

History

The Rustler's Valley Festival **started** in 1992 as a small annual gathering of hippies who dreamed of a South African equivalent to Woodstock or Glastonbury, and the music was mainly South African white alternative rock. As the 1990s wore on, the music changed, with live music receding, and the dance scene – in all its mutations – taking over. The shift drew a younger crowd, though there were plenty of older hippies glad to discover that hallucinogens were back in fashion. At its height, Rustler's was pulling in five thousand punters to its major events, but the start of the twenty-first century has marked a change in the festivals' character.

The growing corporatization of South African entertainment, with South African Breweries becoming the main sponsor of the once-alternative Splashy Fen, and the fact that South Africa now hosts around 85 annual music festivals nationwide (nine of these over the Easter weekend alone), have seen the organizers return to their roots, ditching their anthemic Easter Festival and taking to heart the "small-is-beautiful" eco-philosophy that underpinned Rustler's in the first place. Now, several parties are held over the summer, but they are far smaller than before (500–1000 people) – and much mellower. If any event could be considered a highlight, then the New Year party would be it.

a veritable New Age checklist of tepees, healers, astrologers and crystals

The focus of the Rustler's Valley Festivals is the centrepiece **World Stage**, which has hosted a mixture of chart-topping headline acts, a bit of rock, and, most recently, a uniquely southern African blend of experimental jazz and folk. Whatever the tunes, there is always a heavy percussion element in the music. In the early 2000s, live music was ditched at Rustler's because the organizers felt the same old bands were doing the rounds, and line-ups had become far too predictable. DJ sounds now dominate, but as a new wave of local musos emerges, live bands, mostly from Cape Town, are gradually being reintroduced into the festivals' programmes. For a break from the 24-hour-a-day musical action at the World Stage, the *Saucery Restaurant* doubles up as a **chill space** dishing up mellower sounds that include large dollops of music from across the continent.

Part of the Rustler's scene is the veritable New Age checklist of tepees, eclectically inspired shamanic ceremonies, healers, astrologers and crystals. In keeping with the eco spirit of the place, energy is provided by windmills and solar panels. At some stage during the parties a lot of people take to the surrounding hills to chill out, and from the festival site you can see dozens of small convoys traipsing over the beautiful Maluti sandstone.

Insider info Tickets cost R150 (in advance from the website; see p.284) or R200 (at the gate), but once inside all events are free.

Basics

Rustler's Valley is in the eastern Free State, very close to the Lesotho border – the nearest domestic **airport** is Bloemfontein. While there's no public transport direct to Rustler's, from Cape Town and Durban you can catch one of the Intercape **buses** that stop in nearby Ficksburg; if you call in advance, someone from *Rustler's Valley Mountain Retreat*, the festival organizers (see below), will pick you up (R20). From Johannesburg, you'll have to rely on minibus taxis or drive yourself. If you're **driving**, it's not too hard to find – Rustler's is signposted off the R26 between Ficksburg and Fouriesburg (the nearest towns). The final approach is a dirt road so be prepared for a rough ride. There's plenty to keep you busy around Rustler's if you feel like staying on for a while – horse-riding, hiking, fishing or just making the most of the rural hippiedom.

Accommodation

Rustler's is **camping only** and it pays to come prepared. In summer, the valley usually cooks in the day but can be chilly at night, and it can also pour with rain. At the very least you should have a change of clothes, a waterproof tent and a warm sleeping bag. A limited range of **equipment** can be bought on site or in neighbouring towns, although most retail outlets are closed for Easter and New Year. Long-time Rustler's festivalgoers are increasingly organized, and come replete with all the counter culture's camping comforts – from run-down camper vans to state-of-the-art sound systems.

Eating and drinking

For **food**, you can either buy curried vegetarian fare from the Hare Krishna stall or else sit down for a meal at *Rustler's* own á la carte *Saucery Restaurant*, where the emphasis is on organic produce from their own garden.

Event info

Rustler's Valley (☎ 51/933 3939, ⓦ www.rustlers.co.za). Well-assembled website, with details of forthcoming parties, and a description of everything else that goes on at the farm. There's also an online booking service for accommodation at Rustler's outside the festival season.

Free State Province Tourism (ⓦ www.dteea.fs.gov.za). Provides information on routes, attractions and accommodation throughout the region.

Time zone GMT +2   **Country Code** +27   **Currency** Rand (R)

Africa and the Middle East
The best of the rest

Ben Aïssa Moussem

Where? Meknes, Morocco
When? March
How long? 1 day

Held at Mouloud (the Prophet's birthday in the Islamic lunar calendar, usually mid- to late March), this is the largest of all Morocco's *moussems*, or pilgrimage festivals, with galloping horses and fairground rides, and crowds of people converging on Meknes for the event. On a more subdued note, the festival is also devoted to Ben Aïssa, whose tomb lies just outside the city's old town, and whose devotees (once the most popular cult in Morocco) celebrate by testing their powers of endurance under trance. This used to mean harming themselves – swallowing glass and other such feats – but the Moroccan government has cracked down on this in recent years.

Cape Minstrels Carnival

Where? Cape Town, South Africa
When? January
How long? 1 month

Cape Town's traditional New Year's Day carnival – the Kaapse or Cape Minstrels Carnival – has grown enormously in size, duration and decibel level since its introduction over a hundred years ago, and now preliminary parades build in fervour over consecutive Saturdays in January, climaxing in the dazzling Grand Parade at month's end.

Cape Minstrels Carnival

Originally dubbed the "Coon Carnival" but renamed so as not to scare off the tourists, it's an exuberant celebration of the culture of Cape Town's black and Malay population, and it clearly has added poignancy in the post-apartheid era. Over twenty thousand people of all colours enjoy the summer sunshine and join in with the parade's Black and White Minstrel-style fancy dress – satin suits, fancy bowlers, cheeky parasols – accompanied by jazz bands, floats and booming sound systems.

Cape Town Jazz Festival

Where? Cape Town, South Africa
When? March–April
How long? 2 days

Bringing together major South African and international artists, the high-profile Cape Town Jazz Festival (Ⓦwww.capetownjazzfest.com) takes over the massive Cape Town International Convention Centre for some seriously mellow music-making. A couple of days beforehand, as a consolation gesture to those who haven't managed to grab tickets for the star-studded main events – headlining acts have included Manu Dibango, Hugh Masekela, Herbie Hancock, Youssou N'Dour and Miriam Makeba – there's an outdoor Community Concert in the city's Greenmarket Square, offering a great chance to catch up-and-coming local artists; it's a lot of fun and it's free.

Cape Verde Mardi Gras

Where? Mindelo, Sao Vicente island, Cape Verde
When? February
How long? 2 days

Though one of the biggest towns in the Cape Verde islands, Mindelo is ordinarily a rather conservative sort of place. But each February it comes alive for Mardi Gras, with a fantastic carnival procession on the Monday, followed by fireworks and dancing. Shrove Tuesday itself is a public holiday; everyone recovers from the previous day's carousing in the morning, then things get going again in the late-afternoon, when there's another great, family-friendly carnival parade. It's very much a local event for local people, but extremely welcoming nonetheless.

Cure Salée

Dubai Shopping Festival/Dubai World Cup

Where? **Dubai, UAE**
When? **January**
How long? **1 month**

It's hard to imagine how the shopping capital of the Middle East could improve on the opportunities it offers to shop till you drop, but Dubai somehow manages to, devoting itself to a month-long shopping festival, with lots of special offers in its stores and hotels, raffles, and competitions for things you never thought you could afford. It's very much the place to be if you fancy your chances of landing that Ferrari, or for some serious shopping, since there's nowhere better for luxury items, carpets, or haggling in one of the souks. And when you've reached your credit-card limit, there are fireworks, street shows and the added attraction of the Dubai World Cup – which offers the biggest prize money of any horse race in the world, and as such is attended by anyone who's anyone in the sport of kings.

Cure Salée

Where? **Agadez, Niger**
When? **August/September**
How long? **1 day**

Traditional festivals are stitched firmly into the pattern of daily life in the ancient Agadez region of northwest Niger, and one of the most famous is the festival held after the rains – usually in August or September, when the area's large salt flats fill with water and animals are fattened with the cure salée ("salt cure") – by the nomadic Fulani community. Gerwol, the much-photographed male beauty pageants that are a central part of the proceedings, are unique. Young men seeking a wife adorn themselves with thick face paint to accentuate the features they consider most attractive, namely a high forehead, a long nose, white teeth and the clear whites of their eyes, then set about displaying their sex appeal to maximum effect through ritual teeth-baring and eyeball-rolling. Visitors don't have much opportunity to participate, but you'll certainly see plenty of highly decorated desert-dwellers if you happen to be passing through.

Eid al-Fitr

Where? **Damascus, Syria**
When? **November**
How long? **3 days**

Marking the end of Ramadan, Eid al-Fitr – literally, the breaking of the fast – is celebrated all over the Muslim world, but nowhere more enthusiastically than in Damascus, where festivities include fireworks, music, dancing – and food, the first before sundown for a month. Everyone gets dressed up and takes to the streets, and the city enjoys a carnival atmosphere, with street stalls, fairground attractions and general revelry. It's a fine time to be in town, although truly authentic participation should really include the month of fasting beforehand.

Festival of World Sacred Music

Where? Fes, Morocco
When? June
How long? 1 week

Rabat may be the political capital of Morocco, but Fès el Bali – old Fez, the most complete living medieval city in the world – is the nation's beating heart; and the Fes Festival of World Sacred Music (ⓦ www.fesfestival.com) offers visitors the opportunity to tap straight into its rich, multi-layered cultural and spiritual life. The festival styles itself as "a beacon of peace from the Islamic world" and deliberately draws performers from many different faiths and traditions. Alongside internationally acclaimed world music stars such as master sitar player Ravi Shankar and Malian superstar Salif Keita, both of whom headlined in recent years, are offerings as diverse as African-American gospel choirs, English chamber singers, Japanese court musicians and Spanish flamenco artists. The ticketed concerts, held in the palace courtyard of Bab Makina or the wonderful, cedar-scented gardens of the Musée Bathar, are glamorous, high-society events, attended by well-groomed locals keen to see and be seen. There's a daily programme of free events, too, held at dusk in Bab Boujloud, one of the city's main squares. Late in the evening, people move on to the Dar Tazi Gardens, to sway to hypnotic hadras, traditional Sufi chants. Between performances, you can explore the spice-scented souks, dodge muffled-hoofed donkeys in the winding alleyways, and sip mint tea to the call of the muezzin.

Festival of the Dhow Countries

Where? Fes, Zanzibar
When? July
How long? 10 days

Though this started life as the Zanzibar International Film Festival, even before it had got off the ground the programme was extended to feature music and performing arts. The eighth festival showcased over 250 films, 40 performing artists and 10 exhibitions; seminars and workshops included Filmmakers, Musicians, Dance, Women, Children and Village; there was a literary forum, a "dhow culture" symposium and batik classes; and, of course, plenty of beach parties.

Festival of the Oases

Where? Tozeur, Tunisia
When? November/December
How long? 4 days

If you're after danger, wildness and a good knees-up in the desert, then Tozeur's Festival of the Oases has got the lot. During the Bedouin event the endlessly undulating sand dunes south of town (off Avenue Aboue el Kacem Chabbi) contain a sprawling tent-city where several thousand desert nomads take up residence. The diversions include horse racing, whip-cracking, snake charming, knife-throwing competitions and the extraordinary hissing, spitting and biting spectacle that is camel-fighting.

Festival of the Sahara

Where? Douz, Tunisia
When? December
How long? 4 days

This festival for nomads and other fun-loving desert dwellers is situated smack in the middle of the rolling sand dunes of the Tunisian desert, in and around the pleasant town of Douz – the so-called Gateway to the Sahara. If the landscape seems familiar it's because it was used as the backdrop for Star Wars, and the best thing to do is buy yourself the full Obi Wan Kenobi robe and search out one of the tents where the bubbling hookah action is going on. There's a huge variety of events and spectacles – ranging from dog-racing to camel-fighting to belly-dancing – and displays of traditional local crafts, most of them taking place in the tourist zone, a couple of kilometres south of town, in the oasis. There are also music and dance events held in the town itself (at the Maison de la Culture in Place des Martyrs), leading up to a grand finale on the fourth day that's attended by Tunisian politicians and various local bigwigs. Despite these establishment credentials, there's a great atmosphere and it's a fantastic location, although women should be aware that they may often find themselves the centre of unwanted attention. Bear in mind also that you'll need to book early – Douz isn't a big town, and its hotels fill quickly during the festival.

Festival on the Niger

Where? **Segou, Mali**
When? **February**
How long? **3 days**

For those who can't make it all the way to Essakane for Mali's Festival in the Desert (see p.275), the lesser-known Festival on the Niger (ⓦwww.festival segou.org; tickets available online), held in the riverside town of Segou, makes an appealing alternative. Featuring an exuberant mix of music, dance, art, puppets, craft workshops, theatre and debate, it may not boast the exotic location of the desert, but at night the setting on the banks of the Niger, with a full moon hanging low above the water, processions of fire-lit pirogues (dug-out canoes), and bats weaving in the air above the main stage, has its own special magic.

The Festival on the Niger only began in 2005, the brainchild of local businesspeople who sought to promote the region's culture and boost economic development, but it's become a regular item on the Mali festival calendar, enjoyed by locals and tourists alike. While leading acts – including, in 2006, renowned balafon player Neba Solo, griot Abdoulaye Diabate, and rising reggae star, Tikken Jah – play long into the night, there's plenty to do and see in the daytime: you can learn how to make bogolans (blankets decorated with dye made from mud and tree bark), meet artists eager to discuss their work, marvel at puppets in the form of turtles, fish and scorpions wrestling by the water, join huddles of teenage girls swooning and giggling at the sexy antics of local boy band, Maya Maya, or simply sip a beer in the shade. Segou is a pleasant, lively town, relatively prosperous by Mali standards, and the whole event has a gentle, laid-back feel.

Fêtes des Masques

Where? **Pays Dogon, Mali**
When? **April**
How long? **5 days**

Famous for their unique cosmology, their beautifully carved granary doors and their fairy-tale, shaggy-topped, pepper-pot houses, the Dogon have fascinated anthropologists for decades. Their belief in the afterlife is such that they celebrate funerals with great gusto, and masks have a crucial role in these and all other ritual proceedings. Masked dancers, some on stilts, take centre stage for the dramatic and colourful Fêtes des Masques, in which rival troupes compete against each other to re-enact scenes from tribal history. Purists argue that the spiritual roots of these dances have been corrupted for the benefit of visitors – ruggedly remote though it is, the Pays Dogon is far from undiscovered by tourism – but you're still left with the feeling that you're witnessing an ancient and thrillingly authentic event.

Gnawa and World Music Festival

Where? **Essaouira, Morocco**
When? **June**
How long? **4 days**

The music of the Gnawas (or Gnaouas), a spiritual brotherhood that has its origins in sub-Saharan Africa and melds animist, Berber and Arab influences, is mysterious, hypnotic, trance-inducing stuff that can send the musicians spinning (literally) into another plane. Essaouira makes for a beautiful setting – its picturesque lanes and squares, sparkling light and relaxed, tranquil atmosphere have attracted many painters, woodcarvers and other artisans over the years – and, during the festival (ⓦwww.festival-gnaoua.co.ma), the pounding rhythms of drums, reed pipes and castanet-like garagabs ringing out from Place Prince Moulay el Hassan, deep inside the city's medina, or old town, only adds to the atmosphere.

Grahamstown Festival

Where? **Grahamstown, South Africa**
When? **July**
How long? **8–10 days**

Every year during the first week or so of July, the cultured and historic settlement of Grahamstown overflows with visitors descending for the annual arts festival. The hub of the Grahamstown Festival (ⓦwww.nafest.co.za) is the 1820 Settlers Monument, which hosts big dance, drama and operatic productions in its theatres, free art exhibitions and early evening concerts. Having begun in 1974, when the building first opened, the festival has grown to become the largest arts event in Africa. Food stalls and markets sprout up on every street corner, and you can hardly order a beer for the number of Chinese acrobats or Irish dancers propping up the bars around town. Several hundred shows are staged in Grahamstown's many parks, church halls and restored Victorian buildings, and span every type of performance, from traditional Xhosa dance to New Orleans cabaret.

Hermanus Whale-Watching Festival

Where? **Hermanus, South Africa**
When? **September**
How long? **5 days**

The once-sleepy little seaside town of Hermanus, an hour and a half's drive from Cape Town, is South Africa's self-appointed whale-watching capital, and during its festival the whole town really pushes the boat out in celebration of the mighty mammals. The event's mascot and MC is Zolie Baleni the Whale Crier, who blows a traditional horn of dried kelp whenever a southern right whale hoves into view indicating which way you should look with his Morse Code-like blasts. The festival (ⓦwww.whalefestival.co.za) is held in South Africa's peak season for whale-watching; it's common for whales to swim so close to shore that you can see them clearly from the cliff paths just outside Hermanus – and even from the town itself. Often, tantalizingly, all you'll see is a dark flank; more rarely but much more thrillingly, a muscular tail will flip right out of the water. As well as whale-watching parties, the festival programme includes concerts, cabaret nights, an innovative craft fair and plenty of stalls selling all manner of whale-shaped souvenirs.

Imilchil Wedding Moussem

Where? **Imilchil, Morocco**
When? **September**
How long? **3 days**

Once upon a time, or so the story goes, two lovers from rival Berber tribes killed themselves in grief because their parents wouldn't let them marry. To stop this from ever happening again, the tribes agreed to let their children marry freely, and every year, at the September moussem held around the tomb of their patron saint, members of the Ait Hadiddou tribe gather to find their partners. Men looking for a wife wear white turbans, women looking for a husband wear all their jewels, and in the three days of the festival they celebrate their engagement and subsequent wedding. The moussem also marks the time when the tribes no longer have to move their livestock to summer pastures, and come home to settle in for the winter, so there's a massive livestock market with paddocks for the different animals, as well as souks selling provisions, and a whole sea of tents (Berbers head here from all over the Atlas mountains to celebrate). Singing, dancing and music lasts throughout the festival, but it's pretty much spontaneous, so follow your ears to find it. Accommodation is spartan – you'll need to bring a sleeping bag and rent a tent and mattress, and you'll also need water, toilet paper and a flashlight. Imilchil also takes a bit of getting to, but it all adds to the fun.

International Roots Festival

Where? **Banjul, The Gambia**
When? **June**
How long? **1 week**

Inspired by author Alex Haley's book, *Roots*, and his journey back to the land of his ancestors, the International Roots Festival (Ⓦ www.rootsgambia.gm) is only a few years old, but is gaining credibility – and popularity – for its focus on black culture. There is drumming, music, fashion shows and a film festival, all designed to draw the black diaspora to the Gambia to celebrate their common culture.

Lake of Stars Festival

Where? **Lake Malawi, Malawi**
When? **September**
How long? **3 days**

Easy-going but famously conservative, Malawians don't have a particularly strong home-grown musical tradition. Very few Malawian bands have made any impact on the international scene, and it's the exception, rather than the rule, for bars and clubs to specialize in local sounds – you're far more likely to hear music from the west or from the country's neighbours and near-neighbours: South Africa, Zimbabwe, Tanzania and Mozambique. It's partly thanks to this musical outlook that the relatively new festival (Ⓦ www.lakeofstarsfestival.co.uk) has begun to take off. Taking place on the banks of Lake Malawi, it hosts cool European and African bands and DJs; in recent years, guest stars have included Groove Armada's Andy Cato, and Felix from Basement Jaxx. For a laid-

International Roots Festival

back vibe, the setting couldn't be better: the main stage, at Chintheche, is close to a dazzling strip of sand where fish eagles call shrilly across the crystal-clear water; accommodation is in one of several castaway-style lodges and campsites. After the long drive to get there – four hours from Lilongwe, or eight from Blantyre – you'll be ready to kick off your shoes and chill out. Who says you need to head to the ocean for the best beach parties?

Maherero Day

Where? **Okahandja, Namibia**
When? **August**
How long? **1 day**

This very local festival is unique to the Herero people of Okahandja, a quaint little provincial town that's around an hour's drive north of the Namibian capital, Windhoek. The Herero are cattle farmers whose history is littered with bloody conflicts, both with their tribal rivals, the Nama, and with German colonialists who almost wiped them out in the early twentieth century. On Maherero Day, the clans don traditional dress and parade through town in military style to honour their war dead, starting from the cemetery at the graves of two great chiefs, Kahimunua and Nikodemus, both felled by German bullets. It's the women's costumes that make the day a remarkable occasion – they wear elaborate dresses based on a style introduced by German missionaries in the 1800s, with long-sleeved jackets and bodices over voluminous, crinoline-like skirts. Topping off each ensemble is a huge cloth headdress shaped like cow horns, a symbol of wealth in traditional Herero society.

Mampoer Festival

Where? **Cullinan, South Africa**
When? **May**
How long? **1 day**

The Boers have been distilling mampoer, South African moonshine, since trekking up onto the Transvaal in the

Maherero Day

1830s and seeing the elephants getting blind drunk on fermented poer berries. (A less romantic version of the tale has a local chieftain named Mapuru showing them how.) Today, peaches and apricots are the favoured fruit for the volatile brew, which has an alcohol content in excess of sixty percent and delivers a kick powerful enough to save you from snake-bite – indeed, after a slug of this you wouldn't care what bit you. Fortunately for those who like their spirits just so, this is one of the few places in the world where moonshine is legal, and even agricultural colleges and museums are allowed to make their own mampoer. Naturally enough, the festival is held at the local museum in the town of Cullinan, near Pretoria, and after a short time you'll find yourself amazingly fluent in Afrikaans.

Maralal Camel Derby

Where? **Maralal, Kenya**
When? **August**
How long? **3 days**

Residents of the quiet, remote town of Maralal, deep in the Samburu district of northern Kenya, are used to having camels around – the dromedary plays a crucial role in the lives of the nomads in this wild and arid region – but for a few days every August, Maralal is invaded by scores of the hairy beasts, in preparation for its prestigious Camel Derby. Camel riding is not a routine part of daily life in this part of Kenya – the animals generally carry goods rather than people – but their owners tend to be excellent handlers, with a canny eye for a mount with strength and speed. Winning the 42-kilometre "Professional Camel Race" means the world to the participants, and every year the title is hotly contested; for anybody else who feels like a go, there's a novices' event, which follows a twelve-kilometre course around town.

Maulidi

Where? **Lamu, Kenya**
When? **May**
How long? **4 days**

On the Indian Ocean island of Lamu, Maulidi, the birthday of the Prophet Mohammed, is the undisputed highlight of the Islamic year. The island atmosphere is usually laid-back in the extreme, but in the run-up to Maulidi, the narrow streets of Lamu town swarm with visitors from all over the region, and you'll find yourself rubbing shoulders with pilgrims, who gather here for the all-night recitation of the Maulid. All are welcome at the four-day knees-up that concludes the festival, complete with dhow competitions, and donkey races along the waterfront.

Moulid of Sayyid Ahmed al-Bedawi

Where? **Tanta, Egypt**
When? **October**
How long? **8 days**

Egyptians love a good moulid (festivals honouring local saints), and they don't come much bigger than the Moulid of Sayyid Ahmed al-Bedawi, when the otherwise nondescript Nile Delta city of Tanta is besieged by some two million pilgrims, who converge on the triple-domed mosque where al-Bedawi is buried. Moulids are especially associated with Sufis – Islamic mystics, who use singing, chanting and dancing to bring themselves closer to God. Some fifty Sufi brotherhoods put up their tents around Tanta and set to work chanting and beating out a rhythm on drums or tambourines, as devotees perform their zikrs (ritual dances). In the less frenetic tents, you can relax with a sheesha (water-pipe) or a nice cup of tea, while scoffing festive treats such as roasted chickpeas and sugared nuts. The atmosphere is intense, the crowds dense, and pickpocketing rife (so leave your valuables at home). Tanta doesn't have much in the way of accommodation, and most people just bunk down in the tents, but if that doesn't appeal and you can't get a room, it's near enough to Cairo to take in on a day-trip. The climax comes on the last night, a Friday, when the Ahmediya, the Sufi brotherhood founded by al-Bedawi, parade with drums and red banners behind their sheikh.

Mwaka Kogwa

Where? **Zanzibar**
When? **July**
How long? **1 day**

Celebrating the Shirazi (Persian) New Year, Mwaka Kogwa is entirely organized and performed by the locals: the men take on each other in mock "fights", armed only with banana leaves; the women parade around in their finest outfits choosing suitors; and there's ritual burning of a grass hut – the direction of the smoke supposedly determines the prosperity of the village in the coming year.

Ncwala

Where? **Swaziland**
When? **December**
How long? **3 weeks**

Swaziland's Ncwala or "First Fruits" festival is a raucous thanksgiving celebration, praising the king and his people while simultaneously fêting the new harvest – and the New Year. Starting on a date decided upon by Swaziland's royal astrologers (basically 3 weeks from the full moon), the first days of the festival see the Bemanti or "Water People" travelling to the coast to capture foam from the waves. They then return to celebrate "Little Ncwala" by collecting shrubs and ritually slaughtering a bull. Once the full moon has arrived, the chief tastes the first fresh produce of the year, royal objects representing the previous year are burnt amidst much colourful pageantry, and the people throw themselves into all-night dancing, drinking, feasting and merrymaking – "Big Ncwala". Ncwala is also celebrated in Zambia, towards the end of February, when the Chewa chief ceremonially samples the harvest and then slaughters a bull and drinks its blood.

Nederburg Wine Auction and Paarl Wine Festival

Where? **Nederburg and Paarl, South Africa**
When? **April**
How long? **3 days**

These two festivals follow on from each other in April every year, and attract up to thirty thousand visitors keen to make sure that the region's wine season opens well. The wine auction attracts lots of buyers, but it is more than just a business event, with a great atmosphere that flows through to the festival, when the first wines of the year are carried up the mountain slopes behind town in a variety of novel ways, and there's plenty of sampling and general enjoyment. It's not something to race down from Cairo for, but good fun if you're in the area.

Panafest

Where? **Ghana**
When? **July**
How long? **10 days**

Gold-rich Ghana was a cornerstone of European trading interests in West Africa during the colonial era, so it makes perfect sense that it's latterly become a focus for homecomers from the African diaspora. Riding this wave, Panafest (short for Pan-African Historical Theatre Festival; ⓦ www.panafest.org), a biennial celebration of African culture and freedom, is a lively mixture of events – part-pilgrimage, part-party. Movingly, pilgrims gather at Cape Coast, one-time hub of the transatlantic slave trade, for a candlelit Emancipation Vigil to honour the victims of slavery. Then, on a more boisterous note, there's booty-shaking entertainment from traditional West African musicians.

Sauti Za Busara Festival

Where? **Stone Town, Zanzibar**
When? **February**
How long? **5 days**

A feast of East African music, this relatively new festival rocks Stone Town and around with a wide variety of Swahili music and dance. Whoever the participants might be, the locations can't be beat: four days in Stone Town's Omani Fort, followed by a big finale on the beach at Kendwa, in the north of the island, where the acts are accompanied by crafts, food, fire-eaters and all manner of Swahili entertainment. If you can only be here for one day, make it this last one.

Splashy Fen

Where? **Underberg, South Africa**
When? **April**
How long? **4 days**

Woodstock and Glastonbury meet Africa at Splashy Fen, a farm in Underberg, at the foot of Natal's Drakensberg Mountains, for one of the southern hemisphere's greatest music festivals. Over ten thousand people turn up to the Easter weekend camp-out at the Fen (ⓦ www.splashyfen.

co.za; tickets R350 or R200 per day) to catch sessions ranging from township musicians pounding out the bqanga beat to the latest big names in South African pop, along with a handful of international acts. Now is the time to go, as the festival is growing, and has lost a lot of its raw spirit over recent years, having accepted an increased amount of corporate sponsorship. Nonetheless, it's still South Africa's biggest music event.

Timket

Where? **Adis Ababa, Ethiopia**
When? **January**
How long? **2 days**

Ethiopia's largest festival celebrates the Epiphany according to the Julian calendar. It's chiefly a religious occasion – and the priests take centre stage, resplendent in velvet and sequins, whirling `bejewelled velvet umbrellas – but it's certainly not a sombre one. In Addis Ababa, a carnival atmosphere takes hold of the city as thousands camp out around the Jan Meda area on the eve of Timket, their fires and torches blazing in the night sky. The day itself is marked with all-out feasting, singing, dancing and consumption of great quantities of specially brewed tej – strong Ethiopian beer – before a mass at 2am and a baptism ritual at dawn.

Windhoek Carnival

Where? **Windhoek, Namibia**
When? **December**
How long? **2 weeks**

A long way to travel for a bit of carnival fun, but this is one of the best you'll find. The former German colony lets rip for a riotous fortnight of atavistic music, food, beer tents, barbecues and leather-slapping drunkenness. German traditions, complete with a cabaret evening and a night-long masked ball, are all served with such a heavy dash of Africa that the festival – locally known as "Wika" – is utterly unforgettable. And if you think at any time that you might have slipped back to the Fatherland without remembering how, just take a quick peek out beyond the town's boundaries, where the dark of the Namib Desert will bring you straight back to reality. A large carnival parade takes place on the final Saturday, to which all are invited.

Sauti Za Busara Festival

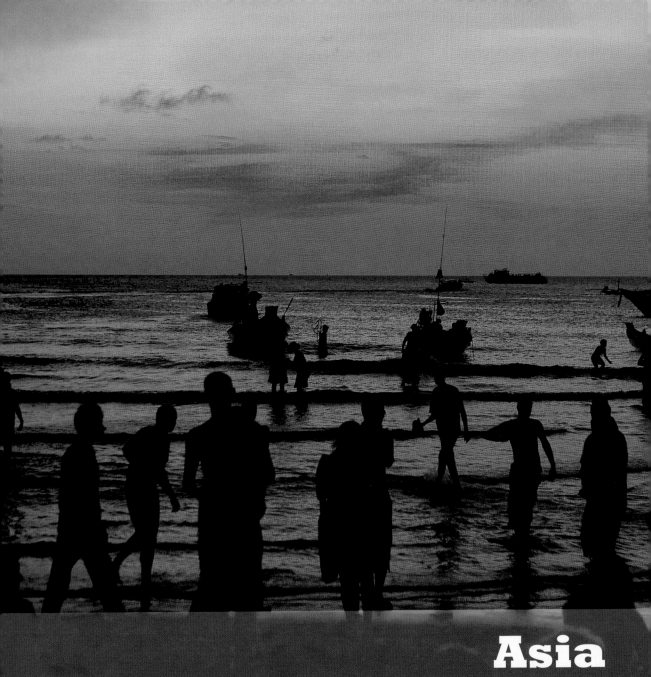

Asia

Asia

Ati-Atihan
Esala Perahera
Full Moon Party
Gion Matsuri
Holi
Kumbh Mela
Naadam
Phalgun Festivals
Pushkar Camel Fair
BEST OF THE REST

Ati-Atihan

Bigyan mo ako ng lechon at kangkong.
Okay na yan sa iyo, mahal?

Ati-Atihan

Where?
Kalibo, Panay Island, The
Visayas, The Philippines

When?
Mid-January

How long?
2 weeks

In the sixteenth century, a pious Spanish friar noted that among the Visayan people of the Philippines it was not quite proper to drink alone or to appear drunk in public. Drinking was always done in small groups or in "gatherings where men as well as women sat on opposite sides of the room". The good friar would have revised his opinion if he had been to Ati-Atihan, a quasi-religious Mardi Gras where much of the fervour is fuelled by free-flowing locally brewed grog. Throw in the unending beat of massed drums and the average Filipino's predisposition for a good party, and the result is a flamboyant al fresco rave that claims – with some justification – to be the biggest and most prolonged in the Philippines. And this, remember, in a country where fiestas are as common as sunny days.

You'll find all the elements for a spectacular carnival parade – extravagant costumes, lavishly decorated floats and a legion of up-for-it participants – but absolutely none of the organization. Nor will you find that sometimes welcome distinction between spectators and parading dancers as you would in, say, Rio. In Kalibo, wherever you are, you'll be in the thick of it. You'll be hauled onto a float by a bunch of mermaids, made to dance with a group of schoolgirls dressed as nuns, and forced to drink ludicrous quantities of rum until you can barely stand. The whole shindig rages until sunrise, by which time you will be totally disoriented, sky-high and probably in the clutches of a beautiful, if somewhat sexually ambivalent, Filipino. But hell, what better way to start the year?

The Ati-Atihan mantra *Hala Bira, Puera Pasma* translates as "Keep on going, no tiring", and you'll need all the energy you've got if you want to take in the whole fortnight. However, it's the final three days that are the most important, with the costumed locals taking to Kalibo's streets in a riot of spontaneous partying, music and street dancing. Ati-Atihan is still partly a religious festival, but it's also the one time of the year when Catholic Filipinos aren't afraid to poke fun at a few of their treasured icons. Transvestites – accepted in the Philippines as a legitimate "third sex" – get out their best frocks, and schoolgirls with hats made of coconuts join aborigines, national heroes, drag queens and spacemen in the final Sunday's spectacular fancy-dress procession. Some of the costumes are so big they almost block the street.

History

Ati-Atihan's **origins** can be traced to 1210, when refugees from Borneo smeared their faces with soot in affectionate imitation of the Filipino natives – political correctness was evidently not an issue in the thirteenth-century Philippines. The Borneans, ten ruling families and their followers, had fled to escape the tyranny of an enemy and found themselves on Panay Island, in the heart of the Philippine archipelago. Panay's Negrito natives, known as Atis, were quick to capitalize on the refugees' arrival, selling them land in exchange for a solid gold hat and a basin. In addition, the Ati chief's wife wanted an ankle-length necklace, for which the natives gave a bushel of live crabs, a long-tusked boar, and a full-antlered white deer. The Purchase of Panay wasn't the most lucrative real estate deal ever done, but both parties were satisfied and held a feast that same night to celebrate, the Atis slaughtering livestock and the Borneans blackening their faces.

The Ati-Atihan's religious element is in honour of the ubiquitous **Santo Niño** (the Holy Child), whose image appears throughout the archipelago, in churches and homes, and on the dashboards of taxis, tricycles and pedicabs. In the Filipino saintly hierarchy, Santo Niño has few rivals, and people carry reminders of him as *anting-anting* (talismans), to ward off the unholy.

Santo Niño was introduced by Spanish friars to the Philippines – and, in turn, to Ati-Atihan – through a deliberate act of cunning. The unprotected northern coast of Aklan province, of which Kalibo is the capital, had always made it vulnerable to **Muslim invasions** and, in 1813 and 1835, Muslim *vinta* (ships) carrying a thousand pirates attacked the seashore town of Buswang, taking away with them slaves and loot. Following another raid, this one unsuccessful, the opportunist friars spread word among the islanders that the baby Jesus had appeared and had driven off the attack. It was a cynical move to hasten the propagation of Catholicism throughout the Philippines, and it worked, giving rise to the ritual of *patapak* in local churches, during which revellers hold aloft images of the baby Jesus on their shoulders shouting, "Viva el Señor Santo Niño!" ("Long Live the Holy Child").

The build-up

Although the festival doesn't really get into top gear until the third week of January, the build-up starts a week earlier with events like craft fairs, cock fighting, snake dancing and a re-enactment of the Purchase of Panay, whetting the appetite for the three-day frenzy that ends it all. Most of the action, including the fancy-dress procession, takes place in Kalibo's town centre, with **Magsaysay Park** and **Pastraña Park** hosting various events day and night.

Inter-island boats docking at the nearby seaports of New Washington and Dumaguit are greeted by a corps of deafening tribal drummers; tourists are ferried across rice fields and coconut plantations to hotels in Kalibo, while others are accommodated in private homes and public buildings. Some camp on the beach, where fires are lit and fisherfolk make a few extra *pesos* selling barbecued grouper. By the last weekend of the fiesta, there's no room at the inn, although it doesn't seem to matter because no one sleeps anyway.

The procession

By mid-morning on the Sunday, small groups from all the nearby *barangays* (villages) gather in their respective neighbourhoods and dance their way to the town centre. Numbers increase exponentially as different groups from outlying areas merge into one.

The **main procession** starts at the south side of Pastraña Park and takes a circular route to St John the Baptist Cathedral, just north of the park. The Kalibonhons have an unwritten rule that there are no wallflowers at Ati-Atihan and no choreographed steps that isolate participants from spectators. If the best you can muster is a drunken conga line, that's fine. But come what may, you must participate – if you don't, they'll make you.

Beauty pageants

No fiesta in the Philippines would be complete without a beauty pageant and **Miss Ati-Atihan** is the chance for all the local beauties to compete for prizes for the best costumes and the coveted title of Miss Ati-Atihan. Pretty teenagers in sparkling dresses and rouged cheeks glide around hoping that this will be their year. They look as if they were made from icing sugar, shading themselves from the melting sun under brightly coloured parasols.

No less desirable is the title of **Miss Gay Ati-Atihan**, as transvestites are embraced by Filipinos as arbiters of fashion and style. Glamorously tossing their lustrous hair, the entrants dispense perfumed kisses to embarrassed foreigners, but the competition is no joke. For the winner, success brings respect, and, who knows, maybe even a ticket to mini-stardom in Manila.

The morning after

After the hangover, the hair of the dog. The majority of visitors to Ati-Atihan make the most of the prevailing festive spirit by continuing the party on the tiny nearby island of **Boracay**, famous for its white sand, sunsets, and shoals of girls offering beach massage for less than the price of a beer. The drill is simple: after Ati-Atihan, hop on a bus from Kalibo heading west along the coastal road to Caticlan, where you take a *banca* – a pumpboat with outriggers – to Boracay. The whole journey takes about three hours and costs very little, even allowing for some loose change to placate the unrelenting waves of porters.

you'll be hauled onto a float by a bunch of mermaids and forced to drink ludicrous quantities of rum until you can barely stand

Once on Boracay, you can vegetate, scuba dive or spend raucous nights in bars such as *Moondogs Shooters Bar. Moondogs* is known for its "Shooters Test", where the barman lines up fifteen bilious cocktails, and you drink them in quick succession – if you're still standing at the end you get a free T-shirt.

Insider info For a glimpse of the more religious side to the celebrations, take in one of the many ceremonies that are held either at St John the Baptist Cathedral or, for the huge Sunday-morning mass, at Pastraña Park.

Atihan wannabes

Kalibo's Ati-Atihan has become so popular that similar festivals have cropped up at the same time of the year all over the Visayas. Elsewhere in Aklan province, Ati-Atihan is celebrated in the towns of Makato, Altavas and Ibajay, all of which claim to be the birthplace of the Ati-Atihan, as do countless other small towns throughout Panay. Antique, a rural and almost tourist-free province on the island's rugged west coast, has its **Binirayan** and **Handugan** festivals, and Panay's capital, Iloilo City, has a more lavish and choreographed version, called **Dinagyang** (see p.357). The busy coastal town of Bacolod, on neighbouring Negros Island, also has an annual Ati-Atihan, while every January Cebu City, on the next island to the east, has the **Sinulog**, which is also dedicated to the veneration of the Santo Niño. Historians generally agree, however, that Kalibo's Ati-Atihan is the real thing.

Basics

Kalibo is 216km south of Manila – the capital of the Philippines and the nearest international **airport**. The town's provincial **tourist office** is in the Provincial Capitol Building (daily 8–11am & 2–5pm; ℡036/262 4692), about 400m east of Pastraña Park.

Accommodation

Good **accommodation** can be hard to find during Ati-Atihan and prices increase significantly, starting at about P550 a night for a very ordinary double room, often with a shared toilet and shower. More sophisticated places cost from around P1000 for a double. But this is a special event for locals and it would be unheard of for any visitor not to be received with the utmost hospitality – townspeople open their houses and the mayor allows bleary-eyed travellers to lay down their heads in village halls and schools. *The Beachcomber Inn* on N. Roldan Street (℡036/262 4846) is a comfortable and quiet accredited resort with nineteen air-con rooms (about P1800 for a double). The *Glowmoon Inn & Restaurant* on South Martelino Street (℡036/262 3073) is a good budget choice, with fifteen rooms (around P900 for a double) and a popular restaurant, or there's the *Apartelle Marietta* (℡036/262 3353) and the *Garcia Legaspi Mansion* (℡036/262 5588), two reasonable places on Roxas Avenue, the main road from the airport. Both charge P1300 for a double room. The *Hotel Casa Felicidad Alba* in Archbishop G. Reyes Street (℡036/268 4320) has eight air-con rooms (P1200 for a double) and a coffee shop, while the slightly more expensive *La Esperanza Hotel* (P1600 for a double) is a good middle-of-the-road option in a central location in Osmeña Avenue (℡036/262 5858). *Sampaguita Gardens* at 506 Rizal St (℡036/264 3422; ⊛www.sampaguitagardens.com), in a suburb called New Washington, is upmarket by local standards, but comfortable and quiet – a double here will cost around P2000.

Eating and drinking

There is nothing urbane about **Filipino cuisine**, and that's the way people like it. Food is there to be enjoyed and shared, not pontificated over – a feeling typified by the phrasebook line *Bigyan mo ako ng lechon at kangkong. Okay na yan sa iyo, mahal?*, which translates as, "Waiter, give me a roast pig and some spinach. Is that all right for you, darling?". The humble *baboy* – the pig – is the **meat of choice** for all fiestas and the Ati-Atihan is no exception. Roast pig is known as *lechon*, and a significant amount of care and attention goes into its preparation. It's a simple dish, but cooked for many hours, often overnight. The beast is slaughtered the night before it is to be eaten and the skin scraped to remove the hair. It is then stuffed with herbs – pandan or lemongrass – and roasted slowly over coal on a bamboo spit, turned by volunteers who have to stay up all night, whipping the skin with banana leaves to infuse extra flavour. The crispy skin is considered the most delicious part of the pig and is fought over first at the expense of the tender meat inside. Nothing goes to waste and even the ears are coveted. Other **fiesta delicacies** include home-made sweets such as *pastillas de leche* (milk sweets) and "Food for the Gods", a brownie-style sweetcake with dates and walnuts. There's no point in recommending anywhere in particular to try all this stuff; it's on sale everywhere you go – just tuck in!

As for **drink**, the faint sense of sedition in the air is in part fuelled by *lambanog*, a vigorous native confection made from leftover jackfruit or mango fermented in cheap containers buried in the earth. It's passed around everywhere, either in an old diesel can, which gives the sweet liquid inside a faintly industrial aftertaste, or a plastic bottle, with labels that say things like, "Brewed in the Philippines: Zombie Flavour." Other native drinks include *tuba* (rice wine) and fresh *buko* (coconut milk). Ice-cold San Miguel beer is ridiculously cheap (P12.50 a bottle from the little *sari-sari* stores), while Tanduay rum (P30 a bottle), is also a bargain source of inspiration: Filipinos tend to drink this neat in *barkadas* (groups of friends), often passing around the same cup as a sign of solidarity. It isn't a particularly sophisticated intoxicant – adding a splash of Coke will remove the rough edges.

Event info

Ati-Atihan (⊛ www.ati-atihan.net). Excellent site with flight schedules, event diary, photo gallery, accommodation, maps and more.

| **Time zone** GMT+8 | **Country code** +63 | **Currency** Philippine peso (P) |

Esala Perahera

The smoke and pungent fumes add to the full-on assault on the senses

Esala Perahera

Where?
Kandy, Sri Lanka

When?
The last ten days of the Buddhist lunar month of Esala (usually late July and early August), ending on the full moon day of the lunar month of Nikini

How long?
10 days, plus an afternoon "day *perahera*" on the day after the conclusion of the festival proper

SRI LANKA

• Kandy
• Colombo

In terms of noise, colour and crowds, there's nothing else on earth quite like Kandy's Esala Perahera, a ten-day extravaganza dating back to the fourth century AD and the early days of Buddhism in Sri Lanka. Forget Ibiza's club scene, for truly all-out sensory assault, this is hard to beat. Held to honour the Buddha's tooth, the festival is based around a series of increasingly lengthy and spectacular night-time parades involving drummers, dancers, torch-bearers, whip-crackers, fire-eaters and, most spectacularly, over a hundred costumed elephants. The final parade is the best part of a kilometre long, and can take several hours to wind its way around the city streets.

Whatever you might hear in the press about outbreaks of **violence in Sri Lanka**, Kandy remains a perfectly safe destination – clashes between the Sri Lankan Army and the separatist LTTE (Tamil Tigers) remain confined to the remote eastern and northern parts of the island, and political and military targets in Colombo. Apart from a single bomb blast in 1998, timed to disrupt a visit by Prince Charles, the city has never experienced any fallout from the long civil war between the Tamil Tigers and the Sri Lankan government that traumatized parts of Sri Lanka from 1983 to 2002. Even if the civil war does resume (a tenuous ceasefire is currently in place, and has been since 2002), Kandy itself is extremely unlikely to experience any problems.

Sri Lankans call **Kandy** "Maha Nuwara", the "Great City", and although it's long been overtaken by the country's capital, Colombo, in terms of size and population, Kandy remains the centre of the island's ancient Buddhist cultural and religious traditions, of which the Esala Perahera is the most spectacular example. Located just 100km northeast of Colombo, amid lush green hills in some of Sri Lanka's most beautiful and rugged countryside, the Kingdom of Kandy was the last part of Sri Lanka to be conquered by invading Europeans – the king of Kandy held out against the British until 1814 – and the place least affected by foreign influences. It is home to the country's most famous temple, the Dalada Maligawa, or the **Temple of the Tooth**, which houses the Buddha's Tooth Relic, the *raison d'être* for Esala Perahera, while other important temples throughout the city contribute performers and elephants to the festival.

Kandy is also the centre of traditional Sinhalese performing arts, in particular the exuberant styles of dancing and drumming that play such an important role in the Esala Perahera – outside festival time, displays of Kandyan drumming and dancing are held nightly at several venues, offering the chance to sample the acrobatic and adrenaline-charged performances that are typical of the city.

History

Gautama Siddhartha – or the **Buddha** – lived in India from 560 to 483BC; his teachings first arrived in Sri Lanka in 247BC and very soon become the predominant religion of the Sinhalese majority there. According to legend, one of the Buddha's teeth was snatched from his smouldering funeral pyre by a devotee and then smuggled into Sri Lanka in the hair of an Orissan princess in around 300AD. King Meghawanna received the Tooth Relic (as it is now known) with great honour, laid it in a gold urn and had it carried around the then capital, Anuradhapura, in a celebratory procession – the origins of today's festival. During the following centuries the Tooth Relic was moved around the island, being variously used to prevent famine (the Tooth Relic is popularly believed to protect against drought) and defeat invaders, before arriving in Kandy in 1592, where it has remained since, residing in Sri Lanka's most sacred temple, the Dalada Maligawa, or Temple of the Tooth. Reports of the first Sacred Tooth Perahera date back to the sixth century AD, though the event has continued uninterrupted in its present form since the early seventeenth century.

The parades

Although originally a Buddhist celebration, the Esala Perahera was also spiced up with a fair dash of Hinduism during the seventeenth and eighteenth centuries, when the Kingdom of Kandy was ruled by Hindus from the Nayakkar dynasty of southern India, and when Hindu deities became absorbed into local Buddhist traditions. The four most important of these deities – Natha, Vishnu, Kataragama and Pattini – each have a dedicated temple in the city, from which **separate nightly parades**, or *peraheras*, emerge, to join up with the main parade from the Temple of the Tooth, so that the complete procession is actually made of up five separate parades joined together – a kind of giant religious conga, with elephants.

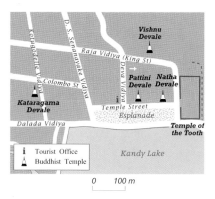

> **Insider info** If you're not keen on crowds, Kandy hosts a so-called day *perahera* on the afternoon following the final night parade, a scaled-down version that's good for photography but a lot less atmospheric than the original.

The nightly parades start between 8pm and 9pm, though you'll need to be in place at least an hour before. As dusk approaches, the flood of humanity lining the route turns into a solid and almost impenetrable mass. With the streets closed to traffic, the smell of jasmine, incense, frangipani – not to mention the spicy picnic suppers everyone is tucking into – is intense, and the trees, shop fronts and streetlamps drip with tinsel decorations and coloured lights. Large crowds of tourists merge with the thousands of Sri Lankans who descend on the city for the event.

You'll hear the parade before you see it. Depending on the night, there could be up to a thousand drummers involved in the *perahera*, and the boom of their powerful drums carries for miles around the city, heightening the sense of anticipation that precedes the arrival of the elephants – scores of them, decorated with golden balaclavas, yards of beautiful silks, embroidered cloth and silver thread. Some are even rigged with flashing lights. Surrounding them are brightly attired dancers, drummers and torch-bearers, each either carrying a bundle of sticks that have been dipped in oil, or swinging burning

a kind of giant religious conga, with elephants

Watching Esala Perahera

It's doubtful whether even Buddha himself would have had the patience to attend all ten nights of the Esala Perahera. Although an awesome spectacle, the disorganized melee of onlookers can be pretty overwhelming, and you've got to be comfortable in crowds if you want to take in the spectacular final night – the fifth and sixth nights offer a good compromise between avoiding the worst of the throngs and seeing the procession in something approaching its full glory.

Where to see it

There are two ways of actually watching the parades. You can do as the locals do and claim a spot amidst the densely packed crowds that line the route of the procession – this is free, and will get you right in the thick of things, but you'll have to be prepared to spend four or five hours sitting on the ground before the parade even begins. Otherwise, you can reserve one of the thousands of street-side seats that are rented out by houses, shops and hotels along the route – buy them through your guesthouse rather than off a tout on the street. Seats up on the higher floors of street-side buildings, or with restricted views, can cost as little as US$10, though expect to pay closer to US$50 for the better seats. Even with a reserved seat you'll need to be in place at least an hour before the parade begins.

coconut husks from chains. Either way, the smoke and pungent fumes add to the full-on assault on the senses. Troupes of dancers, acrobats and musicians accompany the pachyderm procession, along with local dignitaries dressed in traditional finery, and men wielding mighty whips, which they crack every minute or so, supposedly to scare away demons but more useful for keeping over-zealous devotees and over-curious tourists at a respectable distance.

Near the head of the parade is the mighty Maligawa tusker elephant, the beast entrusted with the job of carrying the Tooth Relic on its back, secured in a solid gold casket (although nowadays only a replica of the Tooth Relic is carried in the procession). Kitted out more ostentatiously than all of the other elephants put together, the Maligawa tusker marches through the streets with stately dignity, his appearance triggering wild cheering in the crowds, many of whom have patiently waited for hours just to catch a glimpse of him.

Water-cutting

Shortly before dawn on the morning after the final night of the *perahera*, a "water-cutting" ceremony is held at the Mahaweli Ganga river, near Kandy. The Kapurala, the most senior official from the Temple of the Tooth, "cuts" the waters of the Mahaweli Ganga with a golden sword, symbolically dividing the pure from the impure and, thanks to the Tooth Relic's perceived ability to protect against drought, ensuring a ready supply of water for the coming year. A goblet of water is then taken back to the temple where it is stored until the following year, when it is used in the initial tree-planting ritual that signals the beginning of the festival.

Basics

The nearest **airport** is at Colombo, from where you'll need to catch a taxi or hop on one of the frequent buses or trains that make the one-hundred-kilometre trip northeast to Kandy. The city's **tourist office** is near the entrance to the Temple of the Tooth (see below).

Accommodation

Kandy boasts an incredible number of hotels and guesthouses, and during festival time many private homes rent out rooms. Most of the best **guesthouses** are based along Saranankara Road; those worth trying include: *Freedom Lodge*, at 30 Saranankara Rd (☎081-222 3506, ✉freedomomega@yahoo.com); *Expeditor*, at 41 (☎081-223 8316, ✉expeditorkandy@hotmail.com); *Sharon Inn*, at 59 (☎081-222 2416, ✉sharon@sltnet.lk); and *Highest View*, at 129/3 (☎081-223 3778, ☎www.highestview.com). These places offer a range of comfortable rooms, for US$20–50.

If you can afford to spend a little more, good three- and four-star **hotels** include *Thilanka*, 3 Sangamitta Mawatha (☎081-223 2429, ☎www.lanka.net/thilanka), *Topaz Hotel*, Anniewatte (☎081-222 4150, ✉topaz@eureka.lk), and *Hotel Suisse*, on Sangaraja Mawatha, on the south side of the lake (☎081-223 3024, ☎www.ccom.lk/suisse) – count on US$100–$150 for a room at one of these. For local five-star luxury, look no further than the sumptuous *Mahaweli Reach* (☎081-447 2727, ☎www.mahaweli.com) or the *Earl's Regency* (☎081-242 2122, ☎www.aitkenspenceholidays.com), both a few kilometres outside Kandy on the Mahaweli Ganga; doubles go for US$300 and upwards during the *perahera*. Alternatively, you could try bagging a room at one of the two city-centre hotels that overlook the route of the parade, so you can watch the festival from the comfort of your own room. The modern *Hotel Casamara*, 12 Kotugodelle Vidiya (☎081-222 4688, ✉casamara@senfini.com) and the venerable, colonial-era *Queens*

Hotel, on Deva Vidiya (☎081-222 2813, ☎www.ccom.lk/suisse) have rooms that range from US$150 for a standard double up to over US$1000 for the presidential suite at the *Queens Hotel* – if, that is, it hasn't already been booked up by the president of Sri Lanka.

Eating and drinking

Rice and **curry** is the staple diet of Sri Lanka, and these boys like it hot. If you watch the parades with the locals, you'll probably be besieged by people offering you a huge array of snacks that they've brought along – *biryani* (rice cooked with coconut milk and fried in *ghee*) is a festive favourite. If you find yourself in need of an emergency fire extinguisher, then the small crisp *papadams* are an excellent counterpoint to the curries, but watch out for the notorious *pol sambol*, made with ground chillies.

As a Buddhist festival, Esala Perahera is strictly **alcohol-free**, though away from the festival, booze is freely available, so all you need to do is hang on for a few hours. The local firewater is called *arrack*, made from fermented coconut sap and usually mixed with coke or lemonade or used as a base for cocktails. It goes down very easily – and so will you after a few glasses.

Event info

Dalada Maligawa (☎ www.daladamaligawa.org). History and cultural background to the Esala Perahera.

Useful websites

Temple of the Tooth (☎ www.sridaladamaligawa.lk). Official website of the sacred temple.
Sri Lanka Tourism Deva Vidiya (☎081-222 2661, ☎www.srilankatourism.org). Islandwide, tourist-board website.

Time zone GMT+5.5   **Country code** +94   **Currency** Sri Lankan rupee (Rs)

Full Moon Party

*Fire-throwing jugglers, day-glo body paint
and the fat moon herself*

Full Moon Party

Where?
Hat Rin, Ko Pha Ngan, Thailand

When?
Every month, on the night of the full moon (though it's sometimes moved forward or backward by one day if the full moon coincides with a Buddhist holiday)

How long?
1 night

THAILAND

• Bangkok

• Hat Rin

The tourist party season in Southeast Asia traditionally gets underway at the end of the year with huge, head-thumping parties at Hat Rin beach on Thailand's Ko Pha Ngan island. Hat Rin has firmly established itself as Southeast Asia's premier rave venue, especially in the high season around December and January, but every month of the year travellers flock in for the Full Moon Party – something like *Apocalypse Now* without the war. Tens of thousands of party fiends from all corners of the world kick up the largely good-natured, booze- and drug-fuelled mayhem, dancing the night away on the squeaky white sand.

Despite Hat Rin's elevated profile, you won't find any megaclubs here, only half a dozen beach bars with outdoor tables and beach mats, and banks of hastily erected sound systems. Instead of fancy laser shows, the lighting effects are provided by flimsy fireworks, fire-throwing jugglers and day-glo body paint – and, of course, the fat moon herself. This DIY approach carries over to the music, too: although big names such as Paul Oakenfold and Danny Rampling often fly in to check out Hat Rin, you're quite likely to find yourself dancing to a have-a-go DJ, who's registered interest on the Full Moon Party website, playing anything from psychedelic trance to drum 'n bass, from handbag house to garage.

To make the most of a Full Moon Party, get yourself to Hat Rin at least a couple of days in advance. That way, you'll be able to maximize the stunning beach location, soak up the growing buzz as the crowds pour in and, more importantly, snag yourself somewhere to stay – Hat Rin only has beds for around two thousand people, so the numbers just don't add up on party night.

You have three basic choices for **accommodation**: full-on ravers will try for a bungalow on the main beach, Sunrise, or Hat Rin Nok (Outer Hat Rin), to have their own chillout zone on the big night; the less committed, and anyone contemplating at least a wink of sleep, will head for the much less attractive Sunset beach, or Hat Rin Nai (Inner Hat Rin), a few minutes' walk away across the neck of the peninsula; others head up the slopes towards

History

The **origins** of the full-moon parties are lost in the swirling, herbal mists of time. What is clear is that foreign travellers have been coming to Hat Rin at least since the 1970s, attracted by its remoteness on the southeastern headland of Ko Pha Ngan (until the road was paved a few years ago, the only regular way to get there was by boat), the beauty of its main beach, and the brain-warming teas containing the local fungus, *hed khi kwai* (literally, buffalo-shit mushrooms). Some time in the late 1980s the hippie, prog-rock sensibilities of the full-moon "happenings" were displaced by techno-driven Acid House parties, and dance music has prevailed ever since.

Dismayed by the levels of drug taking, the authorities have sporadically tried to **ban the parties** – only to be shouted down by the locals who make a living from techno tourism. As well as run-of-the-mill drug excesses, police are also concerned about dodgy Ecstasy and diet pills, spiked drinks, occasional accidental deaths, assaults and psychiatric admissions. Accordingly, they have started clamping down in earnest, setting up a permanent police box at Hat Rin, instigating roadblocks and sometimes even bungalow searches around full-moon night, and drafting in scores of uniformed and plain-clothes officers for the parties. It doesn't seem to have dampened the fun, though, only making travellers a lot more circumspect (the going rate for escaping a minor possession charge is a 50,000 baht "fine"). Fortunately, recent, risible plans by the Tourism Authority of Thailand to turn the parties into family affairs, complete with beauty contests and sporting events, seem to have died a death.

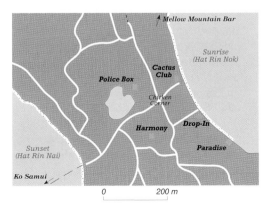

partygoers can still be seen splashing in the shallow surf towards noon, when the last of the beach DJs pull the plug

"Have-a-go DJ" Iain Stewart recounts his part in the legend of Ko Pha Ngan

In 1991, when I first visited Hat Rin, expecting a serious rumble in the jungle, dance music was pretty unpopular. Most of the Thai bar-boys were heavy rock and reggae fans, and the only meeting point for techno-heads was the *Bongo* bar, situated midway between Sunrise and Sunset beaches, beneath a spiky crop of coconut palms. Here, an oddball assortment of party people (mainly Brits) gathered in the nights before the full moon to slug on a Singha beer and plot how we were going to "take" the travellers' bars on Hat Rin's magnificent Sunrise sands. In these beach bars, the accepted traveller wisdom was that techno was "utter shite" – and the nightly soundtrack was a strict diet of MOR rock and a student union-style playlist of REM and The Smiths interspersed with reggae-lite.

As the full moon approached, the party momentum gathered pace and a dozen of us made a foray down to Sunrise with a tape to test the water. A deal was struck with one of the less popular bars – we'd order drinks if the owner would play our music. By the full moon, a party posse had materialized, and after a lengthy session warming up at the *Bongo* on a diet of magic-mushroom tea, special omelettes and "Sang Tip" Thai whisky, we descended en masse to our beach bar.

It went off. Pounding techno trance erupted from the bar's PA and rows of dancers formed to face the sea, massed onto a tiny wooden dance floor that bounced to the beat. More and more gathered until it became impossible to get anywhere near the place. Wide-eyed travellers stood and stared at the scene from a safe distance. Along the beach, rows of entrepreneurial, grinning Thai ladies had set up stalls dispensing mushroom teas and sizzling barbecued chicken. At the southern end of the bay, the self-styled party hosts, *Paradise Bungalows*, had the biggest speakers but the worst DJ in town. But this was where the volume was, so, through a mixture of negotiation and sheer willpower, we took over their DJ box to unleash our repetitive beats.

I've returned to Hat Rin for full-moon parties several times since and have witnessed the scene develop and mutate. Numbers have swollen from around two thousand to tens of thousands, as more and more boatloads of tourists from Ko Samui are heading over to Hat Rin, diluting the intensity somewhat. By the mid-nineties, a couple of bars on Sunrise bay boasted turntables and mixers, and the *Backyard* bar up on the hill extended the event for days – a glorious, though very messy spectacle as legions of frazzled dancers partied on and on in a chaotic test of sybaritic stamina.

Commercialism may be creeping in – today, you can even book a Full Moon Party package holiday – but some things never change. Much as I love the place, Hat Rin still retains a dark side. The undeniably edgy energy is partly because amphetamines are the main stimulants available, and tropical comedowns can be horribly twisted. It can all get too much for some – I've seen a visiting foreigner or two flip out completely, and a wasted farm worker from Wiltshire get a serious pasting courtesy of some local criminals for acting the wrong way. I've also seen a girl beaten with a stick by a Thai man for bathing naked at sunrise (locals find public nudity deeply shameful).

But despite the tensions, the appeal is obvious. The setting is simply stunning, and in a world of corporate clubbing and DJ millionaires the parties remain free and gleefully unorganized, with a funky bunch of beachside bars offering a spicy selection of choice tunes. I've since found other great, less-hyped party scenes in other remote parts of the globe, but as the full moon nears – whether I'm on a 159 bus to Brixton or half way up a volcano in Guatemala – my mind wanders, and a palm-fringed vision of Hat Rin returns.

the southern tip of the headland, where the bungalows are quieter still and the sunset views even better.

If this race for space sounds like too much hassle, it's worth knowing that on party nights frequent speedboats make the trip over to Hat Rin from the larger island of Ko Samui just to the south, while boats and shared vans (*songthaews*) ferry ravers in from other beaches on Ko Pha Ngan.

> **Insider info** If you're hitting Hat Rin for just one night, bring a swimsuit and sarong, to act as towel, beach rug or bed sheet.

First up on the night of the party, it's advisable to eat as it's going to be a long haul (and a lot of beachfront restaurants stay closed the following morning to let their workers get some kip). Once you're fuelled up, there's nothing for it but to plunge in. The **main action** happens on the southern end of Sunrise, spreading out from *Paradise Bungalows*, which styles itself as the original party host, to places like *Drop-In* and the *Cactus Club*. Each has a small concrete dance floor inside if rain stops your play, but you're more likely to be making a grab for one of the lamp-lit tables on the foreshore.

The party's unofficial **chillout zone** is *Mellow Mountain Bar*, perched high in the rocks at the northern end of Sunrise, with the chaos on the perfect crescent of a beach arrayed like a movie set below, to an eclectic backing track of ambient sounds. Most partygoers make it through to the dawn, and some can still be seen splashing in the shallow surf towards noon, when the last of the beach DJs pull the plug. Some ravers will then trudge up the hill to the *Backyard Bar* for morning-afters, and a hardcore few will manage to roll back down to *Harmony* for evening-afters.

Full Moon Party, Goa, India

Full-moon parties aren't confined to Ko Pha Ngan – or even Thailand. **Goa** was once home to some of the biggest events. Started in the 1960s by hippies wintering in north Goa after long hauls across Western Asia, the party scene came of age in the 1990s with the advent of digital micro technology, when a full-on PA could be erected on the remotest Goan hilltop and the latest dance tracks beamed in from the clubs of Amsterdam and London. Goan Trance was born and rapidly popularized by DJs such as Juno Reactor and Goa Gill who regularly showed up for the full-moon parties that took place every month. But, over New Year in 2000, just when the Goa scene seemed poised to live up to its somewhat exaggerated reputation as a prime rave venue, on a par with resorts such as Ibiza and Ko Pha Ngan, a government-led clampdown pulled the plug on the party scene. However, reports in the international media that India's rave era was at an end were premature. Six years on, the scene survives, albeit in a more subdued style. Parties tend to be smaller and better hidden – except that is, over the Christmas and New Year period, when they're as full-on as ever.

Goa was, until 1961, a Portuguese colony, and around one-third of its 1.3 million population remain fervent Catholics, for whom Christmas is the most important time of the year. For Western tourists, however, Christmas in Goa offers the chance to escape the conventional yuletide at home for a night of unbridled hedonism under a South Indian moon. Goa is nothing like the fleshpot dance resorts of the Mediterranean – not least because of the paucity of parties. Since they're technically illegal now, the Christmas/New Year raves aren't advertised, and the big events are held only in out-of-the-way spots – on cliff tops, down densely wooded valleys or on mown rice fields near the state border with Maharashtra. To find one you have to keep your ear to the ground: ask around the shack cafés, chat to the taxi drivers and hawkers on the beach, and listen out for the tell-tale roar of massed Enfields thumping through the paddy fields. This clandestine aspect adds a spark to tracking down a party, and to the overall impact of the music, lights and crowd when you finally arrive.

Regardless of your taste in nightlife, Goan raves are a compelling spectacle. Heaving beneath a palm canopy strung with UV, strobe and fairy lights, the tanned masses look appropriately exotic in their retro-psychedelic dance gear, bought, more often than not, at the Anjuna flea market, India's trendiest and most outrageously colourful open-air boutique. No self-respecting Goa ravehead would be seen without a tool belt to stash all those party essentials: papers and keys (thefts of passports and possessions from rented rooms on party nights are very common), imported Rizlas (Indian ones don't stick) and a bottle of mineral water. Those brave, or foolish, enough to run the gauntlet of the inevitable police roadblocks also carry their *charas* (Indian hashish) in Velcro wristbands that can be discreetly ripped off and ditched in a hurry.

The pace builds steadily to a peak at around 3 or 4am, after which the rhythms mellow and the dancers are drawn to the kerosene lamps of *chai* ladies' stalls, to chill out on straw mats and sip reviving, sweet Indian tea as the moon turns pale cream, to yellow, then pink, before finally sinking into the sea. With the first rays of sunlight shining through the palms, the survivors slip on their shades and kick-start their Enfields, leaving behind a graveyard of plastic bottles, which kids from the nearest village sift through in search of coins and lost lumps of hash.

For more **information**, contact the India Tourism Office on Church Square in Panjim (☏+91 832/222 3412, ⌨www.tourismofindia.com).

Basics

Daily **boats** run to Thong Sala, Ko Pha Ngan's main town, from Ko Samui (site of the nearest **airport**, with flights from Singapore, Bangkok and elsewhere in Thailand); Surat Thani, on the mainland; and from the next island out, Ko Tao. From Thong Sala, *songthaews* and motorbike taxis cover the steep, roller-coaster ride out to Hat Rin – only to be attempted with caution if you hire a motorbike. The most painless way into Hat Rin, however, is to catch one of the daily **ferries** from Ko Samui's north coast direct to the pier on Sunset beach. The nearest tourist office is on Ko Samui at Na Thon (daily 8.30am–noon & 1–4.30pm; ☎077/420504, ✉tatsamui@tat.or.th), though there is an equally useful one on Bangkok at 4 Rajdamnoen Nok Rd, Dusit (daily 8.30am–4.30pm; ☎022/8297773).

Accommodation

The beaches at Sunrise and Sunset are both lined with simple **bungalow resorts**. Owners are continually looking to upgrade their facilities, but you can expect to pay 200–400 baht for a basic, two-person hut, rising to over 1000 baht if you feel the need for air con. If you want to be right at the throbbing heart of the party action, try to make camp at *Paradise Bungalows* (☎077/375244) as far in advance of the big night as you can. The beachside restaurant is good, all bungalows are en suite, and some of the cheaper options, spreading across the slope at the southern end of Sunrise, offer fine views over the bay from their verandas. At the slightly quieter northern end of Sunrise is *Palita* (☎077/375170), a clean, well-run place with a variety of bungalows (all en suite, some air-con), giving on to the beach or sheltering under the coconut palms behind. A typical set-up across the isthmus on somewhat tamer and cheaper Sunset beach is *Neptune's*

Villa (☎077/375251), a popular, laid-back choice set in grassy, shady grounds and offering basic but cheap huts or pricier rooms with hot-water bathrooms, some with air-con. However, for the best chance of a room on full-moon night, you'll need to try places that are further away from the action. *Leela Beach Bungalows* (☎077/375094, ✍www.leelabeach.com), on the beach of the same name, a twenty-minute walk along a signposted route from Chicken Corner, is a good budget choice with en-suite, no-frills bungalows and plenty of space under the palm trees. Beyond, right out at the tip of the peninsula (30min from Chicken Corner), friendly *Lighthouse Bungalows* has concrete or wooden bungalows, either sharing bathrooms or en-suite.

Eating

For somewhere so remote, Hat Rin sports an unnervingly good choice of international **restaurants** from Italian to Indian, but they all close around 11pm, after which you'll be left to forage snacks from the stalls on the beach or at *Nira's* 24-hour bakery at Chicken Corner, the main junction in the resort village between the beaches. You can get good simple Thai fare at many of the bungalow resorts, but it's worth dragging your buns off the beach on full-moon night for a blowout at one of the village restaurants. Standouts are *Casa Nostra* for its reasonably priced pasta, pizza and other good Italian dishes; the *Old Lamp*, where delicious Western and Thai food is served at relaxing low-slung tables; and *Om Ganesh*, an excellent Indian restaurant with cheerful service, whether eat-in or delivered to your bungalow (☎077/375123).

Event info

Full Moon Party (✍www.fullmoon-party.com). Gives the dates of forthcoming parties, news of big-name DJs, and has a well-subscribed message board.

Time zone GMT+7   **Country code** +66   **Currency** Baht (B)

Gion Matsuri

The floats come by in a compelling drone of drums, bells, voices and flute

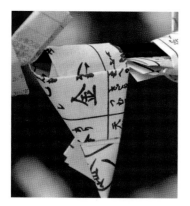

Gion Matsuri

Where?
Kyoto, Japan

When?
July

How long?
10 days

Japan can be a weird place, at least to the uninitiated. Sometimes, it's the epitome of modern, urban life; at others it's as if the country is stuck in the Middle Ages. Nowhere is this more evident, or perhaps more jarring, than in Kyoto, and there's no better time to be here than during the annual Gion Matsuri – a series of events dating back over a thousand years that culminates in a massive, full-on procession through the modern main streets of the old capital. Thousands of people of all ages line the route: youngsters in colourful summer kimonos, wobbling precariously on wooden sandals while they pose for pictures or chat on mobile phones, and tour buses full of middle-aged country folk, videocams out waiting to capture the moment when the floats – some of them two storeys high, and dragged by locals in loincloths – come by in a compelling drone of drums, bells, voices and flute.

Gion Matsuri actually encompasses almost a month of events, but the first ones of interest to visitors happen on July 10, when the construction of the **hoko and yama floats** for the parade begins. Starting at 7am, the pieces – which weigh between 1.2 and 1.6 tons each for the 23 *yama*, and from 5 to 12 tons for the nine huge *hoko* – are fitted together, then tied with rope, to guarantee that none of them falls and squashes a spectator.

The piecing together of these giant jigsaws continues every morning until July 13, after which the *hoko* are on view

History

The **origins** of Gion Matsuri date back to 869 AD, when a great plague raged through Kyoto. To appease the angry gods, a priest led a procession of 66 men, one for each of the provinces of Japan, through the streets of the city, carrying halberds (*Hoko*, the word for the larger, wheeled floats, originally referred to these halberds.) The tribute was a success, and the ritual was repeated frequently, developing into an annual event by the end of the tenth century.

The festival was suspended during the Onin War of the 1460s, and when it was revived the nature and purpose of it had changed – developing from a ceremony of the nobility to more of a street festival and spectacle, and a chance for the merchants to show off their wealth and wares. Gion Matsuri continued to gain popularity throughout the Momoyama and Edo periods, and was an annual event until it was interrupted again by the Second World War. It re-emerged afterwards, on a new route along the major thoroughfares (some say for the benefit of the occupying forces and other foreign tourists), and is now one of the country's biggest annual events, drawing visitors from all over the world.

until the parade on July 17. The easiest place to get a view of this process is on Shijo-dori, near Karasuma Station, but the construction and display actually occur all around the city centre, with each district having responsibility for its own *yama* or *hoko*. You can pick up a map in the tourist office at Kyoto Station, detailing where to see what floats. Or you can simply wait for the parade, and watch them all go by. The floats are often exquisite structures, hand carved and painted in vermilion and gold with scenes from the mythology, history and courtly life of a culture that has all but disappeared in modern-day Japan. Among the most elaborate are the *fune boko*, in the form of a massive ship, and the *toroh yama*, topped with a gigantic, moving mantis.

The **mikoshi arai**, or purification ceremony of the portable shrines (*mikoshi*), also takes place on July 10, at 8pm at the Shijo Ohashi bridge. *Arai* means "clean" or "purify", and the mythical purpose of this ceremony is to prepare the *mikoshi* to receive the gods again after a year of gathering dust. The three shrines are brought down to the river, where a priest performs the cleansing ritual.

with a huge heave-ho, sixteen men jerk the ten-ton cart around

The festivities continue on July 15, when in the early afternoon there's dancing and theatre – and large crowds – at the Yasaka-jinja, a focal point of the festival, at the easternmost end of Shijo-dori. There's more dancing the following afternoon, at Yasaka-jinja, where, in a performance popular at many Shinto festivals, a male and female white heron dance to please the divinities of the shrine. But for most Kyoto-jin, the heart of the Gion Matsuri is the evening of July 16, the **yoi-yama**, when crowds of teenagers, dressed in *yukata* (summer kimono), tottering on wooden clogs, come out and stroll in mobs down Karasuma-dori

and Shijo-dori. Street hawkers sell all manner of useless items, from Hello Kitty masks to *Star Wars* light sabres, and, for a price, you can climb inside a *hoko*. More interesting, and for free, walk a couple of blocks west of Karasuma to Shinmachi-dori and Muromachi-dori, where a number of merchants' homes, many dating from the Edo period of the early seventeenth century, have their front rooms open to the public and are stocked with gorgeous kimono, wall hangings and painted screens – a rare chance to see inside a sumptuous, traditionally furnished Japanese home.

The parade

Try not to overdo it on the evening of the 16th, because you'll want to be up early the next morning for the parade, which starts at 9am and begins to wind down after noon, with the last of the *hoko* and *yama* rolling off the streets by 2pm. You'll hear it before you see it, the distinctively monotonous kon-chiki-chin of the Gion-bayashi, the festival music, wafting ahead of the floats.

> **Insider info** The excellent monthly glossy *Kyoto Visitors' Guide*, available free anywhere foreigners are found, is a great source of information about the city and the festival, including special events and openings.

One of the best – if most congested – places to be is the **intersection of Shijo and Karasuma**, where the parade begins, and where the *chigo*, the young boy chosen to initiate the parade, gets things going by cutting a rope hung across the street with a samurai sword. (The child doesn't do the actual cutting; rather, he is manipulated by adults like a puppet, sparing countless generations the inauspicious start of accidental dismemberment.) The other good – and subsequently popular – spots are the corners of Shijo/Kawaramachi or Kawaramachi/Oike, where the floats turn. Watching this is quite something, as the *hoko* are built not only without the use of nails, but without the benefits of steering devices, and turns are effected by laying bamboo poles out in front of the wheels, and dragging the *hoko* on top. Water is thrown on the bamboo to make it slippery, and with a huge heave-ho, sixteen men jerk the ten-ton cart around, eventually making it to a ninety-degree angle and proceeding up the street.

If you don't like crowds, your best bet is to make friends with someone who works in one of the office buildings on Shijo-dori, Kawaramachi-dori or Oike-dori – a second- or third-floor window is an ideal vantage point. Or set yourself up on Shinmachi-dori: the *hoko* and *yama* split up at Oike/Shinmachi, heading back to their respective districts, and a number of the floats head down Shinmachi-dori, a small street that's probably the best place to get a closer view of some of the more interesting floats, including the giant mantis.

Basics

Most people arrive at Kyoto's shiny new JR **train** station – either from other cities in Japan, or from Osaka's Kansai **airport**. There are two helpful **tourist information centres** in the station, where you can usually find someone who speaks English (see below).

Accommodation

One dubious advantage of Kyoto's cosmetically disastrous building boom is that there's no shortage of **accommodation**; that said, booking in advance for the Gion Matsuri is essential. *Pension Higashiyama* at 474-23 Umemiya-cho, Shirakawa-suji, Sanjo-sagaru (☎075/882-1181) is a fairly cheap guesthouse in the centre of the city, near the Higashi-Hongan-ji temple, where private rooms with shared bath start at ¥8000; while *Three Sisters' Inn* at Kurodani-mae, Okazaki, Sakyō-ku (☎075/761-6336), is a homely *ryokan* with beautifully appointed rooms for around ¥10,000. For a cheaper option, the friendly *Tour Club* at 363 Momiji-chō Kitakoji-agaru, Higashi-Nakasuji-dōri, Shimogyō-ku (☎075/353-6968, ⓦ www.kyotojp.com), has dorm beds for ¥2415.

Eating and drinking

There are hundreds of eating places along the main parade route, and if you stick with **Japanese food**, you'll rarely go wrong in Kyoto. One good place among many is the four-storey *izakaya Heno Heno Mo Heno* (☎075/205-1441), a pub-style diner a block south of Sanjo-dori, which has an English menu (but no English sign – look for the face formed by phonetic characters). Others include *Gontaro*, Fuyacho Shijo-agaru (☎075/221-5810), a well-priced noodle bar, and *Chikyu-ya*, Kawaramachi Shijo-agaru (☎075/344-6159), another *izakaya*. If you've got a craving for pizza, the delicious thin crusts at *La Botte* (☎075/241-7765), right at the entrance to the Kamo-gawa, half a block south of the Sanjo Ohashi bridge and with nice views over the city, should do nicely.

Event info

Kyoto Tourist Information Centre 2nd floor (daily 8.30am–7pm; ☎075/343-6655) and 9th floor, JR Kyoto Station, Shimogyo-ku (daily 10am–6pm closed 2nd and 4th Tues of the month; ☎075/344-3300).

Time zone GMT+9   **Country code** +81   **Currency** Yen (¥)

Holi

Soon no one is recognizable, lost beneath the layers of colour that cake their faces and bodies

Holi

Where?
Primarily North India, but other states such as West Bengal, Manipur, Maharashtra, Gujarat, Himachal Pradesh and Goa also join in the revelry. Mathura, in Uttar Pradesh, hosts perhaps the biggest Holi party

When?
February or March

How long?
About 4 days

Holi is one of the most vibrant Indian festivals. It has its origins in Hinduism, but revellers today span the entire country, regardless of their religion, caste or class. Although a springtime festival, and hence a celebration of the arrival of the harvest season, Holi is essentially about colour, and everyone gets involved, showering friends, family and passers-by with multi-coloured powders, and assaulting complete strangers with water balloons and spray guns. No one seems to mind; indeed, some people don't even notice after indulging in *bhang*, an intoxicating substance culled from cannabis leaves, and usually mixed with seasonal food and drink, or made into chewy balls, or *golees*. Colour may be the common feature of Holi, but each region adds its own unique touch to the spectacle – from Mathura's mock battles between the sexes to Phalen's full-moon bonfire.

History

Other than its importance as a spring festival, there are various Hindu myths surrounding the **origins** of Holi. Some believe the festival derives its name from the demon princess, Holika. Her brother, the megalomaniac king, Hiranyakashipu, wanted everyone to worship him as god. Prahlad, his son, preferred the powers of Vishnu and refused to be bullied by the king. An outraged Hiranyakashipu ordered Holika to kill Prahlad, but the devout young boy survived the fire that she had prepared for his murder, and instead it was she who perished in the flames. The bonfires that burn the night before Holi, all over North India, are associated with the burning of Holika.

Other myths involve Lord Shiva incinerating Kamadeva, the god of carnal love, and the relationship between Lord Krishna and Radha, concentrating particularly on the blue-skinned Krishna applying colour to Radha's enviable luminous complexion; many worship Kamadeva during Holi, especially in the southern state of Tamil Nadu, while images of Krishna and Radha are often carried through the streets – Mathura, Krishna's birthplace, celebrates the festival with a gusto unrivalled in the rest of the country.

Holi reaches its vigorous climax on the full-moon day of the Hindu month of Phalgun, but the **build-up** generally begins a few days earlier, when devout Hindu families get together in the evening to perform the formal sprinkling-of-colour ceremony. On the second day of the festival, *Puno*, bonfires are lit as part of the community celebrations and people gather around the flames in festive bonhomie.

Celebrations peak on the **final day**, *Parva*. Children rush around squirting everyone with dyed water from their water guns, and people gather on the streets, smearing each other with powder called *abeer* and *gulal* – soon no one is recognizable, lost beneath the layers of colour that cake their faces and bodies. Holi has always been a chaotic event, but these days things are more full-on than ever, with eggs and mud baths added to the mix. Competing with the general mayhem are the sounds of *dholaks*, or Indian drums, as revellers belt out the songs of the season.

Participating in Holi is not always your choice to make, especially in the north, where it's hard to avoid being dragged into the festivities at every street corner. If you'd rather stay clean, then remaining indoors and watching the powder-slinging from the window might be a better option – Holi also involves a number of performances, parades and other pageantry that you can watch from a distance, wherever you are in the country.

Where to go

Although Holi is celebrated all over India (and in other Hindu countries, such as Nepal; see p.347), it's primarily a North Indian festival. Partying in the Uttar Pradesh towns of **Mathura**, **Vrindavan**, **Barsana** and **Nandgaon** – places associated with the birth and childhood of Krishna – lasts all week, with each major temple devoted to Radha and Krishna commemorating the occasion on a different day. People flock to these shrines to be drenched in coloured water, a shower of which is considered a blessing from God – devotees at the Bakai-Bihari Temple in Vrindavan appear almost

in a trance, rapt in the spiritual atmosphere. The region also hosts *Lathmaar Holi*, a particularly boisterous event – best watched from the vantage points set up by the tourist board on the outskirts of town – where Nandgaon men shield themselves from stick-wielding Barsana women in a playful mock battle. The men try to raise their flag over Shri Radhikaji's temple, and those that are "captured" are made to dance in public in women's clothes. At **Phalen**, a full-moon bonfire depicting the Prahlad-Holika legend is performed, and local priests walk through the fire to prove their devotion, while **Jaipur**, in Rajasthan, holds an annual Elephant Festival during Holi, with a royal procession of pachyderms painted in brilliant floral patterns, accompanied by lancers on horses, chariots, camels, cannons and palanquins. Elephant polo and tug-of-war are also part of the festival, as is a hotly contested elephant beauty pageant.

Towns in **West Bengal**, on the other hand, perform the *Dol Yatra*, where idols of Krishna and his consort, Radha, are placed on swings and sprayed with coloured water. A great place in the region to visit at this time is Shantiniketan, where India's Nobel laureate, Rabindranath Tagore, was so inspired by the spirit of Holi that he introduced the festival to his university. The students here wear yellow, the colour

of spring, sing and dance to special Holi songs composed by Tagore, and coat each other with *abeer*, or dry colour made from natural products.

In **Manipur**, festivities last six days, blending into the ancient Yaosang festival that follows. Thabal Chongda, a Manipuri folk

everyone gets involved, showering passers by with multi-coloured powders

dance, is traditionally performed on each of the six days, and there are a lot of high jinks, with girls letting the boys splatter them with colour, and then extracting money from them. The Shri Govindaji Temple in Imphal is the venue of most of the activities, with white- and yellow-turbaned devotees gathering for worship, song and dance, and on the last day moving on to the Vijay Govindaji temple for more festivities.

In the states of **Gujarat** and **Maharashtra**, men form a human pyramid to break a pot of buttermilk hanging high on the street – whoever succeeds is crowned the Holi king of the locality for that year. In **Himachal Pradesh**, colder areas such as Kulu celebrate "Ice Holi", mixing colours with the snow that's often still on the ground at this time of year, while **Goa** has its own brand of Holi – *Shigmo* – which it celebrates with drum performances, plays and cultural events, and with processions of enormous effigies that wind their way through the streets at dusk.

Most foreigners are likely to find themselves in **Delhi** or **Mumbai** during Holi. Vibrant celebrations at areas such as Colaba and Juhu Beach in Mumbai draw huge crowds, while various shows and concerts take place in Delhi, with the Habitat Centre holding an annual Holi Festival, with talks, dance and music performances and art exhibitions, and the India International Centre featuring its own share of recitals.

Insider info Coloured powder is available at all marketplaces, but be careful what you buy – many colours contain toxic chemicals and dyes, which are harmful to both the people using them and to the environment, seeping into the soil and the underground water table. In Delhi, the *Central Cottage Industries Emporium*, on Janpath, and the stalls at Dilli Haat sell natural coloured powders made from flower petals and sandalwood. The *Bombay Store* and *Spencers Hyper Mart*, in Mumbai and Pune (Maharashtra) respectively, also cater to a safe and natural Holi.

Basics

The closest **international airport** to the northern states of Uttar Pradesh, Himachal Pradesh and Rajasthan is Delhi. Mumbai is the gateway to Gujarat and Maharashtra, while West Bengal is accessed from Kolkata. Several companies, such as Tourism of India (Ⓦwww.tourism-of-india.com), run Holi **tour packages**, which include everything from transportation to accommodation.

Holi is great fun, but the uninhibited atmosphere can sometimes lead to unwanted attention, especially for women. It's often safer to enjoy Holi with people you know or in more organized surroundings, at clubs or cultural centres, as Holi in the streets is not always a pleasant experience, particularly if you don't like big crowds.

Event info

Mathura and Vindravan (Ⓦ www.mathura-vrindavan.com). Detailed information on these North Indian towns, plus the area's temples, festivals and a potted history of Lord Krishna.

Time zone GMT +5.5   **Country code** +91   **Currency** Indian rupee (R)

Kumbh Mela

The largest single gathering of humanity on the planet

Kumbh Mela

Where?
Allahabad (2007)
Haridwar (2010)

When?
When Jupiter enters Aquarius and the sun enters Aries (January or February, roughly every three years)

How long?
1 month

Delhi • **Haridwar**
Allahabad •

• **Ujjain**

• **Nasik**

INDIA

The Indian subcontinent hosts more mass religious festivals than anywhere else on the planet, but the Kumbh Mela is the biggest, weirdest and most mind-boggling of them all. It is, in fact, the largest single gathering of humanity on the planet – in January 2001, an estimated seventy million pilgrims gathered to bathe in the Ganges near Allahabad, in Uttar Pradesh. From the tip of tropical Kerala to the snow valleys of Kashmir, and the swampy Bengal Delta to the Thar Desert, Hindus converge on the Kumbh Mela for the chance to immerse themselves in river water, which, during a short but highly auspicious alignment of certain stars and planets, is believed to wash away not only the sins of one lifetime, but of 88 previous generations, ensuring liberation from the eternal cycle of rebirth for oneself and one's ancestors.

Comemmorating the triumph of good over evil, the Kumbh Mela is held roughly every three years, rotating among four different riverside locations: Ujjain, a sacred city in Madhya Pradesh; Haridwar, in Uttar Pradesh; Nasik, in Maharashtra; and Prayag, near Allahabad, at the confluence, or Sangam, of the Ganges, the Jamuna and the (mythical) Saraswati rivers. In addition to the Kumbh Mela, there is an Ardh (Half) Mela in Allahabad every six years, and a Maha Kumbh Mela every twelve years, also in Ahallabad.

The culmination of the Kumbh Mela takes place when the various sects and monastic orders process at dawn to the waterside, brandishing traditional weapons to protect their revered leaders, seated atop elephants or in gilded chariots. It's a mesmerizing spectacle, but one that in past years has turned sour, as opposing groups, following heated arguments over precedence, get stuck

the overwhelming atmosphere is one of fervent devotion, as millions of worshippers file to and from the river

into each other with their tridents, maces and swords. Carnage has also resulted from stampedes sparked off by rampaging elephants, the appearance of rabid dogs and, in the 2003 Kumbh Mela at Nasik, holy men throwing coins into the crowd, causing the death of 39 people. But despite these dangers, inevitable with an event as massive as this, the overwhelming atmosphere at the *mela* tends to be one of fervent devotion, as millions of worshippers file to and from the river, after days of travel from their homes. No statistics, nor film footage, can hope to convey the sheer scale and intensity of the ritual. To believe it, you have to be there, mingling with the biggest crowd on earth.

History

Watching the sun rise over a city of pilgrims several times the size of New York is to witness an event whose roots date back more than a thousand years. Historians claim the great *mela* was **founded** by the eighth-century philosopher Shankarcharya, who masterminded the triumph of Hinduism over Buddhism in the subcontinent, and called for a celebratory gathering of all ascetics, *sadhus*, temple priests and monastic orders. According to ancient Sanskrit scriptures, however, its origins lie in a conflict between the demi-gods and demi-demons that arose after the two had joined forces to find an immortality-giving *amrit* in the Cosmic Ocean. Using Vasuki, the Snake King, as a rope, they churned the primordial depths of Mount Mandara until Dhanavantri, the Divine Healer, surfaced holding a *kumbh* (pot) of the nectar. A twelve-day chase ensued as the gods attempted to make off with it, during which four drops of *amrit* fell to earth – the four locations where the Kumbh Mela now takes place.

Maha Kumbh Mela

The biggest Kumbh Mela of them all, the **Maha Kumbh Mela**, literally, the "Mother of All Pot Festivals", happens every twelfth year when the cycle returns to the Sangam (the next time this occurs will be in 2013), and the festival is attended in the largest numbers because the waters where the rivers merge are believed to flow with *amrit*, or nectar, during the festival. However, disputes over how to calculate the astrological conjunctions mean that the whole cycle may in fact take thirteen years, or that two *melas* may occur in the same or successive years. Information is hard to come by and often contradictory – the only thing to do is to cast your net wide for information, and plan well in advance.

The mass bathing

Whichever of the four *mela* locations you attend, the main event is always the mass bathing at the river. These invariably follow a familiar routine – you'll gain a clearer sense of what that is if you get here several days before the peak, before the crowds become too much. Pouring in from the railway and bus stations, the pilgrims, carrying camping gear and provisions on their heads, first make for the *ghats*, or sacred steps, on the waterfront, where their ritual specialists, *pandas*, wait under ragged raffia sun shades. *Pandas* have responsibility for specific regions of the country, and the castes and villages in those regions, so every pilgrim has to track down the right person, whose ledgers will list each family's records, dating back twenty or more generations. Renowned for their venality, *pandas* tend to be brusque and stroppy, and have little time for camera-toting tourists. The area they preside over, however, forms the religious focal point of the *mela* and is thus the best place to hang around at dawn, when the day's ritual cycle kicks off.

> **Insider info** If you find yourself swept off track in the build-up to a big bathe, talk your way up one of the observation towers that punctuate the site to get your bearings again.

Hindus from all castes, regions and walks of life are drawn to the *mela* for the immortality-inducing dip, from poor rural villagers to government ministers and millionaire businessmen. Pride of place on the riverbanks, however, and priority access to the water at the key times, are reserved for India's hardcore holy men, or *sadhus* (see box on this page). Every shade of the Hindu spiritual spectrum features in their ranks, from gold-robed, Transcendental Meditation-propounding Maharishi Yogis to naked Naga Babas smeared in cow-dung ash and sandalwood powder.

Between dips, the pilgrims wander around in family groups in search of *sadhu darshan* – glimpses of these holy men. Moving between the camps around the rivers' confluence, you'll soon get a feel for the different *sadhu* sects, discernible by their attire (or lack of it), headgear, ritual paraphernalia, weapons and make up. As you move through the various *sadhu* encampments, it's a good idea to gauge the reaction of their doorkeepers – not all sects welcome visitors, while some only admit foreigners to certain "open" portions of their camps. The time when you should really keep your wits about you, however, is during the build-up to a big bathe (see festival website on p.334 for exact dates). At certain times of day or night, the flow of people in one direction can make it impossible to get where you might want to go. The danger spots, where the risk of stampede is greatest, are along the riverbank on the key bathing days. At such times, you'll be much better of watching from the fringes of the festival, although this will mean missing the awesome *sadhu* processions, when the *sadhu* sects, or *Akharas*, make their way to the river.

Sadhus

For eight or nine months of the year at least, most **sadhus** travel alone between temples and other sacred sites across India, begging for alms, or, if they're less serious questers, bumming tips off hippy tourists in exchange for hits on their chillum pipes. They've a reputation – not always deserved – for being aloof, wild and unscrupulous. None, however, miss Kumbh Mela.

One of the most prominent of the sects is the **Juna** *Akhara*, warrior *sadhus* with a reputation for ferocity, who cover themselves in blue-grey holy ash and grow long dreadlocks, denoting their devotion to Lord Shiva. Their arch-rivals are the **Bairagis** and members of the **Niranjani** *Akhara*, followers of Lord Vishnu. Then there are the **Sakhis**, holy transvestites who dress in saris and simulate sex with male deities, and, more obscure and arcane still, the **Aghoris**, who believe that the fastest route to enlightenment is to spurn all taboos, especially those normally espoused by Hindus. Most of these live in and around cremation *ghats*, amid human remains, drinking from skulls and eating excrement.

But perhaps the most eye-catching of all the *sadhus* are those who perform **tapasya**, or austerities, to demonstrate their yogic powers. Standing on one leg, or holding an arm in the air, for years until the unused limb atrophies, is standard; and you'll often come across naked *sadhus* skewering or hanging heavy rocks from their genitals, or wearing heavy chastity belts. Then, of course, there are the one-off spectaculars, like Houdini stunts without the escape element. In 2001, for example, a Japanese female *sadhu* caused a stir when she survived being "buried alive" for 72 hours, though the semi-furnished pit in which she was interred was far from the hole you might imagine.

Surviving Kumbh Mela

The most recent twelve-yearly Maha Kumbh Mela, in 2001, was particularly significant, coinciding with an astrological alignment that occurs once every 144 years, and therefore attracting an unprecedented seventy million pilgrims. Geronimo Madrid was there.

I've been in crowds before – concerts, protests and the local IKEA on weekends – but none of these gatherings could compare to Kumbh Mela. In fact, my first ten minutes in Kumbh City, the great fifty-square-kilometre tent city erected along the Ganges, were as intimidating a stretch of time as I can remember, engulfed as I was in the kicked-up dust and campfire smoke of tens of millions of pilgrims, all struggling to get down to the riverside. I finally got my bearings and headed toward the Ganges with them, dodging curio sellers and keeping pace with the scrum-like masses in an effort not to get trampled on. The odd thing was, once I got in step, marching with the riverbound crowd was like joining a massive queue at bath time. Everyone has assorted toiletries tucked under their arm, whether it be a simple towel, or some soap and shampoo, and everyone is eager to get cleaned up – not just ridding themselves of the grime of the day but of eighty-odd generations of sin. Some bath...

The confluence of the rivers is of course the most popular spot, but the crowds thicken the closer you get, so only true believers and those who've staked out the area earlier can reach it. I settled for a stretch of river upstream from the confluence and found no shortage of bathers. The water was afire with brilliant saris trailed by women; the riverbank dotted by the orange robes of passing *sadhus*; on both banks of the river tents spread as far as the eye could see; and on the fifteen pontoon bridges erected to facilitate river crossings an unceasing tide of people shuffled from bank to bank. Overwhelmed as I was at first, I soon realized why the Western media and tourists alike are drawn to the Kumbh. While the festival is one of Hinduism's holy of holies, the actual events themselves have a carnivalesque feel. There are lots of circus-like tents, for a start, full of carved and painted likenesses of Shiva, Ganesh and the whole pantheon, where, after walking by the gods, you make a donation. Meanwhile, *sadhus* bearing tridents and strutting about in their *lungis* add a freak-show element.

Surface appearances aside, it didn't take me long to realize that logistics for the Kumbh are astounding. Though dusty, Kumbh City's streets are some of the cleanest I've seen in two months in India; somebody is picking up garbage, and the latrines at least manage to keep the waste away from the living spaces. Loudspeakers make all sorts of announcements, including the whereabouts of the inevitable lost children (at the last Kumbh, 252 children disappeared without a trace), and post offices, telephone booths and, yes, Internet cafés, allow pilgrims to contact home. Surprisingly, I didn't see any of the rich telephoto-toting Western tourists vilified in the Indian news (branded neo-colonialists for their voyeuristic exoticizing of the event). I did, however, notice an inordinate number of hippies playing hackeysack and wowing Indian children with magic tricks, even having chillum-inspired chats with *sadhus*, on their way to a nearby Rainbow Gathering upriver. I talked to some of these bummed-out Rainbows, who, predictably, are gaga over India – full of half-baked theories of how much more spiritual the East is by comparison to the West. Whatever you think about this, and however great it is to get stoned off your tree at these kind of things, there's no doubt how big a spiritual event the Kumbh Mela is. And I guess jiving with *sadhus* and jumping in the river side-by-side with devout Indians, many of whom have come from far-flung, often isolated parts of the country, is about as close to a shared cultural experience as you're ever going to get.

So, determined to get into the spirit of things, I joined the loud, passing 4x4 and elephant train of an *ashram* that's decided it's as good a time as any for a dip in the Ganges. A long line of Western yoga practitioners played tambourine and trumpet, while atop the lead vehicle was a big, bearded American who looked eerily like Jerry Garcia. "Isn't it awesome, man?" he said to me. "Yeah, it is!" I yelled up to him. The Indians stood agog at this parade of Western wannabes, and we headed down to the river.

Basics

The **organization** behind each Khumbh Mela is mind-boggling. The 2001 event near Allahabad, the biggest ever, saw the construction of an entire temporary city with its own water and electricity supply, 90km of roads, hospitals and security forces, and fire-fighting stations. Fourteen shopping complexes were set up and stocked with raw vegetables, milk, cooking gas, firewood and other necessities to cater to the vast numbers of pilgrims and visitors. What this means is that the site has most of the facilities you're likely to need – food, water, medical aid, even Internet cafés.

As you might expect given the sheer volume of humanity here, the **toilet facilities** will be the biggest challenge you have to face. You'll have to join the throngs using the massive "trench latrines", partially covered with tin plates with holes cut in them. When full, they are covered with insecticide. To clear up the vast amount of mess left by those pilgrims who don't avail themselves of the trench latrines, "picking squads" are also dispatched each morning. Ironically for a faith obsessed with cleanliness and pollution, shit is the big downside of any Hindu religious festival, and the Kumbh Mela breaks all records in this department, too.

Ahallabad's central train station, Allahabad Junction, lies on the Delhi–Calcutta main line and serves as the principal jumping-off place for pilgrims arriving at the *melas*. It's a seven-kilometre rickshaw ride across town from the sacred-river confluence.

You can also get to **Haridwar** by direct trains from Delhi, though for journeys during *mela* times advance booking is essential. Tickets can be reserved online at ⓦ www.indianrail.gov.in.

Accommodation

Finding decent **accommodation** at the height of the festival is impossible unless you book months in advance; most pilgrims in any case sleep rough on the riverbanks, cooking over open fires. In 2001, however, the British travel agency Cox and Kings (ⓦ www.coxandkings.co.uk) set up a luxury camp for tourists (and film crews) at the Kumbh Mela, costing £130–230 per night for a tent with beds, fans, electric light, a safe locker and, most importantly of all, proper toilets – check for packages. In **Ahallabad**, a dependable, central hotel with modern, western amenities is the *Hotel Kanha Shyam* (0532/256 0123). Situated a short walk from the Ganges River, the *Hotel Suvidha* (☎ 01334/227023; ⓦ www.hotelatithi.net/hotel_suvidha.html) is one of the best choices in **Haridwar**.

Event info

Kumbh Mela (ⓦ www.kumbhmela.net). A full rundown of the *mela's* key bathing dates, with quality photos and links.
Allahabad Tourist Office Hotel Ilawart, 35 MG Marg, Civil Lines, Allahabad (Mon–Sat 10am–5pm; ☎ 0532/260 1873).
Haridwar GMVN Tourist Office Upper Road, Haridwar (Mon–Sat 10am–5pm; ☎ 01334/224 240).

Time zone GMT+5.5   **Country code** +91   **Currency** Indian Rupee (Rs)

Naadam

*You will understand how the Mongols
once conquered half the world*

Naadam

Where?
Ulaanbaatar, Mongolia

When?
The national Naadam is held in Ulaanbaatar on July 11–13. Regional naadams are held across the countryside throughout July

How long?
3 days

Mongolia's Enin Gurvan Naadam – Naadam, for short (literally, "Manly Games") – is one of the world's oldest and most spectacular annual events. After seeing it, you will understand how the Mongols once conquered half the planet. Basically a sporting contest, the festival pits the nation's best athletes against each other in tests of skill in the "manly sports" of archery, horse racing and wrestling – the very talents with which Genghis Khan forged an empire. It's an experience you won't forget easily: you know you've done Naadam when you're squeezed into a nomad's tent, swilling Genghis Khan vodka with a pair of 300-pound wrestlers sweating in their bikini briefs while a woman in traditional silk robes sets before you a platter full of sheep parts.

Held every July on Mongolia's vast grassy steppes, Naadam brings the country to a standstill. The grandest event is staged in **Ulaanbaatar** on July 11–13, a commercial affair nowadays, with plenty of modern touches and side attractions, and all the hustle and bustle you'd expect from Mongolia's lone metropolis. It's still a traditional occasion though, with a strong countryside flavour, as nomads fresh off the steppes strut around town on horseback. **Outside the capital**, Naadam remains an intimate gathering that has changed little since the days of the Mongol hordes. You can get closer to the action here, meet more people, and even participate if you feel like it (some brave foreigners have entered wrestling tournaments). The problem is finding one – there are no set schedules, so your best bet is to ask around in Ulaanbaatar or try contacting the tourist office or tour agencies (see p.342). Most years, the town of Zuunmod, 43km south of Ulaanbaatar, holds a Naadam in mid-July. It's easy to reach – public minivans head there (daily 7am–8pm) from the long-distance bus station, 7km west of Sükhbaatar Square – but check it's on before you head out there.

Naadam is a time of rest as well as a celebration of sport and manly virtues. Life is hard on the steppes – herding livestock and moving encampments – and the festival offers Mongolians a chance to visit friends, discuss current events and enjoy life before the winter sets in. In Ulaanbaatar, the commercialized Naadam also gives entrepreneurs an opportunity to earn hard currency, as the city becomes swamped

History

The **origins** of the Naadam games in fact date back long before Genghis Khan. The competition is thought to have evolved when clans and tribes came together to celebrate weddings, the enthronement of a leader, or to honour the spirits of the land – the accompanying feasts and colourful sporting events lightened what was an otherwise precarious existence. It was Genghis Khan, however, who presided over the first organized Naadam celebrations – in the 13th century – when the focus shifted from venerating ancestral spirits to glorifying military campaigns; though Genghis also used the occasion to scout out talented youths for the front lines of his army. Winners were granted titles and battle gear – wrestlers and archers received helmets and armour, while the best equestrians earned new saddles.

In the sixteenth century, Mongolia adopted Tibetan Buddhism as its state religion, and Naadam began to serve as a gathering place for nomads ready for conversion. The grandest of all naadams was held in 1641 to honour the Bogd Gegen, Mongolia's equivalent of the Dalai Lama, after which it took place every three years until the end of the nineteenth century, when it became an **annual event**. In 1921, the new communist government swept away much of old Mongolia, but Naadam managed to hang on, albeit in a slightly modified form, showcasing Soviet military strength, with tanks replacing brawny horsemen in the opening cortege. The festival date was set for July 11, the Day of Independence (from China). After Mongolia's democratic revolution in 1990, Naadam reclaimed its roots. Old traditions now reign supreme, and the event is as much a symbol of an independent Mongolia (from Russia) as it is a sports festival.

Tickets

Although regional naadams are free, some of the main events in Ulaanbaatar require tickets. Two-day passes to the Naadam Stadium – which will get you into a part of the stadium that offers protection from the sun and rain – cost $16–20 for foreigners, and are available at the stadium itself, through a hotel or from one of the scores of tour operators in Ulaanbaatar; a single-entry ticket for the same section costs $8. Just before the opening ceremony, scalpers will be selling tickets for the cheap seats; these shouldn't cost more than $3.

You don't need a ticket to watch the horse racing, archery or anklebone shooting events. Most concerts are free during Ulaanbaatar's Naadam, although a few might charge $5 or so.

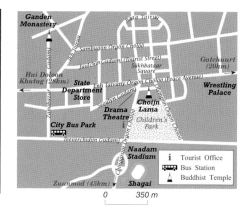

with foreigners. The opening ceremony kicks off two days of sporting endeavour – the third day is mainly one of rest, when most visitors take in the sights – with Mongolia's biggest street fair taking over the Children's Park and, after dark, Sükhbaatar Square, each evening. The programme changes from year to year, but you can expect a variety of music – rock, rap, classical, traditional Mongolian folk tunes, perhaps even some operetta – with live bands and other performers playing under a magnificent fireworks display. Jump into the fray and have fun, but watch out for the horsemen who have wandered in from Yarmag on their mounts – their steeds can pack a powerful kick. The party ends about 1am, but bars and clubs may stay open later.

The opening ceremony

The celebrations begin on July 11 at around 9am in Ulaanbaatar's Sükhbaatar Square, as a brass band belts out regal music announcing the arrival of a mounted guard of honour, neatly decked out in blue-and-red regalia, and parading white, horsehair banners around the square – in Genghis' time, the colour white symbolized peace (black meant war). The procession then moves to the Central Stadium, where the **opening ceremony** is in full swing by 11am. Give yourself lots of time to get there and find a seat; it's a 25-minute walk from Sükhbaatar Square (just follow the crowds). The ceremony proceeds with a mixture of singing, dancing, and mock battles performed by actors dressed as medieval warriors. The guard of honour then charges into the stadium on white ponies, planting their banners in midfield. Once an assortment of wrestlers and archers have joined them in the stadium, and the president has delivered his opening speech, it's time for the grand finale: a troupe of skydivers bearing the national flag, which adds a surreal modern touch to proceedings.

Wrestling

The **wrestling tournament** starts after the opening ceremony. More than five hundred of the country's top wrestlers compete, and the draw is seeded so that, theoretically, the best wrestlers face each other in the later rounds. Matches are notoriously long in the countryside, often taking hours to complete, but new rules in the Ulaanbaatar finals keep the action going at a fairly decent pace. Even so, you might want to save yourself for the final rounds, which take place on day two. There's no way of knowing when the last match will be, but it's likely to happen between 6pm and 8pm. You'll want to time your arrival to see the best of the action, when the hours of waiting are rewarded with the final spinning take-down – after which the beefy winner does his traditional celebratory eagle dance and charges into the stands to receive praise from the president. The adoring crowd will then try to swipe off some of his sweat for good luck (foreigners usually avoid this tradition). The closing ceremonies are brief – the guard of honour trots around the stadium on horseback and rides off with the white banners. If you're still standing, go and hit the clubs again.

Archery and anklebone shooting

Just outside the main stadium, a concrete amphitheatre provides the stage for the **archery** events. Decked out in their finest silk *dels* (traditional robes), the archers fire heavy, dull-tipped arrows at a stack of small cylindrical baskets placed on the ground. The judges, rather than calling out the score, sing a verse of praise for each successful shot. Likewise, the archers might also sing to their arrows – requesting a straight and true flight. You can watch the contest from the grandstand or near the targets where the judges stand (watch out for stray arrows!).

A relatively new addition to the Naadam line-up is *Shagai*, or **anklebone shooting**. Basically a Mongolian version of darts, the game sees crouching competitors flicking a sheep's anklebone from a small board at a target of bones. The more bones they knock down the more points they score. As in archery, the judges kneel near the target and sing praise for each direct hit. The competition is held in a tent next to the archery stadium.

the archers also sing to their arrows - requesting a straight and true flight

Bows and arrows

Mongolian **bows and arrows** were originally designed for hunting and later for warfare – the bows made during Genghis Khan's day could launch an arrow an incredible 300 yards. Although the archery practised today is a considerably tamer affair, producing the unique bows and arrows is a painstaking process carried out by only a handful of master craftsmen. One bow takes six months to make and must be left to dry for two years before it can be used. The range of materials used in construction includes birch bark, fish glue, bamboo, antlers, silk threads and animal tendons. Unsurprisingly, such fine craftsmanship doesn't come cheap – a bow and arrow set costs a minimum of $150.

Horse racing

The most dramatic of the manly games is **horse racing**. The races are staged at Hui Doloon Khutag, around 30km west of the city, a temporary tent city that, for horse trainers and race fans, becomes the centre of the festival during Naadam. *Gers* (the traditional felt tent used by nomads) are lined up and transformed into small restaurants, and patrons queue up to enjoy the national drink, *airag*, a fizzy concoction made from fermented mare's milk and tasting like bitter yogurt. Mongols down *airag* by the bowl-full; it has the strength of weak beer, but don't drink too much or your stomach will erupt.

Insider info For a full schedule of Naadam events in Ulaanbaatar, pick up the two weekly English newspapers, *The Mongol Messenger* and *UB Post*.

There are three or four races per day, varying in length from 15km to 20km according to the age of the horses – the older the horse the longer the race (though all can last an hour or more). The race begins when the jockeys, who are between the ages of five and ten years old, sing a song called "Gingo" to their horses, which helps to pacify the half-wild steeds. After officials check the teeth of each horse (which determines the age), the riders are off. The best way to see the start – it's usually located well away from the crowds – is to hire a jeep driver to take you to the starting line and then drive you further up the course for another look.

If you haven't got money for a jeep you can just hang out with the locals at the finish line, biding your time with bowlfuls of *airag* and vodka. Many Mongolians jockey for position behind the finish line where they can wipe the sweat from the top five finishers – touching the sweat is auspicious, so mind the stampede. The winner is pronounced *Tumny Ekh*, or "Leader of 10,000" – a reference to Genghis Khan's army, which was organized into units of tens, the largest being made up of ten thousand troops. The jockey is then honoured with a cup of *airag*, which is sprinkled on the horse's head and rear end, and the appreciative crowd sings to the winners. A special song is recited for the horse that finishes last in the two-year-old race, encouraging it to lead the ten thousand horses the next year.

Making a song and dance of it

Another attraction of the festival – and a must-see – are the spectacular **song and dance shows**, put on at the Cultural Palace on Sükhbaatar Square and the Drama Theatre, just south of the square. The shows include a variety of traditional routines, including the famous *khöömii* (throat singing) and the *moriin khuur* (horsehead fiddle) orchestra.

Basics

Mongolia isn't your average tourist destination – if you don't want to go it alone, the best tour companies to contact are Boojum Expeditions (ⓦ www.boojum.com) and Karakorum Expeditions (ⓦ www.gomongolia.com). Otherwise, the **airport** is 18km southwest of the city, and the **train** station 2km southwest of the centre. There are **tourist offices** at the airport, train station and central post office.

You'll need your **own transport** to get out to the horse racing – hire a taxi or get a group together from your guesthouse. Otherwise, *Chez Bernard* (☎ 11 32 46 22), a pastry shop at Peace Ave 27, also organizes transport.

Accommodation

There are plenty of **hotels** in Ulaanbaatar, though you'll still need to book for Naadam. Most of the backpacker places are located inside old Soviet apartment blocks. One of the best is *Khongor Guesthouse*, Peace Ave 15, Apt 6 (☎ 11 31 64 15, ⓦ get.to/khongor), located just beyond the landmark State Department Store, 500m southwest of Sükhbaatar Square. Others include *Bolod's Guesthouse*, Peace Ave 61, Door 20, Room 22 (☎ 99 19 24 07, ⓦ www.bolodtours.com), opposite the Central Post Office, and the rustic *Gana's Guesthouse*, Gandan Khiid Ger District, House 22 (☎ 11 36 73 43, ⓦ www.ganasger.mn), which consists of several *gers* located near Gandan Monastery, a kilometre or so southwest of Sükhbaatar Square. They all charge $5 per night, and the owners will pick you up from the train station and airport.

The mid-range *Hotel Örgöö*, on the corner of Juulchin Gudamj and Jigjidjavanyn Gudamj (☎ 11 31 37 72), is very central, and charges $40 per night per room including breakfast. More upscale is the *Bayangol Hotel*, Chingisiin Örgön Chölöö 5 (☎ 11 31 22 55, ⓦ www.bayangolhotel.mn), which charges $90. If you're feeling adventurous, you could try camping in Gatchuurt, a quiet village 20km east of the capital.

Eating and drinking

Most of the Mongolian-style **restaurants** in Ulaanbaatar actually cook Russian-influenced food these days (the best of these are on the Little Ring Road, near MIAT, on the east side of Sükhbaatar Square) – an OK option if you're after a filling, low-cost meal. For real **Mongolian food** (boiled mutton, basically) you're better off in the countryside, though there are plenty of stalls selling traditional food in the Children's Park, five minutes' walk from Sükhbaatar Square, such as *buuz* (steamed dumplings), *huushuur* (fried mutton pancakes) and, the real treat of Naadam, *shashlyk* – barbecued strips of fatty meat (usually mutton and beef). Ulaanbaatar also has an excellent supply of international restaurants, many of them owned by European, Japanese and Korean entrepreneurs. If you're craving some Western food, try *Millie's Café*, Marco Polo Bldg, for lunch, or *Silk Road*, Jamiyan Gunii Gudamj, for dinner. Both are located near the Monastery-Museum Choijin Lama, close to the Children's Park. The best place for Italian food is *Marco Polo*, Seoul St 27, which is incongruously modelled after a Bavarian hunting lodge. One of the most bizarre places is the *Arirang Pyongyang Restaurant*, on the corner of Seoul Street and Undsen Khuliin Gudamj, which serves Korean dishes and has its own "Friendship Cultural Centre of North Korea".

You will probably be invited to **drink** with a crowd of Mongolians. Vodka and beer are the usual tipples, and it's quite normal to drink until you are unconscious. Some of the best late-night dancing and debauchery spots include the Tahitian-themed *Face Club*, on Juulchin Gudamj; student-favourite *Muse*, Maral Tavern Bldg, Little Ring Road; and the ultra-chic *Medusa*, *Chinggis Khaan Hotel*, Tokyogiin Gudamj 5. *River Sounds*, Olympiin Örgön Chölöö is good for live music. The drink of choice is straight vodka, knocked back in one go, so good luck! If you need a break from the vodka-swilling hordes, you can retreat to the popular *Dave's Place*, in the Cultural Palace on Sükhbaatar Square, which is filled with beer-guzzling Englishmen. Mongolia's nouveaux-riches can be found drinking pints on the sunny front deck of the *Khan Brau*, Chingisiin Örgön Chölöö, a great place to watch the crowds go by.

Useful websites

Mongolia Tourism (ⓦ www.mongoliatourism.gov.mn). Official website of Mongolia's tourist office, containing a useful calendar of events.
Mongolia Matters (ⓦ www.mongoliamatters.com). Useful website with discussion forums, book reviews and current events.
Mongols.com (ⓦ www.mongols.com). History and culture features.
Mongoluls.net (ⓦ mongoluls.net). A great review of Mongolian history and culture, plus book reviews.

Time zone GMT+8   **Country code** +976   **Currency** Tugrik (Tug)

Phalgun Festivals

Campfires burn all around, and a constant pounding of drums, wailing of flutes and chanting of Shiva's many names carries in the smoky air

Phalgun Festivals

Where?
Kathmandu Valley, Nepal

When?
Losar Late January or early February
Shivaratri The fourteenth day of the "dark fortnight" (the full moon) of the month of Phalgun
Holi Begins a fortnight after Shivaratri, culminating on the day of Phalgun's full moon

How long?
Losar 3 days
Shivaratri 1 day
Holi 8 days

NEPAL
Kathmandu

Kathmandu is blessed with not just one but two religions that seriously like to party. As spring drives away the winter chill from the Kathmandu Valley, the Nepalese start turning up the spiritual heat as well. Buddhists kick off the season with the Tibetan New Year festival, Losar, celebrated most spectacularly in the Tibetan settlements around the sacred dome, or *stupa*, at Boudha. Hindus come back with Shivaratri, roughly a fortnight later: this is the call for the god's fervent followers to head for Pashupatinath, site of one of Hinduism's holiest temples, where tens of thousands of pilgrims and holy men flood in from India to bathe, fast, pray – and get stoned out of their minds. Then, during Holi, or Phalgun Purnima, Kathmandu's youth take to the streets in gangs, throwing water bombs and bright-red powder at anyone in their way in a ritual laden with springtime sexual symbolism.

Losar

Don't expect anything austerely enlightened during Losar the three final days of the old Tibetan year: this is Tantric country. Tibetans and Sherpas have a simple formula of massive boozing and feasting, with fireworks (to chase off the old year's devils) and ritual throwing of *tsampa* barley flour (it's a bread fight – who needs a reason?). Colourful, heavily symbolic ceremonies take place on the morning of the final day, with yellow-hatted lamas gathering en masse around the main stupa at **Boudha**. Later on, it isn't too hard to get yourself invited to an evening feast. But if hedonism palls, New Year is a good time to work on that karma, and Boudha is awash with Western-friendly meditation centres and monasteries.

Shivaratri

Shivaites veer to the wilder side of Hinduism, particularly within Nepal's Tantric tradition, and Shivaratri – also known as Mahashivaratri, or Shiva's Big Night – is the night where they let rip. During the four-day build-up to the main event, and especially on the night itself, the place to be is on the east bank of the **Bagmati River**. The paved area facing the *ghats* (river platforms) is a sort of royal enclosure – though nudity and dreads are more *de rigueur* than a hat. From the terrace above you can look down on pilgrims massing around the Pashupati temple (it's closed to non-Hindus), praying and

History

Losar began as a farmers' spring festival, later taking on Buddhist ritual concepts based around the lunar calendar. Resolutions are made, lamas bless the people, and the "devils" of the old year are chased out with fireworks, bright colours and a good spring clean.

As Pashupati, the Lord of the Animals, Shiva embraces darker, pre-Hindu elemental forces – from the days before the Brahmins came along and wrecked everything with awkward rules about drinking, smoking and roaming the universe as a pan-dimensional phallus. **Shivaratri** is celebrated as the night on which the god first assumed material form in the shape of a giant lingam (phallus). In order to save the universe from destruction, Shiva swallowed the poison of the mythical primeval ocean, but was instantly struck down by an appalling fever. The Ganges poured out all her waters as an antidote, but it was only the coolness of the moon, settling among his dreadlocks, that could slake his fever. Consumed with joy, he danced the Tandav, his cosmic dance, and midnight on the moonless night of Shivaratri – calculated using the Brahmanical lunar calendar – is now seen as the perfect moment for the ecstatic mind to see through the illusion of the world and achieve unity with god. A racier story fits Shiva's nature as god of reproduction and all-round sexual champion. One night, on the new moon of Phalgun, Shiva was making out with his consort Durga. The other gods came to visit but, being drunk, Shiva ignored them and the couple carried on making love. When they suddenly sobered up they were struck with shame and died on the spot, locked into one of their more advanced positions. Taking new life as the immortal lingam, Shiva decreed that humans should worship him every year on that night.

The usual legend around **Holi** is that it commemorates the destruction of the demoness Holika by her nephew, Prince Prahlad, who tricked her into stepping into the raging fire prepared for his own murder. That explains the bonfires, but Holi is basically a springtime fertility festival, which is probably why Nepali boys get to spray water and blood-red powder (the colour of rejoicing) all over the girls. Traditionally, they're supposed to serenade them with obscene songs as well, but this custom has been stamped out by modern moralists.

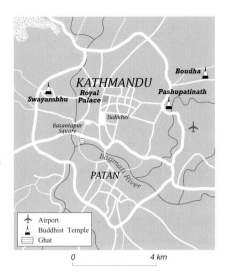

making offerings to the sacred lingam. The devout bathe in the river among thousands of margosa petals. Unless you're used to it, stay well clear – it's an open secret that the river is mostly fed by sewers. The worshippers aren't only ascetics, either, but smart Nepalis in suits and garish *topi* hats, women dressed head to foot in festive red, and the odd shell-shocked traveller wondering if that was one smoke too far.

Around dusk, an interminable gun salute rolls across the city from the king's celebration at the Tundikhel, in central Kathmandu. Small oil lamps and fires light the woods of **Gorakhnath**, the hill on the east bank, where saffron-robed *sadhus* (holy men) and *nagas* (naked *sadhus*) camp out on mats, drawing deep on chillum pipes and practicing austerities. The yogis' freak show would be disturbing anywhere else, but in the middle of Shivaratri it seems fairly cool to coat yourself in ash, lift weights with your penis or stab your flesh with a *trisul* (trident). Campfires burn all around, and a constant pounding of drums, wailing of flutes and chanting of Shiva's many names carries in the smoky air. Midnight is the peak of the event, with things quietening down towards dawn, when many of the Indian pilgrims up sticks and head for home. – Nepalis believe that Shivaratri is usually followed by a last blast of Himalayan winter as Shiva's way of chasing them home.

in the middle of Shivaratri it seems fairly cool to coat yourself in ash and lift weights with your penis

Nepal in turmoil

In the last few years, Nepal's celebrated peace has been disturbed by armed Maoist insurrection in the countryside, and political chaos in Kathmandu. Travel to the capital has been frequently disrupted as general strikes – known as *bandhs* or "shutdowns" of the Kathmandu Valley – alternated with military curfews. The turmoil culminated in the mass protests of spring 2006 (see opposite), which deposed the king as autocratic ruler and brought the Maoists back into the political fold. Since then the atmosphere in the city has been significantly calmer. The backcountry, however, is still largely run by a parallel government of Maoist revolutionaries whose commitment to the democratic process remains uncertain; many trekkers have had to pay a '"tax" to Maoist bands (though mostly this has been levied with a smiling face and the offer of a receipt). Kathmandu remains a troubled city, no question: packed to the brim with refugees from the countryside and with higher than usual levels of crime. But Nepal remains one of the safest and most welcoming countries in Asia, and at the time of writing the outlook is distinctly positive.

Holi

The much-celebrated colour and water-fights of Holi haven't
worn well. Apart from the final day, when areas of Kathmandu
erupt into sporadic battle, there's little more than a few
kids' bonfires in the streets and giggling schoolboys "Eve
teasing" – read harassing – girls. By all means grab a handful
of vermilion or a lola balloon and go hunting, but Holi only
really hums during the raising and lowering of the *chir* pole.
This twenty-foot expression of virility is raised by a frantic
crowd in **Basantapur Square** (just south of Kathmandu's
Royal Palace) at the beginning of the ceremony. Eight days later
(usually around late afternoon – only the astrologers know,
and boy are they not telling you), it's burnt at the **Tundikhel**
parade ground in the centre of town, attended by the army in
full-on Gorkhali costume. White-clad, scarlet-stained Newaris,
Marwaris and other ethnic groups pray, beat drums, chant, and
grab hot ashes with which to bless their homes. Later in the
night, the hardcore head down to the strange buffalo sacrifices
and burnings at **Itum Bahal**, deep in old Kathmandu, choosing
to ignore the legend that someone disappears at this festival
every year, a victim of the demon Guru Mapa.

Basics

All of the festival sites are within a few kilometres of each other so, if you plan to be around that long, you can easily take in all three, basing yourself in one place and venturing out to the others, by bus, minibus or taxi. **Boudha** is 5km northeast of Kathmandu – best reached by bus (from the City Bus Park) or taxi, as it's not a particularly pleasant road to walk or cycle. The temple complex of **Pashupatinath** is between Kathmandu **airport** and the city centre, 4km east of Kathmandhu.

Accommodation

Boudha has a good range of **accommodation** and plenty of inexpensive guesthouses. Budget options generally cost around Rs250 a night for a double room, or you can pay around Rs100–200 more and get your own bathroom. The *Dragon Guest House* (☎01/447 9562, ✉dragon@ntc.net.np) and *Kailash Guest House* (☎01/448 074) are both good, inexpensive options and only a few minutes' walk from the stupa –but you'll need to book ahead. For a bit more comfort, the *Shechen Guesthouse* (☎01/447 9009), which actually belongs to the adjacent Shechen monastery, has smart rooms arranged around a small lawn, for around Rs1000. For air-con luxury in a faux-traditional architectural style, make for the *Hyatt Regency*, halfway between Boudha and the airport (☎01/449 1234, ⊛kathmandu.regency. hyatt.com), where rooms cost US$100 and up. If you don't fancy bedding down with the yogis in Pashupatinath, try *the Shree Shankar Guesthouse*, though it's the only one and so likely to be booked out; central Kathmandu is a short ride away on a· *tempo* (tuk-tuk), so it's probably easier to stay there (see below). For Holi's *chir* ceremony, Freak Street, the cleaned-up old hippie quarter of Kathmandu, is the closest place you'll find accommodation, and a quieter – and often cheaper – alternative to the tourist mayhem of Thamel. *Annapurna Lodge* (☎01/424 7684) is one of the bigger places, with en-suite rooms for Rs200–300 and cheaper, shared-facility rooms. Failing that, the large and well-established *Kathmandu Guesthouse* (☎01/470

0632, ⊛www.ktmgh.com) is a reliable, safe hotel in the heart of tourist Thamel, with a garden and a wide range of rooms from the perfectly acceptable "ultra basic" (US$4), to deluxe air-con (US$30–50).

Eating and drinking

Even dogs are supposed to be intelligent enough to know to fast during Shivaratri, and most worshippers get by on **marijuana** – Shiva himself is said to have liked a smoke. On this one night, marijuana is legal for worshippers – *sadhus* have theirs supplied by the Nepali government – being considered as *prasad* (blessed food), whether smoked as *charas* or drunk as *bhang*. Be aware, however, that marijuana is never legal for tourists – not that this stops the dealers in Thamel, Kathmandu's tourist honeypot.

During Losar, the classic festival **food** is a U-shaped biscuit called *khabze*. Tibetan families traditionally enjoy *gutuk*, a soup made with nine ingredients containing special fortune-cookie-like dumplings. Each dumpling predicts a different fortune for the New Year: you might get salt (for luck) or butter (for good-naturedness); if you find wool (for laziness) or sheep droppings (for intelligence) you might want to wash them down with *chang*, a murky home-brew.

Otherwise, try to get your hands on a pot of *tongba*, a kind of magic alcohol pot full of fermented millet – just add hot water, drink through a straw, add more hot water.

Useful websites

Nepal Festivals (⊛www.nepalhomepage.com/society/festivals). News and general info on society and culture, with a decent page on other festivals through the year.
Nepal Vista (⊛www.nepalvista.com). Usually has an up-to-date calendar with some festival and holiday dates.
FCO (⊛www.fco.gov.uk/travel). The UK government's official advice for travellers to Nepal. Somewhat alarmist, but it's good to know the facts.

Time zone GMT+6   **Country code** +977   **Currency** Nepalese rupee (Rs)

Pushkar
Camel Fair

You'll smell it long before you see it

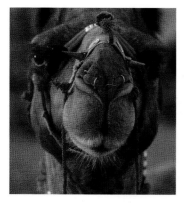

Pushkar Camel Fair

Where?

Pushkar, Rajasthan, India

When?

Over the full moon of the Indian Kartika month, usually mid-November

How long?

3 days

For anyone who has ever wondered what a football crowd-sized quantity of farting camels smells like, the Pushkar Camel Fair, on the fringes of India's Thar Desert in the northwestern state of Rajasthan, is the place to find out. This compact pilgrimage town, clustered around a pearl-shaped lake in the lee of the Aravalli Hills, is overrun by more than fifty thousand flatulent ships of the desert, along with cartloads of their owners, dressed in jaw-dropping traditional costumes. Concentrating the full spectrum of Rajasthani colour onto a sandy canvas the size of New York's Central Park, it's everything foreigners come to India hoping to experience, but usually only catch fleeting glimpses of from train or bus windows.

Having got the harvest safely in their granaries, the Gujar herders, Lohar blacksmiths, and innumerable other castes and tribes from India's arid border region spruce up their camels with fancy fur and other jazzy tack, don their most colourful turbans, wax the ends of their handlebar moustaches into pin-sharp points and head for the fair. Uniquely at Pushkar, the men are also accompanied to the market by equal numbers of women, whose flowing veils and pleated ankle-length skirts, glittering with mirrorwork and elaborate embroidery, outshine even their husbands' candy-coloured headgear. Picture this spectacle against a backdrop of rolling ochre dunes, enveloped in a pall of woodsmoke and dust kicked up by tens of thousands of Hindu pilgrims, ash-smeared ascetics, acrobats, snake charmers, Japanese film crews and Israeli ravers, and you'll understand why Pushkar's camel fair has become the cornerstone of tourist itineraries over the Indian winter.

The local tourist office, which has been muscling in on the camel fair for the past fifteen years or so, promotes the full-moon weekend itself as the core of the festival. However, to see the livestock market in full swing, you should come at least ten days before the culmination of Kartika Purnima. Most of the serious trading is done well before the "official" festival, or *mela*, even starts. By the time the tourist office's camel races and beauty competitions are underway in its specially erected stadium, all but a handful of the Gujars and other tribals have moved off, having blown all their winnings and run out of fodder.

History

Picking your way through all the donkey turds, camel pats and goat droppings, it's easy to forget that the livestock fair is only a sideshow to the main religious celebration of Kartika Purnima. For the three days of the full-moon period, the waters of Pushkar lake (believed to have formed when the Lord Brahma, the Creator Being, dropped a lotus flower to earth to crush a demon) are said to cleanse the soul of all sin. Ancient Hindu scriptures record this auspicious astrological phase as the one chosen by Brahma to convene all 900,000 deities of the Hindu pantheon for a *yagya* ceremony. Brahma also decided to get hitched at the same time, but his fiancée, the beautiful Savitri, failed to show up, and he found another consort, an Untouchable girl from the Gujar (herder) caste called Gayatri. When Savitri found out she'd been jilted, she flew into a cosmic rage and cursed Brahma, saying that henceforth he'd only be worshipped here at Pushkar. The spell has never been broken. Despite occupying a prominent position at the centre of the great Hindu trinity, the Supreme Creator Being only boasts one major shrine in India, overlooking Pushkar lake. From its shores, two hills sweep in gentle curves to rocky summits crowned by a pair of identical toothpaste-white temples: the abodes of Savitri and Gayatri, the jealous wives, locked in an eternal stand-off.

The *yagya* ceremony and Brahma's marriage are the mythological foundations of the Kartika Purnima festival, when tens of thousands of Hindu pilgrims pour in to Pushkar to notch up a few points on their reincarnatory balance sheet with a redemptory dip. Scriptures dating back more than 1500 years mention this annual event, and it is highly likely that the camel fair, which takes place in the dunes west of the lake and temple area at the same time, is just as ancient. Brahma's wife Gayatri was, after all, a Gujar, and for the camel herders Pushkar remains the holiest of holies – "Pushkar Maharahajl", or "Pushkar, King of Kings".

The camel fair

Once you've dumped your luggage at whichever tent camp or guesthouse you've managed to find a space in, follow the tide of humanity down through the Main Bazaar, and past the northern edge of the lake to the **main mela ground**. You'll smell it long before see it. For most of the past decade, something like 200,000 people have converged on Pushkar for the fair, the majority of them camel herders, whose makeshift encampment, strewn over the dunes outside town, is the great sight of the festival. Crouched or leaning on sticks under the knobbly knees and imperious necklines of their animals, the villagers congregate in knots of dealers and family groups to buy, sell, smoke *chillums* and watch the world go by. For the women in particular, dripping in heavy silver jewellery, their eyes heavily lined by black *kohl*, Pushkar represents a rare break from the daily grind of life in the desert villages. This is the time when mothers and aunts fix matches for their daughters and nieces, and when sisters separated since marriage are reunited to swap news.

As an outsider, you may feel a bit uncomfortable amid the sea of camel legs and outsized turbans, but no one seems in the least perturbed by the hordes of white people that mill around these days, not even when they find themselves staring down the barrel of a 200mm lens. Rajasthanis adore dressing up, and pose with evident pride beside their animals, after a last-minute twirl of the moustache or twitch of a sequined *odini* to preserve modesty.

Beside the campground, a good old-fashioned **funfair** provides a hefty dose of subcontinental surreality. Join the queue of Gujar girls in their swirling skirts and veils for a ride on a rickety big wheel, or check out Rajasthan's take on the Wall of Death, in which a Maruti hatchback is driven at top speed around the vertical sides of a drum, with a man leaning out of the window to grab the rupee notes offered by the astonished spectators standing on the rim. Meanwhile, between racks of day-glo party gear and crazy-patchwork bedspreads, crowds start to congregrate around the sideshows: tight-rope walking toddlers balancing brass pots on their heads; folk bands singing desert songs to *tabla*, harmonium and reed-pipe accompaniment; and,

weirdest of all, the masochistic *sadhus* (holy men), smeared with cow-dung ash and sandalwood paste. Brandish your camera and you'll find a gang of them dangling bricks from their penises, sticking skewers through their tongues or rolling around on beds of nails and crushed glass.

Towards the end of the afternoon, however, everyone – even the *sadhus* – packs up and heads to the dunes for sunset. This is the time die-hard druggies hit the *bhang lassi* – a potent psychedelic concoction of marijuana leaves mixed with sugar, spices, milk and yogurt. Even without one, though, the sight of the world's largest camel herd spread across the darkening dunes, with campfires illuminating the faces and silver necklaces of the herders, is pure magic.

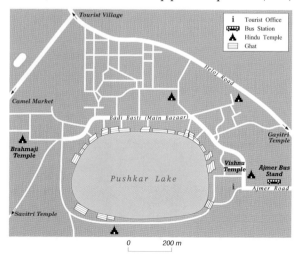

The full-moon fair

If only as an antidote to *bhang-lassi*-induced brain fuzz, the mayhem of the "official" fair, staged at the stadium on the outskirts of town, is worth hanging around for. During the three days of the full moon itself, various agricultural competitions and races attract straggling herders and a stadium full of camera-toting tourists. Adornment and fur-clipping contests, livestock beauty competitions and cow-milking demonstrations are followed by rounds of horse- and camel-dashes, where the spectacle of flapping camel lips and the prodigious quantities of spittle flicked from them, leave the most lasting impression. More hilarious still is the "camel-loading" event, in which villages compete to see how many people can pile on to a growling beast before it flips them off – kind of like a camel rodeo for large crowds.

The weirdest race of all is one in which teams of men with terracotta pots of water balanced on their heads attempt to run through ranks of club-wielding opponents, whose task is to smash the pots and soak the runners, provoking cheers of approval from the stands. The foreigners get their chance to bag a Pushkar prize in the grand Tourists v Locals Tug-O-War. Each year the line of burly Germans and American ex-footballers looks certain to kick sand in the face of the scrawny Rajasthani squad, but the result is always the same: a humiliating defeat for the visitors and unbridled jubilation among the Indian spectators.

The madness of the *mela*'s wacky Olympics is a far cry indeed from the mass devotion of the main **puja**, or religious ritual, which brings Pushkar's Kartika Purnima festivities to a spiritual close on the final day of the full moon. Throughout the afternoon and evening, pilgrims pour in by the thousands from the surrounding villages to be at the lakeside for dawn, the most auspicious bathing time. Thumping drum beats, bells and devotional songs, pumped out by the temples' crackly old sound systems, create a decidedly unholy din that drifts across the still waters of the lake and rises to a crescendo just before sunrise. Standing waist-deep, those lucky enough to have made it to the *ghats* (bathing places) in time savour the moment with the mantra "*Asvodiyov Brahma*", pouring the sacred lake water from cupped hands to worship the source of life – the sun – as it rises above the parched Aravalli ridges.

Insider info You can check the precise dates of the full moon (which vary from year to year according to the astrological calendar), on the tourist-office website (see p.354)

the sight of the world's largest camel herd spread across the darkening dunes is pure magic

Basics

The nearest international **airport** is in Delhi, some 400km to the northeast. The railhead for Pushkar is at nearby Ajmer, on the main Delhi–Mumbai (Bombay) line. Getting there is easy enough – there are two **trains** from Delhi a day (the journey takes between 6hr 30min and 8hr 30min) – but the remaining fifteen-kilometre **bus** or **taxi** ride over the mountains to Pushkar itself can be a slow haul during the festival. To survive the interminable jams, jump out of your bus at regular intervals to buy piping hot *pakora* from the roadside vendors and soak up the festival atmosphere, as the flood of pilgrims, animals and tourists builds. Pushkar's **tourist office** is in the Sarovar Hotel, off Ajmer Road (24hr; ☎0145/227 2040).

Accommodation

Pushkar has a huge number of tourist beds for a town of its size, but don't expect to just turn up over the official period and find one without a reservation. It's best to arrive ten to fifteen days before, when the herders are already trading hard, and there's still plenty of **accommodation**. If that's not possible, don't worry – most guesthouses and hotels will take reservations over the phone, especially if confirmed by email afterwards. The same rules apply to the Rajasthan tourist office's purpose-built camp on the outskirts of the fair, two miles outside of the town, on the banks of Pushkar lake. The camp offers dorm beds for backpackers (US$8 per head) or swisher tents equipped with proper beds, fans, electric lights and safe lockers (US$100 per double). Book in advance through the General Manager, Central Reservations, Hotel Swagatam Campus, Jaipur, Rajasthan, India 30200, or by phone (☎0141/220 0595/3531).

Of the budget guesthouses on or around the lake, the pick of the bunch are the *Lake View* in the Main Bazaar (☎0141/277 2106, ⊛www.lakeviewpushkar.com), whose simple rooms open on to a large rooftop, and the *White House*, back in the town proper near the Marwar bus stand (☎0145/277 2147, ⊛www.pushkarwhitehouse.com), which has a great rooftop restaurant. If you fancy splashing out and sleeping in style consider a tent in one of the luxury camps set up by the state's Maharajas, where you'll be brought tea in the morning by cummerbund-wearing, turbanned bearers for the princely sum of US$250 per night (per double). Bookings should be made as far in advance as possible through the *Hotel Pushkar Palace* (☎0145/277 2001, ⊛www.hotelpushkarpalace.com), a beautiful old Rajput building that itself offers comfortable, pricey rooms with panoramic views over the lake. The other upmarket option, and the only place where you are allowed to drink alcohol and eat meat during the festival, is the *Pushkar Resort*, 5km out of town at Gankera village on the

Motisur Road (☎0145/277 2017, ⊛www.pushkarresorts.com), a modern, purpose-built luxury complex with its own pool and separate air-con cottages costing US$185 per night during the camel fair.

Eating and drinking

One of the most amazing things about India is that as soon as your tummy starts to rumble, someone is bound to appear hawking exactly the sort of **food** you were hankering for. Pushkar is no exception. At the camel fair, a newspaper wrap of hot, crispy *pakora* is the most ubiquitous, and hygienic, fast food. You can also grab little leaf plates of spicy chickpea curry served with deep-fried dough-breads (*channa batura*).

Pushkar's religious importance means that it's a strictly **vegetarian** town; eggs and meat don't appear on any menus. In the Main Bazaar, dozens of tourist-oriented restaurants churn out standard travellers grub – everything from banana pancakes to pizzas, pasta dishes and German pastries. The *Raju Terrace Restaurant*'s great north Indian and Western dishes can be enjoyed from rooftop tables offering a view of the lake. The *Sunset Café*, in the eastern *ghats*, has an even more idyllic lakeside location, at which sizeable crowds gather at sunset to be serenaded by local buskers and techno DJs. The pilgrims, however, pile into soot-blackened *chai* shops for tin plates of mixed vegetable and rice meals, or the local favourite, *dal batti* – a crumbly savoury cake flavoured with *ghee*.

Pushkar's religious status means alcoholic drinks and drugs are also banned, though they can still be found in some of the outlying luxury hotels (for the former) and in the travellers' cafés in the Main Bazaar (for the latter).

Health

With so many people from all over the state crammed into such a confined area, **malaria** can be a serious problem at the camel fair, so come well-armed with a deet-based mozzie repellent and a solid net, and keep taking your anti-malarial pills after you leave. Anyone with dust and animal-hair allergies should also stock up on anti-histamine, as the pharmacy in town invariably runs out. Finally, don't underestimate the sun. This is the cool season in Rajasthan, but without a hat and high-factor sunblock you can easily come down with sunstroke after a day under Pushkar's cloudless skies.

Event info

Pushkar Camel Fair (⊛www.pushkar-far.com). Site dedicated to the fair, and pushing accommodation and package tours based around the event.

Time zone GMT + 5.5   **Country code** +91   **Currency** Indian rupee (Rs)

Asia

The best of the rest

Bonn Om Tuk

Where? **Phnom Penh, Cambodia**
When? **Early November**
How long? **3 days**

This is the biggest festival in the Cambodian calendar and traditionally celebrates the end of the rainy season. There are celebrations all over the country, but Phnom Penh, the capital, is perhaps the place to be, with boat races on the Tonle Sap river, and fireworks contributing to the full-on carnival atmosphere.

Bun Bang Fai Festival

Where? **Vientiane, Laos**
When? **May**
How long? **1 day**

On the full moon in May it's time to light the fuse and stand well clear throughout Laos, as rocket fever grips the nation, and countless home-made contraptions are launched skywards to ensure good rain and a healthy crop as part of the Bun Bang Fai Festival. Vientiane is the place to be, although you'll find smaller events going on all over the country. Buddhist monks are the most expert rocket scientists, using bamboo tubes – up to 5m in length – stuffed with gunpowder, decked in coloured ribbons and capped by a paper dragon's head. For the layman, PVC piping is a less traditional but equally effective material. As it's something of a fertility festival, there's much bawdy singing and dancing through the day, and come the evening everyone assembles in raucous crowds by the Mekong to watch the launchings. There's serious "mine-is-bigger-than-yours"-type competition between builders, and those whose efforts fail to go off or flop badly face ridicule, and often end up getting pushed into the river. Bun Bang Fai is also celebrated in Yasothon, in Thailand's dense, less touristed northeast interior, close to the Laotian border. The firework safety book is thrown out of the window as the locals work their way through crates of Singha beer, and home-made rockets are let off with dangerous enthusiasm all over town.

Chariot Festival

Where? **Puri, Orissa, India**
When? **June**
How long? **1 day**

As the home of Lord Jagannath, Puri is one of the most significant stops on India's Hindu pilgrimage trail, and its annual chariot festival, or Rath Yatra, commemorates the deity's journey with his brother, Balabhadra, and sister, Subhadra, by chariot from his temple in Puri to the countryside beyond. There are other chariot festivals in India, but this is by far the biggest, with three vast chariots, one for each deity, purpose-built each year and draped in

Chariot Festival

coloured cloth, pulled by thousands from the Jagannath temple to their summer residence just outside town and then back again – pulling the chariots is a devotional act for Hindus. Thousands more join the processions, and the whole thing is about as spectacular an Indian festival as you could find.

Chinese New Year

Where? **Hong Kong**
When? **Late January/ Early February**
How long? **3 days**

The best place to welcome in the Chinese Lunar New Year or Spring Festival is, of course, the traditional citadel of good times, Hong Kong. Celebrations last for three days, and feature parades and lion dances accompanied by booming percussion, firecrackers, skyscrapers bedecked in neon – and one of the world's biggest fireworks displays, launched from barges in Victoria Harbour. The tradition of buying a wardrobe's worth of new clothes to welcome in the New Year also means that Hong Kong's shops go crazy, knocking upwards of fifty percent off everything in a massive clearout sale that only adds to the rising fever of the approaching festival. New Year's Eve is usually devoted to gorging at family banquets, which must include chicken (for prosperity) and fish (for good luck), as well as an idiosyncratic stew of dried oyster and a kind of black seaweed known as *fat choi*, which also translates as "prosperity". Buckets of the stuff are downed, along with anything sweet and round – to encourage unity and happiness (through sweetness). For days before the big party, Hong Kong is crammed with a huge fragrant flower market; locals go for kumquat trees in particular. Afterwards, head for Lan Kwai Fong in Central for some great post-parade partying, and then on to the traditional New Year's Day meet at Sha Tin racecourse (where much of the financial abundance so earnestly wished for is flashed around). *Kung Hei Fat Choi*! Prosperous Wishes!

Dinagyang

Where? **Iloilo City, The Philippines**
When? **Late January**
How long? **2 days**

Held the weekend after Kalibo's Ati-Atihan (see p.299), Dinagyang is Iloilo City's chance to go bananas. Similar to the Kalibo event, this too honours the Santo Niño (the Christ Child), and is characterized by drumming, drinking and dancing over the course of a madcap two-day party. The climax – officially speaking, anyway – is the Ati-Atihan competition, in which tribes of costumed, soot-caked "warriors" dance themselves dizzy to the drumbeats – although in the past Dinagyang has been a victim of its own insanity and the mayhem has ended in violence on occasion. In a bid to calm things down, organizers are emphasizing the festival's religious roots, and introducing more sedate spin-off events such as film and food festivals. Even with its corners smoothed, though, this will still be one hell of a party.

Diwali

Where? **India**
When? **October or November**
How long? **5 days**

The Hindu festival of lights – symbols of knowledge, health, wealth and everything that is positive in the world – celebrates Rama and Sita's homecoming in the *Ramayama*. It's the biggest event of the year in India, sort of on a par with Christmas in the West, and as such is not an especially good time to travel here, since everything is closed and everyone stays at home for feasting. But if you know someone in India, taking part in its rituals can be magical: festivities include the lighting of oil lamps and firecrackers and the giving and receiving of sweets and gifts.

Chinese New Year

Ganesh Festival

Where? **Pune, Maharashtra, India**
When? **Early September**
How long? **10 days**

The pot-bellied elephant-headed deity Ganesh is celebrated all over India but is particularly important in Maharashtra, where there are eight temples dedicated to him. In Pune, especially, his birth is remembered every year, when everyone in town makes clay idols of Ganesh for worship. The god is venerated by brass bands and drums, culminating on the last day, when the idols are taken to the river in a massive parade of drummers and musicians, and everyone scatters armfuls of red powder over everything.

Dragon Boat Races

Where? **Hong Kong**
When? **May 31**
How long? **1 day**

Hong Kong's dragon-boat races commemorate the aquatic suicide of an upright regional governor, Qu Yuan, who jumped into a river in central China in 278 BC rather than live to see his home state invaded by a neighbouring province's army. Distraught locals raced to save him in their boats, but were too late; later on, they threw packets of sticky rice into the river as an offering to his ghost. There are festivities all over China remembering the uncompromising Qu Yuan, but the race in Hong Kong's Stanley Harbour (ⓦ www.dragonboat.org.hk) is one of the best, with huge quantities of sticky rice consumed and some fierce competition between the dragon-boat teams, who speed their narrow vessels across the harbour to the steady boom of pacing drums. To soak up the best of the buzz, go down to the waterside with a cold beer and take in the festive atmosphere, though you'll need to get up early to catch the dedication of the dragon-head prows. The celebrations carry on through the evening, with firecrackers and traditional dragon dances. Not to be confused with the much better publicized International Dragonboat Races later on in June.

Dussehra

Where? **India**
When? **October**
How long? **10 days**

A classic good-versus-evil spectacle, this Hindu festival celebrates Rama's victory over the demon Ravana, as described in the *Ramayana*. Effigies of Ravana and his family are filled with firecrackers and attacked by people dressed up as Rama, whereby the whole lot goes off in a giant explosion accompanied by the approving roars of the assembled throng. Each region interprets the festival slightly differently, although Mysore, Karnataka, is one of the best places to be.

Hadaka Matsuri

Where? **Japan**
When? **January**
How long? **1 day**

The Hadaka Matsuri (literally, the "naked festival") is one of Japan's more peculiar events, taking place in many towns across the country at this time. It's a Shinto festival, and a test of manhood and a purification ritual, and although the details differ from town to town, it generally involves the local men and boys stripping down to their loin-cloths and doing something completely inappropriate for the time of year, when it's bitter cold in most parts of the country: jumping and chanting, getting doused in cold water, swimming in the sea or prostrating themselves on blocks of ice. The best-attended Hadaka Matsuri is held in Inazawa, on Honshu, in which some ten thousand naked men compete to touch the so-called *Shinotoko*, or Chosen One, in the belief that this will bring them good luck in the year to come. Other places to head for include Tokyo, Kyoto, Osaka and even the far northern, freezing city of Sendai, where they at least have a bonfire to warm up to. If you're here at this time of year, there's nothing like it.

Dragon Boat Races

Harbin Ice and Snow Festival

Where? **Harbin, China**
When? **Early January**
How long? **1 month**

This exhibition of fabulous sculptures carved from snow and ice, including life-size figures and even exact reproductions of Chinese temples, has been going on for twenty years in the Manchurian city of Harbin. It's spectacular if you can stand the freezing temperatures – sometimes plummeting 40 degrees below – and opened in style with a huge firework display and then closed at the beginning of February when attendees get the chance to smash everything up with ice-picks.

Hemis

Where? **India**
When? **June or July**
How long? **2 days**

Held all over the subcontinent, this Buddhist festival is at its best at Hemis, Ladakh, one of the most important and remote monasteries in India. Honouring the birthday of the founder of Tibetan Buddhism, its parades and lavish masked dances also celebrate the triumph of good over evil. Hemis' monastery alone is worth the trek, but to come here during the festival is special.

Hounen Matsuri

Where? **Komaki, Japan**
When? **March**
How long? **1 day**

It's no-holds-barred at this annual spring celebration of the penis at Komaki, just outside Nagoya, in which a giant, three-metre-high wooden dong is tugged around town on a *mikoshi*, or portable shrine, to the town's Tagata temple, and everyone sucks happily on phallic-shaped sweets and dainties – and drinks prodigious amounts of sake. The festival dates back to the seventeenth century, when local prostitutes figured they should offer something to the gods to avoid getting STDs; nowadays, it's an HIV/AIDS fund-raiser, a lure for couples hoping for children, and a saucy day out all round. Everyone's fairly drunk by the time the parade starts, which makes its way to the shrine to deliver the giant penis; there are women carrying their own, smaller penises, all of them 36 years old (apparently a bad age for conception), and a host of men (all of them 42 – another bad age) carrying the phallus. Once it has been delivered to the temple, dignitaries throw rice cakes to the baying mob below and the whole event turns into a giant food-fight.

Loi Krathong

Where? **Sukhothai, Thailand**
When? **November 11**
How long? **1 day**

Seeking forgiveness from the Mother of the Waters for the filth poured into her rivers the rest of the year, Loi Krathong witnesses millions of tiny boats, made of flowers and leaves and loaded with candles, launched into rivers and harbours around the country under a watchful full moon. You'll certainly be aware of the event wherever you are, as houses and *wats* everywhere are decorated with streamers and lights, but one of the best places to observe the festival is the atmospheric city of Sukhothai, the first Thai capital, situated on the Yom river 480km north of Bangkok. Here, the ruins of the ancient capital are lit up with fireworks and a pretty nifty *son et lumière*.

Lopburi Banquet

Where? **Lopburi, Thailand**
When? **Late November**
How long? **1 day**

Bad table manners? Not to worry. At the Lopburi Banquet (also known as Lopburi Monkey Banquet) in Thailand, you'll fit right in. This strange feast is laid on in the jungle town of Lopburi, 160km north of Bangkok, to thank the primates that are said to guard the well-being of the town, and your fellow diners are several hundred long-tailed macaques who may get nasty if you reach for the wrong banana.

Losar Archery Festival

Where? **Bhutan**
When? **Late January or early February**
How long? **1 day**

Archery is Bhutan's national passion, and every year, as part of the Buddhist New Year, or Losar, celebrations, teams of marksmen across the land compete to hit targets at 140m using old-style bows and arrows. Traditionally, competitors spend the night beforehand sleeping out in a barn or in the forest – it's claimed that spending the night at home with your wife is liable to make your concentration waver during the big event. On the day, there's a big build-up, with competitors calling on shamans, astrology, mantras and other spiritual trickery to ensure their skill and good fortune. In the heat of the moment, though, all that inner tranquillity can go to pot, as rival teams and the hordes of drunken spectators are permitted – and even encouraged – to put the shooters off their stride. Anything bar actual physical contact goes, so there's much cat-calling, insult-hurling – and, bizarrely, a preponderance of cross-dressing. The crowd has a great time – drinking, feasting, shouting, dancing (especially when someone makes a good shot), and generally acting the goat.

O-Mizutori

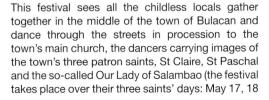

Where? **Nara, Japan**
When? **Early March**
How long? **1 day**

Nara's Todai-ji temple, home to the country's largest Buddha, is also the venue for the annual Buddhist "water-drawing" festival, held every March for over a thousand years. Basically, a large crowd gathers outside the temple while eleven monks stand on a balcony above and wave lit torches around so that embers and flames deliberately drop onto the people below – all while other monks chant and pray behind the veil. Rather than dodge the embers, people try to catch them, as they're believed to ward off evil. After a couple of hours of this, water is drawn from the temple's sacred well and everyone goes home happy.

Obando Fertility Festival

Where? **Bulacan, The Philippines**
When? **May**
How long? **3 days**

This festival sees all the childless locals gather together in the middle of the town of Bulacan and dance through the streets in procession to the town's main church, the dancers carrying images of the town's three patron saints, St Claire, St Paschal and the so-called Our Lady of Salambao (the festival takes place over their three saints' days: May 17, 18

and 19). The dance is a deliberately sexy affair, with lots of grinding hips designed to summon up the mystical forces needed to aid reproduction. The whole thing ends when the dancers reach the church, dance up the aisle and a mass is held.

Onam

Where? **Kerala, India**
When? **August**
How long? **10 days**

A particularly joyful affair, this Keralan celebration of the harvest, has everything: flowers, dance, music, food, fireworks and – its main feature – the snakeboat races or *Vallamkali*, held in the towns of Karuvatta, Payippad, Aranmula and Kottayam, in which up to 150 oarsmen compete hard to win as well as look good, festooned as they are with silk, lace and flags.

O-Mizutori

Puram

Where? **Thrissur, Kerala, India**
When? **Late April/early May**
How long? **2 days**

Introduced over two hundred years ago by the Cochin raja, Shaktan Tampuran, Puram is Kerala's largest festival, a riot of colour and activity in which a host of stylishly decorated elephants parade through town, alongside marching bands of drummers and folk dancers. The frenetic climax to the amazing, seemingly non-stop percussion acts as a signal to the elephant riders, who stand in unison, twirling their feather fans and hair whisks in an incredible co-ordinated sequence. The festivities continue through the night, when the entrances to the Vadukannatha temple, right in the heart of town, are ablaze with colour and a spectacular firework display takes place in the early hours of the morning.

Shandur Polo Tournament

Where? **Shandur Pass, Pakistan**
When? **July**
How long? **1 day**

The highest and most remote polo tournament in the world is staged in the Shandur Pass, in the far north of Pakistan, between six teams from each end of the pass. It's a fantastically remote place for a sports event, 11,000 feet up, and nine hours' rocky and precipitous drive from Chitral to the west or thirteen hours from Gilgit in the east – you have to be either a keen polo fan, or a determined traveller, to make it. But ten thousand or so people do so, including the Pakistani president, and the experience, whether you like polo or not, is pretty unforgettable.

Sisters' Meal

Where? **Taijiang, China**
When? **April or May**
How long? **2 days**

Deep in the hills of Guizhou province, southwestern China, teenagers of the Miao ethnic group get together and celebrate spring by choosing their partners at this huge shindig, which involves scores of villages and more than thirty thousand participants. It all begins on the fifteenth day of the third lunar month in the showgrounds at Taijiang with a dance spectacular, the girls dressed in ornately embroidered jackets and massive silver headpieces, the young men wearing cut-off jackets and leggings that show

their muscles to good effect, and playing four-metre-long *lusheng* pipes. That evening, the main street of town is jammed solid for dragon-lantern dances, where village teams race paper dragons through the streets while onlookers throw fireworks and crackers at them. Noon the next day sees buffalo fights – wrestling matches between bulls – out on the river flats around town; the animals are decked out in ribbons and pheasant tail-feathers, and snort and scrabble as they battle on the grass. Meanwhile, in the Sisters' Meal itself, men are handing out a parcel of sticky rice to the girl of their choice: lucky ones get it back with a pair of chopsticks inside; unlucky ones, with a chilli. There's another big night-time dance, and then the action moves 40km north to the riverside hamlet of Shidong for a day of dragon-boat races, after which rice wine and dancing fever takes over once more, with everyone from toddlers to ancient grandmothers – and foreigners swept up in the rhythms – getting involved.

Songkhran

Where? **Thailand**
When? **Mid-April**
How long? **3 days**

The start of the Thai New Year gives rise to one of the best festivals in the Thai calendar, when the entire nation wishes for good luck and literally washes away the sins by enthusiastically hurling buckets of water over each other. Everyone on the streets, from beggars to police, innocent bystanders and – especially – tourists give and get a good soaking down, which can be something of a relief in the summer heat. There's a serious side, too, with Buddhists attending temple services to sprinkle monks' hands with scented water, wash down statues, build miniature sandcastles in temple grounds, and release cagebirds as an act of charity. The bigger cities, such as Bangkok and Chiang Mai, also hold more commercial events, such as Miss Songkhran beauty pageants, but on the whole it's just a good excuse to get into the streets and have some fun.

Sumba Pasola

Where? **Sumba, Indonesia**
When? **March**
How long? **2 days**

The island of Sumba is one of the more remote Indonesian islands, and its *pasola* is the region's most authentic festival – a series of battles and jousts between hundreds of fabulously attired horsemen, which is supposed to balance the sphere of the heavens and the sphere of the sea by the spilling of blood. Scary stuff, and this is one event in which outsiders are not allowed to take part, even if they wanted to.

Surin Elephant Round-Up

Where? Surin, Thailand
When? Mid-November
How long? 3 days

The Surin Elephant Round-Up, held every year in this small town a few hundred kilometres north of Bangkok, is one of Thailand's best-known annual festivals, but unfortunately this ancient courtesan display is now extremely commercially exploited, complete with wall-to-wall Pepsi posters and miniature plastic elephants to buy – and a lot of tourists. Some of the shows involving over a hundred trained elephants are genuinely compelling, however, particularly the parade of elephants outfitted for medieval warfare and demonstrations of wild elephant hunts, an occupation still undertaken in the receding forests in the north of the country. And there are impressive displays of elephants playing football and engaging in tugs of war. But don't try and wrestle an elephant yourself, unless you want to be dragged through fresh heaps of elephant shit in front of forty thousand spectators.

Thaipusam

Where? Kuala Lumpur, Malaysia
When? Late January
How long? 1 day

Thaipusam is probably Malaysia's biggest religious festival, honouring the Hindu gods Lord Subriaman and Ganesh during the tenth month of the Hindu calendar. After sunset, Hindu penitents carry a variety of *kavadis*, an elaborate steel arch bedecked with flowers and lights, attached to their skin by hooks and skewers, up the 272 steps to the Batu Caves, just north of Kuala Lumpur. Similar events take place in neighbouring Singapore, where local Hindus – mostly Tamils – carry the *kavadi* in the same, painful fashion, along Serangoon Road to the Chettiar Temple on Tank Road.

Torajan Funerals

Where? Sulawesi, Indonesia
When? Year round
How long? 1 day

Funerals aren't usually something you'd go out of your way to visit, but the funerals held in the Tana Toraja region, in Sulawesi, are more celebrations of a life than the gloomy affairs you might be used to. The Torajans have two funerals, a private one, after which the body is preserved until the time and money is found for a public one, to which everyone is invited, whether or not they knew the deceased. It's a party, basically – pigs and water buffalo are slaughtered and then butchered, gifts are brought, and palm wine is consumed with abandon. An extraordinary experience, and not as voyeuristic an affair as you might think.

Surin Elephant Round-Up

Australia and New Zealand

Australia and New Zealand

Birdsville Races
Sydney Gay and Lesbian Mardi Gras
THE BEST OF THE REST

Birdsville Races

The place is so remote that simply getting there is half the fun

Birdsville Races

Where?
Birdsville, Queensland, Australia

When?
First weekend in September

How long?
3 days

Birdsville
AUSTRALIA
Canberra •

Come September, locals flee the dusty desert township of Birdsville, as a six-thousand-strong crowd descends for a weekend of hard drinking and, if they sober up for long enough to work out the odds, the chance to win a packet on the ponies running in the Birdsville Races. This is the archetypal, good-natured Aussie piss-up, in a bizarre Outback setting. The racegoers are a mix of young cowpokes making the most of their one opportunity of the year to whoop it up and meet folks they're not related to, and townies who have just driven 1400km from the coast on atrocious roads to get there. Even by Australian standards, that's a long way to go for a drink. Although you might see the odd fist-fight between drunken mates on account of the effort involved in reaching Birdsville, nobody has anything to prove by the time they arrive, and there's nothing left for it but to down a slab of XXXX and party.

The Birdsville Races (officially known as the XXXX Birdsville Cup Carnival) kick off on Friday, though most people skip the trackside opening ceremonies in favour of spending the day easing themselves onto a liquid diet. After dark, the town fires up in fairground mode, with a host of anachronistic sideshow attractions – whip-cracking competitions, ringing the bell with a mallet, guess my weight, arm wrestling, you name it – setting up along the **main street**. A huge, mainly male crowd materializes at the fundraising auction, impatiently

History

Founded in the 1880s as a customs post for collecting dues on cattle being driven interstate, Birdsville – and its half-a-dozen streets and around 120 residents – is stuck way down in southwestern Queensland, within sight of the Simpson Desert's mighty red sand dunes. The **first race meeting** was held here in 1882 and attended by just a few locals – a far cry from the crowd-pulling event it is now. With the droving days long gone, the town's survival owes a lot to the bar at the **Birdsville Hotel,** a timber and adobe place built in 1884 and the only watering-hole for 400km in any direction – a lifeline for farmhands from nearby cattle stations, and the race weekend's social focus.

Just about all Outback settlements have their own bulldozed gravel racetrack and host race meets, so why Birdsville's has become such a big event is a bit of a mystery. It's probably got a lot to do with sheer Aussie perversity: the place is so remote that simply getting there is half the fun – most people have a few bruises, headaches and tales to tell by the time they arrive on the Thursday or Friday. And they'll have plenty more by the time Sunday morning rolls around.

watching all sorts of farm junk going under the hammer as they wait for the real attraction: the draw at the end to win a T-shirt off the back of a stripper (women can buy tickets for this event at half-price).

After the auction, and on the principle that sex and alcohol are nothing without a bit of violence thrown in, haul yourself over to **Brophy's Boxing Tent**, where contenders from the crowd don gloves to slug it out with Brophy's bruisers for small prize money. Stick to spectating: any drunken bravado will evaporate as you stand on oil drums at the back of the crowd watching a two-hundred-kilo farmhand being hammered unconscious in three seconds flat by a wiry lightweight.

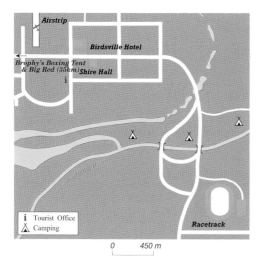

Airstrip
Birdsville Hotel
Brophy's Boxing Tent
& Big Red (35km) Shire Hall

i Tourist Office
△ Camping

Racetrack

0   450 m

Race day

If you haven't made it out there already, Saturday is the day to hit the **racetrack** – a baking hot, shadeless stretch of dust and gravel 3km southeast of town. Ascot it's not, but there's a vague attempt to be noticed and a few women sport flamboyant headgear, though men stick to more practical Aussie Akubras. The **Birdsville Cup**, run over 1600m, is the big one. It usually starts around 3.50pm and, as the race approaches, crowds swarm around the touts, with last-minute betting slips and cash rapidly switching hands. It's also worth catching a **camel race** or two, but here you can forget about favourites and carefully calculated odds – camels run in any direction they feel, and dead-cert winners have been known to give up and sit down a metre from the finishing line.

The races end mid-afternoon, when everyone retires for a wash-and-brush-up before heading back to town to celebrate or drown their sorrows. After dark there's usually a live

band at **Shire Hall**: you need a clean kit – shoes, long trousers, shirt and tie – to get in, though you won't be the first to make it through the door wearing a black sock dangling from your collar. Those whose dress sense falls short of the mark head to the hotel bar instead, where there's a more raucous atmosphere and the action soon spills out onto the street. If you haven't done so already, it's around now that you'll register the weekend's ten-males-to-one-female ratio – women, single or not, will have no shortage of suitors.

The morning after

Don't plan much for Sunday as you'll be in the minority if you surface before lunch. A few die-hards crawl back to the bar for hair of the dog, but the hotel's best avoided on Sunday: the faces of the survivors propped up or passed out on the porch might put you off drink for life. Those with four-wheel-drives and a bit of stamina head west out to **Big Red**, the first of the desert dunes, and spend the afternoon driving up and down its powdery slopes; otherwise, it's time to start packing up camp and planning your return to civilization.

over sixty thousand cans of beer are downed at the Birdsville Hotel, leaving the street outside ankle-deep in discarded tinnies

Insider info The events at Birdsville are charged individually. If you think you've got the stomach – or, more crucially, the liver – for it, then you can save money by buying a "souvenir medallion" (AUS$55) from local businesses, which grants you access to both race days and their subsequent evenings' entertainment.

Basics

Various aircraft companies and bus services organize six-day **Birdsville Races packages** out of coastal Queensland and New South Wales – check the official website (see below) for the current list and contact details. If you're planning to **drive** overland routes yourself, note that all roads into Birdsville are unsealed so you'll need a sturdy vehicle. It's essential to take adequate precautions when travelling on Outback roads – ensure that you have extra fuel, water, food, medical supplies and spare tyres on board, in case of emergency. For road information and local conditions, check out ⓦ www.ExplorOz.com.
The **Wirrarri Information Centre** on Billabong Boulevard (☎07/4656 3300, ⓔwirrarri.centre@bigpond.com) can also provide info on up-to-date travel conditions, as well as the town's amenities, and Internet facilities.

Accommodation

With the *Birdsville Hotel*'s beds reserved for their extra bar staff over the weekend, you'll be **camping**. The official free campsite (ⓔ birdsvillecvanpk@growzone.com.au) is near the bar but far too small to cope with demand, so most people set up in the scrub along the Diamatina River on the town's outskirts, halfway to the race track. The campsite's huge toilet and shower block are a lifesaver, but as Birdsville gets all its water from an underground hot spring, be prepared for scalding showers and steaming toilet bowls.

Eating and drinking

Something over sixty thousand cans of cold **beer** are downed at the *Birdsville Hotel* over the weekend, leaving the street outside ankle-deep in discarded tinnies. But this doesn't take into account the fact that everyone brings at least a carton of beer and a bottle of Bundaberg rum along with them as well – not so much to save money as to keep them going when reaching the bar would involve too many motor skills.
For **food**, the message is simple: bring your own. Otherwise, you'll have to make do with the hotel's famous "seven-course takeaway" (a pie and a six-pack), bread-and-cheese-style supplies from the store, or face the mobile sausage-and-chips wagons that trundle around. They're unlikely to give you food poisoning, but count your change carefully – they're used to everyone being too blurry-eyed to notice shortfalls. Cook or assemble next day's meal after dark, when the flies have settled down.

Event info

Birdsville Race Club (☎07/4656 3300, ⓦwww.birdsvilleraces.com). The website of the Birdsville Race Club, this is an excellent source of information on the town and provides a detailed timetable of the weekend's events – both the two- and four-legged kind.

Time zone GMT+10   **Country code** +61   **Currency** Australian dollar (AUS$)

Sydney Gay and Lesbian Mardi Gras

Partial nudity, G-strings and wild unleashings of inhibitions

Sydney Gay and Lesbian Mardi Gras

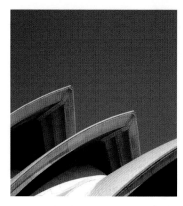

Where?

Sydney, Australia

When?

The Mardi Gras Party is held on the first Saturday in March

How long?

3–4 weeks

AUSTRALIA

Sydney
Canberra •

The Sydney Gay and Lesbian Mardi Gras is a unique Australian festival. It's a party of the rarest – and most uninhibited – breed; it's the single largest night-time parade of its kind in the world, drawing a bigger crowd than any other annual event in Australia. Above all, though, it's a political demonstration, and one that is without equal in colour, drama, spectacle and wit. The Sydney Gay and Lesbian Mardi Gras is, in fact, the umbrella term for a month-long arts, sport and lifestyle festival, which operates throughout February – a feast of theatre, visual arts, film, literature, music, dance, cabaret, comedy and sporting events that combine to make this the largest gay and lesbian festival in the world.

The Sydney Gay and Lesbian Mardi Gras takes place throughout the final, steamy month of summer, beginning with an official launch celebration in early February, and culminating in the parade at the beginning of March – an event with about six thousand participants and half a million spectators.

There's something for everyone in the run-up to Mardi Gras – shows, performances (many held in Sydney's fine old theatres and even in the Opera House), and plenty of sporting competitions, too, including the "Little Black Dress" drag fun run in Centennial Park. Events take place all over the city but it's the NMG's parade and party – both of which take place in the Darlinghurst, Surry Hills and Paddington area, just south of the backpacker (and red-light) district of Kings Cross – that mark the culmination of the festival, draw the biggest crowds and flaunt the most outrageous costumes. In essence, the parade is Mardi Gras' heart and soul, a full-on celebration of gay culture, and a joyous demonstration of pride. But the wild party afterwards is just as huge, involving up to twenty thousand gay and lesbian community members and their friends, with celebrations continuing for days afterwards.

History

The Mardi Gras Parade **began** as a protest march for homosexual law reform in 1978. The original parade took a different route to the current one and ended up in Sydney's red-light district, Kings Cross, where police intervened violently and a scuffle took place, ending in imprisonment for many of the protesters. The *Sydney Morning Herald* published the names and addresses of those arrested the following week, and many leading gay and lesbian business people and rights lobbyists lost their jobs and livelihoods as a result. Not surprisingly, the parade became an **annual focus for protests** against this kind of treatment, and the law in general, and although in 1981 the legal status of homosexuals was reformed, in New South Wales at least, (homosexuality is no longer deemed a psychological disorder, although sodomy is still illegal), the parade has grown in strength and fabulousness year on year. The original marchers still form an important part of the parade each year, and can be seen under the banner of "78ers". However, the over-ambitious SGLMG organization that had developed out of the event collapsed in 2003, owing half a million dollars. Community spirit and the talent and hard work of a few volunteers saw the organization reborn, as the leaner **New Mardi Gras** (NMG), who are responsible for the Launch, the Fair Day, the Parade and the Party.

Insider info For details of what's going on in the month-long build-up, pick up Sydney's gay and lesbian newspaper, the *Sydney Star Observer*, or check it out online at Ⓦwww.ssonet.com.au. For info on NMG's parade and party, get hold of their free *Sydney Gay and Lesbian Mardi Gras Official Season Guide*, which is available at bars and clubs throughout inner Sydney, and also from their website (see p.380).

The Mardi Gras Parade

The **Mardi Gras Parade** is a fantastic event by any standards, and enjoyable for people of any sexuality, provided partial nudity, G-strings, wild unleashings of inhibitions, random acts of love and lewd innuendo don't offend. The parade gets underway at 7.45pm from the Liverpool and Elizabeth street corner of the city's **Hyde Park**, and works its way up Oxford Street, continuing southeast through Taylor Square (the heart of the gay district) and along Flinders Street. The exuberant spectacle terminates at Moore Park, from where it's just over a kilometre walk west along Moore Park Road and south down Driver Avenue to Fox Studios and the Fox Entertainment Precinct, where the massive party is held (see p.378). The route is 1.6km long and the roads are blocked to traffic from late afternoon until after midnight. Needless to say, people start taking their places along the route from quite early in the day – milk crates (brought from home) are the accessories *du jour*, giving a height advantage that can only be matched by the drag queens in their ten-inch heels. (No single event, present or past, leaves more discarded milk crates in its wake than this one – note that they are banned on public transport on the day, though.) The most dramatic place to view the parade is **Taylor Square**, where the media tends to congregate. This is, however, the most crowded section, and the best vantage points are along less glamorous **Flinders Street**.

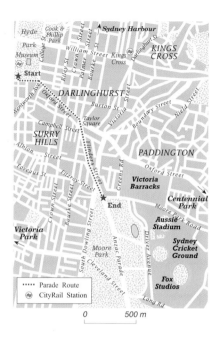

For paradegoers who don't want to battle it out on the streets, tickets for **viewing seats**, situated at the southern end of Hyde Park, can be purchased from the HIV/AIDS charity the Bobby Goldsmith Foundation (see p.380); seats in the grandstand ("Glamstand") cost AUS$115, while a street-level seat will set you back AUS$90. The hefty ticket price includes pre- and post-parade entertainment, and the money goes to those living with HIV/AIDS.

If you're an NMG member (AUS25–45; see p.380), you can get in to a members' area at Taylor Square for AUS$20.

Party and Parade tips

- Wear any gender-bending creation your heart desires, but bear in mind that it gets hot inside, so less is definitely more where clothes are concerned – and the cloakroom is a nightmare.
- Decide on a meeting place with your friends, as everyone always gets lost.
- Cursory bag searches are carried out at the party gates, so be very careful what you carry. Cameras are definitely not allowed and will be taken and returned to you when you leave.
- The medical tent at the party is staffed by very understanding, like-minded volunteers, so don't be afraid to seek their help if anything seems wrong. They are fully aware that people are using all sorts of (illegal) drugs.
- If you leave the party on your own at night, wait for a cab or the shuttle bus to Taylor Square – there can be some unsavoury characters lurking around after the parade.
- Part of the fun of the Mardi Gras Parade is watching the moral wet blankets and right-wing nutters who turn out annually to pray in Hyde Park, usually for rain. God clearly enjoys the event more than they do, as the parade has never been rained out yet.

The parade and its entrants represent all aspects of the gay, lesbian, bisexual and transgender community, and include indigenous Australians and many other ethnic groups. While the NMG organization enjoys a huge amount of sponsorship from business, tourism bodies and the City of Sydney and other councils, no group in the parade can participate in order to promote their enterprises or products – though relevant non-profit community groups are welcome to publicize their causes by participating in the parade. Despite what you might think, the earnestness of these groups seldom makes for dull entries, as whole families, lesbian mothers, leather queens, flight attendants, marching girls and boys, policemen and women, local politicians, major celebrities and virtually anyone else who wants to enter, can lead their float to freedom for their own fifteen minutes of fame.

Before the start of the parade, the waiting crowd is whipped into a not-so-subtle frenzy over several hours by marshalls lining the route. Searchlights, flares, fireworks, strobes, dance music and elaborate lighting effects from all the clubs on Oxford Street, combined with a steady stream of cold beer and champagne, bring the night to a fever pitch of anticipation – a perfect build-up to the gleaming Harley Davidsons of the **Dykes on Bikes**, the not-to-be-messed-with mademoiselles who have heralded the start of the parade for many years. Vast floats, effigies and marching troupes follow in their wake – from dozens of drag Madonnas in cowgirl hats and clingy white pant-suits spilling from the longest stretch limos you've ever seen, to hundreds of Barbara Cartlands in pink-sequined evening gowns, *Brokeback Mountain* cowboys rounding up Mormons from the state of Utah (where the film was banned), mist-enshrouded boats carrying Thai princes and princesses, and six hundred or so bootscooters of all sexes, ages and sizes.

The Mardi Gras Party

The single biggest **party** in Australia takes place at the Fox Entertainment Precinct at 10pm, directly after the parade. Up to twenty thousand people attend – it's meant to be for the queer community and their friends, but anyone can get a ticket nowadays if they get in early enough (see box); scalpers still loiter out front flogging tickets at exorbitant prices, but be warned that they have been known to sell counterfeits, and each ticket has to scan properly for entry. Whatever your sexuality, it's a pretty decadent affair, and you need to be extremely broad-minded.

Party tickets

Mardi Gras Party tickets cost AUS$125 (AUS$79 for NMG members), and are often sold out by the beginning of February; buy them well in advance from NMG (see p.380) or Ticketek (☎013 28 49, ⊛ www.ticketek.com.au).

Party preparation is almost as much fun as the party itself. Who you go with and what you wear matters: there's the tribal grouping, the cocktails, the dressing and the make-up. Friends re-group at pre-party-parties all over the city and make their way to the Fox Entertainment Precinct – usually on foot (it's impossible to get a taxi), which means that traffic literally stops as people clock the outfits and overall antics of the partygoers. The venue itself is more like a small, temporary city than a party, with two huge main pavilions – the Hordern and Royal Hall of Industries – playing host to top DJs

dozens of drag Madonnas spill from the longest stretch limos you've ever seen

from all over the world. There's a variety of musical styles in other spaces, including a smaller, more heavy-duty hall called The Dome, the leather and fetish space of choice. There's also usually a "girls only" area, and a range of bars and food stalls. Throughout the night the larger pavilions offer shows featuring big names – over the years, guest appearances have been made by Boy George, Chaka Khan, Jimmy Sommerville and Kylie Minogue – leading up to the grand finale some time before the 10am finish.

The mornings after

The following day offers little reprieve, with the lanes closed behind Flinders Street, and thousands gathering for a cleansing ale and more dancing. Recovery parties continue through Sunday and into Monday, so be sure to pace yourself if you want to keep going. A recent addition to the hectic schedule is an official morning-after party at **Luna Park**, Sydney's iconic harbourside amusement park; ticket-holders get free access to rides from 10am to noon (the public's response to the dodgem-car-riding, carousel-whirled drag queens is quite a sight) and a dance party attracting around three thousand revellers in the sound-insulated Big Top from noon to 8pm (☎02/9360 6411, ⊛ www.toyboxparty.com.au; around AUS$129).

Other Mardi Gras events

During Mardi Gras, there are several other important annual events that are loads of fun to attend. **Fair Day** is a free festival usually held on Sunday three weeks before the parade, in Victoria Park, just across from Glebe Point Road and next door to Sydney University. The big day, attended by up to eighty thousand people, kicks off at 10am and finishes at 8pm. In between, there's every type of outlandish activity you could wish for, from outrageous dog shows to handbag-throwing championships, plus live music from an outdoor stage, a dance party in the Lounge Tent, face-painting and bouncy castles for kids, stands representing gay and lesbian organizations and charities, and bars and gourmet food stalls. It's a great place to socialize and to see what Sydney's queer community (plus family, friends and pets) looks like in the light of day.

Two weeks prior to the parade, at the Victoria Park Swimming Centre, also in Victoria Park, the **Swimming Carnival** is an alcohol-free pool party that takes place in the evening and features plenty of live entertainment, drag shows and Esther Williams-style water ballet. It's a big queer splash and you've never seen so many blow-up water toys in your life. The Swimming Carnival was cancelled in 2006 – check the NMG website (see p.380) for an update.

Closer to Mardi Gras, **Azure**, the outdoor harbourside party that traditionally takes place on the Sunday prior to the parade (4pm–midnight), is an incredibly popular event, with the AUS$140 tickets usually selling out the day they go on sale (mid-January). If you're in Australia at the time (MCA Tix won't post tickets overseas), you can get them from MCA Tix at 13 Craigend St, in Kings Cross (☎013/0030 6776, ⊛www.mca-tix.com); otherwise, try the classified section of the Pinkboard (⊛www.pinkboard.com.au) or eBay (⊛www.ebay.com.au). The good news is it's worth the hassle: you get to dance with five thousand people under the setting sun on Sydney Harbour, with views of the Opera House and the Harbour Bridge from the vantage point of Lady Macquarie's Chair, next to the Royal Botanical Gardens.

Finally, there's the **QueerScreen Mardi Gras Film Festival**, which offers a fortnight of all the best local and international queer films at screens in inner-city Newtown and Paddington, with opening night at the gorgeous Art Deco State Theatre in the city. The festival produces a comprehensive movie guide each year, and many sessions sell out, so you'd do well to book tickets or passes in advance (☎02/9332 4938, ⊛www.queerscreen.com.au).

Basics

If you're visiting Australia with Mardi Gras in mind, you'd be well advised to use a **travel agent** that specializes in gay-holiday packages, as they will ensure you have tickets to all the important events – at a price, of course.

Accommodation

Inner Sydney has plenty of accommodation options close to the parade route, ranging from cosy, gay-only places through to backpackers' hostels. The only **hotels** with views of the route are the five-star *Marriott*, 36 College St (☎02/9361 8400, ⊛www.mirvachotels. com.au), which has plush modern rooms for around AUS$300, and the *Oaks Hyde Park Plaza*, 38 College St (☎02/9331 6933, ⊛www. theoaksgroup.com.au), with self-catering studios and apartments from AUS$155. But both these options are usually booked out at least six months in advance. Otherwise, the *Wattle Private Hotel*, a long-established gay-friendly place right on the parade route, at 108 Oxford St (☎02/9332 4118, ⊛www.sydneywattle.com), has spacious, contemporary rooms from AUS$110; and the *Comfort Inn Cambridge*, 212 Riley St (☎02/9212 1111, ⊛www.cambridgeinn. com.au), is a comfortable hotel, 150m from the parade route, charging from AUS$145 a room. Centrally located **hostels** include the *Sydney Central YHA* on the corner of Pitt Street and Rawson Place (☎02/9281 9111, ℮sydneycentral@yhansw.org.au), with dorm beds from AUS$28, and the *Sydney Y on the Park*, 5–11 Wentworth St (☎02/9264 2451, ℮y-hotel@zip.com.au), which is metres from the parade route and charges AUS$33 for dorms and AUS$88–130 for private rooms. If you want to arrive earlier and stay longer, well-located *Crown Studio Apartments*, 302–308 Crown St (☎02/9360 1133, ⊛www. sydneyservicedapartments.net), rents out studios with queen-size bed, kitchen and laundry facilities for AUS$140 a night for a minimum of one week. There are also several specifically **gay guesthouses**

including *Pelican Private Hotel*, a five-minute walk from Oxford Street at 411 Bourke St (☎02/9331 5344, ⊛www.pelicanprivatehotel.iwarp.com), which offers budget-priced but comfortable rooms with shared bathroom for AUS$75; and the tasteful *Chelsea Guest House*, in the leafy backstreets of Darlinghurst, at 49 Womerah Ave (☎02/9380 5994, ⊛www.chelsea. citysearch.com.au), which has standard rooms from AUS$143. There is also the quirky nudist option *Oasis* at 106 Flinders St (☎02/9331 8791, ℮admin@oasisonflinders.com.au), offering male-only accommodation for AUS$120–150.

Eating and drinking

Oxford Street is full of eateries, and most of the Asian places here are reliably good. Other restaurants to check out while you're in Sydney include *Longrain*, 85 Commonwealth St, which is an incredibly popular, ultra-chic restaurant and bar, serving modern Thai specialities; and *Bill's*, 359 Crown St, one of three café-restaurants owned by trendy local chef Bill Granger. Bill's **breakfasts** are the best in the city, and ideal after a hard night's partying; he also serves fantastic lunch and dinners as well. Two gay-popular, gay-staffed **cafés** are *The Californian*, at 177 Oxford St (open 24hr Thurs–Sun), serving all-day breakfasts; and *Café Comity*, 139 Oxford St, which does filling café favourites throughout the day and night (until 1am or 2am Fri & Sat).

Event info

New Mardi Gras (☎02/9568 8600, ⊛www.mardigras.org.au). All you need to know about Mardi Gras – photos, online guide, ticket info, and a downloadable Mardi Gras membership form.
The Bobby Goldsmith Foundation (☎02/9283 8666, ⊛www. bgf.org.au). Website of the Sydney-based HIV/AIDS charity set up in memory of Bobby Goldsmith, an active member of the Sydney gay scene, who died of AIDS in 1984.

Time zone GMT+10   **Country code** +61   **Currency** Australian dollar (AUS$)

Australia and
New Zealand

The best of the rest

Adelaide Festival of Arts

Where? Adelaide, Australia
When? March
How long? 2 weeks

This long-running arts festival has been going since 1960 and is modelled on Edinburgh's mix of highbrow culture and cutting-edge experimentalism, with a main festival (ⓦwww.adelaidefestival.com.au), and a fringe festival (ⓦwww.adelaidefringe.com.au) running alongside.

Beer Can Regatta

Where? Darwin, Australia
When? July
How long? 1 day

If you want an Australian festival that fulfils a few stereotypes, then other than the Birdsville Races (see p.367) this may be the one. In a town whose drinking capacity is pretty legendary anyway, even by Aussie standards (after all, there's not a lot else to do), the Beer Can Regatta sees Darwin given over to the single-minded downing of as many tinnies as possible, culminating in a charity "regatta" in which the "boats" are made exclusively out of beer cans. They're bizarre contraptions – ranging from full-scale Viking warships to bathtub lookalikes – but the crowds who head down to nearby Mindil Beach to watch the spectacle take it all pretty seriously. They also know how to enjoy themselves, though, indulging in an assortment of cultural activities either side of the race, with thong-throwing competitions a particular speciality (that's the Aussie word for flip-flops, in case you were wondering).

Big Days Out

Where? Australia and New Zealand
When? January or February
How long? 1 day at each site

Audiences have ballooned since the first Big Day Out (ⓦwww.bigdayout.com) was held in Sydney in 1992, and now 250,000 people gather at six different locations to see this festival-on-tour over successive weekends between late January and early February. It's Australasia's biggest series of outdoor music festivals, taking in Auckland, the Gold Coast, and then Sydney, Melbourne, Adelaide and Perth, and as such attracts big names.

Golden Shears

Where? Masterton, New Zealand
When? March
How long? 3 days

Where else would the world's premier sheep-shearing contest take place but New Zealand? Golden Shears (ⓦwww.goldenshears.co.nz) pits the very best in the world against each other in what – in New Zealand at least – draws enough crowds to be classified a spectator sport. Wool-pressing and wool-handling comps are rounded off with "Shearable Arts", where the catwalk meets the shearing shed. Of course, only devotees of sheep would travel down here specifically to attend. But if you're in the area, how could you possibly miss it?

Henley-on-Todd Regatta

Where? Henley-on-Todd, Australia
When? September 9
How long? 1 day

Faced with the problem of holding a boat race in a dry riverbed, the inhabitants of Alice Springs, slap-bang in the middle of the Australian desert and thousands of miles from any water, came up with an ingenious solution. They kicked a hole in the bottom of the boat, stood inside, lifted the vessel to their thighs like a lady gathering her skirts and ran the length of the course, Flintstones-style. Helped by the huge quantities of cold beer that fuel the crews and crowds of spectators, the event (ⓦwww.henleyontodd.com.au) now attracts teams from around the world. There are a number of different events nowadays, ranging from rowing pairs and rowing eights to "yachting", sand-shovelling and a "triathlon". Get seven buddies together, get training, and go for glory.

Camel Cup

Where? **Alice Springs, Australia**
When? **July**
How long? **1 day**

There are camel races held elsewhere in Australia, but Alice Springs is the best-known and best-attended, with a great atmosphere, lots of people, events and stalls, and the opportunity to witness the extraordinary sight of camels racing – something they're clearly not naturally disposed to. Camel-racing is a serious and venerable sport in many parts of the world, but this event puts a uniquely Australian slant on it.

Melbourne Cup

Melbourne Cup

Where? **Melbourne, Australia**
When? **November**
How long? **4 days**

The highlight of Victoria's spring racing carnival, the Melbourne Cup is one of the world's great race meetings, held at Flemington race course (Ⓦwww.vrc.net.au), just outside Melbourne. The whole of Australia stops to watch the Cup itself, one of the most lavish events in the world, with prize money of around AUS$5 million, and the event is subtitled a "carnival" for good reason: fashion values are high, and people scramble to get trackside to drink champagne, have barbecues and make merry. Not to be missed.

Melbourne International Arts Festival

Where? **Melbourne, Australia**
When? **October**
How long? **3 days**

First staged in 1986, Melbourne's annual arts festival (Ⓦwww.melbournefestival.com.au) is twinned with Spoleto's in Italy (see p.172), and like Adelaide, its high culture agenda is leavened by the coexistence of a vibrant fringe event (Ⓦwww.melbournefringe.com.au), which takes place at roughly the same time.

Moomba Waterfest

Where? **Melbourne, Australia**
When? **March**
How long? **3 days**

Held every March over the Labour Day weekend, the Moomba Waterfest turns the stereotypical Aussie reputation for making everything a giant piss-up on its head. Driven by civic pride, this fifty-year-old event is a deliberately wholesome family occasion, and gives Melbourne a chance to show off and prove that it's the match of its more international rival, Sydney. The key events are the opening night's huge fireworks display over the Yarra River; the Garden Party at the city's Treasury Gardens, where you can rock away the afternoon to Aboriginal bands or spend an hour trying to master the intricacies of the didgeridoo at one of the many music workshops; and the parade that passes down Swanston Street on the Monday, in which Melbourne's iconic trams appear dressed to the nines, and people don budgie suits and giant puppet outfits to stalk passers-by.

Mount Isa Rodeo

Where? **Mount Isa, Australia**
When? **August**
How long? **3 days**

Australia's most remote inland city hosts this huge rodeo event every year at the beginning of August (ⓦwww.isarodeo.com.au). Attracting competitors from overseas as well as from Australia, the event features a two-day country music festival in addition to the traditional rodeo activities; there's also a Rodeo Queen Quest and various kitsch cowboy and cowgirl stunts.

New Zealand International Arts Festival

Where? **Wellington, New Zealand**
When? **February/March**
How long? **3 weeks**

New Zealand's premier arts festival (ⓦwww.nzfestival.telecom.co.nz) showcases theatre, music and dance events at a variety of venues around central Wellington, along with readings by New Zealand writers, and temporary exhibitions of paintings and photographs. A deliberately homegrown event on the whole, there are usually some biggish international talents in attendance too, and a good diversity to the scheduling, with world music and jazz names sitting alongside more local experimental theatre and music productions (a jazz *Tristan and Isolde* anyone?), and a big free outdoor opener on the first Saturday in Waitangi Park.

Pasifika

Where? **Auckland, New Zealand**
When? **March**
How long? **2 days**

Auckland's attempt to celebrate the traditions of the Pacific island communities with which New Zealand historically has such close cultural ties, Pasifika has grown into the region's largest such event, with representation from Tonga, Samoa, Fiji and the Cook islands, among other others. There are hundreds of stalls selling food, crafts, clothes and jewellery, and lots and lots of live music, with four stages on the Saturday itself hosting everything from Pacific pop to traditional dance and war chants, and a grand opening-night concert kicking things off on the Friday evening.

Queenstown Winter Festival

Where? **Queenstown, New Zealand**
When? **End June**
How long? **9 days**

This thirty-year-old event makes the most of the things that bring people to Queenstown all year: adventure activities and good nightlife – and oddly enough, it was started originally to perk up what used to be a quiet time of year. Nowadays, Queenstown Winter Festival (ⓦwww.winterfestival.co.nz) heralds the start of the town's important winter season, celebrating its arrival with mountain biking, snowman-making, dog-racing and any number of wacky outdoor events during the day, and winding up at night with music gigs, comedy nights, off-the-wall dinner balls, and big firework displays, which keep the place bubbling all week.

Sydney Festival

Where? **Sydney, Australia**
When? **January**
How long? **3 weeks**

Sydney Festival (ⓦwww.sydneyfestival.org.au) is less highbrow than its counterparts in Melbourne and Adelaide, an eclectic event that makes the most of the city's great array of locations, with concerts in the Opera House and Hyde Park Barracks and outdoor events in The Domain, in Hyde Park itself and in the park at Darling Harbour.

Wildfoods Festival

Where? **Hokitika, New Zealand**
When? **March**
How long? **1 day**

Now almost twenty years old, the Wildfoods Festival (ⓦwww.wildfoods.co.nz), held in the small town of Hokitika,

World Buskers Festival

on the west coast of New Zealand's South Island, is one of the country's biggest annual events, attracting twenty thousand or so people, who come for miles to tuck into all sorts of food they've never tried before – larvae, shark's penis, scorpions and other such gourmet delights. There's less exotic, but probably more digestible, fare on offer, too, alongside live music and a general ambience of all-round self-indulgence. A good example of a small town deliberately reinventing itself with a slightly bogus theme, but a successful and fun event, nonetheless.

World Buskers Festival

Where? **Christchurch, New Zealand**
When? **January**
How long? **10 days**

This annual competition aims to find the world's best street entertainers – and let's face it, you've got to be pretty good (or pretty mad) to make the trip to New Zealand just to strut your stuff. Masters of the arts of unicycling, escapology, comedy, mime and acrobatics battle it out for laughs and applause in parks and street venues around Christchurch to claim the title. The event (ⓦwww.worldbuskersfestival.com) takes place during the height of the Kiwi summer, at a time when all sorts of special wine and food promotions are going on in the city – so there's plenty to keep you entertained.

End matter

Festivals by month

January
Ati-Atihan
Big Days Out
Cape Minstrels Carnival
Chinese New Year
Dinagyang
Dubai Shopping Festival
Dubai World Cup
Festival in the Desert
Hadaka Matsuri
Harbin Ice and Snow Festival
Ivrea
Junkanoo
Kumbh Mela
La Tamborrada
Losar Archery Festival
Phalgun Festivals
Polo World Cup on Snow
Rustler's Valley Festivals
Sydney Festival
Thaipusam
Timket
Up-Helly Aa
Viareggio Carnival
Vogel Gryff
Winter Carnival

February
Apokriatiká
Basel Carnival
Big Days Out
Binche Carnival
Bob Marley Birthday Bash
Cadiz Carnival
Cape Verde Mardi Gras
Chinese New Year
Cologne Carnival
Dusseldörf Carnival
Festival on the Niger
Fiesta de le Virgen de la Candelaria
Holi
Kumbh Mela
Losar Archery Festival
Mardi Gras, New Orleans
Mazatlan Carnival
New Zealand International Arts Festival
Olinda Carnival
Oruro Carnival
Phalgun Festivals
Recife Carnival
Rio Carnival
Sa Sartiglia
Sauti Za Busara Festival
Tenerife Carnival
Trinidad Carnival
Venice Carnival
Viareggio Carnival
White Turf
Winter Carnival

March
Adelaide Festival of Arts
Ben Aissa Moussem
Calle Ocho
Cape Town Jazz Festival
Dead Rat's Ball
Golden Shears
Holi
Hounen Matsuri
Las Fallas
Moomba Waterfest

New Zealand International Arts Festival
O-Mizutori
Pasifika
St Patrick's Day, Dublin
St Patrick's Day, New York
Spring Break
Sumba Pasola
Sydney Gay and Lesbian Mardi Gras
Vendimia Festival
Wildfoods Festival
World Buskers Festival

April
BVI Spring Regatta
Cape Town Jazz Festival
Feast of St George
Feria de Abril
Fêtes des Masques
French Quarter Festival
Nederberg Wine Auction
New Orleans Jazz and Heritage Festival
Paarl Wine Festival
Phujllay
Puram
Queen's Day
Rustler's Valley Festivals
San Marcos State Fair
Semana Santa, Peru
Semana Santa, Spain
Sisters' Meal
Songkhran
Splashy Fen
Toonik Tyme
Windhoek Carnival

May
Anastenariá
Bay to the Breakers Festival
Brighton Festival
Bun Bang Fai Festival
Cooper's Hill Cheese-Rolling
Corsa dei Ceri
Dragon Boat Races
Fiesta de San Isidro
Los Diablos Danzantes
Mampoer Festival
Maulidi
Monaco Grand Prix
New Orleans Jazz and Heritage Festival
Obando Fertility Festival
Pageant of the Juni
Pink Pop Festival
Puram
Queima das Fitas
Regatta of the Four Maritime Republics
Roskilde Festival
Sisters' Meal

June
Accompong Maroon Festival
Boi Bumba
Bumba Meu Boi
Canelli under Attack
Chariot Festival
Common Ridings
Fes Festival of World Sacred Music
Festa de São Antonio
Festa de São João
Fiesta de Sant Joan
Glastonbury Festival

Gnawa and World
  Music Festival
Hemis
Independence Day,
  Iceland
International Roots
  Festival
Inti Raymi
Isle of Wight Festival
Lajkonik Festival
Midsummer
  Celebrations, Estonia
Midsummer
  Celebrations, Finland
Midsummer
  Celebrations, Sweden
Monsters of Rock
Queenstown Winter
  Festival
Schützenfest
White Nights
Wine War

July
Avignon Festival
Bastille Day
Bayreuth Festival
Beer Can Regatta
Benicàssim Festival
Bumba Meu Boi
Calgary Stampede
Cambridge Folk
  Festival
Camel Cup
Cannabis Cup
Cartier International
  Polo
Cheyenne Frontier Days
Copenhagen Jazz
  Festival
Edirne Oil Wrestling
  Championships
Esala Perahera
Exit Festival
Fastnachtsmontag
Festa de Noantri
Festa del Redentore
Festival of the Dhow

Countries
Fiesta de Merengue
Fiesta de San Fermin
Giants of Douai
Gion Matsuri
Grahamstown Festival
Guilfest
Hemis
Il Palio
Kulmbach Bierfest
Landskronakarnavelen
Love Parade
Montreux Jazz Festival
Mwaka Kogwa
Naadam
Nava Cider Festival
North Sea Jazz Festival
Paleo Festival
Panafest
Reggae Sumfest
S'Ardia
Salzburg Festival
Shandur Polo
  Tournament
Spoleto Festival
White Nights
Wife-Carrying
  Championships

August
Bayreuth Festival
The Big Chill
Brecon Jazz festival
Bumba Meu Boi
Carling Weekend
Cowes Week
Creamfields
Crop Over
Cure Salée
Dragacevo Trumpet
  Festival
Edinburgh Festival
Festival of the
  Assumption of the
  Virgin
Gäuboden Volksfest
Gotland Medieval Week
Il Palio

Inter-Celtic Festival
La Tomatina
Maherero Day
Maralal Camel Derby
Mount Isa Rodeo
Notting Hill Carnival
Onam
Reggae Sunsplash
Salzburg Festival
T in the Park
V Festivals
Westmann Islands'
  Festival
Womad

September
Aloha Festivals
Belize National Day
Bestival
Birdsville Races
Bumbershoot
Burning Man
Cannstatt Volksfest
Clarenbridge Oyster
  Festival
Cure Salée
Galway International
  Oyster Festival
Ganesh Festival
Giostra del Saracino
Henley-on-Todd
  Regatta
Hermanus Whale-
  Watching Festival
Ibiza Closing Parties
Imilchil Wedding
  Moussem
Lake of Stars Festival
New Mexico State Fair
Oktoberfest
Palio of Asti
Pendleton Round-Up

October
Cannstatt Volksfest
Cirio de Nazare
Combat des Reines
Diwali

Dussehra
Fantasy Fest
Festival du Vent
Halloween
Melbourne
  International Arts
  Festival
Mondial du Snowboard
Moulid of Sayyid
  Ahmed al-Bedawi
Oktoberfest

November
Bonn Om Tuk
Day of the Dead
Diwali
Eid al-Fitr
Festival of the Oases
La Diablada
Lewes Bonfire Night
Loi Krathong
Lopburi Banquet
Melbourne Cup
Pushkar Camel Fair
Surin Elephant Round-
  Up

December
Festa de Iemanja
Festival of the Oases
Festival of the Sahara
Fiesta de Santo Tomas
Full Moon Party
Hogmanay
Junkanoo
National Finals Rodeo
Ncwala
Windhoek Carnival

Festivals by country

Argentina
Vendimia Festival

Australia
Adelaide Festival of Arts
Beer Can Regatta
Big Days Out
Birdsville Races
Camel Cup
Henley-on-Todd Regatta
Melbourne Cup
Melbourne International Arts
   Festival
Moomba Waterfest
Mount Isa Rodeo
Sydney Gay and Lesbian Mardi
   Gras
Sydney Festival

Austria
Salzburg Festival

Bahamas
Junkanoo

Barbados
Crop Over

Belgium
Binche Carnival
Dead Rat's Ball

Belize
Belize National Day

Bhutan
Losar Archery Festival

Bolivia
Fiesta de le Virgen de la
   Candelaria
Oruro Carnival
Phujllay

Brazil
Boi Bumba
Bumba Meu Boi
Cirio de Nazare
Festa de Iemanja
Olinda Carnival
Recife Carnival
Rio Carnival

Cambodia
Bonn Om Tuk

Canada
Calgary Stampede
Toonik Tyme
Winter Carnival

Cape Verde
Cape Verde Mardi Gras

China
Harbin Ice and Snow Festival
Sisters' Meal

Denmark
Copenhagen Jazz Festival
Roskilde Festival

**Dominican
Republic**
Fiesta de Merengue

Dubai
Dubai Shopping Festival
Dubai World Cup

Egypt
Moulid of Sayyid Ahmed al-
   Bedawi

England
Bestival
Brecon Jazz festival
Brighton Festival

Cambridge Folk Festival
Carling Weekend
Cartier International Polo
Cooper's Hill Cheese-Rolling
Cowes Week
Creamfields
Glastonbury Festival
Guilfest
Isle of Wight Festival
Lewes Bonfire Night
Monsters of Rock
Notting Hill Carnival
T in the Park
The Big Chill
V Festivals
Womad

Estonia
Jaanipäev
Midsummer Celebrations

Ethiopia
Timket

Finland
Midsummer Celebrations
Wife-Carrying Championships

France
Avignon Festival
Bastille Day
Festival du Vent
Giants of Douai
Inter-Celtic Festival
Monaco Grand Prix
Mondial du Snowboard

The Gambia
International Roots Festival

Germany
Bayreuth Festival
Cannstatt Volksfest

Cologne Carnival
Dusseldörf Carnival
Gäuboden Volksfest
Kulmbach Bierfest
Love Parade
Oktoberfest
Schützenfest

Ghana
Panafest

Greece
Anastenariá
Apokriatiká
Feast of St George

Guatemala
Fiesta de Santo Tomas

Hong Kong
Chinese New Year
Dragon Boat Races

Iceland
Independence Day
Westmann Islands' Festival

India
Chariot Festival
Diwali
Dussehra
Ganesh Festival
Hemis
Holi
Kumbh Mela
Onam
Puram
Pushkar Camel Fair

Indonesia
Sumba Pasola
Torajan Funerals

Ireland
Clarenbridge Oyster Festival
Galway International Oyster
  Festival
St Patrick's Day

Italy
Canelli under Attack
Corsa dei Ceri
Festa de Noantri
Festa del Redentore
Giostra del Saracino
Il Palio
Ivrea
Palio of Asti
Regatta of the Four Maritime
  Republics
Sa Sartiglia
S'Ardia
Spoleto Festival
Venice Carnival
Viareggio Carnival

Jamaica
Accompong Maroon Festival
Bob Marley Birthday Bash
Reggae Sumfest
Reggae Sunsplash

Japan
Gion Matsuri
Hadaka Matsuri
Hounen Matsuri
O-Mizutori

Kenya
Maralal Camel Derby
Maulidi

Laos
Bun Bang Fai Festival

Malawi
Lake of Stars Festival

Malaysia
Thaipusam

Mali
Festival in the Desert
Fêtes des Masques

Mexico
Day of the Dead
Festival of the Assumption of the
  Virgin
Mazatlan Carnival
San Marcos State Fair

Mongolia
Naadam

Morocco
Ben Aissa Moussem
Fes Festival of World Sacred
  Music
Gnawa and World Music Festival
Imilchil Wedding Moussem

Namibia
Maherero Day
Windhoek Carnival

Nepal
Phalgun Festivals

The Netherlands
Cannabis Cup
North Sea Jazz Festival
Pink Pop Festival
Queen's Day

New Zealand
Golden Shears
New Zealand International Arts
  Festival
Pasifika
Queenstown Winter Festival
Wildfoods Festival
World Buskers Festival

Niger
Cure Salée
Festival on the Niger

Pakistan
Shandur Polo Tournament

Peru
Inti Raymi
La Diablada
Semana Santa

The Philippines
Ati-Atihan
Dinagyang
Obando Fertility Festival

Poland
Lajkonik Festival

Portugal
Festa de São Antonio
Festa de São João
Queima das Fitas

Romania
Pageant of the Juni

Russia
White Nights

Scotland
Common Ridings
Edinburgh Festival
Hogmanay
Up-Helly Aa

Serbia and Montenegro
Dragacevo Trumpet Festival
Exit Festival

South Africa
Cape Minstrels Carnival
Cape Town Jazz Festival
Grahamstown Festival
Hermanus Whale-Watching
  Festival
Mampoer Festival
Nederberg Wine Auction
Paarl Wine Festival
Rustler's Valley Festivals
Splashy Fen

Spain
Benicàssim Festival
Cadiz Carnival
Feria de Abril
Fiesta de San Fermin

Fiesta de San Isidro
Fiesta de Sant Joan
Ibiza Closing Parties
La Tamborrada
La Tomatina
Las Fallas
Nava Cider Festival
Semana Santa
Tenerife Carnival
Wine War

Sri Lanka
Esala Perahera

Swaziland
Ncwala

Sweden
Gotland Medieval Week
Landskronakarnavelen
Midsummer Celebrations

Switzerland
Basel Carnival
Combat des Reines
Fastnachtsmontag
Montreux Jazz Festival
Paleo Festival
Polo World Cup on Snow
Vogel Gryff
White Turf

Syria
Eid al-Fitr

Thailand
Full Moon Party
Loi Krathong
Lopburi Banquet
Songkhran
Surin Elephant Round-Up

Trinidad and Tobago
Trinidad Carnival

Tunisia
Festival of the Oases
Festival of the Sahara

Turkey
Edirne Oil Wrestling
  Championships

USA
Aloha Festivals
Bay to the Breakers Festival
Bumbershoot
Burning Man
Calle Ocho
Cheyenne Frontier Days
Fantasy Fest
French Quarter Festival
Halloween
Mardi Gras
National Finals Rodeo
New Mexico State Fair
New Orleans Jazz and Heritage
  Festival
Pendleton Round-Up
St Patrick's Day, New York
Spring Break

Venezuela
Los Diablos Danzantes

Virgin Islands
BVI Spring Regatta

Zanzibar
Festival of the Dhow Countries
Mwaka Kogwa
Sauti Za Busara Festival

Rough Guide credits

Contributing editor: Martin Dunford
Editor: Keith Drew
Picture editor: Mark Thomas
Additional picture research: Harriet Mills & Jj Luck
Design & layout: Diana Jarvis
Cartography: Katie Lloyd-Jones

Icon illustrations: Murray Wallace
Cover design: Chloe Roberts & Diana Jarvis
Production: Aimee Hampson
Proofreaders: David Paul & Stewart Wild
Additional help: Michelle Bhatia & Jo Pickering

Editorial: London Kate Berens, Claire Saunders, Geoff Howard, Ruth Blackmore, Polly Thomas, Richard Lim, Alison Murchie, Karoline Densley, Andy Turner, Edward Aves, Nikki Birrell, Helen Marsden, Alice Park, Sarah Eno, Lucy White, Jo Kirby, Ruth Tidball, Joe Staines, Duncan Clark, Peter Buckley, Matthew Milton, Tracy Hopkins; **New York** Andrew Rosenberg, Steven Horak, AnneLise Sorensen, Amy Hegarty, April Isaacs, Sean Mahoney, Ella Steim
Design & Pictures: London Simon Bracken, Dan May; **Delhi** Madhulita Mohapatra, Umesh Aggarwal, Ajay Verma, Jessica Subramanian, Ankur Guha, Pradeep Thapliyal, Sachin Tanwar, Anita Singh
Production: Katherine Owers, Aimee Hampson
Cartography: London Maxine Repath, Ed Wright, Katie Lloyd-Jones; **Delhi** Jai Prakash Mishra, Rajesh Chhibber, Ashutosh Bharti, Rajesh Mishra, Animesh Pathak, Jasbir

Sandhu, Karobi Gogoi, Amod Singh, Alakananda Bhattacharya
Online: New York Jennifer Gold, Kristin Mingrone, Cree Lawson; **Delhi** Manik Chauhan, Narender Kumar, Shekhar Jha, Rakesh Kumar, Chhandita Chakravarty, Amit Kumar, Amit Verma, Rahul Kumar
Marketing & Publicity: London Richard Trillo, Niki Hanmer, Louise Maher, Jess Carter; Anna Paynton, Nikki Causer, Libby Jellie; **New York** Geoff Colquitt, Megan Kennedy, Katy Ball; **Delhi** Reem Khokhar
Special projects editor: Philippa Hopkins
Manager India: Punita Singh
Series editor: Mark Ellingham
Reference Director: Andrew Lockett
Publishing Coordinator: Megan McIntyre
Publishing Director: Martin Dunford

Writers and contributors

Common Ridings: Dave Dakota
Festa do São João: Matthew Hancock
Fiesta de San Fermin: Dave Dakota & Michelle Chaplow
Galway International Oyster Festival: Dave Dakota & Paul Gray
Glastonbury Festival: Dave Dakota
Hogmanay: Donald Reid
Ibiza Closing Parties: Iain Stewart
Il Palio: Jeffrey Kennedy
La Tomatina: Dave Dakota and Simon Baskett
Las Fallas: Dave Dakota and Damien Simonis
Lewes Bonfire Night: Al Spicer
Love Parade: Dave Dakota & Diana Jarvis
Monaco Grand Prix: Nick Woodford & Tim Beynon
Notting Hill Carnival: Dave Dakota & Polly Thomas
Oktoberfest: Dave Dakota
Queen's Day: Dave Dakota & Martin Dunford
St Patrick's Day: Mark Connolly & Paul Gray
Tenerife Carnival: Christian Williams
Venice Carnival: Richard Schofield
Burning Man: Cali Alpert & Brad Olsen
Crop Over: Adam Vaitilingam & Ross Velton
Day of the Dead: Paul Whitfield

Other writers who have contributed to this book include:
Daniel Jacobs & Emma Gregg (**Africa: Best of the rest**)
Andrew Benson (**Bastille Day**)
David Paul (**Benicàssim**)
Karin Hanta (**Bumba Meu Boi**)
Alex Robinson (**Boi Bumba**)

Fantasy Fest: Jeffrey Kennedy
Fiesta de Merengue: Sean Harvey
Halloween Parade: Don Bapst
Junkanoo: Gaylord Dold & Nathalie Folster
Mardi Gras: Sam Cook
Raggae Sumfest: Polly Thomas
Rio Carnival: Oliver Marshall
Trinidad Carnival: Polly Thomas
Festival in the Desert: Miranda Davies
Rustler's Valley Festivals: Gregory Mthembu-Salter & Tony Pinchuk
Ati-Atihan: David Dalton
Esala Perahera: Dave Dakota & Gavin Thomas
Full Moon Party: Paul Gray
Gion Matsuri: David Tarr
Holi: Reem Khokar
Kumbh Mela: David Abram
Naadam: Michael Kohn
Phalgun Festivals: James McConnachie
Pushkar Camel Fair: David Abram
Birdsville Races: David Leffman
Sydney Gay & Lesbian Mardi Gras: Neal Drinnan & Margo Daly

Miranda Davies (**Festival on the Niger**)
Damien Simonis (**Feria de Abril & Semana Santa**)
Dave Abram (**Full Moon Party, Goa**)
Paul Whitfield (**Our Lady of Guadalupe**)
David Leffman (**Westmann Islands Festival**)
Oliver Marshall (**various European festivals**)

Picture credits

Photography by: Demetrio Carrasco, Philip Cloherty, Martin Dunford, Michelle Grant, Diana Jarvis, Siddharth Khandelwal, James McConnachie, Alex Robinson, Richard Schofield, Damien Simonis, Mark Thomas, Reinaldo Vargas.

All photography © Rough Guides except the following:

FRONT COVER
Main image:
Dancer, Rio De Janeiro © Andrew Woodley/Alamy
Bottom row from left to right:
Costumed reveller, Halloween Parade, New York © Chuck Pefley/Alamy
Festivalgoer, Glastonbury © Matt Cardy/Getty
Dragon dance, Chinese New Year, Beijing © Jack Hollingsworth/Getty
BACK COVER
Top to bottom:
Dancers, Pushkar Camel Fair © Peter Adams/Corbis
Carnival participant, Venice © Altrendo images/Getty
Ati-Atihan, The Philippines © Jim Zuckerman/Alamy
INTRODUCTION
Dancer at the Rio Carnival © Andrew Woodley/Alamy
Crowds celebrating at the Fiesta de San Fermin © Ander Gillenea/Getty Images
Dawn at Burning Man © Rick Egan
Sadhu © Art Wolfe/Getty Images
Man in carnival face paint © Ian Cumming/Axiom

EUROPE
Common Ridings
All photography © P.Tomkins/Visit Scotland/Scottish Viewpoint
Festa do São João
Woman with plastic mallet © Peter M Wilson
View over Porto © Peter M Wilson
Fiesta de San Fermin
Man caught by a bull © Mikel Melero/Mikel Urmenata/sanfermin.com
The bullring © Andrea Pistolesi/Getty Images
Bulls chasing the crowd © Mikel Melero/Mikel Urmenata/sanfermin.com
Bull closing in on festivalgoer © Mikel Melero/Mikel Urmenata/sanfermin.com
Statue diving © Getty Images
Man hit by a bull © Mikel Melero/Mikel Urmenata/sanfermin.com
The Running of the Bulls © Mikel Melero/Mikel Urmenata/sanfermin.com
Glastonbury Festival
Dancer at the stone circle © Matt Cardy/Getty Images
The Pyramid Stage at sunset © Glastonbury Festival
Tents at sunrise © Timothy Allen/Axiom
The Pyramid Stage © Timothy Allen/Axiom
Muddy boots © Glastonbury Festival
People outside the Jazz Stage © Mark Thomas
La Tomatina
Tomato throwing © Desmond Boylan/Reuters/Corbis
Monaco Grand Prix
Passing the Hotel de Paris in Monte Carlo © Vladimir Rys/Bongarts/Getty Images
Celebrating winning the Monaco Grand Prix © Mark Thompson/Getty Images
Blurred Ferrari and Monte Carlo shop fronts © Mark Thompson/Getty Images
Formula One car passing sunbathers © Clive Mason/Getty Images
Negotiating the harbour in Monte Carlo © Pierre Verdy/AFP/Getty Images
Tenerife Carnival
Competitor at the annual Carnival Queen show © Anna Watson/Axiom
Woman in carnival costume © The Tenerife Tourism Corporation
Carnival procession © Anna Watson/Axiom
Carnival Queen © Anna Watson/Axiom
Carnival costume © Anna Watson/Axiom

EUROPE: BEST OF THE REST
Palais des Papes at the Avignon Festival, France © Christophe Raynaud de Lage/Festival d'Avignon
Revellers at the Reading Festival, England © Timothy Allen/Axiom
Cannabis Cup, Amsterdam, The Netherlands © High Times
Contestants at Coopers Hill Cheese-Rolling, England © Patrick Ward/Corbis
Horse and rider at the Fiesta Sant Joan, Spain © Dani Cardona/Corbis
Jousting knight at Gotland Medieval Week, Sweden © Mats Janson
Lovebugs at the Montreux Jazz Festival, Switzerland © Montreaux Jazz Festival
Pageant of the Juni, Romania © Florin Andreescu
Main stage at the Roskilde Festival, Denmark © Roskilde Festival
Westmann Islands Festival, Iceland © Frosti Gislason
Wine battlers at the Haro Wine War, Spain © Neil Philips/Cephas Picture Library/Alamy

THE AMERICAS AND THE CARIBBEAN
Burning Man
All photography © Rick Egan
Crop Over
Crop Over images supplied courtesy of Barbados.org
Bajan Dances © Sean Drakes
Bajan Bootay © Sean Drakes
Fantasy Fest
All photography © Andy Newman/Fantasy Fest
Fiesta de Merengue
The Obelisk on the Malecón, Santo Domingo © Barbara Leslie/Getty Images
Luis Guerra performing at the Fiesta de Merengue © Reuters/Corbis

Junkanoo
Limbo dancer © Philip Gould/Corbis
Close-up of festival costume © Danita Delimont/Alamy
Cowbells on the Junkanoo Parade © M. Timothy O'Keefe/Alamy
Feather costume © Philip Gould/Corbis
Costumed paradegoer © Philip Gould/Corbis
Mardi Gras
Beads thrown from balconies © Lucas Jackson/Corbis
Neon Mardi Gras sign © Richard Cummins/Corbis
Marching band © Ray Laskowitz/Alamy
Zulu Krewe © Bob Sacha/Corbis
Bourbon Street © Vicky Couchman/AXIOM
Revellers in costume © Barry Lewis/Alamy
Reggae Sumfest
All images © Andre McGann
Trinidad Carnival
Harts mas band © Sean Drakes/Blue Mango
Blue Devil drinking beer © Jennie Hart/Alamy
Steel band © Steve Bly/Alamy
Girls in the Poison mas band © Sean Drakes/Blue Mango
Mud-drenched Jouvert band © Sean Drakes/Blue Mango
Canivalgoers dancing to soca music © Sean Drakes/Blue Mango
THE AMERICAS AND THE CARIBBEAN: BEST OF THE REST
Roping a calf at the Calgary Stampede © The Calgary Stampede
Aloha Festivals, Hawaii © Robert Fried/Alamy
Boi Bumba, Brazil © Pavel Chernev
Fiesta de Santa Thomas, Guatemala © Xela/Alamy
The dance of Los Diablos, Venezuela © Reuters/Corbis

Mazatalan Carnival, Mexico © Grant Rooney/Alamy

Devil Dancers, Bolivia © David Merrcado/Reuters/Corbis

Wine-tasting in Argentina © Eduardo Longoni/Corbis

AFRICA AND THE MIDDLE EAST

Camels bottoms © Suzanne Porter

Festival in the Desert

All images © Suzanne Porter

Rustler's Valley Festivals

View of valley © Suzanne Porter

Man in costume © Rustler's Valley

Tents on festival site © Rustler's Valley

Festival gates © Rustler's Valley

AFRICA AND THE MIDDLE EAST: BEST OF THE REST

Festival of the Sahara, Tunisia © Patrick Ward/Alamy

Cape Minstrels Carnival, South Africa © Suzane Porter

Cure Salee, Niger © Suzanne Porter

Dugout sailboat on the River Niger © Michael S Lewis/Corbis

The International Roots Festival, The Gambia © Ariadne Van Zandbergen/Alamy

Festival of the Sahara, Tunisia © Patrick Ward/Alamy

Women in traditional dress, Maherero Day, Namibia © J. Marshall/Tribaleye Images/Alamy

Tamarind band, Sauti za Busara, Zanzibar © Muhidin Issa Michuzi

ASIA

Full Moon Party © Chris McLennan/Alamy

Ati-Atihan

Feathered costume © Peter Adams Photography/Alamy

Colourful tribal costume © Peter Adams Photography/Alamy

Procession © Alain Evrard/Getty Images

Banners © Alain Evrard/Getty Images

Kalibo at dusk © Peter Adams Photography/Alamy

Procession © Alain Evrard/Getty Images

Esala Perahera

All images © Derek Brown/Dbimages/Alamy

Full Moon Party

Couple at the Full Moon Party, © James Pomerantz/Corbis

Thai woman dancing © Paula Bronstein/Getty Images

Dancing on the beach © Chris McLennan/Alamy

Sunset in Goa © Paul Lovichi Photography/Alamy

Sunset on Ko Pah Ngan © Benjamin Lowy/Corbis

Gion Matsuri

Giant float © Chris Willson/Alamy

Fortune paper © Mark Thomas

Geishas © Jeremy Hoare/Alamy

Men pulling float © Jim Holmes/AXIOM

Crane dance © Chris Willso/Alamy

People in ceremonial dress © JNTO

Paper lanterns © Robert Essel/Corbis

Holi

Men covered in powder © Keren Su/China Span/Alamy

Dancer's hands © Piyal Adhikary/Corbis

Coloured power © Siddharth Khandelwal

Crowd covered in powder © Siddharth Khandelwal

Girl in red powder © Siddharth Khandelwal

Crowd throwing powder © Siddharth Khandelwal

Boys taking a drink © Siddharth Khandelwal

Kumbh Mela

Hindu devotees bathing © Reuters/Corbis

Votive candle © Art Wolfe/Getty Images

Sadhus on pontoon bridge © Karoki Lewis/AXIOM

Sadhu drying robe © Reuters/Corbis

Sadhu rushing for a holy bath © Roy Madhur/Reuters/Corbis

Sadhu offering prayer © Raj Patidar/Reuters/Corbis

Saffron procession © Karoki Lewis/AXIOM

Naadam

Boy racing horse © Adam Wheeler/Alamy

Young horse rider © Michel Setboun/Corbis

Children horse racing © Nik Wheeler/Corbis

Riding horses on the Mongolian prairie © Michel Setboun/Corbis

Mongolian Wrestlers © Jeremy Nicholl/Alamy

Archer in competition © Nik Wheeler/Corbis

Young archer © Sue Carpenter/AXIOM

Boy on horseback © Sue Carpenter/AXIOM

Phalgun Festivals

Boudha stupa, Kathmandu © Chris Caldicott/AXIOM

Close-up of Sadhus' hair © Mukunda Bogati/Corbis

People throwing flower © Alison Wright/Corbis

Sadhu practicing tantric Yoga © Craig Lovell/Eagle Visions

Sadhus doing Yoga © Craig Lovell/Corbis

Pashupatinath © David Norton photography/Alamy

Pushkar Camel Fair

Camel and rider © Will Salter/AXIOM

Close-up of camel © Stewart Cohen/Getty Images

Camel traders © Amit Bhargava/Corbis

Fairground ride © Chris Calcicott/AXIOM

Herd of camels © Glen Allison/Getty Images

ASIA: BEST OF THE REST

Dragon-boat racing, Hong Kong © James Montgomery/Jon Arnold Images/Alamy

Painted chariot © Lindsay Robert/Corbis

Chinese New Year celebrations, Hong Kong © The Hong Kong Tourist Board

Ganesh statue floating in the sea, India © Punit Paranjpe/Reuters/Corbis

O-Mizutori, Japan © JNTO

Elephants playing football, Thailand © Alain Evrard/Robert Harding Picture Library/Alamy

AUSTRALIA AND NEW ZEALAND

Men in swimming costumes © Jack Picone/Alamy

Birdsville races

All images © Peter Wallis & Cameron Richardson/Birdsville races

SYDNEY GAY AND LESBIAN MARDI GRAS

Drag queen with tongue out © Suzanne Long/Alamy

Drag queens in the rain © Mick Tsikas/Corbis

Drag queen in costume © Reuters/Corbis

Women on motorbike © David Hancock/Alamy

Man showing off his hairdo © Will Burgess/Corbis

Man wearing a veil © Jack Picone/Alamy

Man in carnival costume © Will Burgess/Corbis

AUSTRALIA AND NEW ZEALAND: BEST OF THE REST

Camel Cup, Australia © Camel Cup Committee

Crowd at the Melbourne Cup, Australia © Kristian Dowling/Getty Images

Bumble Bees at the Wildfoods Festival, New Zealand courtesy of the Wildfoods Festival

Participant at the World Buskers Festival, New Zealand © Inez Grim/World Buskers Festival

Index

A

Accompong Maroon Festival 260
Adelaide Festival of the Arts..382
Africa and the Middle East
..................................273–296
Aloha Festivals 260
Americas and the Caribbean
..................................179–272
Amsterdam 122
Anastenaria 146
Apokriatiká 146
Asia 297–364
Ati-Atihan 299–304
Australia and New
Zealand.........................365–386
Avignon Festival 146

B

Barbados 193
Basel Carnival 147
Bastille Day 148–149
Bay to the Breakers Festival ..260
Bayreuth Festival 147
Beer Can Regatta 382
Belize National Day 260
Ben Aissa Moussem 286
Benicàssim Festival 147
Berlin 95
Bestival 152
Bhang 326
Big Days Out 382
Binche Carnival 150–151

Birdsville Races 367–372
Black Rock City 184
Bob Marley Birthday Bash 262
Boi Bumba 261
Bonfire Societies 91
Bonn Om Tuk 356
Boracay 303
Bourbon Street 229
Brecon Jazz festival 152
Brighton Festival 147
British Summer Festivals 152
Bullfights 39
Bumba Meu Boi 262
Bumbershoot 262
Bun Bang Fai Festival 356
Buñol 77
Burning Man 181–188
BVI Spring Regatta 262

C

Cadiz Carnival 136
Calgary Stampede 262
Calle Ocho 263
Calypso 192
Calypso tents 255
Cambridge Folk Festival 152
Camel Cup 383
Canelli under Attack 153
Cannabis Cup 153
Cannstatt Volksfest................ 119
Cape Minstrels Carnival 286
Cape Town Jazz festival 286
Cape Verde Mardi Gras 286
Carling Weekend 152
Cartier International Polo 153

Chariot Festival 356
Cheyenne Frontier Days 263
Chinese New Year 357
Christopher Street Day 97
Cirio de Nazare 263
Clarenbridge Oyster Festival ..45
Cologne Carnival 154
Combat des Reines 154
Common Ridings 19–24
Contrade 70–71
Cooper's Hill Cheese-Rolling 154
Copacabana 247
Copenhagen Jazz Festival 154
Corsa dei Ceri 155
Cowes Week 155
Creamfields 152
Crews 222
Crop Over 189–194
Cuban Son 211
Cure Salée 287

D

Day of the Dead 195–200
Dead Rat's Ball 155
Decompression Street Fair 187
Dinagyang 357
Diwali 357
Dragacevo Trumpet Festival ..156
Dragon Boat Races 359
Dubai Shopping Festival 287
Dubai World Cup 287
Dublin 129
Dussehra 359
Düsseldorf Carnival 156

E

Ed al-Fitr 287
Edinburgh 55
Edinburgh Festival 156
Edirne Oil Wrestling
   Championships 156
Ernest Hemingway 36, 205
Esala Perahera 305–310
Essakane 276
Europe 17–178
Exit Festival 157

F

Fantasy Fest 201–206
Fastnachtsmontag 157
Feast of St George 157
Feria de Abril 158–159
Festa de Iemanja....................264
Festa de Noantri 157
Festa de São João.............. 25–30
Festa del Redentore 160
Festa do São Antonio 160
Festival du Vent 160
Festival in the Desert 275–280
Festival of the Dhow
   Countries............................288
Festival of the Oases 288
Festival of the Sahara 288
Festival of World
   Sacred Music 288
Festival on the Niger 289
Fêtes 253
Fêtes des Masques 290
Fiesta de la Virgen de la
   Candelaria 264
Fiesta de Merengue 207–212
Fiesta de San Fermin 31–40
Fiesta de San Isidro 160
Fiesta de Sant Joan 161
Fiesta de Santo Tomas 265

French Quarter Festival 264
Full Moon Party,
   Thailand 311–316
Fully Moon Party, Goa 315

G

Galway 43
Galway International
   Oyster Festival.................41–46
Ganesh Festival 358
Gäuboden Volksfest 161
Giants of Douai 161
Gion Matsuri 317–322
Giostra del Saracino 162
Glastonbury Festival 47–52
Gnawa and World
   Music Festival 290
Golden Shears 382
Gotland Medieval Week 162
Grahamstown Festival 290
Guilfest 152
Guinness Oyster Trail 44
Gunpowder Plot 89
Guy Fawkes 89

H

Hadaka Matsuri 359
Halloween 13–218
Harbin Ice and Snow Festival 360
Hat Rin 313
Hawick 21
Hemis 360
Henley-on-Todd Regatta 382
Hermanus Whale-Watching
   Festival 290
Hogmanay 53–58
Holi, India 323–328
Holi, Nepal 347
Hounen Matsuri 360

I

Ibiza Closing Parties 59–64
Il Palio 65–74
Imilchil Wedding Moussem ..291
Independence Day, Iceland ...163
Inter-Celtic Festival 163
International Roots Festival..291
Inti Raymi 266
Ipanema 247
Isle of Wight Festival 152
Ivrea 79

J

Jaanipäev 164
Jouvert 256
Junkanoo 219–224

K

Kalibo 301
Kandy 307
Key West 203
Krewes 230
Kulmbach Bierfest 163
Kumbh Mela 329–334
Kyoto 319

L

La Diablada 266
La Tamborrada 163
La Tomatina 76–80
Lajkonik Festival 164
Lake of Stars Festival 291
Landskronakarnavelen 164
Larry Harvey 183

Las Fallas 81–86
Lewes 89
Lewes Bonfire Night 87–92
Loi Krathong 360
Lopburi Banquet 360
Los Diablos Danzantes 266
Losar 345, 360
Losar Archery Festival 360
Love Parade 93–98

N

Naadam 335–342
Nassau 221
National Democracy Day,
    Nepal 347
National Finals Rodeo 268
Nava Cider Festival 166
Ncwala....................................294
Nederberg Wine Auction 294
New Mexico State Fair 268
New Orleans 226
New Orleans Jazz and Heritage
    Festival 268
New York 216
New Zealand International
    Arts Festival 385
North Sea Jazz Festival 166
Notting Hill Carnival......105–112

O

Oaxaca 199
Obando Fertility Festival 361
Oktoberfest 113–120
Olina Carnival 268
O-Mizutori 361
Onam 361
Oruro Carnival 269

P

Paarl Wine Festival 294
Pageant of the Juni 166
Paleo Festival 167
Palio of Asti 167
Pamplona..................................33
Panafest 294
Panorama finals 254
Panyards 255

Pasifika 385
Patzcuaro 199
Pendleton Round-Up 269
Phalgun Festivals 343–348
Phujllay 269
Pink Pop Festival 167
Polo World Cup on Snow 167
Porto 27
Puram 362
Pushkar....................................351
Pushkar Camel Fair 349–354

Q

Queen's Day 121–126
Queenstown Winter Festival..385
Queima das Fitas 168

R

Reading Festival 152
Recife Carnival 268
Regatta of the Four Maritime
    Republics 168
Reggae Sumfest 233–238
Reggae Sunsplash 237
Rio Carnival 239–248
Romeria del Rocio 169
Roskilde Festival 168
Running of the Nudes 38
Ruster's Valley Festivals 281–284

S

Sa Sartiglia 169
Sadhus 332
Salvador Carnival 247
Samba Schools 242
Sambodromo 243
San Francisco........................ 217

M

Maherero Day 292
Mampoer Festival 292
Maralal Camel Derby 293
Mardi Gras 225–232
Mardi Gras Indians 228
Mas bands 251, 252
Masks 143
Maulidi 293
Mazatlan Carnival 267
Melbourne Cup 384
Melbourne International Arts
    Festival 384
Mexico City 198
Midsummer Celebrations,
    Estonia 164
Midsummer Celebrations,
    Finland 164
Midsummer Celebrations,
    Sweden 164
Monaco 101
Monaco Grand Prix 99–104
Mondial du Snowboard 165
Monsters of Rock 152
Montego Bay 235
Montreux Jazz Festival 165
Moomba Waterfest 384
Moulid of Sayyid Ahmed
    al-Bedawi 293
Mount Isa Rodeo................... 385
Munich....................................114
Mwaka Kogwa 293

San Marcos Street Fair 269
Santo Domingo 209
S'Ardia 73
Sauti Za Busara Festival 294
Sazlburg Festival 169
Schützenfest 169
Selkirk 23
Semana Santa, Peru 270
Semana Santa, Spain 170–171
Shandur Polo Tournament 362
Shivaratri 345
Siena 67
Sisters' Meal 362
Songkhran 362
Splashy Fen 294
Spoleto Festival 172
Spring Break 270
St Patrick's Day, Dublin..127–132
St Patrick's Day, New York 131
St Patrick's Day, worldwide ...131
Sumba Pasola 362
Surin Elephant Round-Up 363
Sydney 375
Sydney Festival 385
Sydney Gay and Lesbian
   Mardi Gras.................. 373–380

T

T in the Park 152
Tel Aviv Love Parade 97
Tenerife Carnival 133–138
Thaipusam 363
The Big Chill 152
Tibetan New Year 345, 360
Timket 295
Toonik Tyme 270
Torajan Funerals 363
Trinidad Carnival 249–258

U

Ulaanbaatar 337
Up-Helly Aa 172

V

V Festival 152
Valencia 83
Vendimia Festival 271
Venice Carnival 139–144
Viareggio Carnival 172
Vogel Gryff 173

W

Westmann Islands Festival
  174–175
White Nights 173
White Turf 167
Wife-Carrying
   Championships.....................173
Wildfoods Festival 386
Windhoek Carnival 295
Wine War 176–177
Winter Carnival 271
Womad 152
Worlds Buskers Festival 386